The Lucid Veil

The Lucid Veil

Poetic Truth
in the Victorian Age

W. David Shaw

The University of Wisconsin Press

Published in Great Britain by
The Athlone Press Ltd
44 Bedford Row, London WC1R 4LY

Published in the United States of America by
The University of Wisconsin Press
114 North Murray Street
Madison, Wisconsin 53715

First printing

Printed in Great Britain

Library of Congress Cataloging-in-Publication Data
Shaw, W. David (William David)
   The lucid veil.
   Bibliography: pp. 289–296.
   Includes index.
   1. English poetry—19th century—History and
criticism 2. Aesthetics, Modern—19th century.
3. Languages—Philosophy.   4. Knowledge,
Theory of. 5. Poetics.
I. Title.
PR595.A34S53   1987   821'.8'0938   86-26703
ISBN 0-299-11210-1

For Carol, Jeffrey, and my four daughters

Contents

Acknowledgements

My ever compounding debts to Northrop Frye, F. E. L. Priestley, J. M. Robson, Patricia Parker, and Francis Sparshott, whose conversations and writing have shaped my ideas over many years, are embarrassing to think about. I am also grateful for the encouragement of Brian Southam, Managing Director of The Athlone Press, who expressed interest in my work from an early stage, and for the support and example of my colleagues at Victoria College, University of Toronto, which has been my intellectual home for the past sixteen years. To have had constant contact with minds gifted for experience of intellectual adventure is already to have received more than I can hope to pay back. Cyrus Hamlin, in particular, usefully mixed a bemused tolerance of my own imperfect command of German with great charity both toward me and my longstanding interest in Hegel's ideas and influence.

An anonymous reader for the Athlone Press and several anonymous readers for the journals in which some of my ideas first appeared have combined painstaking care with more expert knowledge and more wisdom than most scholars are able or generous enough to give. Students are usually too politic and colleagues too charitable to criticize my ideas as they should. Many of the sharpest comments have come from my wife, Carol, whose wisdom has been large-hearted and whose patience has been boundless. My debts to her are best recalled in silence, in a silence of long memory and deep gratitude.

Some of my ideas originally appeared in the form of public lectures at Northwestern University in 1979, at the Graduate Center of the City College of New York in 1980, at the annual conference of the Victorian Studies Association of Western Canada in 1983, and at the conference of the Victorian Studies Association of Ontario in 1985. For the hospitality of the conveners and the response of each audience I am grateful. In 1983 Professor Ralph Cohen's faculty seminar on the theory of genres at Toronto also provided indirect criticism of many of my ideas and a liberal, wide-ranging contribution to patterns of thought I was still trying to formulate.

Though I would rather be remembered as the author of books than as a journalist, I must acknowledge that some early formulations of my ideas appeared in portions of the following essays in learned journals: 'Victorian Poetry and Repression: The Use and Abuse of Masks', *ELH, A Journal of English Literary History*, vol. 46 (1979), 468–94; 'The Optical Metaphor: Victorian Poetics and the Theory of Knowledge', *Victorian Studies*, vol. 23 (1980), 293–324; 'The Agnostic Imagination in Victorian Poetry', *Criticism*, vol. 22 (1980), 116–39; 'Browning and Pre-Raphaelite Medievalism: Educated Versus Innocent Seeiñg', *Browning Institute Studies*, vol. 8 (1980), 73–83; 'Mill on Poetic Truth: Are Intuitive Inferences Valid?', *Texas Studies in Literature and Language*, vol. 23 (1981), 27–51; '"The Very Central Fiery Heart": Ruskin's Theories of Imagination', *Journal of English and Germanic Philology*, vol. 80 (1981), 199–225; 'Projection and Empathy in Victorian Poetry', *Victorian Poetry*, vol. 19 (1981), 315–36; 'Mimesis as Invention: Four interpretative Models in Victorian Poetry', *New Literary History*, vol. 12 (1981), 303–28; 'Poetic Truth in a Scientific Age: The Victorian Perspective', *Center and Labyrinth: Essays in Honour of Northrop Frye* (1983), 245–63; and 'Philosophy and Genre in Victorian Poetics: The Idealist Legacy', *ELH*, vol. 52 (1985), 471–501. For permission to quote from my essays, which in most cases have been extensively revised, I am grateful to the editors of the journals and to the University of Toronto Press, publisher of the Frye festschrift.

I want to thank Miss Katharine Duff, who graciously allowed me to quote from an unpublished Clough manuscript to which she holds the copyright. I am indebted as well to the Bodleian Library of Oxford University for allowing me to consult and cite this manuscript and also the 1812 script of Keble's Chancellor's Prize essay. For permission to quote cancelled lines in an early version of Swinburne's poem 'Hertha', I am grateful to the British Library and to the copyright holder, William Heinemann Ltd.

This study was begun with the aid of a Killam Senior Research Fellowship, then laid aside as I began and completed other projects. Unlike Lord Chesterfield's patronage of Dr Johnson, the support of the Killam trustees came early and was kind, even though they denied me their support at a later time when I was really more in need of it. I am also grateful to the Royal Society of Canada for renewing my sense of scholarly vocation by recently electing me a fellow. When I reflect that life is limited and that after twenty-three years of teaching I have received only two sabbatical leaves, I am led to conclude that submission to a tyranny of small vexations is below the dignity of thinking beings and that knowledge is more valued when it is acquired with difficulty. Like the solitude of prisons, a measure of adversity may do more to promote knowledge than all the academies and research agencies combined. My own ideas are the slow and painful product of solitary years, and I am encouraged to think they have laid a foundation on which better scholars will build bolder, more enduring books.

Preface

In an earlier study I observed that 'no scholar has done for the Victorian age – perhaps the feat is inimitable – what M. H. Abrams' *The Mirror and the Lamp* has done so ably for the earlier Romantic age' (1976, p. 310). The present book tries to remedy that deficiency by studying the connection which exists between Victorian poetics and changing theories of language and knowledge. Because a wide and rough but genuine consistency of outlook is manifest equally in the poetry, the science, and the philosophy of the Victorian period, it is rewarding to see what changes in one field coincide with similar changes in another. What developments in the theory of knowledge, for example, reinforce or challenge the representational and the expressive axioms of early-Victorian poetics? And what changes in science, metaphysics, and Victorian theology parallel the emergence after 1870 of new theories of art for art's sake? To ignore such questions in the name of literary purity is a philosophical mistake. In some circles historical scholarship now seems out of date. But should we be cowed by such distrust into abandoning all historical research? Or should such distrust of history be viewed itself as a historical phenomenon? Perhaps historical scholarship is the best safeguard against mere slavery to current fashions.

If contemporary literary theorists have taught us anything, it is that philosophy is just as indispensable as history to an understanding of the theory and practice of poetry. And since Victorian Idealism, the single most important influence on Victorian poetics, is now in disfavour among professional philosophers, it seems as if only a literary critic or historian of ideas is likely to reread with profit such major idealists as F. H. Bradley, John Grote, J. F. Ferrier, and T. H. Green, as well as more minor figures like John Caird and F. C. S. Schiller, whom posterity has more justly consigned to oblivion.

In the well-honoured tradition of using prefaces to disarm predictable criticisms of what authors have written, I should say at the outset that, though my approach is inclusive, it is not inclusive enough. The important topic of Goethe's influence on Tennyson, Arnold, and other Victorians is treated only in passing, and limits of space have forced me to omit altogether any discussion of French influence. The political and economic implications of Victorian poetic theory have an important polemical history. I allude to that history briefly in the Introduction, but I have not been able to find a proper niche for it elsewhere. Except in one or two cases, I have also avoided debating the ideas of other scholars. To do so I would first have had to restate their own formulations of the Victorian period. And if these were the formulations I wanted to adopt, I would have continued to write notes and articles, not a book. Like Arnold, I believe that the function of criticism is not merely an academic question but a life-and-death issue. Though my subject is the living moment of struggle and conflict, the storm front itself, my consolation is that, as in any storm front, most serious imbalances will rectify themselves.

In a book on poetics and theories of knowledge, no philosophical apparatus has any prior authority. The historian of ideas has to justify the balance and quantity of philosophy and theory by establishing their critical fertility. By showing how modern hermeneutical techniques are applicable to liberal and conservative traditions of biblical interpretation in the Victorian period, and how the solvents of deconstruction may be used to analyse agnostic theology and poetry, a study of this kind should also be able to show where these same techniques are inapplicable and alien. When dealing with concurrent changes in science, theology, poetics, and epistemology, the 'game of influences' may often seem about as profitable a study as 'who caught cold from whom when', in Virgil Thompson's phrase, 'they were all sitting in the same draught'. Perhaps the best argument for the influence on Browning of Strauss's theories of biblical interpretation or of Fox's theory of dramatic impersonation is my demonstration in Chapters II and VI that these theories help the reader see new elements of Browning's art.

Readers who are interested in the overall design and argument are invited to read the Introduction first. I had originally hoped to use each topic in critical theory or philosophy to elucidate the poetry, as the students do in my seminars, and a few representative poems to test and modify the theory. When poetic examples began to impede the flow of the larger argument, however, I realized I was writing two different books. I decided that, whenever an analysis of poems was not essential to an understanding of the theory, I had to discard it. Economy has meant giving up many ornamental illustrations, including practical criticism of entire poems and most references to the critical works on Victorian poetry that have appeared in recent years. To include all these secondary references would have drowned my primary sources in a flood of notes. Many scholars and critics will recognize my indebtedness to their work. They will not, I hope, think it unscholarly or ungenerous to have omitted reference to them here or in the notes. Paring away these references and illustrations has been a painful process, and the result may seem skeletal and austere. But I accept the adjectives as tersely descriptive of a desirable feature of all theoretical argument, which each reader can supplement with critical examples of his or her choice.

The overlapping contexts in which I have been obliged to discuss complicated poets like Tennyson and Hopkins, Browning and Arnold, do not, I believe, invalidate the distinctions I have drawn. On the contrary, it was an awareness in their poetry of complex interactions that led me to distinguish among axioms of cognition and among expressive, purist, and oracular lines of theorizing in the first place. Theories of language and knowledge would be of little critical interest if they could not be combined in many different ways in a poet's work. The exceptions to that statement are the agnostic poems of James Thomson and the devotional poems of John Keble, which I have been able to study in single contexts.

'To look into the Victorian mind,' W. E. Houghton says, 'is to see some primary sources of the modern mind.' One purpose of this study is to show how this observation is as true of poetic theory as of any other branch of knowledge. I show in the first chapter how Mill's attempts to differentiate the emotive discourse of the poet from the normal descriptive discourse of science anticipates the poetic theories of I. A. Richards. Radically different are the assumptions of Ferrier and the other theorists I discuss in Chapters II and III. In anticipation of Cassirer and Collingwood, they argue that poetry is more than a mere expression of emotion. Without poetic imagination, John Grote argues, there would be no recognizable unities which could serve as the foundation of human culture and education. Agnostic theologians like Mansel and Herbert Spencer are pioneer semioticians. Are our words for God indices, icons, or mere empty signifiers? An analogical understanding of God presupposes a theory of the icon in which some similarity or fitness of resemblance is proposed by the sign. If our knowledge of God is univocal, then our words for God are as concrete and actual as Fra Lippo Lippi's. They are an index of His presence. By contrast, a merely arbitrary relation between the sign and what it represents produces Arnold's and Clough's distressingly equivocal knowledge of deity. As the agnostic godson of Keble, on whom the mantle of the priest descends, Arnold is a forefather of the New Critics, substituting his authoritative critical touchstones for the dogmas of religion. Like many classrooms I attended during the 1950s and early 1960s, Arnold's lecture hall becomes a chapel in which the Oxford Professor of Poetry initiates the faithful into the appropriate critical mysteries. In a few years many of my analyses and ideas will be swallowed up and lost in the general multiplication of later articles and books. But some of the intellectual history may not be done again, and my hope is that a few of the facts I have recovered will be serviceable to future students of the subject.

What hope of answer, or redress?
Behind the veil, behind the veil.

Tennyson, *In Memoriam*, LVI, 27–8

And then I know the mist is drawn
A lucid veil from coast to coast,
And in the dark church like a ghost
Thy tablet glimmers to the dawn.

Tennyson, *In Memoriam*, LXVII, 13–16

For the truth I come back always to the doctrine of Hegel, that 'there is nothing behind the curtain other than that which is in front of it'.

F. H. Bradley, *Essays on Truth and Reality*

It is manifest that behind the so-called curtain, which is to hide the inner world, there is nothing to be seen unless we ourselves go behind there, as much in order that we may thereby see, as that there may be something behind there which can be seen.

Hegel, *Phenomenology of Mind*

Perhaps nothing more sublime was ever said and no sublimer thought ever expressed than the famous inscription on the Temple of Isis (Mother Nature); 'I am all that is and that was and that shall be, and no mortal hath lifted my veil.'

Kant, *Critique of Judgement*

Introduction: The Lucid Veil

Philosophers since Bacon and Hobbes have generally assumed that normal language is scientific. If other forms of discourse like poetry are to be accepted as forms of education, they must be made to conform with the empiricist's search for knowledge and with his metaphor of the mirror of nature, on which the inductive sciences are based. Many Victorians dispute T. H. Huxley's claim that science, rather than a study of poetry or of the classics, must be made the foundation of education. Critiques of the mirror image assume several forms. In revising the *tabula rasa* theory of Locke, J. F. Ferrier teaches that the minimal unit of cognition is the framed event, or the world 'mecum' (1854, p. 93). A more radical critique is the subject of my third chapter, where I show how thinkers as diverse as Bradley, Green, Trench, Ruskin, and John Grote all champion the holistic axiom that because vocabularies are not mirrors of nature but take their meanings from other words and images, they have no representative character in isolation. Words are not pictures but tools, and acquire such privileges as they possess only from their use. The metaphor of the mirror may apply to successful normal discourse. But it does not apply to the rest of discourse, particularly to poetic discourse. Some philosophers and critics find poetry less like a mirror of nature than a kaleidoscope of coloured glass or a windowless mansion full of chambers that mirror only other chambers in the mansion.

Before 1870, however, most Victorians still accept and use, even when they try to modify, the scientific theory of knowledge and its representational metaphors of the window, the mirror of nature, and the lucid veiling of that mirror – metaphors which both empirical and idealist philosophy in the nineteenth century had made the foundation of all systematic knowledge and education. If the only source of truth is the mirror of nature, then the levity of the poet's fictions will be no substitute for the burden of science. Poetry becomes the organ, not of truth, but of mere illusion or make-believe, what Bacon calls 'feigned history' (1955, p. 244). Such is the dominant assumption of most Utilitarians, though J. S. Mill introduces some important qualifications. Other Victorians who would reject the authority of scientific models still defer to a representational theory of language and knowledge deriving from Aristotle. The theory of imitation in Aristotle's *Poetics* is taken to be a semi-divine revelation, which even an expressive theorist like Keble casually equates with his own antithetical doctrines. 'It would seem,' Keble says, 'that the analogical applications of the word "poetry" coincide well enough with Aristotle's notion of it, as consisting chiefly in Imitation or Expression' (1838, p. 435). Few passages in Victorian poetics better illustrate Stephen Booth's assertion that Aristotle 'has lost his place as the fourth member of the Trinity . . . in all but one field' (1983, p. 82). And yet even in being as deferential to Aristotle's authority in poetic theory as he is to the authority of the Church Fathers in theology, Keble finds he is more concerned than Aristotle with the role of analogy, which may tell us as much about the interpreter as about the subject he is interpreting. A poet's words, like his mind, are neither a mirror that clearly reflects the world nor a mask that hides it, but what Tennyson calls a 'lucid veil'.

I prefer the metaphor of the lucid veil to that of the mirror of nature because by suggesting a norm of transparent knowing that is in practice rare, the mirror blunts the force of Wittgenstein's insight that 'we predicate of the thing what lies in the method of representing it' (1972, proposition 104, p. 46). Indeed, transparency is a limit, and when the mind reaches that limit the metaphor breaks down. As Richard Rorty explains, 'the notion of an unclouded Mirror of Nature is the notion of a mirror which would be indistinguishable from what was mirrored, and thus would not be a mirror at all'. Sartre suggests that 'the notion of a human being whose mind is such an unclouded mirror, and who *knows* this, is the image . . . of God'. As Rorty wryly adds, however, 'He can be called "God" if we think of the advantages of this situation, or a "mere machine" if we think of the disadvantages' (1979, p. 376). Apart from a few advocates of innocent seeing, most Victorians recognize that nature is always an ideal construction. Any unclouded mirroring of the world would have more in common with the disintegrating perceptions of Tennyson's Lucretius or with the barrage of sensory atoms that assault Browning's Caliban than with Sartre's image of God or Bradley's Absolute.

In choosing the image of the lucid veil, which filters both God and nature through a screen of analogy, I may be accused of introducing an idea which, however important to Aquinas and to scholastic theology in general, plays only a minor role in nineteenth-century poetics and thought. In fact, however, Aquinas was read by Ruskin and Hopkins, and the important medieval distinction between analogical and merely equivocal uses of words survives in Coleridge's influential distinction between analogy and metaphor in *Aids to Reflection*. H. L. Mansel quotes extensively both from Coleridge's *Aids* and Aquinas' *Summa Theologica* in support of his own understanding of analogy in *The Limits of Religious Thought*. Tennyson's familiarity with these ideas is evident from a conversation with William Knight. After stating his belief that 'the ladder of analogy' is 'very useful in metaphysics', Tennyson concedes that 'the outward world, where the ladders and symbols are, is surely more of a veil which hides the Infinite than a mirror which reveals it' (Page, 1983, p. 182).

Each poetic theory shares with a corresponding philosophical tradition an axiom of cognition which can be described with the aid of some analogy or picture. As these axioms change from one tradition to another, so does the corresponding poetic theory. The first axiom, which is shared by Mill's inductive scientist with certain expressive and descriptive theories of poetic language, is best compared to a mirror of nature. Language is a mirror of some antecedently existing fact. This image is modified in later Victorian science by two other axioms. The physicist John Tyndall argues that scientific language is less accurately described as a mirror of nature than as a picture which 're-presents' reality in a medium of the physicist's choice. A picture of waves in ether provides a pictorial analogy of the transmission of light and sound. There may be no actual waves in space or air, and ether may turn out to be a fiction. But at least a pictorial model which 're-presents' the world presumes to find some authentic analogy between what antecedently exists and what Tyndall's physicist can most readily understand. In a pure presentation, by contrast, as in art for art's sake, there is no pretence of re-presenting or of analogizing anything. A mere symbolic shorthand like the algebraic notations of the mathematical physicist is valued by such late-Victorian philosophers of science as T. H. Huxley and Karl Pearson, not for its capacity to mirror or re-present, but for its powerful predictive and its elegant heuristic properties. Whereas the mirror of nature represents a world of facts, and a pictorial analogy like the waves in ether re-presents these facts in a medium of the interpreter's choice, a symbolic shorthand presents a kaleidoscope of fictions which renounce any pretence of duplicating anything. Ferrier's idealist axioms presuppose a different model. They posit a self-consciously framed picture or event in which frame and picture space may change position at any moment. The holistic axioms discussed in Chapter III replace a single subjectively framed picture with a whole gallery of pictures. And these pictures are presented in a hall full of mirrors that allow them to recede from view in an infinite regress. Holistic theories of language and knowledge try to redress the atomism of Mill's empirical psychology without subsiding into the solipsism inherent in Ferrier's refusal to unhinge either God or the world from a framing subject. Holistic theorists conclude that as soon as the mind is resolved into a stream of flaring atoms there is no longer any mental substance to 'stand under' or 'understand'. In a purely atomic world, 'substance' becomes one of Bentham's fictitious entities.

In Chapters IV and V I show how agnostic thought replaces the mirror of nature and the framed picture with metaphors of the darkening glass and the kaleidoscope of self-contained forms. Meaning is originally a lucid veil. But the more agnostic the interpreter, the darker and more veiled his meaning becomes. Agnosticism also replaces the representational mirror with portraits or paintings that re-present some biblical original in a story or myth of the artist's choice. Though there is no longer any attempt to produce a photograph or Xerox-copy of a real-life original, some unanalysable likeness allows the observer to recognize the portrait as showing Perseus representing Christ. But the more such analogizing resists analysis, the purer the re-presentation becomes. Ultimately, in pure forms of presentation where the medium becomes the message, the coloured glass of a kaleidoscope replaces the image of the unclouded mirror or window. To the degree that the 'abnormal' discourse of poetry aspires to the condition of unclouded mirroring, it aspires to abolish itself by dying into one of Mill's inductive sciences. To the degree that it aspires to the formality of a self-contained world which admits no shapes or colours external to itself, poetry tries to renounce its own cognitive worth. Many Victorians would agree with John Grote that, without poetry, they would have no expressible emotions and ideas. But many Victorians would also agree with Arnold and Pater that art is justified by the cognitive *pleasure* which it offers. As poetry replaces God as the new sacred centre, there is no longer any higher religious or moral authority by which poetry can be judged.

To recover more constructive methods of representation, the Victorians try to revive historical analogy. Such an analogy is at the base of all biblical typology, which discerns a resemblance between an Old Testament type and a New Testament antitype. Historical analogizing is also used in cyclical theories of history pioneered by Vico and Herder and adapted both by Comte and by the liberal Anglican historians. It operates as a kind of bifocal lens which brings foreground figures into sharp outline without developing myopia about the past. The two most ambitious axioms of cognition are the Platonic and the Hegelian. For Hopkins, the Platonic realist of the early undergraduate essays, the world is conceived as a diatonic scale of nature, with hierarchically fixed intervals that prevent any promiscuous merging or blending. All this is changed in the Hegelian model, where the static scale of nature is turned into an escalator, a moving altar-stair that slopes through darkness up to God.

At each stage of the argument I try to show how changing theories of language and knowledge are reflected in changing images of the mirror of nature, the picture that re-presents an original in a medium of the painter's choice, and the kaleidoscope of presentational forms that renounce unclouded mirroring altogether. Ferrier's analogy of the framed picture, the holistic image of the infinite regress of pictures in a hall of mirrors, the darkening glass of the agnostics, the bifocal lens of historical analogy, the fixed diatonic scale of the Platonists and the chromatic escalator of the Hegelians are all used as weapons in battles over ideology and values. The holistic axioms studied in Chapter III, for example, tend to be politically conservative. Atomism, by contrast, is the doctrine of *laissez-faire* liberalism. T. H. Green's political holism harks back to the conservative teachings of Coleridge and Burke. There are also similarities between Green's appeal for corporate identity and the totalitarianism of Carlyle. Maurice Mandelbaum believes that Green 'is too infrequently compared' with Fichte (1971, p.

221), a lay preacher in the Prussian army whose *Address to the German Nation* suggests he was the only immediate follower of Kant in Germany who might have supported the German National Socialist Party had he been alive during the 1930s. On the other hand, Arnold's appeal for more inclusive vision in *Culture and Anarchy* and in his essay 'Equality' is directed against 'the hardness and vulgarity of middle-class liberalism' (1965, vol. 5, p. 107). With an almost Marxist zeal for social equality, Arnold uses the holistic axiom to attack bourgeois defence of the class system.

Since almost no theory of language and knowledge is ideologically innocent, the study of epistemology is seldom a cloistered or even a disinterested inquiry. For psychological and aesthetic rather than purely logical reasons, the holistic search for an undifferentiated language in which all discourse is contained continues to appeal to synthetic thinkers like Coleridge, Green, and Müller. More analytic thinkers like Bentham and Mill prefer a highly differentiated language in which each word mirrors a different fact. Most poets are afraid that in Bentham's analytic language 'there will be objectively true or false answers to every question we ask . . . This is frightening,' as Richard Rorty has said, 'because it cuts off the possibility of something new under the sun, of human life as poetic rather than merely contemplative' (1979, pp. 388–9). Poets try to turn the axioms of the scientific tradition inside out by redefining what is normal. They find an advocate in F. H. Bradley, who announces that what he used to admire and love in the poets he now accepts as literal truth. Reversing Plato's campaign of dialectic against poetry, the English Hegelians argue that the primary meanings are metaphoric and that they bear the same relation to discursive meanings that myth bears to history. It is less accurate to say that the language of the poets illustrates the commentary of the philosophers than to say that metaphysical discourse, like the discourse of logic, theology, or ethics, is one possible commentary on that language.

The same conflict over values and ideas underlies the ascendancy of late-Victorian formalism, whose kaleidoscope of presentational forms tries to escape from the grime and contagion of a world covered with the fingerprints of matter. Victorian disciples of Coleridge might well deplore the purist vogue of art for art's sake. They might see it as a betrayal of the high vocation of the poet as creator, who is asked to impose order on an alien world. And Hegelian critics might see it as a sad decline from the high calling of the poet as prophet or seer, who is privileged to turn poetry into magic or liturgy, disclosing the secrets of a lucidly veiled Absolute or God. And yet the free play and disinterestedness that Arnold praises in his poet and critic are more than just the dedication of any dilettante to his hobby. As Aristotle recognized, the freedom of art is a celebration of the natural delight people take 'in the disengaged use of their cognitive faculties'. And, as one commentator says, 'for a free, rational being, there is no higher activity than this and, therefore, none by which it can suitably be justified' (F. E. Sparshott, 1982, p. 101).

Axioms of cognition never change often or quickly. But I show that during the period 1860–1900, as the darkening glass of the agnostics and the colourful kaleidoscopes of the purists begin to replace representational images of the mirror, the subjectively framed picture, and the lucid veil, it is possible to chart a fairly direct relation between changes in poetic theory and practice and the ascendancy of new scientific theories designed to explain the mathematical physics of Faraday and Clerk Maxwell, the rise of new agnostic theologies, and the gradual deconstruction of Platonic metaphysics, first begun by Jowett in the early 1870s and completed by Pater two decades later. Before poetry becomes too pure or impoverished, too uncontaminated or empty (depending on one's perspective) to be true of anything but itself, most Victorians assume that poetry is a source of knowledge and meaning. But I argue that the precise nature of that knowledge and meaning tends to be lucidly veiled, even from the poets themselves. The primary reason for such veiling is that the dominant representational axioms of the age are crossed with Romantic theories of spontaneously achieved creation. According to these expressive axioms of the subjectively framed picture or event, the world is already ordered by the poet's imaginative perception of it. But is it not to the poet's advantage to veil the discovery that all poetry is really about other poems? Is there not something disquieting and subversive about the conclusion that perception is only primary imagination, and that (instead of representing an existing world) the poet presents a world that is already prearranged by his imagination and words? These doubling inventions of the expressive line of theorizing are further complicated by the assumption of typological critics like Keble and of idealists like Carlyle that the oracular utterances of the poet as prophet or as seer testify to his link with supernatural truth. In this oracular tradition, poetry is not an end in itself but only a means to an end. Keble's biblical God, Hegel's self-unfolding Mind, or even the unknowable God of Hamilton and Mansel, could just as easily achieve that end by other means. By a sort of Newtonian law which posits for every action an opposite and equal reaction, the impurities of this oracular line of criticism produce the revolt of late-Victorian critics like Pater and Wilde. W. P. Ker's essay 'On the Philosophy of Art' (1883) marks one such moment of transition. His criticism wavers uneasily between Hegel's teaching that aesthetics is 'a science about art' which 'goes beyond art' and the new purist teaching that art is its own end and can have no reference to anything beyond itself.

THE MIRROR OF NATURE:
SCIENCE AND THE EXPRESSIVE TRADITION

Except for J. S. Mill, who is hard pressed to explain how the poet's violation of descriptive norms can qualify as knowledge, all the theorists studied in Part One are determined to refute Thomas Love Peacock's assertion in 'The Four Ages of Poetry' (1820) that the poet's effusions are neither useful nor true. 'While the historian and the philosopher are advancing in, and accelerating, the progress of knowledge,' Peacock complains, 'the poet is wallowing in the rubbish of departed ignorance . . . The march of his intellect is like that of a crab, backward' (1961, pp. 577–8). In order to educate, most Victorian theorists assert, it is not necessary for the poet to imitate Peacock's philosopher or historian. Only for empiricists like Mill is the educational value of scientific induction prior and unquestioned. In Mill's view, poetry can express, refine, or allay emotion. But, being unscientific, it cannot directly educate.

According to the more constructive lines of expressive theorizing explored in Chapters II and III, the poet does more than merely express his feelings. He also articulates a world. When expressing his grief in *In Memoriam*, for example, Tennyson's mourner defines a world which has already been brought into focus for him by the more primary form of imaginative framing described by J. F. Ferrier in his treatise *The Institutes of Metaphysics*, where every perception of the world is said to be inseparable from the contribution of a perceiving subject. In Coleridge's familiar phrase, the poet's secondary imagination is an echo of a prior and more primary imaginative act. Poetry is educational, not because it is a source of knowledge, but because it is a source of meaning, which is an antecedent condition of knowledge. The opposite of meaning is not error but nonsense, the absurdity of a world of unorganized sensations.

Many theories of poetry reflect political as well as aesthetic preferences. Utilitarian attempts to demystify poetry by comparing its abnormal emotive language with the normal descriptive statements of science are clearly an attempt to simplify poetry, making it more intelligible to the masses. Art is no longer the sacred preserve or

9

sanctuary of an élite, but the property of a democratic society freed of the last vestiges of priestly authority and metaphysical tyranny. This democratic ideal is clearest in Mill, but it is also implicit in Wordsworth, who values poetry for its expression of communal emotion, proving 'we have all of us one human heart' ('The Old Cumberland Beggar', l.153). A similar ideology informs the criticism of G. H. Lewes, who in *The Principles of Success in Literature* (1865) tries to reduce aesthetics to three 'scientific' principles, including a Wordsworthian principle of sincerity. In his *Biographical History of Philosophy* (1845–6), Lewes praises Comte for making philosophy scientific. Metaphysics, by contrast, is rejected as a highsounding name for obfuscation and for ignorance.

The more constructive versions of Victorian expressive theory trace their descent, not from Mill and Lewes, but from philosophic idealists like J. F. Ferrier and from such holistic theorists of knowledge and language as Coleridge. Without human creation, these theorists argue, there would be no humanity. The idealist doctrine that man is by birth and by instinct an artist and architect of nature reaffirms Vico's precept, 'Verum factum'. According to historians like Thomas Arnold, A. P. Stanley, and Connop Thirlwall, all so-called historical description is really interpretation in disguise. Their axioms are already implicit in Browning's theory of 'the Maker-see' in *Sordello*. At a rudimentary stage, the poet or historian may simply assert *that* he has seen. But Browning knows that to see Caponsacchi is already to see him as a Perseus-St George or to see him as a seducer and betrayer. It is to see him in some determinate way. The interpreter's next task, therefore, is to say *what* he has seen. But since there are many different figures in the carpet, the poet must become the highest kind of poet, a 'Maker-see' who allows the reader to see some figures and not others. Every observer has to interpret what the otpic nerves transmit. And every historian has to read what the documents in the archives say. But the moment the poet or historian tries to reconstruct the past, he generates a fiction. As one critic says, 'the passage of real experience into the past is not itself fictional, but all attempts to reconstruct are precisely that: fictions. Fiction is not what is lost but what is constructed' (Scholes, 1982, p. 32). In showing how fictions are used by his 'Maker-see', Browning is also showing how every one of us constructs a world we call real. There could be few more important projects for any poet.

I Poetry and Science:
Mirrors, Pictures, and Symbolic Shorthand

Most Victorian poets are resolved to justify Wordsworth's faith that 'poetry is the breath and finer spirit of all knowledge ... the impassioned expression which is in the countenance of all science' (1963, p. 253). But if this is the poet's function, in what sense is his 'impassioned expression' true? How can his language give us knowledge? Lying at the heart of the debate which Arnold and Huxley waged over the virtues of a literary as opposed to a scientific education, these questions seem to me as important today as they were a hundred years ago. In this first chapter I study changing conceptions of poetic truth by examining the impact on Victorian poetics of three scientific models: the mirror, the picture, and the non-representational symbol or fiction. I begin with Mill's account of scientific induction in his *System of Logic* (1843). In analysing and refurbishing the empirical axiom of the mirror of nature, Mill reaffirms the mind's power to represent accurately the physical world. This axiom of the mirror is modified in later Victorian science by two other axioms. In a pamphlet entitled *Scientific Use of the Imagination* (1873), of which Tennyson owned a copy, John Tyndall argues that physicists make use of pictures of waves in ether to 're-present' nature in a medium of their choice. What we predicate of light or sound may lie in the method of picturing it. More sceptical is the conclusion of T. H. Huxley, expounded most fully in his essay 'On the Physical Basis of Life' (1868), that scientific theories are mere symbolic shorthand designed to economize mental labour. They make no more pretence of mirroring an external world than do the pieces of coloured glass in a kaleidoscope.

From Mill's early confidence in the capacity of language to reflect as in a mirror what is already there, most Victorian poets and scientists tend to pass to the increasingly sceptical conclusions of Huxley and Karl Pearson. They speak of scientific theory as a mere pragmatic instrument or tool, more or less elegant, economical, or convenient to use. I conclude the chapter by turning to F. H. Bradley's

The Principles of Logic (1883), where I consider the consequence for poetry of his famous critique of scientific abstraction. I show that whereas earlier Victorian theories subordinate poetry to a scientific model of induction, later idealist thought subordinates science to poetry. In a treatise on 'The Problem of Philosophy at the Present Time', originally given as an address to the Philosophical Society at the University of Edinburgh in 1881, the Oxford Hegelian Edward Caird repeats Plato's prophecy that the 'old quarrel between the poet and the philosopher' can 'be reconciled only if poetry [is] shown to be truth, or truth, in its highest aspect, to be poetry' (1881, pp. 42–3).

1 Mill, Wordsworth, and Tennyson on Poetic Truth

In *A System of Logic* (1843) Mill methodically reduces all knowledge to a process of induction. The mind is a mirror that reflects physical nature. Knowledge depends on the accuracy of its reflections. Unless everything has entered through the senses and the scientific belief in an ordered world is justified by repeated empirical obser-vations, it is impossible, Mill argues, to arrive at general laws. As a critic of poetry, however, Mill revolts against this empirical mirror of nature, because he knows that by expressing all the niceties of his own intimate elation or awe a poet like Wordsworth rightly refuses to surrender to some crudely defined induction of the geologist or botanist all the psychological refinements of his response to Mount Snowdon or a daffodil. Without a theory of induction, the logical distinction between sanity and insanity would be impossible to maintain. But no genius is confined to empirical laws. And the Mill of 'On Liberty', the great champion of intellectual minorities, is sworn to defend the essential sanity of genius and to denounce the madness of commonplace minds. The imagination of the poetic genius must absorb descriptive details, but it can never be confined to them. Poetry must be recomposed beyond the simplicity of a scientific induction and must, as Mill says in his *Autobiography*, appeal 'to the feelings on [some] basis of reason' (1981, vol. 1, p. 73).

Apart from idealists like John Grote and later F. H. Bradley, Mill is one of the few Victorian philosophers to take art no less seriously than science and logic as a means of enlarging knowledge and of discovering repressed or forgotten truths. Having recovered from his breakdown after experiencing the 'healing power' of Wordsworth's poetry, the young Mill is eager to refute Jeremy Bentham's opinion that because poetry is fictitious and untrue it is a dangerous enemy of the Utilitarian philosophy. Mill's earliest articles on poetry, which he published in 1833, try to vindicate the poet against Bentham's charge. Mill argues that to judge poetry by the same criteria as we judge a scientific treatise is to commit a form of the descriptive fallacy. To demand full reducibility to the descriptive statements of the scientist is to forget that there may be other standards of truth – criteria of felicity or aptness, for example. These other criteria will be no less rigorous than those applied in science, but they will be more appropriate for evaluating truths that are conveyed in poetry, which addresses itself, not to 'matter of fact', as Mill says, but 'to the feelings' (1981, vol. 1, p. 344).

For Mill, then, science is a language of true-or-false propositions, whereas poetry is a language of more or less felicitous proposals. When the geologist identifies the stones of a hill as terminal moraine, he proceeds to classify the range of hills by providing a scientific explanation of their glacial origin. We judge the geologist's classifications as true-or-false judgemental inferences, capable of being empircally tested. Reading *In Memoriam*, however, we judge Tennyson's classification of the solid lands as mist and clouds by different criteria.

> There rolls the deep where grew the tree.
>   O earth, what changes hast thou seen!
>   There where the long street roars, hath been
> The stillness of the central sea.
>
> The hills are shadows, and they flow
>   From form to form, and nothing stands;
>   They melt like mist, the solid lands,
> Like clouds they shape themselves and go.
>
> (*In Memoriam*, CXXIII, 1–8)

Tennyson's lines have all the immediacy of wonder and dread conveyed through an idea of terrifying dissolution in which everything solid and definite seems to slip away into the void. No reader can respond to Tennyson's powerfully restrained proposals to see land as mist and hills as shadows unless he has been properly educated by metaphor. By metaphor I mean the association of ideas, not by contiguity, but by similarity, or, as Mill would argue, by the logic of their emotional as well as their representational links. In order to clarify the distinction between poetic proposals and scientific descriptions, Mill argues that poetic utterances about lions which look like statements made by naturalists 'intent upon stating the truth, the whole truth, and nothing but the truth' (1981, vol. 1, p. 347), are not designed to state the truth at all. The mistake of construing as descriptions of lions utterances which record the reactions of an observer is the mistake of confusing two modes of discourse, one referential, framed on the representational notion of the mirror of nature, and the other emotive. Though Mill does not use the term, the confusion which arises from attempts to subordinate poetic discourse to a scientific induction is an excellent example of what more recent philosophers of language have called the 'descriptive fallacy'.

The failure to see that poets use language in ways beyond the scope of traditional description, in order to evince emotion and to do things with words, is also the same failure to which J. L. Austin draws attention when trying to extricate from descriptive statements the kind of utterance he calls 'performative' (1962, p. 25). There is a primary sense, Austin concedes, in which all utterance is performative. To say something is to perform an act, if you will – the act of saying something. It is important to distinguish, however, between Hopkins' mere act of saying in 'Hurrahing in Harvest' that the stooks are rising in the fields (ll. 1–2) and his performance of an act of ritual naming, a kind of baptism, when he pronounces the hills a part of God's anatomy (ll. 6, 9). Only the second action is performative in Austin's sense. What is said has no existence prior to Hopkins' saying it.

Mill's axiom in an 1833 essay that poetry is 'the expression or utterance of feeling' (1981, vol. 1, p. 348) leads him to ascribe to poetry two features of language which Austin ascribes to all performative speech. In the first place, both are activities, mental performances. Poetry expresses, Mill says, 'state[s] of awe, wonder, or terror' (1981, vol. 1, p. 347). When Wordsworth's heart fills with pleasure, and he joins with the daffodils in a sacramental dance, his elated diction gives a verdict or estimate of the daffodils' worth. His language has less in common with a botanical description of flowers and trees than with the words used in christening ships or making wagers. The private stage on which the dance of the flowers will be repeated is more like a sanctuary than a chorus hall. To re-enact the dance on the stage of the 'inward eye' is nothing short of felicity. Wordsworth's ritual naming of this felicity, which he calls 'the bliss of solitude', is really an act of faith. It is a wager about his ability to renew felicity now and in the future. Like a poet's emotive reactions to lions, such ritual naming would not normally be construed as a use of words to mirror facts that exist before they are described. Nor are such decrees and wagers thought to predict, like scientific laws, the kind of future event – the outcome of a race or the throw of a dice – on which a gambler makes a wager. For unless the future were unpredictable, there would *be* no wager.

A second characteristic of both poetic and performative speech is that neither can be said to advance a strictly 'true-or-false' proposition. Both are what Kant would call a form of 'trowing', a holding true that is recognized to be 'insufficient *both* subjectively and objectively' (1881, p. 705). Since no logical proof or demonstration is involved, there is nothing for the 'trower' to 'unbelieve'. Or as Austin whimsically insists, when propounding his 'doctrine of the *Infelicities*' (1962, p. 14), the poet is not judged by true-or-false criteria. What he says will be evaluated as more or less happy or apt. In anticipation of I. A. Richards' doctrine, Mill asserts that poets may represent lions 'falsely or with exaggeration' (1981, vol. 1, p. 347), and be all the more 'felicitous' as a result.

For Mill's inductive logician, a scientific fact is incapable of being modified by anything he can do or say about it. A geological fact like the age of the earth simply is the case, whether or not a poet like Tennyson can understand and use the fact. Poetry, by contrast, is something we 'make up' about the facts. If it yields knowledge at all, it is the kind of *a priori* knowledge which the mind possesses only of its own artefacts and fictions. One such fiction, Wordsworth's lyric 'The Solitary Reaper', which Mill must have known, breaks the dominant indicative mood of factual report with injunctions and questions. To involve the reader in the value of a music that each listener must hear and celebrate privately, Wordsworth opens with a series of marvelling injunctions: 'Behold her', 'Stop

here, or gently pass!', 'O listen!' (ll. 1, 4, 7). In abruptly switching
the scene from the Highlands to the Arabian desert, then back to the
farthest Hebrides, Wordsworth is inviting the reader to experience
faith in a power which Mill says it is the office of the poet 'to declare
. . . and make impressive' (1962, vol. 12, p. 163). In a letter to
Carlyle dated 5 July 1833, Mill concedes that 'the . . . more
numerous kind of people will consider' the truths of the poet 'as
nothing but dreaming or madness' (1962, vol. 12, p. 163). But by
asking in bewildered awe, 'Will no one tell me what she sings?' (l.
17), Wordsworth celebrates a faith that is inclusive enough to value
what it cannot know or understand. Such faith has less in common
with 'dreaming or madness' than with Keats's faith in the holiness of
the heart's affections. As the celebrant mounts the hill, bearing 'The
music in [his] heart . . . / Long after it was heard no more' (ll. 31–2),
he becomes to the Highland Lass what Wordsworth hopes the ideal
reader will become to his own poem. The lyric, like the Highland
song, directs the listener to the silent meanings. The listener
becomes the kind of reader Mill describes to Carlyle, a 'hearer or
spectator' who 'will . . . receive' the poet's 'truths at once' and 'lay
them to heart in proportion to the impressiveness with which the
artist delivers and embodies them' (1962, vol. 12, p. 163).

By evoking a peace which may not antecedently exist, the ritual
blessing which Wordsworth pronounces on Dorothy at the end of
'Tintern Abbey' shows how words may reach a listener from the
other side of silence. Prayerfully transforming the indicatives of de-
scriptive poetry into the language of benediction, 'let the moon /
Shine on thee' (ll. 134–5), Wordsworth uses subjunctive verbs of
possible rejection and loss to make the death of imagination pre-
figure literal death: 'If I should be where I no more can hear / Thy
voice' (ll. 147–8). In saying to Dorothy like a voice from the grave,
'Nor . . . / . . . wilt thou then forget / That on the banks of this
delightful stream / We stood together' (ll. 146, 149–51), Words-
worth is drawing upon the auxiliary verb of prophecy and volition
to reach into the silence and to commemorate by an odd kind of in-
verted *déjà vu* his sister's future commemoration of a love which,
after his death, she alone will be able to keep alive in the 'dwelling-
place' of memory.

In the sonnet 'It is a beauteous evening, calm and free', Words-
worth and his listeners require a comparable faith in the benedictory

language of meanings felt, considered, and remembered in silence. Unless the reader responds to the poet's exhortation to listen imaginatively, he will be deaf to the 'sound like thunder' which the 'mighty Being' makes 'everlastingly' (ll. 6, 8) only in the ears of those who have the aptitude to listen for meanings in a new and deeper silence. Such faith, the 'willing suspension of disbelief', as Coleridge calls it, does not require the kind of notional assent we give to a theorem in geometry or a logical proof. Since the young girl who walks by Wordsworth's side appears 'untouched by solemn thought' (l. 10), the poet cannot be describing a capacity to be attuned to silent meanings which exists in advance of affirming and celebrating the power. Instead, Wordsworth's ritual blessing of the girl, 'Thou liest in Abraham's bosom all the year' (l. 12), beautifully illustrates Mill's contention that the reader's faith in the poet must be a trust or assent, a confidence that the man of words loves silence better. For as Mill explains in a passage that strikingly anticipates Newman's distinction between real and notional assent, 'the artist's is the higher part ... by him alone is real *knowledge* of such truths conveyed'. It must be possible, says Mill, in a sentence that could easily have found its way into Newman's 'Essay in Aid of a Grammar of Assent', to 'convince' the logician 'who never could *know* the intuitive truths, that they are even very *probable*, and that he may have faith in them when higher natures than his own affirm that they are truths' (1962, vol. 12, p. 163).

Though Mill tries to liberate the poet from a descriptive theory of language, his essays of the eary 1830s confuse the issue by using the same verb 'describe' to cover two dissimilar forms of reference. Misled, in my view, by the analogy of painting, Mill uses 'describe' both for the first facts of perception and for the last facts of explored emotion. Mill speaks metaphorically about the 'colours of the imagination' and the need to 'paint' emotion 'with scrupulous truth'. Because a poet paints in exaggerated colours and uses images of 'striking likeness and contrasts', Mill assumes that a poet describes his emotions in the same way that a portrait painter records his visual impressions of a model. Perhaps a less pictorial analogy – a comparison of poetry and music – would have prevented Mill from assuming that poetry, like a representational painting, provides a transcript of emotion. When Hartley Coleridge, for example, in an essay contemporary with Mill's, maintains that 'the highest poetry has no analogy whatever with painting', because poetry, like music, has the power of 'suggesting infinitely more than words can say' (1839, pp. 529, 537), he is drawing attention to a distinction between a mere description of emotion and the artistic expression of emotion. This is an important distinction which Mill's pictorial thinking obscures. Mill's failure to distinguish between the description of emotion and the description of a lion (1981, vol. 1, p. 347) prevents his grasping the difference between the mere transcription of feeling, as in Tennyson's dry and official affirmation of faith in the Prologue of *In Memoriam*, where private consolations have become part of a public testament or at most catchwords, and the lucid articulation of emotion, well illustrated by Tennyson's consoling optatives of prayer in section LXXXVI of the same poem.

> Sweet after showers, ambrosial air,
>   That rollest from the gorgeous gloom
>   Of evening over brake and bloom
> And meadow, slowly breathing bare
>
> The round of space, and rapt below
>   Through all the dewy-tasselled wood,
>   And shadowing down the hornèd flood
> In ripples, fan my brows and blow
>
> The fever from my cheek, and sigh
>   The full new life that feeds thy breath
>   Throughout my frame, till Doubt and Death,
> Ill brethren, let the fancy fly
>
> From belt to belt of crimson seas
>   On leagues of odour streaming far,
>   To where in yonder orient star
> A hundred spirits whisper 'Peace'.

                              (*In Memoriam*, LXXXVI)

The grammatical kernel of Tennyson's prayer is the petition 'Air, fan my brows, and sigh the full new life.' But 'air' is heavily qualified by the clauses that come after, so that until we reach the end of the second quatrain we tend to read the lines as opulent description. Only the optative mood of the principal verbs 'fan' and 'sigh' forces us to construe the preceding descriptions as prayerful apostrophes. From this point on, the springtime landscapes that Tennyson evokes in the lyric become less and less descriptive. They are elements now of a dedicatory formula, of a prayer to God to bind the soul with obligation and affection. No longer confined to what Mill calls the descriptive use of words, Tennyson draws upon optative verbs and subjunctive moods to refine and transform the impressions he receives. The power of nature to console depends on the efficacy of his petition. The meteorologist's statement that the air is purer after a rainfall has a different philosophical grammar from Tennyson's statement that the 'ambrosial air' has sacramental power. A meteorologist's reading of the pollution index is unaffected by anyone's believing or disbelieving it. But Tennyson's statement depends on what his belief in the healing properties of 'ambrosial air' allows him to do with it. Whereas the language of Mill's inductive logician describes a prior state of affairs, Tennyson's poetic language makes something happen.

2 The Dualist Legacy: Two Solutions in Tennyson and Mill

Mill is the great enemy of finality. His ability to criticize and enlarge his premises about poetry gives to his early essays a delightful and exhilarating life. In Mill's 1833 essays on poetry, for example, originally published in the January and October numbers of the *Monthly Repository*, 'the poetry of culture' and of 'a naturally poetic temperament' are set in contrast to each other. But in the article of July 1835, published in the *London Review*, Mill asserts that the poet-philosopher, because he combines two virtues, is naturally to be preferred to the mere poet. What distinguishes, not simply dialectic, but intelligence itself from mere observing is the power of revising and synthesizing thought, which Mill displays to an unusual degree. Because he is always ready to inhibit dogma and quicken truth in pursuit of the wider premise, we can learn more from Mill when he is wrong than from most philosophers when they are right.

I have suggested that Mill's early essays on poetry contain 'in more than embryonic development', as M. H. Abrams has said, 'I. A. Richards' influential distinction between "scientific statement, where truth is ultimately a matter of verification", and the "emotive utterance" of the poet, which is composed of sentences which look like statements, but are actually "pseudo-statements"' (1953, p. 323). In fact, I think Mill's position is more complicated than Abrams' comparison suggests. Mill's early tendency to equate poetry with feeling and to deny it any cognitive worth derives originally from his father's comments on the 'wild imagination' of the Hindus, whose poetical excesses are unfavourably compared with the more mature and sober art of the Muslims. 'Poetry is the language of the passions,' James Mill asserts in his *History of British India*, 'and men feel, before they speculate' (1817, vol. 2, p. 33). But in his letter and diary entries the younger Mill also makes it clear that poetry, no less than science, deals in speculations and beliefs.

The true Victorian precursor of I. A. Richards is Alexander Smith of Banff, in whom we find a flexible but straightforward version of the emotive theory. In his 1835 essay, 'The Philosophy of Poetry', Smith concedes that poetry is often referential, but he insists that it is never *merely* so. Smith observes that often no grammatical clue exists to differentiate a merely descriptive use of language, like 'my son Absalom', from a poetic use. His example of the latter is the biblical passage, 'oh! Absalom, my son, my son'. The interjection 'oh' and the repetition of 'my son' add nothing to the content. But they clearly align the poetic language of the biblical David with two functions of discourse which differentiate poetry from an equivalent assertion of fact. These are the use of words to realize vividly, and to appraise (Alexander Smith, 1835, p. 830).

Unlike Smith, Mill himself is never entirely happy with the distinction he draws between the descriptive language of science and the emotive language of poetry. He believes there is a poetic way of arriving at truth, just as there is a scientific and a philosophic way. But if poetry is purely emotive, if it is only 'feeling, confessing itself to itself in moments of solitude' (1981, vol. 1, p. 348), in what sense can poetry be true? A pure poet like Shelley subordinates the association of his ideas to the course of his emotions. But even in his earliest essays Mill tries to amend an emotive theory of art. He admits that a poet who combines the reflective powers of a Wordsworth with the native gifts of a Shelley is to be preferred to either type by itself. 'Truth is more certainly arrived at by two processes, verifying and correcting each other, than by one alone' (1981, vol. 1, p. 364). By recovering some of the many useful suggestions about poetry which lie buried in Mill's letters and in his treatises on logic and education, which are not explicitly devoted to poetics, it should be possible to show how Mill is constantly revising his premises. In order to make the study of poetry an authentic part of education, Mill extends the meaning of the prize word 'truth' so that it can include versions of the world that can be still judged as right or wrong but by different, though no less exacting, criteria than those the philosopher applies to a logical induction or to a hypothesis in science.

Mill accepts the beliefs of science at full value. But he realizes that poets like Wordsworth and Tennyson also solicit our belief in very different kinds of worlds. These worlds cannot always be reduced to the scientific models of Darwin or Newton. The world views of these poets are of independent importance for Mill because the correctness of a scientific induction itself depends upon and implies, not so much an antecedently existing world, as a world that is revealed to its observer only in all *right* interpretations of it. Included in such right interpretations are not only scientific and philosophic but also poetic ways of imagining the world. Just as Mill's essay 'On Liberty' champions *laissez-faire* in the realm of ideas, so his speculations on poetry champion a form of pluralism. Worlds can be built in many different ways.

In his later essays, there are three ways in which Mill proposes to make poetry true without surrendering its prerogatives. The least satisfactory way, proposed in the 1835 essay on Tennyson, is for a naturally poetic author, incapable of writing a long poem, to make himself a poet of culture. Such a hybrid author may be able to produce an extended work that is logical and poetical by turns. But what Mill really seeks is an explanation of the poet's capacity to be rational and expressive simultaneously. How can deep thinking and deep feeling be inseparable? Mill's thoughts on the subject are never fully formulated. They are clearly implicit, however, in his theories of inference, which allow the mind to check apparent against actual resemblances. A second answer to the question is also provided in Book VI of *A System of Logic*, in Mill's doctrine of ends, which allows the artist to supply the major premises of belief and desire. From various remarks that Mill has made, I shall try to reconstruct and critically examine each of these two last attempts to move beyond the dualism of his early essays on art.

Even when formulating an emotive theory of art, claiming that the poet's function is to describe, not the lion, but the emotions it evokes (1981, vol. 1, p. 347), Mill is unwilling to eliminate the lion altogether because he is reluctant to discard the representational axiom of the mirror of nature as the canon of truth. On Utilitarian premises, poetry would seem to be feigned history, as it was for Bacon. If this is so, then how is Mill to reconcile an empirical theory of knowledge with anything but the narrowest empirical conception of poetic truth? An answer can be found in Mill's belief that the emotional associations of the poet, which are founded on feeling and affective memory, are not an exception to empirical laws. Mill is actually burying a theory of description only to revive it in a different form. His poet is not really composing without the aid of mirrors. By recovering sense impressions once reflected in the mirror, but since forgotten, Mill's poet is continually restoring mirror images. The emotions evoked by the poet's descriptions revive a set of facts, stored for retrieval in the unconscious mind, and actually corresponding to past events. Such a view of displaced or repressed description is never made explicit in Mill's essays on poetry. But a study of his *System of Logic* (1843) and of his notes to his father's *Analysis of the Phenomena of the Human Mind* (1869) confirms our suspicion that, in struggling to vindicate the truth claims of poetry, Mill is trying to explain the practice of Wordsworth and Tennyson, the two contemporary poets he most admires and wants to defend.

According to Mill's *System of Logic*, 'in almost every act of our perceiving faculties, observation and inference are intimately blended' (1974, vol. 8, pp. 641–2). The inferences may be of two kinds. They may be judgements, 'belief grounded on evidence', or intuitions, belief 'independent of external evidence'. Strictly speaking, a truth that is known directly, by pure intuition, like the mind's emotions and volitions, is not an inferred truth, and lies outside the province of logic. As R. F. McRae explains, some truths 'are known directly, that is, by intuition; some are known by means of other truths, that is, inferred. Logic has no concern with the former kind of truths, nor with the question whether they are part of the original furniture of the mind or given through the senses' (Mill, 1974, vol. 7, p. xxiv). There is much in our knowledge, however, including perhaps poetic knowledge, which may seem to be intuited but which is actually inferred, and which is therefore subject to logical study. Such a disguised inference, to distinguish it both from the pure intuition which McRae identifies and from a scientific inference, may be called 'intuitive'. Evidence, Mill believes, is supplied by memory, by the recollection of past sensations. In cases of judgement, the mind compares present sensations of yellow colour, heavy weight, brilliant lustre, for example, and past experiences of gold, to reach the inference that the mineral it now perceives is gold. In all so-called description we infer. Because the mind is not an unclouded mirror of nature, its images must be supplemented with comparison and inference at every stage.

Intuition, the alternative mode of inference, is an activity firmly rooted in imagination, just as judgement is rooted in memory. Like Hobbes and Hume, Mill ascribes to the imagination a constructive power which enables it to form out of goats, lions, and snakes a composite image of chimeras. Pure intuitions of chimeras, however, are not to be confused with intuitive inferences about dinosaurs, for example. The truth or falsity of an inference can always be checked. Whereas there exist no past sensations of chimeras to confirm the mind's present intuition of them, a poet's presentation of a dinosaur – which is my example, not Mill's – can be judged by a paleontologist as either true or false, because intuitive inferences are easily convertible into forms of judgement based on memory of past sensations. In the case of dinosaurs, the memory is collective and geological, preserved for the scientist in the fossil record. Unlike the paleontologist, who simply combines his ideas as they are found in nature, in existing spatial connections between the dinosaur's jawbone, say, and other fossil remains of its skull, Mill's poet compounds his ideas under the influence of dominant feelings, under emotions of awe or terror, for example, which allow him to substitute one idea for another. Mill is anticipating, without in any way influencing, Roman Jakobson's influential distinction between metonymic combination of ideas and metaphoric substitution of them. Many studies of historical influence come to ruin on the obvious but neglected truth that the mind, though rich in its accidental varieties, is poor in its essential types. It is possible to speak of influence, however, in the case of Mill and his father. For the distinction between two methods of compounding ideas, the younger Mill is indebted to the elder. And he owes to James Martineau's articles on Joseph Priestley, the first of which appeared in the same number of the *Monthly Repository* (January–April, 1833) as Mill's essay 'What is Poetry?', the specific application of his father's distinction to the poet's synchronous and the scientist's successive methods of associating their ideas.

If only scientific knowledge is genuine, then all education is education by metonymy. But poets want to associate their ideas synchronously. Unpredictable breaks in logic and abrupt cross-cuts from one idea to another allow them to celebrate the sovereignty of their ideas over the temporal and spatial connections of the scientist. The poets show what it means to think in and be educated by metaphor.

For a full account of the theory of synchronous association which Mill develops in the 1833 essay, we must turn to his editorial remarks in his father's *Analysis of the Phenomena of the Human Mind* where he speaks of feelings as complex psychological states caused by sensations yet connected with ideas of aversion or desire that allow the poet to experience pain and pleasure simultaneously. Earlier empiricists like Locke and Hume deplore the process of synchronous association because it may so transform present sensations that they lose all correspondence to their sequence in nature. But Mill commends these changes. Without forcing him to abandon the empirical basis of his theory, they explain how poets may merely seem to be composing without the aid of mirrors. If the feelings the poet associates correspond to no sensation he is conscious of mirroring, they continue to be logically valid intuitions only if they are inferences in disguise. And feelings can be inferences in disguise only if they correspond to sensations once registered on the mirror of the mind but now forgotten or obscured. Though the mind's unconscious memory is not a faculty that Locke or Hume recognizes, it is of central importance in the autobiographical poetry of Wordsworth and Tennyson. When forgotten sensations come suddenly alive, they strike the mind with the force of a recognition, as Wordsworth discovers when he encounters his 'spots of time' in *The Prelude* or as Tennyson discovers when, in exorcizing his grief, he uncovers the meaning of past events in *In Memoriam*.

To see what Mill means we may turn once more to section CXXIII of *In Memoriam*, where there seem at first to be no sensations in nature which correspond to Tennyson's elated sense of being invulnerable to change.

> But in my spirit will I dwell,
> And dream my dream, and hold it true;
> For though my lips may breathe adieu,
> I cannot think the thing farewell.
>
> (*In Memoriam*, CXXIII, 9–12)

If Tennyson's feeling of elation and release corresponds to no phenomena he is now conscious of experiencing, there is only one way in which it can be a valid intuition, or a disguised form of inference. It must correspond to forgotten or evaded sensations, to experiences repressed in the poet's memory. There are indeed several earlier experiences in *In Memoriam* which arouse the same curious amalgam of dread and exaltation. I am thinking of frightening sensations of lucid veils and glimmering gravestones, or of the strange experience of dim light waging battle against boundless day. In finally submitting to the geological truths and allowing the dizzying depths of duration to be dispelled before his eyes, Tennyson is bringing to consciousness a truth about the soul's fragile hardihood, about its power to create its own enduring worlds. Though the poet's conjunctions of dread and exaltation are disguised or intuitive forms of inferences, which his earlier experiences confirm, the truth to which they point – the soul's sovereignty over nature – has formerly been repressed, perhaps because it seemed too daring a claim to urge.

I argued earlier that Tennyson's association of hills with shadows and of solid lands with clouds in the first eight lines of section CXXIII, from which I have just quoted the next four lines, is really only a felicitous proposal. But Mill's theory of intuitive inferences in *A System of Logic* suggests that this association may be something more. Sensations of awe and terror which Tennyson experiences simultaneously rather than successively in the presence of the hills are compounded under the influence of powerful feelings. But far from losing all correspondence to their sequence in nature, the alternation of fluid and solid elements – the displacement of the tree by the deep and of the central sea by the roaring street – corresponds to a sequence in time that could actually be observed if we were to replace the conventional mirror of nature with a time-lapse photograph of the earth extending over billions of years.

I have shown that by enabling the poet to check his sensations against events which have actually occurred but been repressed in memory, or which have been forgotten with the passage of time until a scientist like Lyell or Chambers rediscovers them, Mill's doctrine of intuitive inferences allows him to affirm that the dignity of art resides in its power to be true descriptively while still remaining free. I should now like to consider a second way in which Mill tries to overcome the dualism between the poet's emotive and the scientist's descriptive meanings. In Book VI of his *Logic* Mill argues that art is ultimately a source of knowledge, for it ennobles as the architect of our purposes and inspires as the poet of our dreams. The artist's high vocation is to discern and proclaim the ends we should pursue, then relinquish to science the task of determining how to reach them.

Mill's doctrine of ends is anticipated by his letter to Carlyle, which assigns to the poet the persuasive function of making truth impressive to those who already know it. But in the last chapter of the *Logic* Mill takes one crucial step beyond his earlier position. 'The only one of the premises . . . which Art supplies, is the original major premise, which asserts that the attainment of the given end is desirable. Science then lends to Art the proposition . . . that the performance of certain actions will attain the end' (1974, vol. 8, pp. 944–5). In the letter to Carlyle, truth resides with the logician alone. In order to be moved by the poet, the reader must have an antecedent faith in what he says (1962, vol. 12, p. 163). In the *Logic*, by contrast, the artist's intuitions are the antecedent condition of truth. The antithesis of art is no longer the truth or falsehood of logical inquiry, but the meaninglessness of a world from which human purpose has been banished. Until the artist has intuited man's ends, there is no intelligible world which the logician can mirror or the scientist can study.

In trying to clarify the nature of aesthetic and moral truth, which will not quite formulate in logical terms, Mill acknowledges his debt to Kant, the philosopher who tries hardest to make the mysteries of reason intelligible. According to Mill, 'the Art of Life' consists of 'three departments' – ethics, politics, aesthetics. And 'every art is . . . a joint result of laws of nature disclosed by science, and of the general principles of what has been called Teleology, or the Doctrine of Ends, which, borrowing the language of the German metaphysicians, may also be termed, not improperly, the principles of Practical Reason' (1974, vol. 8, pp. 949–50). The ends that art intuits may be indirectly descriptive of man's moral nature, rather like Kant's ideas of God or of immortality, which function more as lucid veils than as unclouded mirrors of Kant's moral axioms. Such ends are not just fictions. But they are not constitutive truths either. They are regulative truths, required by our moral nature and descriptively true only in the sense that our moral experience demands them.

As a discoverer of these moral ends, Mill's poet must bring into focus an ideal world, as Tennyson does at the climax of *In Memoriam*, where his spiritual insight, aroused by the blended might of natural oppositions, makes powerful contact with something beyond faith, with a vision that speaks to him from the far side of death. Because Tennyson is engaged in a search for possibilities greater than those already domesticated, he is able to recover the sublime, to bring it home and naturalize it, in a description of events which could actually have taken place on a northern midsummer night in an English garden. 'Death is a leveller,' Northrop Frye suggests, 'not because everybody dies, but because nobody understands what death means' (1982, p. 230). For Tennyson, however, 'boundless life' seems just as certain, just as much a natural fact, as the exhilarating midsummer phenomena he describes. What speaks to Tennyson across his own death is the visionary extravagance of a talking breeze – something that allows his mind to expand, to move beyond the discursive arguments at the centre of the poem and the sacramental processing of the Prologue. Like Mill's ideal poet, Tennyson adds to the description of his world an invention of its value. He is a poet who, even in reaching out to take in the extravagant, knows how to tame what is vagrant or daring in his intuition of man's moral goals. He uses his intuition of these goals to restore meaning to his life, to humanize his world, and to find his way back home.

So far I have tried to make as strong a case for Mill as I can. I have argued that both Mill's doctrine of ends and his doctrine of intuitive inferences try to overcome the dualism of emotive and referential meanings bequeathed by Baconian axioms of the poet's feigned histories and by empirical axioms of the mirror of nature. Mill's theories are designed to confer an emotive freedom on the poet without making poetry descriptively untrue. Having tried to argue as an empiricist, however, I must now show why both Mill's theories, his revised version of a descriptive account of language and his doctrine of ends, have serious limitations when applied to poetry. Mill posits the prior existence of a physical world which the poet's words then mirror. But as Tennyson realizes, all description is interpretation. Apart from an observer's perception of the world, there exists no world which either the scientist's judgemental inferences or the poet's intuitive inferences can be said to mirror. As I shall show in the next chapter, Tennyson was a student of metaphysics and an admirer of J. F. Ferrier, the shrewdest of the early-Victorian idealists. As Ferrier asserts, 'the whole material universe by itself', which Mill would make the test of his correspondence theory, is 'absolutely unknowable'. 'The object of knowledge' is always 'the object with the addition of oneself . . . Object . . . plus subject is the *minimum scibile per se*' (1854, pp. 93, 106, 117).

Sometimes, as in section CI of *In Memoriam*, where Tennyson anticipates a scene of neglect and oblivion after his family leaves Somersby and the garden-boughs and flowers fall into ruin, the mirror of nature seems momentarily to detach itself from a self-conscious observer. Tennyson's anxiety may be felt in his uneasy syntax: 'And year by year our memory fades' (l. 23). Is the possessive pronoun 'our' a subjective or objective genitive? Does the poet's memory of the hills fade, or the hills' memory of him? The second possibility is the more unexpected and disturbing. Refusing to concede that the mind and its memories are fragile and will fail, however, Tennyson expects the reader to perceive that no mirroring of place, however bleak, can be unhinged from the memorial or testament of a self-conscious mind. Even the imagination of nothingness, the imagination of the hills' power to endure, simply to stand there and be – mute witnesses of oblivion – powerfully offsets the bleakest impressions of loss.

As Tennyson's lotos-eaters recognize, the past becomes dreadful when we lose all memory or imagination of it. But because no object or thought can ever be unhinged from a self-conscious observer, not even Tennyson's imagination of the world's grand annihilation, 'When all that seems shall suffer shock' (*In Memoriam*, CXXXI, 2), can entail the supposition of the mind's annihilation. The problem with Mill's mirror of nature is that it obscures the counter-truth that the sovereignty of the self-conscious mind prevents the poet who 'dream[s] [his] dream, and hold [s] it true' (*In Memoriam*, cxxiii, 10) from experiencing his own dissolution. Despite the soul's apparent fragility, the impossibility of unhinging Mill's impressions of sense from a perceiving subject gives Tennyson's soul a rocklike durability (*In Memoriam*, cxxxi, 1–3). As Ferrier concludes, 'we cannot, and we do not think [our death]: we only *think that we think it* . . . In the real thought of [our death] we should be already dead.' But 'in the mere illusive imagination of the thought', we 'are already an immortal race' (1842, p. 819).

Also beset with difficulties is Mill's doctrine of ends, his second proposed solution to a dualist theory of art. According to this theory, Tennyson's classification of the hills as shadows, for example, is not primarily an attempt to provide us with a true-or-false geological description of the hills. Its response of mingled awe and dread is rather an attempt to clarify man's place and final value in the world.

> The hills are shadows, and they flow
> > From form to form, and nothing stands;
> > They melt like mist, the solid lands,
> Like clouds they shape themselves and go.

> > > > (*In Memoriam*, cxxiii, 4–8)

Because Tennyson's proposal to classify the hills as shadows is at least a classification which has some verifiable basis in geological science, Mill's teleological doctrine is found in a purer form in the audacious proposal of a younger Victorian poet, G. M. Hopkins, to classify 'the azurous hung hills' as the shoulder of God.

> And the azurous hung hills are his world-wielding shoulder
> > Majestic – as a stallion stalwart, very-violet-sweet!

> > > ('Hurrahing in Harvest', ll. 9–10)

More stubborn than Tennyson's lines in their refusal to be tested or evaluated like a scientific hypothesis, Hopkins' proposal to telescope God, geology, and a muscular horse is neither a tautology like $2 + 2 = 4$ nor a synthetic proposition like the statement, 'The hills are strewn with rocks.' Nor is it a synthetic *a priori* judgement, like the geological classification of the rocks as terminal moraine. Does this make Hopkins' proposal about man's ends, which is the kind of proposal men have lived and died for, a non-cognitive proposal? No man has ever died for the propositions of a geologist. But in becoming one source of moral and axiological meaning, have the normative recommendations of Mill's poet not been required to pay too high a price? Have they not been deprived of truth value altogether? This is a conclusion that Mill himself would be reluctant to reach. For as Mill grows older he comes to reject the view of his own father, of Comte and of Macaulay, that poetry necessarily declines in importance as education becomes increasingly scientific. Even in an 1835 article Mill maintains that poetry 'flourishes equally with reason' (1969, vol. 10, p. 571). As Peter Morgan says, Mill expresses his conviction in this essay that 'the autonomous and educational roles of the imagination [are] both important' (1983, p. 153).

A brief consideration of the similarity between the poet's language and the language of the moral philosopher or metaphysician may clarify, if not answer, the question of how education by metaphor can be just as indispensable as education by metonymy. For if the poet's metaphorical proposals about man's ends or goals are non-cognitive, then is most philosophical language, as the discourse of normative recommendation, not non-cognitive as well? A philosophic statement such as a Berkeleyan idealist might propound, 'The hills continue to exist as long as they are perceived by my mind or God's mind', is like the metaphoric recommendations of Mill's poet. It is a proposal to classify the hills among existing objects: that is to say, among objects perceived by God. But because such a perceiving deity cannot be derived from ready-made facts, then, unlike the descriptive statements of Mill's inductive logician, Berkeley's proposal, like most poetic proposals, would seem to be incapable of either proof or disproof. Such a proposal has no direct claim to truth as Mill conceives truth. It depends for its validity on the truth of a value judgement, that Berkeley's or Hopkins' proposal to view God as our end or Tennyson's proposal to view universal flux and dissolution as our end is the best one available.

We may want to conclude that the best proposal for perceiving the hills is to view them as the anatomy of God or as shadows flitting by in a form of time-lapse photography extending over millions of years. But if we follow Mill's line of reasoning, we cannot reach this conclusion because neither of the two proposals has a truth value as such. Each proposal derives its truth or lack of truth from the cognitive status of a value judgement, from the assertion that Hopkins' proposal to be elated by the hills is somehow better than Tennyson's proposal to be depressed or terrified by the hills or vice versa. But two problems remain.

In what sense do we know that a poet's classifications and his metaphoric substitutions of shadows for hills and mist for lands are proposals about values or ends to be attained, rather than the kind of true-or-false proposition that Mill analyses in his *System of Logic*? And even if we know they are proposals, how can we agree upon the value judgements which determine the truth claims of conflicting proposals?

In the first place, what is meant by the verb 'know' when we say that the recommendation to classify the hills as shadows, or as shoulders, or as the content of God's mind, is *known* to be not a true-or-false proposition, but a normative classification that is more or less happy or apt – better or worse – than some other classification? Do we *know* this in the same sense the geologist *knows* the rock-strewn hills to be a product of glacial deposits? Our very distinction between poetic proposal and scientific proposition insists we cannot. If our distinction is true, then it would seem to follow it cannot be true. As one commentator notes, this paradox 'would not mean that' our distinction 'would be false, but only that the assumption of its truth' – the notion that the language of poetry, like the language of philosophy, is a language of classification and of metaphoric substitution neither true nor false but more or less happy or apt – 'would lead one to deny its truth, in this case to deny that it has any truth value at all' (Lange, 1970, pp. 64–5).

Even if the philosopher can resolve this 'cognitivity paradox', as I think he can, he must solve the second, more difficult problem of determining how value judgements can be cognitive. What allows us to say that the proposal of Berkeley's idealist or of Hopkins' religious celebrant is a better proposal than Tennyson's? What, in fact, is meant by 'better?' Hopkins' proposal to see the hills as a feature of God's athletic body may be more ennobled by emotion or by a capacity for concern than Tennyson's proposal to see the hills as insubstantial shadow. After all, if humanity were really a footnote to geological history, would it be in the interest of man's self-esteem and dignity to know this truth? But to maintain that a given proposition represents a better 'end to be attained', as Mill says, is to maintain that it better conforms to some set of ideal conditions about which no consensus by an individual poet or philosopher or by any community of poets and philosophers seems likely to be reached.

3 Huxley and Pearson: Symbolic Shorthand

The subordination of even myth and art to scientific axioms helps explain the ascendancy during the last third of the nineteenth century of Absolute Idealism. As a reaction toward Buddhistic metaphysics, this influential movement sidetracks representational axioms of the mirror of nature by relegating them to a world of mere appearance. To understand the cause of this reaction we have only to see what happens when scientific axioms of the mirror of nature are uncritically accepted as the norm by two Victorian theorists of myth, Max Müller and George Grote. Müller argues that behind the concealed metaphors of myth, which he calls 'a disease of language' (1869, vol. 2, p. 74), lies a non-metaphorical, representational use of language which Müller believes it is his task as a scholar to expose. In contrast to Müller, Grote asserts that myths evoke 'a past which was never present', which was 'neither approachable by the critic nor measurable by the chronologer' (1869, vol. 1, p. 43). Like other Utilitarians, however, Grote believes all language should aspire toward the normal representational use of words. He differs from Müller only in placing such unclouded mirroring of nature, not in an idealized Aryan past, but in a positivist Utopia of the future. Both critics make the same mistake. They fail to see that there is no representational norm, either in Müller's past or in Grote's future, which would allow the theorist to say that the language of a myth is either literal or figurative. The fact is that the language of myth is the only possible way of expressing what it says.

Representational axioms of the mirror of nature remain the dominant scientific model until 1870. But in later Victorian science they are replaced by two other axioms. T. H. Huxley teaches that scientific theories are a mere symbolic shorthand. John Tyndall argues, less sceptically, that scientific theories are pictures, not pure descriptions but not mere symbolic fictions either. Both teachings have important consequences for poetry. I want to show how theories of the physicist's fertile pictorial models and fictions help turn the arguments of Müller and Grote inside out by making the meanings of myth and metaphor primary.

The extreme form of the first theory is enshrined in Karl Pearson's *The Grammar of Science*. His theory of symbolic fictions stands in the same relation to the descriptive axioms of an early-Victorian scientist like John Herschel as the late-Victorian formalism of Arnold or Pater stands to the earlier representational postulates of G. H. Lewes, say, or Ruskin. John Herschel may not have been 'very confident of a close connection between current [scientific] theories and unseen Nature'. But as David B. Wilson says, 'he regarded such a correspondence as [in principle] *attainable*' (1977, p. 207). By contrast, Karl Pearson in *The Grammar of Science* treats physical theories as mere '"shorthand" methods of distinguishing, classifying, and resuming phases of sense-experience' (1892, p. 214). With comparable candour T. H. Huxley confides that all scientific hypotheses are 'more or less imperfect and symbolic' (1893, vol. 3, p. 150). If the symbolic language of science still refers to phenomena, it refers to them at two removes, the way the earthly paradise of William Morris discloses formal principles that seem to stand behind the brazen world of nature, but which in Huxley's words are 'neither self-evident' nor 'strictly speaking, demonstrable' (1893, vol. 1, p. 61). A more complete account of science's symbolic shorthand can be found in Huxley's essay 'On the Basis of Life' (1868):

> With a view to the progress of science, the materialistic terminology is in every way to be preferred... But the man of science, who, forgetting the limits of philosophical inquiry, slides from these formulae and symbols into what is commonly understood by materialism, seems to me to place himself on a level with the mathematician, who should mistake the x's and y's with which he works his problems, for real entities. (1893, vol. 1, p. 165)

The merely provisional or fictional status of such a theory provides Matthew Arnold with a belated scientific justification of Wordsworth's claim that poetry is 'the impassioned expression which is in the countenance of all science'. If poetry is truly 'the breath and finer spirit of all knowledge', as Arnold polemically reasserts in 'The Study of Poetry' (1961, vol. 9, p. 162), it is presumably because Arnold's poet can design elegant symbolic structures. He can express with more emotion than the physicist, but with as much concision and clarity, the laws that govern an ideal world. Unlike Bacon's poet, Arnold's is not simply submitting the shows of things to the desires of the mind. He is remoulding nature, but always like the nineteenth-century physicist in accordance with symbolic fictions and models that make it possible to speak intelligibily (and in the case of physics, even correctly) about phenomena that are not basically known. Arnold's defence of provisionality and fiction is most explicit in his later theological writings. But as Ruth apRoberts has shown, these writings owe less to scientific developments than to theories of fiction in Herder, Vico, and Joseph Glanvill, who argues that 'the best Principles, excepting Divine, and Mathematical, are but Hypotheses' (Glanvill, 1661, p. 195).

To retain vestiges of Newton's mechanical model of simple substances and their qualities, which had been systematized by Locke, nineteenth-century scientists had tried to explain sound and light by postulating the model of a mechanical wave moving through a semi-rigid medium called the ether. But after Clerk Maxwell had translated Faraday's fields of force into mathematical language and developed them into a theory of electromagnetic waves, the postulate of the ether came to be viewed by theorists like Helmholtz, Huxley, and Karl Pearson as mere symbolic shorthand, no more descriptive of external reality than the obsolete fiction of phlogiston in chemistry. The pictures of a universe of atoms 'floating in ether', says Pearson, 'do not exist in or beyond the world of sense-impressions, but are the pure product of our reasoning faculty' (1892, pp. 214–15).

Tennyson was a close reader of Helmholtz and Huxley as well as of John Tyndall, an agnostic physicist and former colleague of Faraday. His abiding interest in the philosophy of science and in its implications for poetics, theology, and for a theory of knowledge is evident from his owning such works as John Tyndall's *Scientific Use of the Imagination* (1873), F. L. Büchner's *Force and Matter* (1864), and Samuel Brown's *Lectures on the Atomic Theory* (1858). Tennyson owned Tyndall's *Six Lectures on Light Delivered in America in 1872–1873* and pamphlets by Tyndall on cometary theory and on Helmholtz's theory of ice and glaciers. Science's 'counter-terms', as Tennyson calls them in 'The Ancient Sage' (l. 250), make clear that the reality which lies beyond space, time, and atoms, beyond the antinomies 'Of this divisible-indivisible world' ('De Profundis', l. 43), is 'unconceivably' itself, ultimately unknowable and hence, in Tennyson's phrase, 'unshadowable in words'. Huxley's idealist critique of mechanical Newtonian models is also exactly analogous to Tennyson's critique of the atomic philosophy in an earlier poem, 'Lucretius'. In that monologue Tennyson shows how the atomistic model of a physicist like Tyndall, who quotes extensively from Lucretius in his Belfast Address, delivered before the British Association in 1874 (1889, vol. 2, pp. 144, 162–9), fashions a mechanical mythology that is just as fantastic an exaggeration of partial knowledge as the religious mythology it supplants, and a good deal less consoling.

The parallel between Huxley's theory of symbolic fictions and the unreality of all antinomies which fashion 'This double seeming of the single world' is explored not only by Tennyson in 'The Ancient Sage' (l. 105) but also by Browning in his monologue 'Mr Sludge, "The Medium"'. The spiritualist's hypotheses, Sludge concedes, may have originated as poetry or the mere 'knack of story-telling' (l. 192). They are not to be confused with strictly true-or-false propositions. But then neither are the supreme postulates of the theologian or the molecular hypotheses of the biochemist and physicist. Like Pascal's two immensities, the unknowable God of the theologians 'comes close behind a stomach-cyst' ('Mr Sludge, "The Medium"', l. 1117). He permeates in an infinite regress the least of the scientist's atomic models, which, as Mr Sludge observes, 'turns our spyglass round, or else / Puts a new lens in it' (ll. 1110–11). An X-ray machine may photograph a 'stomach-cyst' or tumour. But no microscope or lens has ever allowed the eye to see an atom, which remains a mere chemical hypothesis, mere 'fabling' or 'story-telling' of a sort. When reading Benjamin Jowett's comments on Plato's *Republic* in the volume Jowett gave him, Browning would have encountered a remarkably similar formulation. The model world of Plato – and, by implication, of much modern poetry – illuminates natural phenomena in much the same way as do the hypotheses and fictions of modern chemistry and physics. The poetic 'anticipations or divinations' of Plato, Jowett concludes, 'stand in the same relation to ancient philosophy which hypotheses bear to modern inductive science' (1871, vol. 2, p. 80).

4 *Tyndall on Pictorial Analogy*

The physical theories of John Tyndall, a physicist whose works Tennyson owned and apparently read with interest, are based upon the mind's picture-making power. Equally critical of empirical axioms of the mirror of nature and of axioms about the scientist's mere heuristic fictions, Tyndall adopts an intermediate position. He acknowledges that what is said about the world often lies in our method of picturing it. But he believes that these pictures also reveal a concrete feature of what is really there.

Tyndall sets forth his theory most persuasively in a pamphlet entitled *Scientific Use of the Imagination*, which he originally delivered as an address to the British Association at Liverpool in 1870. A member of the Metaphysical Society Tyndall attended, Tennyson owned a copy of this pamphlet, which is now in the Tennyson Research Centre at Lincoln. Praising imagination as 'the architect of physical theory', Tyndall argues that the scientist will begin by observing some phenomenon like the propagation of waves through water, which Tennyson describes in vivid detail in 'Timbuctoo' (ll. 119–29). To explain less obvious effects the scientist will then use the propagation of waves in water as a pictorial analogy of the transmission of sound waves through air and of light waves through a medium, the ether, which, though invisible, the scientist is forced to imagine or invent. Tyndall argues that these pictorial analogies are 'not less real than the world of . . . sense'. As properties of the physical world, the wave motions of light in ether, like the lines of force connecting magnetic poles, may be veiled from view. But since 'the world of sense itself is the suggestion' of these pictures, 'and to a great extent [their] *outcome*' (1889, vol. 2, pp. 104, 107), Tyndall insists not only that they are real entities but also that they are the living 'garment of God', as he provocatively calls them, quoting Goethe and Carlyle (1889, vol. 2, p. 132).

Tyndall's picture of light waves in ether is precisely the form of divine vesture Tennyson uses a year earlier to endow the sacramental cup in 'The Holy Grail' with physical existence. Like Tyndall, who argues that the concept of ether, trembling with waves of light, bears the same relation to the observable phenomenon of ordinary wave motion as the theological postulate of a Universal Father shaping nature to his own will bears to 'the ordinary actions of man upon earth' (1889, vol. 2, p. 43), Tennyson gives to the sacred object a base in such optical phenomena as the surging waves of the aurora borealis. The great gusts of auroral light, startling and ephemeral as shooting stars, and of constantly shifting shape, are properties of the real that veil the Holy Grail from view. But the Grail also gleams radiantly through the shimmering auroral waves. Tennyson is claiming to define in the volatile fire that imitates in its magnificent coruscations the spiritual change in Galahad, a principle that underlies nature. Without the characteristic accuracies of Tennyson's picture of the auroral fire, neither metaphysical nor physical laws could be given a habitation and a name. For like God's kingdom, 'the kingdom of science', as Tyndall says, 'cometh not by observation and experiment alone, but is completed by fixing the roots of observation and experiment in a region inaccessible to both, and in dealing with which we are forced to fall back upon the picturing power of the mind' (1889, vol. 2, p. 208).

Tennyson's poem 'De Profundis', which was not completed until 1880, may well reflect the influence of Tyndall's *Scientific Use of the Imagination*. In the 'divisible-indivisible' conjoining of the material and spiritual universes which constitute the two halves of 'De Profundis', Tennyson's stirring account of the human embryo's ability to recapitulate the evolution of the whole race 'for a million aeons' (l. 3) draws adventurously, as Tyndall says, upon 'the power of matter to divide itself and distribute its forces'. Allowing his mind to run back with awe over the whole length of biological succession, Tennyson channels through subtly varied caesural pauses and carefully placed trochaic inversions his marvelling sense that, in Tyndall's phrase, matter and spirit are 'equally worthy, and equally wonderful . . . two opposite faces of the self-same mystery'. As in the psalm by which Tennyson is inspired, a discipline is imposed upon the poet by the perfect parallelism of his phrasing – 'Out of the deep, my child, out of the deep' (ll. 1, 26) – and by the many felicities of his syntax, as, for example, the way each successive epithet proves more expansive than the preceding one: 'million', 'vast / Waste', 'multitudinous-eddying' (ll. 3–4). Exalting the material

universe of part one, and repealing as Tyndall would say 'the divorce hitherto existing between [the two universes]' (1889, vol. 2,
pp. 126, 132), Tennyson moves through a spacious sequence of
expanding clauses and phrases, relieving the overflowing emotions
that in the coda, 'The Human Cry', he expresses too directly.

But like Tyndall, Tennyson is still at a loss to explain the 'main-
miracle' ('De Profundis', l. 55). In his Belfast address, which he delivers four years after his lecture on *Scientific Use of the Imagination*,
Tyndall proclaims his faith that the two universes, material and
spiritual, 'go hand in hand. But we soar in a vacuum,' he admits,
'the moment we seek to comprehend the connection between them.
An Archimedean fulcrum is here required which the human mind
cannot command' (1889, vol. 2, p. 194). In 'De Profundis' the evolutionary atomic and physical models of the first half of the poem
and the evolutionary spiritual models of the second half seem to run
in tandem as parallel phenomena. But because man the physical
object is still separated by an impassable gulf from man the subject,
Tennyson finds he cannot quite command Tyndall's 'Archimedean
fulcrum'. The near-hysteria of the coda betrays that sense of failure.

> Hallowed be Thy name – Halleluiah!
>   Infinite Ideality!
>   Immeasurable Reality!
>   Infinite Personality!
> Hallowed be Thy name – Halleluiah!
>
> ('De Profundis', ll. 57–61)

It seems incredible that a poet of such fertile metrical invention as
Tennyson could write a stanza so obdurately heavy-footed and
graceless. The three-line clump of banal rhymes, framed by unintegrated quotation from the Lord's Prayer, provides too little resistance
to the poet's impulse to vent affirmations he would not venture on
in prose. If the clichés of hymn-singing are recalcitrant materials, it
is not because their emphatic metres are too resistant, but because
they yield too readily to an uncritical formulation of Tennyson's
antecedent faith in a mysterious unity of spirit and matter he cannot
quite compass or express. Once launched on his primitive raft of
Sunday-school faith, the poet rides the deep buoyantly. But what
he really seeks, I suspect, is not the assurance of the Lord's Prayer.
Nor is it the uncertain consolation provided by the evolutionary

atomic model of the two universes, physical and spiritual, he has just explored. In Christ's physical containment of an 'Infinite Ideality' Tennyson seeks an answer to the question that puzzles both himself and Tyndall: how from the combination and separation of mere insensate atoms can the miracle of consciousness come to birth?

The Incarnational faith of the Christian is not a solution available to the agnostic Tyndall. And I think even Tennyson wants to 'stand under' the mystery. It is not enough to be awed by the mind's mysterious connection with matter. Tennyson also wants to understand how finite minds can comprehend the incomprehensible. Recalling in his Belfast address that even 'the great Leibnitz felt the difficulty' of explaining how consciousness can arise from matter, Tyndall strains to envisage a new cosmology in which dead atoms will be replaced by self-conscious monads all capable of functioning as 'more or less perfect mirrors of the universe' (1889, vol. 2, p. 168). But it is not, I believe, to Leibniz's monadology but to philosophic Idealism that historians of thought must turn for a metaphysical doctrine of the kind Tennyson and Tyndall are seeking. Tennyson was familiar with the Idealism of Edward Caird, and owned a copy of Caird's monograph *The Problem of Philosophy at the Present Time*. The most systematic exposition of such thought is to be found in the writings of Caird's fellow idealist, F. H. Bradley, whom I must now briefly consider.

5 F. H. Bradley and the Poets: The Critique of Abstraction

In his last book, *Essays on Truth and Reality*, F. H. Bradley confesses that he does 'not know whether this in my case is a mark of senility, but I find myself now taking more and more as literal fact what I used in my youth to admire and love in poetry' (1914, p. 468). Bradley wrote no treatise on aesthetics, but the scepticism with which he successively erodes the representational axioms of the historian, the moral philosopher, and the logician, seems not in the end to erode the authority of the poet. Why should this be? Is it possible that a poet like Shelley, whom Bradley admired, gave the universal meaning of Bradley's Idealism, the germ out of which it grew? Did the Romantic poets come closer to the genesis of Bradley's philosophy than that philosophy itself could ever come by the use of representational language?

Bradley's whole career, it may be said, parallels the movement away from representational mirrors and pictures toward the symbolic fictions that I have been studying earlier in this chapter. His first published pamphlet is a sustained critique of the assumption that historical discourse mirrors facts that antecedently exist, waiting to be recovered. As Richard Wollheim says, Bradley 'had been amongst the first to insist . . . that to mean something cannot be equated, as the empiricists would, with having an image or representation of that thing' (1973, p. 234). In *Ethical Studies* Bradley tries to picture ethics as a pilgrimage of self-realization. But he would be the first to concede that the picture is imperfect, because the goal of ideal morality, the destination of the moral pilgrim, is always out of reach. Morality cannot exist unless the pilgrimage it posits is also a failed pilgrimage, thwarted by detours and traps. 'Most progress is most failure,' as Browning's Cleon says in a different context ('Cleon', l. 272). In other words, the pictures Bradley uses tell us as much about the philosopher and his pictures as about the nature of morality as such. The very concept of ideal morality, like the concept of a limit in calculus, may be a mere heuristic fiction.

The fictive status of Bradley's axioms is clearest in the first book of *Appearance and Reality*, where everything he says about the real turns out to be a fiction which, taken by itself, does as much to hide the Absolute as to reveal it. If even the philosopher's pictures are fictive, then how much more fictive and 'unreal' must be the abstract concepts of the scientist? Though this 'unreality' helps explain the surprising vigour of Bradley's attack on abstraction in *The Principles of Logic*, what cure does Bradley think poetry can offer? One answer seems to be that poetry provides an immediately felt unity of experience, and so prefigures the unity of the Absolute. When experience is immediate, there is nothing left over to the mind as its content. The closest approximation to such immediacy seems to be the non-relational unity of many in one that is sometimes experienced in music or in visionary poetry like Shelley's. The images in the fourth act of *Prometheus Unbound*, for example, may be so pure, so devoid of representational content, that, like any truly immediate experience, they predate the moment at which the distinction between subject and object begins to apply.

It is also possible that poetry provides Bradley with an example of a difficult and obscure concept which continues to elude definition in *The Principles of Logic.* Because the logician can merely gesture inexpressively at the immediate experiences which are given to him as a subject, he inevitably sunders this concrete but unnameable whole from a host of partial predicates which, however abstract, can at least be talked about. Presumably, if the developments of these predicates are exhaustive enough, a concrete subject and its richly differentiated predicates will eventually come together again at infinity. There they can form at last what Bradley, following Hegel, calls a 'concrete universal'. But outside of poetry or music, the very idea of such a convergence may be barely intelligible.

If logicians and scientists predicate of the subject what is different, they ascribe to it what it is not. And if they predicate what is not different, they say nothing at all. They limit themselves to the one kind of proposition which we never make, the tautology that coal is coal, diamond is diamond. Bradley believes that the deadlock results from philosophers' attempts to extend the law of non-contradiction, the law that A cannot be both *a* and *non-a*, from the realm of logic, where it is valid, to the realm of concrete particulars and facts, where it may be possible, as Hegel argues, for unity to exist only through multiplicity and difference. In poetry, for example, we see how a subject may assume diverse forms, allotropes of being like Hopkins' coal and diamond, without ceasing to be itself, a concrete particular distinctive as the taste of alum.

> In a flash, at a trumpet crash,
> I am all at once what Christ is, since he was what I am, and
> This Jack, joke, poor potsherd, patch, matchwood, immortal
>   diamond,
>   Is immortal diamond.
>   ('That Nature is a Heraclitean Fire', ll. 21–4)

The poet's recovery of his true identity is marked by strong reversion to truncated three-stress lines (ll. 21, 24). The reverberatory lift of the half-echoing internal rhymes, 'at a trumpet', 'ash', 'flash', 'crash' (ll. 20–1), and the sharp blows of the final full repetitions (ll. 23–4), show the firmness of the soul, staunch under attack. Linking solidity with finely faceted beauty, Hopkins' identification with

Christ confers on him the only genuine identity he has: 'I am all at once what Christ is, since he was what I am' (l. 22).

The near-chiasmus of this last line suggests the trope most often associated with what Northrop Frye has called 'the royal metaphor' (1982, p. 87), the figure of speech which identifies an individual, Christ, with his class, humanity, so that the whole is presented as a single body. Frye calls this trope 'the royal metaphor' because 'the function of the king is primarily to represent, for his subjects, the unity of their society in an individual form. Even yet Elizabeth II can draw crowds wherever she appears, not because there is anything remarkable about her appearance, but because she dramatizes the metaphor of society as a single "body" ' (1982, p. 87). Though there is a jump from the concrete particular to the concrete universal in Hopkins' lines, the individual is not blotted out. Alchemized from coal to diamond, Hopkins reaffirms the mystery of archetypal identity, a mystery that is celebrated not just in biblical myths but in all the ancient fertility myths of resurrection and rebirth.

According to J. H. Stirling, the whole 'secret of Hegel' resides in his ability to make '*explicit* the *concrete* Universal that was [merely] *implicit* in Kant' (1898, p. xxii). To understand Hegel's 'secret', in other words, we must understand the logic of the royal metaphor. Like Hegel, Bradley develops a new logic to explain how it works. But the ability of the royal metaphor to reverse 'a metaphor of integration into a wholly decentralized one,' as Frye says, 'in which the total body is complete within each individual' (1982, p. 100), is perhaps easier to grasp in poetry than in logic. To understand what is meant we have only to see how the unity of Hopkins' Logos in the poem I was just quoting can unite Christ and Hopkins without subordinating the second to the first, and so differentiate itself from other more totalitarian forms of integration. The power of the royal metaphor to contain particulars as the Word contains the world can also be studied in an unusually subtle form in Hopkins' hermeneutical sonnet from 'New Readings,' 'Although the letter said'. Hopkins shows how, in a spiritual alchemy more rare than any Ovidian metamorphosis, the banquet of grain and wine harvested by Christ from the thorns of his death and resurrection transforms the meaning of the parable of the sower by putting the nature described inside a body, a royal metaphor at once individual and infinite, in which the whole universe can be contained.

If reality is a concrete universal, as Bradley maintains, then it must be intuited from such concrete manifestations of its power as Tennyson's description at the climax of *In Memoriam* (xcv, 53–64) of the rocking of the full-foliaged elm trees, the throwing into wavelike motion of the scents that stream from the rose and the lily, and the final astonishing apparition of the speaking breeze, which seems to materialize out of the looking-glass world of *Maud*'s talking flowers, then just as mysteriously vanishes. Bradley assumes that the more truth the mind attains, the more it can lay aside Mill's representational mirror of nature. Instead of evolving poetry from the world, the world can be evolved from poetry and from its coherence model of truth. Because the real is both concrete and universal, it is less accurately defined through Mill's mirrors, through Tyndall's pictures, or even through Huxley's symbolic fictions, than through that powerful but subtle form of identification which Northrop Frye has called the 'royal metaphor'. But if reality is metaphoric in its structure, is the converse proposition not equally valid? Are statements about poetry's non-relational unity of many in one not also statements about the structure of a world we are entitled to call real? And if they are, is any scientist likely to accept this poetic model of truth?

It might seem at first that Bradley provides exactly the solution Tyndall and Tennyson are looking for. We have seen, for example, that Tyndall believes it is just as accurate to say that the world itself is deduced from our pictorial models of the world as to say that a metaphorical proposal about the wave properties of light is directly inferred from physical facts. The scientist's pictures resemble Keats's metaphor for the poetic imagination. They are like Adam's dream: he awoke and found it truth. But it would be wrong and unhistorical to minimize the widespread scientific hostility to Hegel's thought. The scientists' contempt for Hegel is well expressed by Helmholtz, who observes that Hegel's 'system of nature seemed, at least to natural philosophers, absolutely crazy' (1873, p. 5). Though Helmholtz retains great respect for Kant's 'Critical Philosophy', and argues that scientists have much to learn from philosophical 'criticism of the sources of cognition', he cannot forgive Hegel for launching out 'with unusual vehemence and acrimony, against the natural philosophers, and especially against Sir Isaac Newton, as the first and greatest representative of physical investigation'.

It is true that in the later nineteenth century the distinction Mill originally draws between a scientific language of true-or-false propositions and a poetic language of metaphoric proposals ceases to be valid for all but the most uncritical materialists like Büchner. But the increasing approximation of scientific to poetic models does not mean that scientists are prepared to subordinate science to a poetic model of truth. Few of them would have approved Friedrich Schlegel's conclusion that 'many of the chief founders of modern physics should not be considered philosophers, but artists' (1971, p. 224). And like most Hegelian systems, Bradley's *Appearance and Reality* must have struck most Victorian scientists as an abdication of intelligence. We should not, after all, expect philosophers of science like Pearson and Huxley to expose the merely fictive status of the scientist's models only to embrace with open arms a massive reification of such fictions. But would this not be the result of accepting the kind of poetical ontology which turns the merely formal and logical account of the concrete universal that Bradley offers in his *Principles of Logic* into a metaphysical theory that makes existential claims as well?

For Huxley the strict truth or falsity of a scientific model, like its ontological status, is never really at issue. The symbolic shorthand of the physicist is devised solely for the mind's convenience or delight, like a tool we might use, or like a poem we might admire for its verbal economy. In *The Grammar of Science* Karl Pearson had developed a theory of the conceptual understanding designed to defend the validity of the scientific method against Hume's critique. Kant argues that the scientist's propositions are both true and cognitive. They are true because they are *a priori*: they organize experience according to spatial and temporal forms that the mind itself supplies. But unlike the analytic *a priori* propositions of mathematics, the propositions of science also give us knowledge of the world, because they are *synthetic* propositions that add information in the predicate that is not given in the subject. The truths of ethics and religion, by contrast, are mere postulates of the practical reason. Once Pearson and Huxley, however, show that science itself is only a tool or a convenience, an invention of the practical reason rather than a representational mirror of nature, then Kant's influential distinction between the pure and the practical reason, designed to preserve the authority of science by distinguishing between mirrors and tools, is found to be invalid. Nor can theologians any longer accept the Kantian conclusions of the Dean of St Paul's, H. L. Mansel. In his Bampton lectures for 1858, *The Limits of Religious Thought*, Mansel had argued that our practical reason requires us to believe in a God whose conceptual definitions are riddled with the logical contradictions that are generated whenever a concept like the infinite or the absolute is not directly convertible into sense impressions, as are the concepts of the scientists. But if all language is more like a tool than a mirror, there can be nothing privileged about scientific usage.

Having called into question science's capacity to mirror nature, late Victorians like Karl Pearson and T. H. Huxley are likely to be deeply suspicious of F. H. Bradley's attempts in the second book of *Appearance and Reality* to reconstruct their world by baptizing the poet's concrete universals in the name of the real and calling them the Absolute. Like later philosophers, these scientists are far more sympathetic to Bradley the sceptic, who in the first book of *Appearance and Reality* systematically unmasks the abstractions and contradictions of conceptual thought. All abstract thinking is relational, he argues, and the relational is unreal. More relentlessly and incisively than any other Victorian, Bradley exposes what A. N. Whitehead calls 'the major vice of the intellect', 'the intolerable use of abstractions' (1925, p. 18). He provides the most searching critique of the fatal tendency of all conceptual thought to strip away and abstract, producing only a dissection of the warm and living world the poets know. For this reason alone scientists and humanists alike owe a lasting debt of gratitude to Bradley.

I have shown how in his essay *Scientific Use of the Imagination* John Tyndall tries to remove science's Achilles' heel, its tendency to impoverish concrete reality by making its models too generic and abstract. For despite the efforts of late Victorians to minimize the difference between scientific and poetic fictions, thinkers as dissimilar as Tennyson, Tyndall, and F. H. Bradley all recognize that in order to retain their ability to control and predict events the scientist's models are condemned to be incomparably more attenuated, more naked and skeletal, than the poet's. The atomic theories of the scientists disclose only 'some spectral woof of impalpable abstractions', as Bradley says, 'or unearthly ballet of bloodless categories. Though dragged to such conclusions, we cannot embrace them. Our [scientific and logical] principles may be true, but they are not

reality. They no more *make* that Whole which commands our de-
votion, than some shredded dissection of human tatters *is* that warm
and breathing beauty of flesh which our heart found delightful'
(1883, p. 533). To escape from the fallacy of misplaced concrete-
ness, from the tendency of science to invest atoms and ether with a
reality they do not possess, many Victorians find they must turn
away from the abstractions of science to the delights and pains of
the affective life, which are preserved for them, as they were for
F. H. Bradley and for J. S. Mill after his mental breakdown, in the
imagination of the poets. Only the poets seem able to repair the
sense of injustice we feel whenever our individual experiences,
which we believe to be unique to ourselves, are described in the
abstractions of the scientist, who uses concepts common to every-
one. Because the poet's presentations are wholly individual, he may
greatly diminish Bradley's sense of loss, his sense that 'the sensuous
curtain is a deception and a cheat' (1883, p. 533), by countenancing
the belief that in all its idiosyncratic detail – single, unrepeatable,
compelling – a poem like *In Memoriam* or *The Prelude*, even in speak-
ing to and for our common humanity, is speaking to each of us
alone.

II The Idealist Revolt:
Theories of Self-Conscious Response

Despite its immensity, the rest of the universe is denied the gift possessed by man. This is the gift of self-consciousness, man's knowledge that, though he is only 'one ripple on the boundless deep', he is at least a thinking and self-conscious ripple, a wave which '*feels* that the deep is boundless' ('The Ancient Sage', ll. 191–2; my italics). Such, at least, is the claim of the English Romantics – the claim of their major poets, philosophers, and critics, for whom man is by birth and by nature an artist and builder, a self-conscious fashioner of worlds. In revolt against the axioms of inductive science I analysed in Chapter I, these idealists assert that the minimal unit of cognition is always 'the object *mecum*', as the Scottish philosopher J. F. Ferrier says: the world framed by a self-conscious subject.

In this chapter I explore five theories of self-conscious response developed by Victorian idealists to express and refine this new axiom of cognition. I show how Ferrier himself speaks of the mind's self-conscious response as a frame around the world, and how F. H. Bradley uses a similar analogy to explain how historical reconstruction is possible. Every theory of self-conscious response can be described as the framing of a picture. If the picture contains the major meaning and the frame the minor meaning, then the framing consciousness merely qualifies without supplanting the descriptive axioms of the inductive sciences. Such is the strategy of Ferrier and of Bradley in his pamphlet on history. The generic equivalent of Ferrier's axiom, 'the world *mecum*', is the use of narrative and lyric frames. Bradley's axiom of the self-consciously framed historical event tends to work better for such multiply framed historical confessions as St John's last testament in 'A Death in the Desert'. The more important the frame becomes, the more important becomes the self-conscious response of the observer or interpreter. When it becomes impossible to assign either major or minor status to the poet's consciousness and the consciousness of the character he impersonates in a mask lyric or in a dramatic monologue, then the frame becomes as important as the picture. Hallam and Fox develop theories of empathy and projection to explain how Tennyson in describing a scene or a character in a poem like 'Mariana' is also describing a region of his own soul.

As the self-conscious response of an observer begins to dominate the picture that he frames, frame and picture space may begin to switch position. This is what happens in the theories of repressed or subliminal awareness developed by Keble and Carlyle. The awareness that is repressed in Browning's 'Childe Roland' is an awareness of the sovereignty of the framing mind. Because Roland is at first unconscious that his consciousness is lord and master over outward sense, he is unaware that his framing mind and the picture space that it frames have in fact changed places. Such a theory of repressed awareness is advanced by Carlyle. Keble accounts for similar effects by developing theories of displacement and reserve. His ideas are most applicable to elegies like Patmore's 'Departure' or Hardy's 'Without Ceremony', where the apparent major meaning, a breach of decorum, is really the minor meaning. The true major meaning is repressed because it is too painful to face. When the picture at the centre turns out to be a hole in the canvas or a mere empty space, then the observer who frames the picture must move in to fill the void. The true subject of these elegies becomes the mourner's response to the blank space at the centre, which is the frightening void of a soul assaulted or a loved one gone.

1 Ferrier's Philosophy of Consciousness: The Framing of the Object

The realistic portrayal of the houses, manners, and habits of speech of different classes in Tennyson's immensely popular English idylls is the generic equivalent of Locke's *tabula rasa*, on which data are inscribed in the form of synthetic *a posteriori* judgements. The common domain that is transcribed in such genres consists of the primary qualities and of the judgemental inferences which empiricists like Locke and J. S. Mill had identified and described. But in its effort to show how all experience is uniform, empiricism had an unforeseen effect. The secondary qualities, Locke discovered, are unique. Each taste or perception is different. And Mill's acknowledgement of intuitions, which cannot be accommodated in any inductive science based on inference, threatens to pull his world apart. Poetic proposals that are descriptively untrue begin to separate themselves from scientific propositions that are true but banausic. For the synthetic *a posteriori* judgements of the descriptive poet, the vatic poet or seer substitutes the analytic *a priori* judgements of a mere tautology or trance. Hoping to short-circuit the normal transit through experience of the quest or journey poem, Browning's Paracelsus, for example, wants to bracket history as an obstacle course full of detours and traps. He hopes to leap to the truth all at once, before he has any experiences to relate. Browning's critique of his hero's restless move away from history is also a critique of the familiar Faustian quest, which is exposed as a form of immaturity and impatience. As Mill perceived, Browning's early quest poem *Pauline* is the quest of a seer who has never really quested. Passing too briskly from psychology to vision, *Pauline* presents no effective history compassing change and development.

More important in Victorian poetics than either the descriptive or the prophetic genres are the many experimental genres of framed narration. These are the generic equivalent of J. F. Ferrier's teaching that all events are subjectively framed. Ferrier's commanding two-part volume, *The Institutes of Metaphysics: Theory of Knowing and Being* (1854), and his earlier series of seven articles appearing in *Blackwood's Magazine* between February 1838 and March 1839, entitled 'An Introduction to the Philosophy of Consciousness', are the most spirited and inclusive Victorian critique of Locke's empirical premise that data are literally gifts, facts given to the mind in a ready-made form. In Locke's judgements, the predicate contains information not found in the subject, and the knowledge conveyed is *a posteriori*, or dependent on experience. By exploring the contribution of the framing subject to the picture that it frames, Ferrier revives a form of synthetic *a priori* judgement to refute the naïve empirical assumption that it is ever possible to mirror an unmediated world of primary facts, plain, exposed, and naked to the eye. Ferrier's judgements are still synthetic, because the framed event brings information to the subject. But because Ferrier insists it is impossible to sunder objects from a mind that is conscious of them, the human subject now provides an essential ingredient of its own knowledge. Since we have been using the word 'subject' in a double sense, as both the human subject and the grammatical subject of a logical proposition, we can borrow Kant's term and say that the logical structure of Ferrier's axiom of cognition, 'the world *mecum*', is synthetic *a priori*. It is important to see that new poetic genres of framed narration display the same formal structure as Ferrier's axiom.

When Tennyson writes his English idylls, which are a kind of social novel in verse, he is using language descriptively. In logical terms, his judgements are synthetic and they depend upon experience. By framing events subjectively in poems like 'The Lotos-Eaters', Tennyson is modifying this norm. When a poem's minor meaning is clearly assigned to the frame, its function is usually to criticize or defend the action that is framed. Least successful are the dedicatory frames that Tennyson uses to introduce poems like 'The Palace of Art' and 'The Day Dream'. The dedicatory frame that summarizes the allegorical meaning of 'The Palace of Art' is too self-conscious and defensive. And in a frame appended to 'The Day Dream', called 'The Moral', Tennyson finds himself in the self-contradictory position of having to undertake an unambiguous defence of ambiguity. In other frames which enclose 'The Day Dream's' graceful retelling of the Sleeping Beauty legend, however, Tennyson proves he is capable of writing against the kind of self-interpretative poetry which is about itself and its own potentialities. In a frame at the end of Arthur's quest in 'Morte d'Arthur', where the poet assumes the mask of Everard Hall, an undergraduate who is mildly ridiculed by the non-poetic narrator for trying to write an epic fragment, Tennyson is able to tell the reader, not only about his efforts to revive heroic genres, but also about his own need to restrain heroic extravagance, to remain critical and detached.

In 'The Hesperides' and 'The Lotos-Eaters' the framed event precedes the framing subject. The minor meaning still comes first, but what is framed is not the narrative but the song or chorus of the speakers. Tennyson frames the song of the Hesperides with a narrative proem recounting Hanno's sea voyage. And he repeats the technique in 'The Lotos-Eaters', where the narrative proem that is used to frame the mariners' chorus ironically foreshadows their return to sea. Because these narrative frames are clearly subordinated to the choruses or songs they frame, emphasis is beginning to shift from the framed event to the framing subject. Already the picture and the frame are about to switch roles. In general, Tennyson is adhering most faithfully to the spirit of Ferrier's teaching when he uses the multiple framing of a narrative poem like 'The Gardener's Daughter' to show that, apart from an observer's framing of the world, there exists no world for the poet to describe. By framing Rose within the narrative of her own wooing, and then placing that frame within the frame of the actual portrait Rose's husband shows his unnamed friend, Tennyson satisfies the same desire as is fulfilled by Daguerre's diorama and many Victorian optical inventions ranging from the panorama and stereopticon to the magic lantern. Like the window-opening or perspective effects that Tennyson creates through many of his epic similes in *Idylls of the King* and *The Princess*, a principal effect of these framing devices is to present the experience of Ferrier's self-conscious observer, who can shift his pictures at will, and for whom 'the object of knowledge' is always framed, always 'the object with the addition' of the 'I's' self-conscious response: the 'thing, or thought, *mecum*' (Ferrier, 1854, p. 93).

According to his grandson, Tennyson was a close student of Ferrier's work (Charles Tennyson, 1949, p. 279). One of the entries in Lady Tennyson's journal under 2 December 1854 records that she and her husband 'read Ferrier's *Institutes of Metaphysics*'. Five years later, on 1 July 1859, the same journal notes that Ferrier dined with the Tennysons at Farringford (Hoge, 1981, pp. 41, 137). Though Ferrier's *Blackwood*'s articles on the philosophy of consciousness were published too late to influence an early poem like 'The Two Voices', Ferrier's teaching reflects many of that poem's concerns. When Tennyson's 'I' tries to unhinge 'the simple senses' from an observer's consciousness, these unframed impressions bleakly affirm that death is horrible, for it is the end; ' "The simple senses crowned his head: / 'Omega! thou art Lord,' they said, / 'We find no motion in the dead!' " ' ('The Two Voices', ll. 277–9). But like all testaments of faith, the sceptic's creed, 'Omega! thou art Lord', requires future interpreters to assess whether the quoted witness is right or wrong to defer to the evidence of the senses. Every quotation places a frame around experience. And these two quotations within the 'I's' larger quotation invite every reader who interprets these frames to relive the empiricist's faith within the larger consciousness of his own mind. As G. H. Lewes explains in a lucid exposition of Fichte's thought which Tennyson may have known, since he owned the first edition of Lewes's *Biographical History of Philosophy*: 'To be, and to be conscious, are the same. The existence of the Ego depends upon its consciousness. But to be conscious of Self is at the same time to be conscious of Not-Self,' as Ferrier, like Fichte, concludes. It is true that the 'Not-Self' of a motionless body 'is given in Consciousness as a *reality*, and therefore we cannot suppose it to be a phantom'. But as Fichte also argues, in anticipation of Ferrier's own philosophy of consciousness, 'the existence of the very Ego itself is *determined* [not caused, but defined or rendered definite, as in the German verb 'bestimmen'] by the Non-Ego' (Lewes, 1845–6, vol. 4, p. 167). Because the evidence of Tennyson's 'simple senses' can never be severed from a framing consciousness, Ferrier concludes that a self-conscious 'I' can never for a moment entertain a proposition 'which involves the supposition of [its own] annihilation'. Citing the evidence of Wordsworth's poem 'We are Seven', Ferrier affirms 'this great law of human thought – the natural inconceivability of death' (*Blackwood's Edinburgh Magazine*, June 1842, vol. 51, p. 819).

In his most ambitious work, *The Institutes of Metaphysics*, Ferrier argues that the gulf between the individual framing consciousness and the consciousness of God, between epistemology and ontology, can be bridged by means of carefully constructed argument. The keystone of the causeway he constructs is his so-called agnoiology, or theory of ignorance. Distinguishing between mere ignorance and nescience, Ferrier argues that ignorance is only a privation of knowledge. We can be ignorant only of framed objects, of matter in synthesis with mind. But as Ferrier paradoxically observes, 'the ordinary thinker . . . supposes . . . that he can know *less* than he can really know; hence he supposes that *mere* objects can be known.' The main purpose of his agnoiology is to show 'that we cannot be ignorant of less than can be known – and that, therefore, *mere* objects cannot be what we are ignorant of, but only objects along with some self or subject' (1854, p. 438). Ferrier's ironically constructive use of the limits of ignorance wins the respect of even the antimetaphysical Lewes, who praises Ferrier's *Institutes* as 'one of the most remarkable books of our time'. It 'is like a lonely obelisk on the broad flat plain: there are not even cairns beside it' (1880, vol. 2, p. 755).

Tennyson seems to be recalling the key role assigned to framed negatives in Ferrier's agnoiology when he allows his Ancient Sage to use negatives framed by second-person pronouns to subdue the sceptic into an awareness that, in Ferrier's phrase, '*mere* objects cannot be what we are ignorant of', but only propositions which are self-consciously framed by some self or subject.

> Thou canst not prove the Nameless, O my son,
> Nor canst thou prove the world thou movest in,
> Thou canst not prove that thou art body alone,
> Nor canst thou prove that thou art spirit alone,
> Nor canst thou prove that thou art both in one.
>
> ('The Ancient Sage', ll. 57–61)

But only some of these framed propositions are in principle unknowable. In the rest of the poem we discover that our mere ignorance of body and spirit 'in one' is a potentially remediable privation of knowledge. Like our mere ignorance of the Nameless, it is not to be confused with our nescience of mere 'body alone' and of mere 'spirit alone'. We can neither know nor be ignorant of these objects, because each alone is too small a unit of cognition. But there is nothing intrinsically unknowable about the Nameless, 'a supreme and infinite eternal Mind', as Ferrier says, 'in synthesis with all things' (1854, p. 511). It may not be possible to *prove* the Absolute. But because the mind's framing of the Absolute represents a synthesis of subject and object, it is possible, as the sage later shows, to *experience* the Absolute by passing from the contemplation of the self 'into the Nameless, as a cloud / Melts into Heaven' ('The Ancient Sage', ll. 233–4).

2 Browning, Strauss, and Bradley: The Framing of the Past

Browning's concept of historical reconstruction stands in the liberal Anglican tradition represented by Julius Hare, Connop Thirlwall, Thomas Arnold, and A. P. Stanley, who are all indebted to Barthold Niebuhr's *History of Rome*. His historical re-enactments also anticipate the systematic defence of this practice in F. H. Bradley's earliest published treatise, *The Presuppositions of Critical History*. Browning shows that any effort to unhinge facts about the past from the re-enactment of those facts in the mind of an interpreter is an attempt to descend below the limit of what can legitimately be known. For Browning, as for Ferrier, that limit is the 'object *mecum*'. According to Bradley, who like Browning writes as an opponent of the biblical criticism pioneered by Strauss and F. C. Baur, the only criterion of critical history is the historian himself. A miraculous event like Elisha's resuscitation of the corpse (II Kings 4: 31–5) becomes historically probable only when some analogy can be established between the miracle itself and a phenomenon like artificial respiration or the inspiration of the historical interpreter, Robert Browning, who breathes life into the dead facts of the Roman murder case in *The Ring and the Book* (i, 760–72).

Most paraphrases of *The Ring and the Book* distance us from what actually happens to us as we read. They translate the discomforts and anxieties into safer, less demanding fictions. To return to the text is to stretch oneself out on the rack of a tough, obscure poem. By combining the tortures of the Roman murder trial with a real trial of the reader's own endurance Browning uses the physical extent of his poem, its great duration, to disclose the inconclusiveness and agony of history. To read *The Ring and the Book* is to undergo exquisite and refined torture. Browning's actual story is over almost as soon as it begins. The reader's own vulnerability is made inescapable by the way the rest of this long poem pushes inexorably beyond its natural limits. Almost from the start we have wanted the interminable interpretations to end. This does not mean that readers necessarily dislike *The Ring and the Book*, but it does mean that they are made to experience the anxieties of a critical historian. If Browning is trying to protect Pompilia's noble but fragile love against the heartless black comedy of Guido's intrigue, why does he make us feel so close to Guido? The villain's two monologues are like traps. Even in inviting us into Guido's mind, they conspire to keep us out. Browning writes simultaneously against and on behalf of interpretive precision. He limits and defines the scope of critical history, then shows how every interpretation of the past shades off into a project of limitless amorphousness. The poem as poem – as a test of interpretive capacity and of sheer endurance in each of its readers – is precisely analogous to the dilemma of historical reconstruction Bradley describes.

If scientific historiographers like Leopold von Ranke were right, there would be nothing problematic about historical reconstruction. Once the documents were available, history would write itself. This scientific approach to history reaches a *reductio ad absurdum* in H. T. Buckle's *History of Civilization in England*. Originally published in 1857, eleven years before Browning completed his own critique of scientific historiography in *The Ring and the Book*, Buckle's *History* assumes that all historical scholarship aspires to the status of a statistical science. For example, 'it is now known,' Buckle says, 'that marriages bear a fixed and definite relation to the price of corn; and in England the experience of a century has proved that, instead of having any connexion with personal feelings, [marriages] are simply regulated by the average earnings of the great mass of the people' (1864, vol. 1, pp. 23–4). I have no evidence that Browning read Buckle's curious book. I cite it as a crude example of a scientific tendency represented with greater subtlety by David Friedrich Strauss. Though Browning's limited command of German would not have allowed him to read Strauss's *Das Leben Jesu* when it originally appeared in 1835, he appears to have read it in the translation by George Eliot from the fourth German edition, which was published in three volumes in the late spring of 1846. Strauss argues that historical myth must consist in 'a simple narration of facts'. But how, we might ask, are such facts to be isolated and recognized? Indeed Strauss's concept of historical myth appears to be self-contradictory. If a narrative is genuinely mythical, then it will be characterized by 'the rich pictorial and imaginative ... thought ... of the primitive ages' (1846, vol. 1, p. 26). But to that degree a narrative would seem to be unhistorical. Conversely, if a narrative is genuinely historical, in substance as well as form, how can it be a myth, which Strauss defines as 'the representation of an event or of an idea' which is 'historical' in 'form' only (1846, vol. 1, p. 26)?

The answer seems to lie in Strauss's positivist assumption that all ancient narratives, however factual, 'confounded the divine and the human, the natural and the supernatural' (1846, vol. 1, p. 26). In other words, what was historical for a primitive intelligence is unhistorical for us. According to Strauss, as our intelligence has evolved we have all become positivists. We have come to recognize that 'mental cultivation mainly consists in the gradual recognition of a chain of causes and effects connecting natural phenomena with each other' (1846, vol. 1, p. 2). Genuine historiography is scientific: what cannot be made to conform with Strauss's causal model does not deserve to be called history at all.

In *The Ring and the Book* Browning both uses and challenges these methods of scientific historiography. Though Browning redefines historical truth as any item that can be recovered from the court records of the seventeenth-century Roman murder trial, then fitted into the tropes and schemes of newspaper epic, as into a Homeric filing system, for storage and retrieval, he also recognizes that historical knowledge, far from consisting of archival fragments waiting to be scrutinized, is an imaginative framing and enactment of past events. The historian's knowledge is also self-knowledge, a discovery of his own place in history.

One could argue, however, that both Browning and Bradley make a category mistake about historical writing. They subtly confuse its genre by assuming a law of uniformity that is applicable to treatises on physical nature but alien to works of historical reconstruction. The faith of the inductive logician that what is true of seventeenth-century Romans will be true of nineteenth-century Italians or Englishmen is not a faith that is justified by historical knowledge itself. It is justified by knowledge of another kind, by knowledge of causal laws, which Browning and Bradley inappropriately borrow from the physical sciences. As one commentator concludes, 'it was Bradley's consciousness' of this indebtedness to scientific knowledge, 'based on induction from observed facts on the principle that the future will repeat the past', which 'led him after composing [*The Presuppositions of Critical History*] to devote himself to the searching examination of Mill's *Logic* whose results he published in his *Principles of Logic* nine years later' (Collingwood, 1946, p. 139).

I do not mean to imply that Browning never successfully exorcizes the last traces of a scientific approach to history. In 'A Death in the Desert', for example, written five years before *The Ring and the Book* was completed, St John recognizes that a scientific induction from past facts, however appropriate in the study of natural law, is an inappropriate model for historical knowledge. Apprehending that human nature is not a constant, like the law of gravity, but that it is subject to change, St John foresees that a loss of the faculty to experience miracles may make it impossible for future readers of the Gospels to accept their testimony as ready-made evidence of Christ's divinity. If John says, for example, that Christ rose from the dead, and future historians accept his statement, then their own inference that John was right to say that Christ rose from the dead requires them to re-enact in their own minds not only the events narrated in the Gospels but also the thoughts of St John and the other disciples. As Browning and Bradley both realize, the Gospels are not factual reports or chronicles, but fictions of a rather special kind. They are a sort of midrash or *aggiornamento* of the old texts, a retrospective consideration of what ought properly to have occurred some thirty years before. Using the commentary of Pamphylax the Antiochene to frame the deathbed testament of St John, 'A Death in the Desert' encloses its first narrative enclosure with second and third enclosures. These include the gloss of Theotypas on John's doctrine of the three souls and the concluding gloss of Cerinthus, a gnostic opponent of St John. In all such texts of interpretive framing and enclosure, as in the Bible and its commentaries, retrospective fictions of what ought to have occurred allow Browning to replace the inductions of scientific historiography, which can suffice 'the eye' alone, with a framing model of self-conscious response that, even in sufficing 'the eye' by extracting secrets from the book of the world, has power to 'save the soul beside' (*The Ring and the Book*, XII, 867).

Since in a poem like 'A Death in the Desert' we are constantly moving from the frames to the picture, from the multiple interpreters to the story they interpret, it is impossible to say one is more important than the other. The curious nesting structure of this genre, which turns the scrolls into a cupboard of sacred texts, reminds us that interpretation and description, frames and picture, are inseparable. The complex interplay between the two dramatizes a paradox that besets all generic criticism. This is what I like to refer to as the Heisenberg principle of generic study. Like any form of synthetic *a priori* judgement, a theory about a poem's generic type alters the features to which an interpreter like Browning's St John or the modern critic appeals in support of his conclusion that the Gospels, for example, are a history-like fiction of the kind the Higher Critics of the Bible were discovering, or that as an elaborately nested commentary on commentaries a poem like 'A Death in the Desert' is a member of the same generic family. Such an interplay of interpreting subject and interpreted character or story, where picture and frame are of equal interest, is the outstanding generic feature of Tennyson's and Browning's early monologues, where the portrayal of people like Mariana and Ulysses becomes inseparable from the poet's exploration of his own consciousness.

3 Projection and Empathy: Hallam, Fox, and the Dramatic Monologue

The two theories of self-conscious framing which anticipate and explain the achievements of Tennyson and Browning in the monologue form are enunciated early in the 1830s by Arthur Hallam and W. J. Fox, friends of these poets. In an influential theory of poetic empathy, published in 1831 in *The Englishman's Magazine*, Hallam praises poets of sensation like Shelley, Keats, and Tennyson for their remarkable ability to find in the 'colours ... sounds, and movements' of external nature, 'unregarded by duller temperaments', the signature of 'innumerable shades of fine emotion', which are too subtle for conceptual language to express (1831, pp. 850, 856). In a *Westminster Review* article earlier in 1831 on Tennyson's *Poems, Chief Lyrical*, published in 1830, Fox argues that the poet can best concentrate his energies by sketching his relation to a desolate landscape or to some ruined paradise, as in Tennyson's 'Mariana' or 'Oenone'. Since Fox's poet dramatizes his interior landscapes through projection, and since Hallam's poet internalizes his pictures, they tend to converge on common ground. Despite their different starting-points both critics are agreed that the poet must find in some external object the focus or medium of his truest self-expression.

Insisting that the sensory correlatives of feeling can convey, like music, complexities of meaning and subtly nuanced moods for which no dictionary words exist, Hallam is the prophet of a symbolist aesthetic later endorsed by Yeats. Fox, on the other hand, writes as a disciple of James Mill.[1] Just as Addison is liberated by Locke's theory of the ideality of the secondary qualities, according to which sounds and colours are truly a poem of the perceiver's creation, so Fox is liberated by the penetrating power conferred on the mind by the empirical psychology of James Mill's treatise, *Analysis of the Phenomena of the Human Mind*, which had been published two years earlier in 1829. Tennyson, says Fox, 'seems to obtain entrance into a mind as he would make his way into a landscape; he climbs the pineal gland as if it were a hill in the centre of the scene' (1831, p. 76). Every mood of the mind has its own outward world, or rather it fills the world with objects that the mind can inhabit. Such objects, resistant enough for the exercise of conscious energy, are placable enough for the mind to dominate. Though Fox illustrates his theory by analysing Tennyson's 'Mariana', we are most aware of dramatic impersonation in poems that were not yet written when Fox published his article in 1831. I am thinking of monologues by Browning, a close friend of Fox, who was almost certainly familiar with Fox's *Westminster Review* essay, and of poems by Tennyson like 'Tithonus' and 'Ulysses' which simulate the activity of a person imagined as virtually real, but behind whose speech or manners we are often aware of the poet himself, exploring and refining his deepest concerns.

Fox's poet seems forever searching for some revelation which is inside him all the time. The true subject is the self, the impersonator's soul, which in its myriad facets can be seen only as it is reflected from other characters, like an image recomposed by mirrors. It is important to remember, however, that Fox's theory of impersonation requires more than free projection. It is not enough for the poet to force his own will of aesthetic intention on a character. He must not become another Duke of Ferrara, who makes a tyranny not only within his own domestic life but also within his conversation with the envoy, whom he controls as a mere stage property or puppet. Fox insists that the poet must be modified and changed by the character he becomes. After writing 'Ulysses' Tennyson is presumably a sadder and a wiser man. But to be changed and educated by a character like Ulysses Tennyson must first entertain attitudes foreign to his temperament. In Ulysses' instinctive recoil from the 'eternal silence' (l. 27), for example, Tennyson gives potent expression to a pagan rejection of the soul's immortality, even though it must have wrenched his soul to do so. To be enriched and tutored by Ulysses' splendid resolution is to risk offence and pain as well. It also entails generosity, negative capability, lack of envy, and love. For Tennyson must not only give away part of himself to Ulysses. He must also be willing to take Ulysses back into himself. Such readiness and vulnerability on the poet's part, such openness to pain, are essential qualities of the impersonator's art.

Precariously balanced between empathy and free projection, Fox's poet must perform a difficult high-wire act of the mind. On the one hand, his personality must be 'modified' and even changed by the characters he becomes. On the other hand, that personality can never, Fox insists, be wholly 'absorbed' (1831, p. 77). Total absorption leads to promiscuity or death. Even in seeing the world through the eyes of dead authors, Tennyson cannot be so loyal to his sources that he fails to see where Homer's Ulysses, in speaking of death as 'the eternal silence', has failed to do justice to his theme. Unless Fox's poet remains firmly in control of the licentious process of casting his spirit 'into any living thing, real or imaginary', he degenerates into a moral cipher. No impersonation can lack the authority of a presiding personality who 'gives' generously of himself even while taking back from others. When such authority is lacking, the poet becomes a mere 'poetical harlequin', a chameleon like Keats's poet of negative capability, who may gain the whole world yet lose his own soul.

The impersonator must rule, therefore, and govern. But he must not become too tyrannical in the process. Unless he is a democrat of the spirit, a 'transmigrating Vishnu' (in Fox's striking phrase), who can assume the nature of such 'elemental beings as Syrens . . . mermen and mermaidens' (Fox, 1831, p. 77), he will grow too godlike in his office. Open to the indignities of even the lowliest incarnations, Fox's Vishnu must avoid the despotism of the dictatorial impersonator, who is at best a ventriloquist speaking through his puppet as a mere partisan or apologist. The true impersonator knows how to receive as well as give, and is capable of taking back from his characters more than he is conscious of putting in.

Keats's fear that the chameleon poet of negative capability may lose his identity in dramatic extroversion comes, I think, from a failure to distinguish between an identification so complete that it demands a total abdication of the artist's personality – an extreme that is extraordinary and in practice rare – and two more common forms of identification. In one mode the artist of roles lends himself to a character like the Duke of Ferrara or the Bishop of St Praxed's: there is empathy but no discernible projection. In the other mode the dramatic poet projects his own ideas and feelings, substituting himself or a part of himself for a character like Fra Lippo or Ulysses. Deep forms of caring are not to be confused with the self-annihilating kind of empathy that allows Browning to efface his personality, emptying himself into the Spanish monk, or into the court lady in 'The Laboratory'. Indeed the self-annihilating kind of empathy and the more sympathetic forms of identification appear to exist in reverse ratios. A reader is less gripped by Andrea del Sarto in a purely empathetic way, far less carried away by him, than he is by the raucous swearing song of the Spanish monk or by the hypnotic incantations in 'The Laboratory'. But Browning himself was not greatly moved by these swearing songs. In a letter to Elizabeth, dated 11 February 1845, he calls them 'scenes and song-scraps', 'mere and very escapes of [his] inner power' (1969, vol. 1, p. 17). In 'Andrea del Sarto', however, a poem Browning liked to read publicly and considered one of his best monologues, the viscera and pulse are much less involved. And yet the less physically swayed he is, the more Browning's mingled sympathy and contempt for Andrea can create the conditions of deep caring and concern. Browning clearly empathizes with the uxorious Andrea, the 'weak-eyed bat no sun should tempt / Out of the grange whose four walls make his world' ('Andrea del Sarto', ll. 169–70). The poet's own devotion to Elizabeth and his unflattering comparison of himself to 'those crazy Mediterranean phares ... wherein the light is ever revolving in a dark gallery' (1969, vol. 1, p. 17) give the uncanny feel of a submerged pattern running through the monologue, a pattern of repressed resemblance, like the hidden purposes of Andrea himself. If Browning were more involved in the primitive participatory sense, as he is involved in his 'scenes and song-scraps', his own sense of failure and betrayal would be much less engaged. He would be much less deeply stirred by Andrea.

When Keats expresses his fear that because the artist of roles 'is everything' he is therefore 'nothing' and strictly speaking 'has no character' (1958, vol. 2, p. 81), he is ignoring the paradoxical counter-truth that the idea of involvement always implies some separation, some distance to be crossed. Once a poet is deeply moved by a person or idea, his attention may be safely drawn to his own anxieties and fears by the false sense of his being totally involved with something else. Certainly the power of the most unforgettable monologues – 'My Last Duchess', 'Caliban Upon Setebos', 'Demeter and Persephone' – resides in intrigues and conspiracies, in stirring indictments of creation, which seem deeply and frighteningly to implicate the poet at the moment he seems most secure and detached.

When a strong connection exists between the poet and another person, the sense of their intimacy tends to increase as the dramatic distance between them widens. Thus in *In Memoriam* Tennyson can evaluate his love for Hallam only when Hallam's death has brought them into poignant focus for each other. Before he can closely involve his soul with Hallam's, he must once more magnify the distance to be crossed: 'If any vision should reveal / Thy likeness, I might count it vain / As but the canker of the brain' (xcii, 1–3). Even the conceit of reaping through Hallam's death 'The far-off interest of tears' (i, 8) allows Tennyson to revive in the forgotten etymology of 'interest' ('it exists between', 'it makes a difference') the importance of separation and deferral. Conversely, Andrea's 'close-up' of Lucrezia's face has the curious effect of increasing psychic distance at the same time as it reduces physical distance. His domestic experience is hardly one of closeness or intimacy. Tithonus seems to be closest to Aurora in some kind of middle distance, not as her consort but not as her rejected suitor either. Only his reversion to 'earth in earth' can bring Tithonus into focus for Aurora, just as Tennyson attains a strangely powerful intimacy with Hallam partly because Hallam is dead.

The poet's monologues are a self-reflecting mirror. They are also framed portraits in which the framing consciousness of the poet is at least as important as the portraits. Poetic dramas are attempts to efface the playwright, but dramatic monologues allow the poet to see himself as others see him. Even in taking the 'senses, feelings, nerves, and brain' of the people he impersonates, Fox's poet is still 'himself in them, modified but not absorbed by their peculiar constitution and mode of being' (1831, p. 77). When a dramatic poet like Browning appears to become deeply involved with Paracelsus and Sordello, he may in fact be exhibiting self-love, since such characters are mainly unmodified projections of himself. When, at the other extreme, instead of trying to assimilate the world to his own quickening spirit, Browning tries to empty himself into the thick viscous weight of the Spanish monk's soul (if the monk has a soul), the poetic impersonator is in danger of forgoing the simultaneous 'being-outside' which the fullest involvement with a character requires. As physical distance shrinks between the impersonator and his masks, psychical distance increases, and the empathetic artist of roles loses the greater intimacy that can be experienced only in some sort of middle space, halfway between projection and empathy. Respect for an impersonated character demands a giving of self. In the dramatic act of impersonating, of projecting and empathizing, the artist of roles does not extinguish his personality but brings his whole self to bear.

4 Carlyle and the Unconscious: The Lucid Veil

In many monologues the poet's framing consciousness and the portrait which he frames are in perfect balance. But in other genres of framed narration, as the consciousness of the poet begins to gain ascendancy over the ostensible subject of his narrative, the balance between frame and picture is once again upset. To shift emphasis from the picture space of its landscapes to the framing consciousness of the mourner, for example, *In Memoriam* frames events twice. In the Prologue to his poem, Tennyson uses the knowledge of a recording self, fully conscious of order and meaning, to pass judgements on the neurotic, doubting self whose history is recorded. In other poems, like Browning's *Sordello*, the commentaries of a self-conscious narrator may be used to make the epistemological problems of framed narration the poet's most important theme. The narrator in *Sordello* is excited primarily by the complexity of his own narrative project. If *Sordello* is an epic poem that can scarcely survive the manner of its telling, it is because Sordello's story is continually being interrupted by the observations of the narrator, the poet Browning, living not in medieval Italy but sometimes in Venice, sometimes in London, during the period 1833 to 1838, and forever explaining his choice of topic, his generic experimentations, and the inner meaning of the broken story he relates. To approach *Sordello* with the generic expectations appropriate to an epic poem or a novel in verse is like trying to read *Tristram Shandy* for its plot. Browning tells us not only about the lives of historical characters but also about the making of his own life in the writing of the poetry and about his rescue of a life for history and myth.

The ascendancy of the framing consciousness in such genres of framed narration is best explained by Carlyle's theory of the unconscious. We live in a highly self-conscious age, Carlyle argues, but our intense self-consciousness is a disease. Influenced by Friedrich Schiller's teaching that man's health originally consisted in a 'naïve' state of unconsciousness, Carlyle argues that modern man's self-consciousness has veiled and all but effaced 'the memory of [Adam's] first state of Freedom and paradisaic Unconsciousness' (1899, vol. 28, p. 3). But once the Fall into self-consciousness has taken place, the exile's memory of Eden may partly be restored by his demon of self-conscious response, which is like a serpent with two natures, able to heal as well as wound. For without this demon, how can man ever be conscious of the unconscious? Yet how can Carlyle reconcile his consciousness of the truth of his theory with the general condition of unconsciousness which must exist if the theory is true? The difficulty of being conscious of any truth which lies outside of consciousness arises in an especially vexing form in 'The Poet as Hero', where Carlyle's defence of Dante's sincerity, of Dante's absence of self-consciousness, commits Carlyle to the paradoxical conclusion George Landow has noted (Landow, 1971, p. 328). It leads Carlyle to conclude that in writing allegory in *The Divine Comedy*, Dante (like any sincere poet) did not know what he was doing.

Since only the unconscious is healthy, it is in the interests of our moral health to mask our illness by hiding our self-consciousness from view. By pretending that the picture he presents is an objective portrait, freed of all morbid introspection and subjective taint, Carlyle's poet will demote the mind's diseased self-consciousness to the secondary status of a mere frame around a picture. And in order to conceal the fact that the frame is really more important than the picture space it encloses, the poet may foster the delusion that there is some secret at the centre waiting to be unveiled. Carlyle practises just such an art of narrative strip-tease in *Sartor Resartus*, where the readers are led deeper and deeper into the text by the expectation that Carlyle will eventually remove the veil that holds secret meaning – or some ultimate absence of meaning – in reserve. The editorial frames force the readers to chart their way through a similar maze in prose fragments like 'The Opera' (1852), where everything seems to be on the upholstered periphery and nothing at the centre, or 'On the Sinking of the Vengeur' (1839), in which the editor's last-minute disclosure of a 'discovery not worth communicating' and his 'entire silence concerning it' (Carlyle, 1899, vol. 29, p. 225) leave everything in doubt.

No poet better dramatizes the truth that narrative is always a product of self-conscious veiling, constructed over a loss, than Carlyle's friend Browning, who owned a presentation copy of Carlyle's *Life of Schiller*, and whose 'Essay on Shelley' appears to be influenced by Carlyle's book.[2] Combining a subtle and incessant intellectual activity with an incapacity to understand anything, specialists in priestly election like Browning's cleric in 'The Confessional', spiritual con-men like Mr Sludge the medium, and casuists like Bishop Blougram, all show why Carlyle should yearn for the sincerities of a less self-conscious age. But the masking of an Edenic unconsciousness is not confined to monologues which resort to self-consciously dishonest uses of a dramatic mask or veil. More important are poems like *La Saisiaz*, whose framed debate is far less memorable than either the earlier conversation between the poet and his friend or the concluding colloquy, in which the real grounds for Browning's beliefs are disclosed. Even the self-consciously framed landscape in 'Childe Roland' is less important than the speaker's framing consciousness, which lucidly veils the truth that salvation lies in the mind's sovereignty over landscapes and pictures. And so massive are the interpretive frames in *The Ring and the Book* that the picture space which is framed shrinks to insignificance. The secret truth seems to be that there is no secret truth. Eloquent silences and pregnant indications keep intimating that the sphinx is without a secret after all.

Every frame around a past event is a fiction, a story we make up. But this does not mean the story is untrue. As Schiller explains in a passage Browning may have known because it was a favourite passage of Carlyle, who quotes it twice, first in his *Life of Schiller* and later in his essay on the 'State of German Literature' (1827), 'truth still lives in fiction, and from the copy the original will be restored' (Carlyle, 1899, vol. 25, p. 202; vol. 26, p. 58). Few aphorisms better illuminate the status of fancy and fact in *The Ring and the Book*, where there are at least two sides to every truth. If Perseus rescues Andromeda, Andromeda also rescues Perseus. And if the rescue is heroic, it is also pointless. Pompilia is tragically killed, just as the rescued Elizabeth dies an exile in Italy. Exploiting the mind's capacity for multiple response, *The Ring and the Book* dramatizes Schiller's aphorism that the 'truth still lives in fiction'. The truth about the past is precisely what is lost. Every frame around this loss is a fiction, a story we construct over a missing history. Since it is impossible to penetrate to the innermost core of this history, Browning must keep the story going, allowing the multiple frames to repeat themselves endlessly in their acknowledged incompleteness.

Something similar happens in *La Saisiaz*, where the multiple framing is connected to the double guilt of the narration. Browning is recalling 'in London's mid-November' a debate with himself on the afterlife of the soul which took place some three months earlier on Mount Salève, and which was itself a recollection of a debate held a week earlier with a friend, Anne Egerton Smith, who had died in the interval. For the unresolved outcome of their original debate, death had written a more powerful ending. A question posed in intellectual play, as part of a game, is now posed by life itself, and in meeting life's test Browning must confront the question in a personal way. But the more intimate Browning's questions become, the more he must use multiple frames to hide the empty space at the centre of his picture. Browning's deepest feeling for his dead wife revives a memory so irrepressible that only by dint of the most strenuous reserve can he keep closed the fissure of pain that starts to open up. If Browning fails to penetrate to the core of his story, he will be guilty of opening up an old wound and allowing it to fester. On the other hand, if he pierces all the way in, he will be guilty of desecrating his wife's grave. His use of multiple frames leads simultaneously *toward* and *away* from the void at the centre of his life and his poem. Not only does Browning twice remove the central colloquy in *La Saisiaz* from his original debate with Miss Smith. He also twice removes it from the event in his life – the death of Elizabeth – which gives both the multiply framed debate and the death of Miss Smith their poignancy and power.

5 Keble's Poet of Reserve:
Repressed and Subliminal Awareness

In a poem like *La Saisiaz*, we may at first be unaware that the multiple frames and the picture space that is framed have in fact switched places. Such switching also occurs in elegies. There is always a blank space at the centre of an elegy which only the framing consciousness of the elegist can fill. In Patmore's elegy 'Departure', for example, the apparent domestic meaning is only a minor meaning, and the true meaning is at first sublimated or repressed. The Victorian critic who contributes most to our understanding of sublimation and repression is John Keble. In outward form, Keble's theory of displacement and reserve is more conservative and theological than Carlyle's. But in practice it is more revolutionary, because Keble works out his theory in more detail. He argues that the most permanently interesting features of poetry – Lucretius' 'passion for the Infinite' or 'Virgil's 'master passion' for pastoral celebration (1912, vol. 2, pp. 334, 417) – are so artfully veiled that a reader can glimpse them only indirectly, out of the corner of the eye. Fed by unconscious sources, the primacy of a poet's 'master passion' is preserved by being disguised, by *not* being named directly. Just as one result of the Oxford Movement's theory of reserve is to keep the uninitiated herd at bay, so one result of Keble's poetic theory is to show that a direct representation of the inner life is neither possible nor desired.

The germ of Keble's theory can be found as early as 1812 in his undergraduate prize essay 'On Translation from Dead Languages'. The good teacher, the young Keble argues, needs a proper balance of enthusiasm and restraint. Though a spirited translation will give vent to self-expression, it will be displaced self-expression, a disguised testament that will be all the more spirited for the obstacles overcome. For what the translator reads 'engraven on the tablets of antiquity impress[es] [him] the more strongly for the difficulty he had in deciphering them' (1812, folio 53). In his later criticism Keble argues that the poet's urge to vent his feelings and his accompanying desire to draw over these feelings a 'veil of reserve' (1838, p. 436) advance and adjust their claims most productively in two main areas of composition, in the poet's generic displacements and in his experiments with prosody. I shall briefly consider each of these areas in turn.

In his *Praelectiones Academicae* (1832–41), which I shall refer to more simply as his *Oxford Lectures on Poetry*, and in his review of Lockhart's *Life of Scott*, Keble argues that all epic and dramatic genres are displacements of the poet's lyric impulse. Thus Virgil's epic the *Aeneid* is said to disguise a pastoral yearning, indulged most directly in the *Georgics*. If a poet is writing a lyric or an elegy, he is writing under little generic restraint to 'any sudden burst of high or plaintive feeling' in which he may choose to indulge. Such is not the case, however, with classical epic, in which Virgil may have to displace his instinctive 'love of woods and rivers' by forcing that instinct to work 'its way through all the incumbrance of the epic story'. 'Interposed, as a kind of transparent veil, between the listener and the narrator's real drift and feelings', both the narrative structure of a prose romance by Sir Walter Scott and an epic action like Virgil's act 'like a safety-valve to a full mind' (Keble, 1838, pp. 440, 436).

In a partly autobiographical poem like *Maud*, Tennyson uses Keble's principles of generic displacement to veil his confessional impulse, which surfaces briefly in the germinal lyric expressing his love for Hallam (*Maud*, II, 141–4). Keble's generic theories also account for the power of one of the darkest and most familiar wasteland poems of the Victorian age, 'Dover Beach'. At first Arnold seems to be writing a love poem, and he keeps repressing the dark side of truth. Only in the last verse paragraph does his nightmare vision break out unimpeded in a powerful echo of Newman's Oxford sermon on 'Faith and Reason' (1839). At the end of that sermon Thucydides' account of the 'night battle, where each fights for himself, and friend and foe stand together' (Newman, 1887, p. 201), reverses the import of the lover's plea to his bride by summoning up Arnold's true subject – the trauma of pointless conflict, in which each disputant fails to understand what his adversary means. For a panic moment, in which the earlier appeal to love seems swallowed up in nightmare, obliterating everything of value, the speaker breaks out into bereavement. From nostalgia for his grand illusion, to an odd, reverberating, reproachful kind of lament, to the final surge of terror, all the steps of repressed despair, forcing its way slowly to consciousness, are embodied in Arnold's rhymes, grammar, line breaks, and metre.

Tennyson owned both volumes of Keble's *Oxford Lectures*, which are now in the Tennyson Research Centre at Lincoln. Though the second volume is mostly uncut, Tennyson was clearly familiar with Keble's theories. The repression of meaning in Tennyson's lyrics takes several forms. The silences in 'Tears, idle tears' and the disclaimer of ignorance, 'I know not what they mean', intimate a loss which words cannot express. More elusively, 'Break, break, break' uses syntactic breaks and pauses filled with words to gesture in the direction of some indefinable loss. The removal of the human subject accounts for the power of the vanished hand in the elegy and for the poignancy of those lyrics in *In Memoriam* where a material object like the 'dark house' in Wimpole Street, where Hallam no longer lives, is separated from the person who would give it meaning. Some of the mutest poems are also the most moving, because they point despairingly to a meaning that is still half repressed. In *Idylls of the King*, for example, the sheer opaqueness of Merlin's repeated phrases numbs the mind. The cherished opacity of a mantra or riddle induces incomprehension, and incomprehension produces a kind of reverie that leaves the mind open to repressed or subliminal meaning. The refrain in Tennyson's elegy 'In the Garden at Swainston' may seem at first even self-contradictory and silly: 'Two dead men have I known', 'Two dead men have I loved', 'Three dead men have I loved' (ll. 11, 13, 15). What has gone wrong? Has the poet forgotten how to count? Such stupidity or stupor signals the presence of some indefinably stupendous fact, some repressed or subliminal truth, just beyond the threshold of present consciousness. As one of Keble's poets of reserve, Tennyson can often mean most when he seems to say nothing. ' "Unspeakable" he wrote / "Their kindness," and he wrote no more' ('To the Marquis of Dufferin and Ava', ll. 35–6). The silences in these poems illustrate the cryptic Buddhist saying that one who speaks does not know and that one who knows does not speak. When even the meanest root in 'Flower in the Crannied Wall' can represent what God and man are, then even the most sacred symbols may seem trivial and trite. If Tennyson, as Auden says, is the stupidest poet, it may be because he is also one of the most profound.

As I have already indicated, Keble studies the effects of poetry's displacements, not only in a poet's generic experiments and in his repression of meaning, but also in his experiments with metre. It is in this second area of experimentation that Clough's innovations in *Amours de Voyage* connect most directly with Keble. From Keble, who was delivering the last of his university lectures on poetry during Clough's first four years at Oxford, and who was judging the Newdigate competitions in which Clough himself competed in

1839 and 1840, Clough may have learned the advantage of submitting to a strict metrical discipline. A demanding metre has the advantage of 'determining in some one direction', as Keble says (1838, p. 435), the impulses to act and to meditate, to do and to reflect, which keep pulling Clough in opposite directions, threatening to paralyse the poet and impair his art. Despite a general Tractarian reluctance to discuss poetic technique, Keble's shrewd analysis of the psychological discipline afforded by a difficult and complex metre helps explain how Clough's use of hexameters in *Amours de Voyage* makes this metrically demanding form among his most successful.

> I am in love, you declare. I think not so; yet I grant you
> It is a pleasure indeed to converse with this girl. Oh, rare gift,
> Rare felicity, this!
>
> (*Amours de Voyage*, II, x, 254–6)

Like some formal minuet, the finely managed metre leads Claude through steps of decorous wavering; a pace forward in the opening declaration; a hanging back in the next two clauses; a slackening resistance as he tacitly qualifies his qualification; then, in a rare violation of Clough's metrical practice, in a terminal foot of triple stresses ('Óh, ráfe gíft'), a drawing nearer, with a fullness of emotion, and a momentary attainment of all the heart can wish. The hovering tone and metre deflect conflicting impulses in Clough and his speaker. Without using metre to shape out channels in which the competing claims of action and knowledge can begin to flow, could Clough write the poem at all?

A recent commentator on Keble, G. B. Tennyson, takes both M. H. Abrams and Alba H. Warren to task for developing the psychological rather than the strictly theological implications of Keble's theories. 'Terms like "repression" and "neurosis" . . . are subversive of what Keble was trying to convey,' he argues, 'although they may convey the modern critic's attitude to Tractarian theory' (1981, p. 60). It seems to me, however, that Keble's poetic is no more separable from a theory of psychological displacement or reserve than is Victorian aesthetics itself from theology. And as Tennyson well observes, 'aesthetics and theology do not in the nineteenth century grow in alien soils; they are branches of the same tree' (1981, p. 61). I have focused on Keble's review of Lockhart's *Life of Scott* because Keble's own emphasis is more secular and psychological in that essay than in his 1814 article on Copleston's *Praelectiones Academicae*, than in his essay 'Sacred Poetry' (1824), or than in his better-known *Tract 89*, 'On the Mysticism Attributed to the Early Fathers of the Church' (1840). In these other essays Keble asserts that great poetry exists only as a fall-out from religion. We distort the ideas of displacement and reserve the moment we remove them from a theological setting, because poetry is the expressive evidence of divine power. But when that power is secularized, Abrams' and Warren's interpretations seem to me less to 'misapprehend Keble in crucial areas' (G. B. Tennyson, 1981, p. 59) than to explore the kinds of psychological and dramatic impact his theories were beginning to have on the Victorians themselves. Not only in modern criticism but also in Victorian poems like *Maud* and 'Lucretius', a monologue spoken by a philosopher Keble discusses at length in the *Oxford Lectures*, Keble's ideas of psychotherapy, of displacement and reserve, are already operating in ways the Tractarians did not foresee. Having met a deep Victorian need for repressed and subliminal expression in poets like Tennyson, Keble's theories begin to diffuse themselves into the Victorian sensibility at large, where they can be studied to advantage in such dissimilar poets as Patmore and Hardy, who memorably evokes Keble's ghost in *Jude the Obscure*, but whose tragic evolutionary theology, more Aeschylean than Christian, is light years away.

Keble's theories of reserve are best illustrated in lyrics of repressed and subliminal awareness like Patmore's poem 'Departure' and Hardy's little elegy 'Without Ceremony'. In both cases the psychological and formal risks are considerable. There is a danger that the reluctance to reduce emotion to the dust of words, to a monotonous inventory of grief, a mere crumbling of values, will simply leave a hole or blank space at the centre. But this is the condition of all elegies. Because no one knows what death means, the framing consciousness of the elegist can make the voice at the centre mean anything or everything that circumstance allows. And curious as it may seem, the silences which put reason and sanity at risk in these poems are somehow more vivid and memorable than anything Patmore or Hardy actually says.

The poem 'Departure' runs the gamut of domestic moods, from the husband's majestic rebuke, 'It was not like your great and

gracious ways!' (l. 1), though the impropriety of the wife's omitted
kiss, to the excruciating social pain inflicted unintentionally by her
desire to soothe with 'harrowing praise' (l. 13). Fear that the journey
into death is dark, sudden, unintelligible, is eased by the wife's
exquisite courtesy, which proves as congenial to the poet as life
itself. Indeed, the intimacy of their social exchange becomes, in an
unexpected way, more important than life. It displaces the shock of
death with the greater surprise that his partner should commit a rare
breach of courtesy. Astonished, not by her dying but by her
discourteous manner of dying, the poet professes to be 'More at the
wonder than the loss aghast' (l. 26). Ironically, the wife's only defect
in social tact, the suddenness of her going, turns out to be her most
gracious act of all. For in leaving with the only 'loveless look' (l. 31)
she ever gave, she is no longer depriving her husband of a partner he
can recognize. And such suddenness and silence spare him the pain
of words. In dying she displays at once a bolder discourtesy and a
finer tact than any she has shown in life.

Though the repetition of the frightening circumstances of the
wife's departure (ll. 6–9, 27–30) seems at first to add few clues about
the purpose of her journey, the redundancy is apparent not real. For
the second time the leave-taking is described it is slightly altered.
The first account is circumstantial. It takes place on a 'July after-
noon' (l. 4), just before the wife's departure on a journey the poet is
expecting her to take (l. 10). If this is an account of death, the little
domestic drama between the offended husband and his thoughtless
wife casts a glimmer of lightness and social comedy over the event.
So finely poised between elegy and domestic comedy is this circum-
stantial narrative that each time we read the poem it seems to offer a
different facet to the mind. But the second time the event is
described (ll. 27–30), slight changes in the repeated elements turn
the separation of leave-taking into a separation that is final. The
'journey of so many days' (l. 8) now becomes the more absolute
'journey of all days' (l. 29). The emotional weight of the earlier
phrase 'Without a single kiss' (l. 9) becomes more unbearable,
because it sounds much bleaker now: 'With not one kiss' (l. 30).
And yet the more final the separation becomes, the more the
distance between the departed wife and the bereaved poet seems to
shrink. By turning the impulse to berate, to feel anger at his wife for
dying, into a contest in gentility, Patmore is able to blunt the pain.

He creates his wife in his own best image – heroic in adversity, as he must be now, letting 'the laughter flash' (l. 22) to conceal her suffering, and yet 'great and gracious' (ll. 1, 32) to the end, in ways he still professes not to understand.

Like Patmore's 'Departure', Hardy's elegy 'Without Ceremony' is a lyric of reserve, stoically restricted in means, and spoken prosaically by a mourner who has put away the genre's traditional consolations. What surprises the reader is Hardy's ability, even in scrutinizing the barrenness of his world, to absorb that barrenness with conversational elegance and ease. Terror is allowed to break out only in a few carefully controlled phrases. Momentary panic is first hinted by the strong infinitive 'To vanish' (l. 2) and by the unusual use of the logical verb 'inferred' (l. 5) for a supposition that seems at first so ordinary.

> It was your way, my dear,
> To vanish without a word
> When callers, friends, or kin
> Had left, and I hastened in
> To rejoin you, as I inferred.
>
> And when you'd a mind to career
> Off anywhere – say to town –
> You were all on a sudden gone
> Before I had thought thereon,
> Or noticed your trunks were down.
> ('Without Ceremony', ll. 1–10)

The phrase 'all on a sudden' (l. 8) is mildly disquieting. But only in the last stanza, in the beloved's awesome plunge into the unknown, in her act of disappearing 'For ever in that swift style' (l. 12), does Hardy's poem seem to switch subjects.

After the memory of familiar farewells in the first stanza, and the homely observation that the trunks have been prepared, Hardy has a glimpse of a break that is absolute, which he describes despairingly, and with the rare – and hitherto disguised – finality of a going that is 'for ever' (l. 12).

> So, now that you disappear
> For ever in that swift style,

Your meaning seems to me
Just as it used to be:
Good-bye is not worth while!'
                    ('Without Ceremony', ll. 11–15)

As if to temper his audacity, however, in disclosing a break that is
'for ever', Hardy uses two-way syntax to leave the speaker poised
between the shock of death and a mere style of disappearing, a
manner that is simply in character. If logic binds the words 'for
ever' to the verb, the poetic line binds them to the adverbial phrase,
'in that swift style' (l. 12), to the mere habitual manner of the going.
Grammatically, the second line may be construed as an adjectival
phrase in apposition to the pronoun 'you' (l. 11). This less alarming
possibility absorbs the terror, affording an easy transition to the
hint of relief, as of a burden lifted, in the last two lines.

Because there is always a hole or empty space at the centre of
every elegy, the framing consciousness of the elegist is more im-
portant than the picture that he frames. But the bedrock of doubt is
also the total nothingness of death. The empty spaces in the poem –
the frightening void of a soul assaulted or a loved one gone – can
never be filled by the elegist without remainder. Coupled with the
large claim of saying goodbye 'for ever', the inadequacy of conven-
tional farewells limits the domesticating of Hardy's grief to a
suddenly impoverished inventory. The little household drama of
Hardy's departed guests and packed trunks, a ceremony which once
entailed the sum of all things cherished, now shrinks to insignifi-
cance, as does Emily Dickinson's domestic chore of 'sweeping up
the Heart' and 'putting Love away', like a dish, 'until Eternity'
('The Bustle in a House,' ll. 5, 6, 8). The strict autonomy of the
infinitive phrases, with their incisive syntactic breaks ('To vanish
without a word', 'to career / Off anywhere,' ll. 2, 6–7), enacts the
absurd brevity of life, reduced to 'essential terms', as Barthes says,
'like so many knives (the knives of asyndeton)' (1974, p. 104). For
Keble's poet of reserve, therefore, language is only a residue, the
trace of a meaning that has passed. It is the trace of something unsay-
able, and therefore 'unceremonious', something which the elegist
who honestly charts the truth of his feeling can never quite put into
words.

III Holistic Theories of Language and Knowledge

Ever since Aristotle asserted a general correspondence of words and things, it has been widely assumed that language has the essential property of referring to the world. Locke and Mill both believe that there are genuine names, objects for which the names stand, and elementary propositions in direct contact with reality. This picture theory of language is an admirable construction, incorporating ideas about the necessary character of language. But many Victorians prefer a more holistic theory. They argue that the smallest unit of understanding is not the individual word or pictured fact but the sentence or proposition. Even Ferrier's theory of the self-consciously framed event is really such a theory of contextual definition. The meaning of each atomic picture depends upon its frame. The theorists studied in this chapter expand the scope of Ferrier's inquiry by showing that, though the meaning of a word is bound to a context, the context may be boundless. An image in a picture depends for its meaning not only on the frame around the picture but also on other images in the picture and on other pictures with which the image can be compared.

I begin with philosophers of language like Dugald Stewart and A. B. Johnson and with Victorian philologists like R. C. Trench. In opposing an atomistic, building-block theory of language, they insist that the smallest unit of understanding is not the individual word but the sentence, and that the proper context for interpretation is the past as well as the present uses of a word. In each successive section of this chapter, the interpretive context keeps expanding. In the mid 1840s, for example, when formulating his theory of the Imagination Associative, Ruskin compares the individual words in a poem, not just to other words in the same sentence, but to a whole chain of words and images which may extend throughout a long passage or entire poem. Twenty years later, when establishing tests of imaginative composition in *The Gay Science*, E. S. Dallas expands the unit of contextual definition even further. Instead of comparing his subject with a mere portion of some other class, the poet will compare wholes with wholes. Instead of saying that man is a rational animal, a mere portion of the genus 'animal', the poet will say that in apprehension man is like an angel and in beauty like a god. For a contemporary like T. H. Green, writing at about the same time as Dallas, the context of knowledge is nothing less than the mind of God. Green's deity sustains a whole web of relations in much the same way that the mind of the reader apprehends the meaning of a whole sentence before he can understand the meaning of any individual word. Swift's Struldbrugs would be unable to extract any intelligible meaning from language, because their memories will no longer serve to carry them from the beginning of a sentence to its end. The most expansive context for interpretation I save for the end. It is to be found in F. H. Bradley, who argues that, although individual judgements do not correspond to individual facts, the whole web of judgements has to be true to one fact, which is the fact of everything. But because no finite mind can hope to grasp the total correspondence of all true sentences to the fact of everything, the horizon of possible contexts recedes from view in an endless regress. Meanings are bound to context, but the contexts of interpretation are themselves boundless.

1 Contextual Definitions: The Living Word

Against Mill's view that language consists of logically simple names in direct contact with isolated facts, all the theorists discussed in this section assert that language is a whole superior to its parts, and a whole upon which each part depends for its meaning. Theorists like Dugald Stewart and Max Müller try to explain how the poet's language presents the world, not as an idea, but as a unit of energy. An essentially poetic language can substitute for analytical discourse a more original 'language of nature' in which distinctions between word and thing disappear. A second group of theorists, including A. B. Johnson and Jeremy Bentham, try to show that language is not a picture but a tool. There is a great deal of concealed poetry, Bentham shows, in abstract legal diction. To understand this language we must restore the rhetorical contexts in which politicians and moralists use applied poetry to affect judgements and decisions. By showing that the so-called descriptive uses of language are often highly rhetorical ways of realigning the emotive and descriptive meanings of words, A. B. Johnson, like Bentham, substitutes for a unitary 'picture theory' of language a theory which argues that the function of words is as varied as the contexts in which they are used. Bentham and Johnson think of language as a bundle of activities that cohere much more loosely than Mill's picture theory supposes. A third Victorian tradition, represented by a philologist like R. C. Trench, is ideologically much more conservative. It nevertheless shares Bentham's desire to substitute for a logic of language a natural history of its use. Instead of trying to theorize like Max Müller about the mythic origins of language, Trench has a more modest aim. It is enough for his philologist accurately to observe and compare the actual past uses of words. One of the real merits of Trench's historical approach to language is that it contains the means of its own supplementation. The history of language is only a measuring rod. There is no preconceived idea of a word's meaning to which each inventive new use of the word must conform.

Coleridge suggests that one function of poetic discourse is to reverse the process of 'desynonymizing' whereby the philosopher establishes distinctions among words 'originally equivalent' in meaning. In collapsing all words back into a single synonym, a single unit of energy, Coleridge's poet is recovering a 'poem-universe' which returns man to his mythic origins. Coleridge believes this original unity is more easily recovered in a synthetic language like German than in an analytic language like French or English. Because there are fewer units of equivalence, prefixes in English 'cannot possibly act on the mind with the force or liveliness of an original and homogeneous language, such as the German is' (Coleridge, 1969, vol. 2, pp. 241–2). The British theorist who comments most precisely on this difference between analytic and synthetic languages is Dugald Stewart, who in his *Elements of the Philosophy of the Human Mind*, published with addenda to the first volume in 1827, distinguishes between languages that are 'analogous' in structure, like modern English, and languages that permit 'transpositive' construction. By transposing syntax a poet may be offering only a distorted picture of the world that language with a more 'analogous' structure might successfully mirror. But in shadowing the world with equivalences of his own making, the poet who reverses the process of desynonymizing may be able to recover in Coleridge's synthetic 'language of nature' an undifferentiated whole which precedes the distinction between subject and object or word and thing.

Poets like Hopkins and Browning want to 'transpose' their syntax. They want to write English as if it were a more synthetic language, like Latin, Greek, or German, because the more fluid syntax of these languages allows them to use such units of equivalence as the marked or abrupt parallelisms which Hopkins in an early essay on 'Poetic Diction' finds essentially poetic. 'The structure of poetry', he argues, 'is that of continuous parallelism, ranging from the technical so-called Parallelisms of Hebrew Poetry and the antiphons of Church music up to the intricacy of Greek or English verse' (1959b, p. 84). The grammar of a naturally 'transpositive' language like Latin or Greek will be highly inflected. Even when meaning is not determined by word order it will be determined by inflection. But as soon as a poet 'transposes' the syntax of a language like English, which is naturally 'analogous' in structure, into less determinate syntax that maximizes the opportunities for parallelism and antithesis, his grammar may become highly energized in Hopkins' sense by pressing language back into an undifferentiated whole where all units are equivalent.

To create such units of equivalence, Hopkins often transposes his syntax. In 'Hurrahing in Harvest', for example, instead of using normal English grammar, 'when these two meet', Hopkins substitutes for the subordinate clause an odd grammatical form which turns the subject into two units of equivalence ('which two', 'they') and which uses alliteration to put this parallelism of sense as strongly as possible.

> These things, these things were here and but the beholder
>   Wanting; which two when they once meet,
> The heart rears wings bold and bolder . . .
>
> ('Hurrahing in Harvest', ll. 11–13)

Like the grammar, which hovers between the normal subordinate construction and a nominative absolute ('which two having met'), the object and its beholder are left suspended, as if poised for contemplation. James Milroy has shown that the resumptive force of repeated subjects like 'which two', 'they', which some linguists call 'left-dislocation', is a feature of spoken rather than of written English (1984, p. 145). But Hopkins' transposition of syntax in these lines is too complicated to be easily decoded in ordinary conversational speech. The units of equivalence in Hopkins' poetry have less in common with actual spoken English than with Coleridge's paradigm that never was, an original language of nature in which all words are synonyms.

To apprehend a subject like the windhover instantaneously and as a whole, Hopkins tries to collapse all words into units of equivalence.

> I caught this morning morning's minion, king-
> dom of daylight's dauphin, dapple-dawn-drawn Falcon, in his
>   riding
> Of the rolling level underneath him steady air
>
> ('The Windhover', ll. 1–3)

Such language is electric with energy. It does not allow us to sort out atomic impressions of dapple colour, dazzling light, and aerial motion. It communicates instead, in a single mounting impression, a parataxis of highly charged sensations: a princelike bird drawn by a chariot of dappled light; a spacious riding-of-the-rolling-level-underneath-him-steady-air. The self-embedding Latin syntax, which sunders the preposition 'of' from the direct object 'air', all but dissolves the bird in undulating air. In such a passage, meaning no longer resides in individual words like 'king- / dom', which is carried across the natural breaking-point at the end of the line, as the bird is carried across the sky. Instead, the smallest unit of interpretation is now the long rambling holophrase or sentence. To determine a word's function we have to grasp the nature of the odd grammatical whole in which 'level' (l. 3) can function simultaneously as an adjective and a noun. Tennyson achieves a similar effect in *Maud* (I, 88–101), where the chains of epithets, made remorseless by the repeated suffix ('gemlike, ghostlike, deathlike'), collapse the language into one fearful synonym. By composing in grammatical wholes, Tennyson's impressionist syntax uses the surge of its pulsing participles to produce something as electrically charged and untranslatable as 'seabeachmadness, wintrygleam, daffodil-stardeath'.

Coleridge's idea that words can be pressed back into an undifferentiated synonym reappears in Max Müller's theory of 'radical' metaphor. A Latin word like *spiritus* originally denoted wind or blowing, and became a 'radical' or 'root' metaphor for wind, breath, life, when thinkers were seeking what we should now call the 'cause' of animation. Instead of being the invention of a primitive age, as Müller argues, radical metaphors are really 'one of the latest achievements of conscious linguistic development'. Owen Barfield has noted that Müller's error is to suppose that 'life actually created language after the manner in which [his] logic reconstructed it' (1952, p. 82). In his *Science of Language* Müller finds that the more primitive the language the more metaphorical it becomes. And yet when all desynonymized meanings are finally collapsed, Barfield criticizes Müller for saying that such a language is 'not figurative at all' (Barfield, 1952, p. 73). Barfield seems to think he has killed the bull. But I think he has only rent the cloak of the matador. In a language in which *spiritus* has not yet split apart into multiple meanings of 'breath', 'life', 'wind', there are, as Müller rightly implies, neither figurative meanings nor literal meanings. Such discourse supersedes all metaphors, because it contains them all in an undifferentiated state. Contrary to what Barfield says, Müller's error is not to deny that the universal language of nature is non-metaphorical. His only mistake is to associate the invention of 'root' metaphors with a primitive phase of language instead of with the inventiveness of analytic thinkers who are trying, in Coleridge's phrase, to desynonymize language.

To make language more synthetic, in a reversal of the process Müller accurately describes, poets like Browning try to turn radical metaphors back into a single, undivided 'root'. In Browning's 'Caliban Upon Setebos', for example, the savage's terrified impression of divine displeasure in the coming storm evokes all the undifferentiated, root meaning of the word *spiritus*. It denotes not just breath, or wind, or spirit, but all three of them together. Instead of breaking up his verbs into solid nouns like 'lightning', Caliban perceives the blow of each 'white blaze' as a single terrifying impression, as a concrete unity of fear and force. 'And fast invading fires begin! White blaze – / A tree's head snaps' ('Caliban Upon Setebos', ll. 289–90). Like the 'holophrase' of primitive peoples, Browning's long rambling conglomerates of sound and sense illustrate how an important function of all poetic language is to restore conceptually the original force of Caliban's divine 'wind-spirit', long after that primordial force has crystallized into separate abstract meanings like hurricane or tempest or the principle of life. In lines like 'Greendense and dim-delicious, bred o' the sun' ('Caliban Upon Setebos', l. 40), Browning is aiming at a simultaneous perception of sensations which the constraints of syntax force him to present in sequence. By dropping connectives and allowing a crowd of images, arguments, theories, to rush all at once to the point of his pen, Browning is trying to restore the original, undifferentiated language of a 'poem-universe' which contains within itself all that can be said.

Other Victorian theorists like Bentham, A. B. Johnson, and R. C. Trench are less interested in the logic of language than in verbal behaviour. As analysis replaces synthesis, the preferred analogy is no longer that of a mirror but a tool. Language is now conceived as a multitude of speech transactions and activities. To understand the meaning of a word Bentham and Johnson examine its use. They become natural historians who explore, not the logic of some imaginary language of nature which, like Borges' Library of Babel, contains all discourse in itself, but the concealed or forgotten uses of everyday words.

Unlike his greatest disciple, J. S. Mill, Jeremy Bentham agrees with other Victorian theorists studied in this chapter that the smallest unit of understanding is the proposition or the sentence. He warns that 'the isolation of any part of such a unit will be liable to generate on its own account what may be called an elliptical fiction' (C. K. Ogden, 1932, p. lxxxviii). But to provide a proper context for words, it is not enough to look at the propositions in which they appear. To understand a word, Bentham believes, it is necessary to retrace the process by which poetic resources have been secretly used to affect the attitudes and actions which the word incites. Instead of a churchman, we say the Church or the Altar; instead of rich men, Property. Metonymies like Altar and Property are 'fictions' or incomplete symbols. The appropriate context for their interpretation is a sentence using only genuine proper names like 'men' and descriptive phrases like 'rich'. To translate in this way is to reverse the synthetic procedures that Müller and Coleridge describe and to carry the analytic process of 'desynonymizing' language to a logical extreme. Bentham recommends the process as the only way of removing all the 'dark spots' in language. The language Bentham envisions should be able to eliminate obliquity in fictional statements by substituting verbal substantives for verbs and by translating parts of speech with purely syntactical functions into their substantive, verbal, and adjectival equivalents.

As Kenneth Burke has said, Bentham's discovery of 'a kind of poetry concealed beneath legal jargon' is 'usually considered the very opposite of poetry' (1962, p. 614). We should be surprised if any poet were inspired by such a view. His theory of fictions makes available, however, a powerful rhetorical tool. Subversive characters like Browning's Guido make effective use of Bentham's theory of legal fictions when trying to demystify legal and religious language in *The Ring and the Book*. When analysing words like guilt and innocence, Guido argues in true Benthamite form that an act is called commendable or criminal depending on whether the defendant labels it sacrifice or murder. If he tried to persuade the court that he was sacrificing Pompilia to 'the Unknown God' or to 'the Genius of the Vatican' (*The Ring and the Book*, XI, 2029–30), Guido believes he would have been invoking the magic formula and prescribed fiction. To discredit further Bentham's theory of fictions, Browning satirizes in the opening pages of *The Ring and the Book* the stylistic consequences of taking seriously Bentham's doctrine of 'phraseoplerosis', or the filling in of such words as will 'serve to remove the oblique or elliptical element in a fictional statement'. The clutter and triviality of Bentham's prescribed mode of speech are well conveyed by the grammar of Browning's opening paragraphs, which are frittered away in a shapeless inventory of the contents of the stall from which Browning finally selects the Old Yellow Book. The substantive Benthamite style, in which verbs and connectives disappear, turns the itemizing of the books into a mere card catalogue. Its thesaurus of trivia has no apparent function. Like the crowding and clutter of the Florentine Square, Browning's grammar seems designed to show that a mere inventory of facts has no containing form. The statements in Bentham's proposed form of discourse refuse to be connected with an explanatory word like 'because'. In the mindless chiasmus of a mere random list, with its

'Pages of proof this way, and that way of Proof', Browning mimes the directionless 'wrangling, brangling, jangling', the mere 'noise by word of mouth' (*The Ring and the Book*, I, 239, 241, 244), that seem to accompany any Benthamite conjunction of non-explanatory statements.

The only Victorian poet who seems to take seriously Bentham's theory of fictions is Arthur Hugh Clough. His poem 'Duty – That's to Say Complying' might have been written as a gloss on one of Bentham's favourite examples of the applied poetry concealed in abstract words. The irrelevant but pernicious images of 'binding' and constraint that lurk in the moral term 'obligation' are delightfully dramatized by Clough's volley of feminine rhymes: 'complying', 'dying', 'relying', 'denying' (ll. 1, 3, 5, 6). Clough's preference for a whole chain of verbal nouns instead of verbs shows how scrupulously Benthamite he is in making clear, complete, and non-elliptical the meaning of the discreditable Victorian mystery word 'duty', which has been conscripted into all kinds of dishonourable service. As the leading Utilitarian adversary of deontology, or the theory of moral obligation, Bentham shows how metonymies like Altar for churchman and Property for rich man give religion and property an intrinsic value they do not possess. In a similar vein Clough turns the exercise of matching sounds into a mockery of the mindless conformity and social echoing that pass in Victorian society for moral obligation, as if man were made for the 'pure nonentity of duty' (l. 44) instead of duty for man.

J. S. Mill often implies that a non-descriptive use of language must be merely emotive, like the language used in poetry. A commentator who should appeal more than Mill to critics of poetry by discriminating among a whole range of speech acts that are not primarily descriptive but allow the speaker to do things with words, is the American theorist of language A. B. Johnson, who anticipates a modern philosopher of language like J. L. Austin. Because Johnson was an obscure writer whose reputation has been revived only recently by contemporary analytic philosophers, it is unlikely that his *Treatise of Language*, published in America in 1836, would be familiar to most Victorian poets and critics. But his distinction among science's use of declarative sentence types, the imperative and interrogative moods of moral discourse, and the exclamations and interjections of the poet, sheds a good deal of light on the grammar of

Victorian verse. In Arnold's sonnet 'In Harmony With Nature', for
example, Johnson's theory that the grammatical mood of moral
discourse is imperative helps explain why Arnold should sound like
a schoolmaster delivering a harsh rebuke to a stupid pupil: 'Restless
fool,' he chides, 'Know, man has all which Nature hath, but more'
(ll. 1, 5). If Johnson is right, then Arnold's impatience is understand-
able. The pupil has made a serious mistake in philosophical gram-
mar. To make nature into a moral norm is to mistake the
prescriptive ends of ethics for the descriptive ends of physical
science. It is to use an indicative verb where an imperative is called
for.

Johnson's analysis of the performative force of imperative verbs
can be studied to advantage in the daring optatives which Hopkins
allows his nun to use when addressing her destroyer in 'The Wreck
of the Deutschland'.

> Do, deal, lord it with living and dead;
> Let him ride, her pride, in his triumph, despatch and have
>   done with his doom there.
>
> ('The Wreck of the Deutschland', stanza 28, ll. 7–8)

The tone of the imperative 'Do, deal, lord it' is colloquial, almost
insolent, as if the nun had not yet found the right names for God.
Her predications do not describe what she already knows, for she is
not yet conscious of her destroyer's identity. By discovering that
the cruel, 'lording' despot is also Christ her Lord, the nun achieves a
faith inclusive enough to embrace what she cannot at first under-
stand. Her power to compress boldness and submission into single
words and to combine protest against her destroyer's severity with
celebration of his triumphal ride allows Hopkins to assimilate her
extraordinary act of christening 'her wild-worst / Best' (stanza 24,
l. 8) to Job's mysterious act of acknowledging that the God who has
given has also taken away. Even in destroying, God is still to be
blessed (Job 1: 21).

R. C. Trench, who represents a third, philological tradition in the
Victorian study of language, is a far more conservative commen-
tator than either Bentham or A. B. Johnson. As an archbishop of the
established Church, Trench wants to avoid controversy about ori-
gins. He prefers to concentrate instead on the history of words.
Trench's pioneer research on etymology in *English Past and Present*

and *On the Study of Words* 'did far more than any previous publication to make language study popular', and as Hans Aarsleff has noted, 'without that popularity it seems unlikely that the *New English Dictionary* would have been able both to get the readers it needed and to arouse the general interest which sustained it' (1967, pp. 234–5). Instead of joining Müller and Coleridge in a quixotic quest for a primordial language which may never have existed, Trench is a patient student of history. He makes us aware, not merely of the former meanings of words, but also of the way in which these meanings may be revived. From an early age Trench probably exchanged ideas with Tennyson, a friend and fellow Apostle. Trench's pioneer work on etymology encourages poets like Tennyson to become joint explorers of the fossil record who restore to life some buried root or some metaphor gone dead in the forgotten origins of words.

The verb 'fluctuate', for instance, when used intransitively has a rare meaning of 'to move like a wave'. More usual is the figurative use of 'fluctuate' in the intransitive sense of 'to vacillate' or 'waver'. By extension the verb acquires a subordinate transitive meaning: to agitate or unsettle. But according to the *OED*, the first transitive use of the rare literal meaning of 'to fluctuate' occurs in the extraordinary passage where Tennyson writes, 'A breeze began to tremble o'er / The large leaves of the sycamore, / And fluctuate all the still perfume' (*In Memoriam*, xcv, 54–6). The departure from the expected intransitive form of 'fluctuate' allows Tennyson to undulate between an infinitive and a finite form in a revived echo of the verb's Latin root. By becoming transitive and acting upon the objects of the verbs, Tennyson's novel use of 'fluctuate' restores as the proper context for interpretation a forgotten etymology. To 'fluctuate' is to act and have power. It is to 'throw' some element 'into a wavelike motion'. In establishing the primordial force of the divine 'breeze-spirit' as it boldly crosses the divide between God and nature, Tennyson's use of a verb that is stranger than it first seems to be also helps cushion the shock of one of *In Memoriam*'s most astonishing transformations.

Similarly, when Tennyson in the same section of *In Memoriam* wants to give familiar words an uncanny force, he enlivens the discreet pun in 'fallen leaves which kept their green' (xcv, 23). The 'leaves', or folds of paper, of Hallam's letters are also a repository.

They are a residue, something that is 'left' like a relic. And they 'leave' the mourner free to commune with Hallam in a free exercise of 'lief' or 'belief'. In permitting a root sense of 'love-lief-belief' to resonate, the pun that provides for Hallam the unexpected immortality of a 'fallen' leaf which keeps its 'green' helps restore, if only subliminally, a 'leaf' or fragment of what was once living in the language of our ancestors.

In 1851, two years before 'Andrea del Sarto' was written, Trench had lucidly expounded the origin of the adjective 'frank' in one of five published lectures 'On Language as an Instrument of Knowledge.' The Franks, Trench observes, 'had . . . virtues which belong to a conquering and dominant race in the midst of an inferior and conquered one. And thus it came to pass that by degrees the name "frank", which may have originally indicated merely a national, came to involve a moral distinction as well' (1853, p. 21). Trench concedes that a word like 'frank' may 'often ride very slackly at anchor on [its] etymology'. But because 'very few [words] have broken away and drifted from their moorings altogether' (1853, p. 180), Browning in praising King Francis and his courtiers, 'Such frank French eyes, and such a fire of souls' ('Andrea del Sarto', l. 160), can create out of the proper name 'Francis' and its cognate epithets 'frank' and 'French' a specimen of living philology.

Many Victorians are critical of the illegitimate inferences that are made from theories of language to theories of knowledge. In his *Prolegomena Logica*, for example, written two years before Trench's book *On the Study of Words*, H. L. Mansel argues that Locke's account of language and knowledge is easily reversible. Locke had argued that names which stand for insensible actions and ideas have been derived from names of sensible objects. But is the reverse not also true? Mansel believes that the language properly belonging to the mental fact of volition has been transferred by analogy to the physical world, where it has been identified as the principle of causality. In Mansel's view, cause means the power of a voluntary agent. When Hume interprets cause as 'one invariable antecedent phenomenon', he is illustrating 'the universal tendency of men to identify . . . other agents with themselves'. But Hume is predicating of nature something that lies only in himself and in his method of representing nature through words. As Mansel says, causality is a purely negative notion of power, when 'applied to any other than a conscious agent' (1851, pp. 141–2).

Tennyson shows in 'Lucretius' that the Roman philosopher's materialism is a result of the same error. Living in bondage to his sensual appetite, Lucretius loses all consciousness of himself as a willing agent. The dissociation of Lucretius' erotic life in Tennyson's poem makes unintelligible the notion of a 'free cause' and deprives a moral word like 'duty' of all meaning: ' "Thy duty? What is duty? Fare thee well!" ' ('Lucretius', l. 280). The only obligation Lucretius can recognize is the binding power of 'the flaring atom-streams' 'Ruining along the illimitable inane' ('Lucretius', ll. 38, 40) in imitation of his own sensual enslavement. Lucretius predicates of the world what lies only in his dissociation of logic from religion, belief from desire. By restoring in the expansive present participle, spanning the horizon of a world in ruins, the original Latin force of *ruere* ('to rush down' or 'collapse'), Tennyson is showing how every excavated piece of fossil history is potentially alive with the projection on to the world of some idiosyncratic way of experiencing the world. The atomic system of *De Rerum Natura* may be nothing more than an illegitimate inference from abnormal psychology to metaphysics. A mere comparison between Lucretius' own dissociated sensibility and a disintegrating world has been misread as an identity of essence.

The unexpected revival of a forgotten meaning allows a poet to redefine a world contextually. When Arnold, for example, evokes 'The unplumbed, salt, estranging sea' in 'To Marguerite – Continued' (l. 24), he is releasing in the words an energy that is latent in Horace's *Odes*, I iii 21–3. But to release that energy Arnold must skilfully deepen the meaning of 'salt' and 'estranging' by defining the anguish of an overburdened consciousness, lonely, isolated, ever on the verge of being destroyed by its own inquisition of a strange and alienating God.

> A God, a God their severance ruled!
> And bade betwixt their shores to be
> The unplumbed, salt, estranging sea.
> ('To Marguerite – Continued,' ll. 22–4)

In the appalling spondees of 'the unplumbed, salt, estranging sea' (l. 24), the slow spectral stresses, weighted with alliteration, bring to

the surface an undertow of analogy, more powerful because un-
stated, between the salt waters of the 'shoreless . . . wild' (l. 3) and
the salt tears of the estranged lovers. 'To estrange' is to remove from
acquaintance with. But because its more specific secondary mean-
ing is 'to render or regard as alien' (*étranger* in modern French),
Arnold's use of the present participle evokes the foreignness of the
Swiss, French-speaking Marguerite, once intimate with Arnold,
but now alien and a stranger. It is as if Arnold's use of 'estranging',
or Tennyson's use of 'fluctuate' or 'ruining', sums up all previous
poetic uses of the word and then takes a step beyond them. Some-
thing similar happens in Christina Rossetti's lyric 'Good Friday',
where the poet seems turned to stone by her own hardness of heart.
'Am I a stone, and not a sheep?' (l. 1). The astonished tone of the
first quatrain recalls the forgotten etymology of the English verb
'astonish', which originally meant 'astoned' or 'astonied,' and
which is sometimes derived from 'stony' and used as a synonym for
'petrified'. As Trench realizes, such lines reveal what is already
there, waiting to flash out in the fossil poetry of the language as
soon as its words are touched to life by a poet of true imaginative
power.

I have shown in this survey of holistic theories of language that
the approaches to holism are diverse. Whereas Max Müller is a
linguist who tries to make the study of words scientific, Bentham
and A. B. Johnson are analytic philosophers critical of any search for
the essence of some primordial language lurking behind the untidy
surface of actual discourse. R. C. Trench, by contrast, is an his-
torian of language. He is content to dig up and compare specimens
of the fossil record. Despite these different starting-points and
assumptions, all of the commentators are agreed that any attempt to
understand individual words is an attempt to know less than can be
known. Even an analytic philosopher like Bentham asserts that the
smallest unit of understanding is a sentence or proposition, or per-
haps even an abbreviated history of a word such as etymologists like
Trench can provide. I have spent most time on Trench because his
excavation of the fossil history of a word like 'frank' can best illumi-
nate the meaning of a line like the one I analysed from 'Andrea del
Sarto'. The weakness of Trench's conservative approach to
language it its absence of speculative reach. Trench, unlike Müller,
makes no attempt to account for the origins of language or for the

nature of its changes. But the merit of his method is its flexibility and suppleness. Trench can be as analytic as Bentham, as subtle as Johnson, and as learned as Müller. He also provides a helpful antidote to theorists who betray an obsessive attachment to some monolithic view about language and to metaphysicians like Tennyson's Lucretius who are in danger of making illegitimate inferences from theories about words to theories about the world.

Wittgenstein says that 'philosophy is a battle against the bewitchment of our intelligence by means of language' (1972, proposition 109, p. 47). If the root of this 'bewitchment' is the ossification of words, philologists like Trench can help poets revive forgotten etymologies and prevent words from petrifying into metaphysical dogmas. As John Caird points out, there is always a temptation to turn metaphors like 'impression' into materialistic dogmas about the mind's receiving sensations 'in the same external and spatial manner' as the paper receives 'the printer's types' (1904, pp. 181–2). In looking at words through a microscope, Trench and the poets who follow his example may guard against the error of predicating of the world what lies only in their method of talking about the world. They may even choose to be obtuse about theoretical speculation so that they can be clearsighted about what can and cannot be done in practice with individual words.

2 Imperfect Parts and Perfect Wholes: Ruskin on the Imagination Associative

According to holistic theorists of language, the smallest unit of understanding is not the word but the sentence. As Ruskin shows in his theory of the Imagination Associative, however, an individual word or image may not be fully intelligible until it is interpreted as part of a whole verse paragraph or poem. It is simply not true, for example, that a poem like 'Andrea del Sarto' can be reduced without remainder to its individual images or to the meaning of an aphoristic line like 'a man's reach should exceed his grasp', whose oracular solemnity begins to effervesce the moment we restore it to its ironic context in Browning's poem. In such cases the unit of understanding is much larger than the single sentence or proposition. Ruskin's holistic axiom that no poem can be properly described as a system of parts, and that the meaning of any sundered part is only imperfectly understood, is not a mere mystification. As Ruskin tries to show, the alternative is sheer idiocy and error.

Because the descriptive theory of art that Ruskin formulates in the first volume of *Modern Painters* leads to uninspired painting, in later volumes of that work Ruskin is no less emphatic that sight is insight: it is a truth of fact, a correspondence, which only the imaginative truth of coherence can make real. To understand Ruskin's most important contribution to a theory of contextual meaning, we must look closely at his theory of the Imagination Associative, developed in the second book of *Modern Painters*. Here Ruskin assumes that no particular images are ever associated by the imagination or ever could be. The units of association are never individual atoms of meaning or perception. When solitary units are combined imaginatively, they are always part of a whole which confers on the particular images whatever identity they have.

Ruskin sometimes seems to think that only a holistic theory of art can explain the paradoxical capacity of a poet like Milton or Dante to combine a sense of the indefinite with a sense of the comforting limitation afforded by a recognizable pattern or context. The comfort seems to come from the knowledge that meanings are bound to a context. And the mystery seems to come from the knowledge that each context is boundless. Contexts are indefinite, unlimited, ultimately beyond the power of any single word or work of art to define. But Ruskin does not really presume to explain the truth of his holistic axiom. His response seems to be that a wise critic does not try to scrutinize the inscrutable. The task of how to say the unsayable by binding the meaning to a boundless context may safely be left to the poets and painters themselves.

Ruskin believes that the hallmark of the Imagination Associative is a mysterious ability to combine component parts, each of which is 'separately wrong', but which together are 'right' (1903–12, vol. 4, p. 234). With the aid of a plate from Turner's *Liber Studiorum*, Ruskin provides a practical demonstration. Inviting the reader to cover any segment of Turner's picture, *Cephalus and Procris*, Ruskin shows how the living unity Turner has created is destroyed with the removal of any part. The elements which the artist combines 'must be faulty when separate'. But the deficiency in each part is 'corrected by the presence' of other elements.

When Ruskin's theory is transferred from the visual to the verbal arts, we can see how it describes the operation of much symbolist poetry. An allegorical emblem like the Satanic serpent, the tiger of wrath, or the goat of lechery represents an extreme development of I. A. Richards' logical model of metaphor, according to which a sensory image is used to convey an explicit preconceived meaning. Ruskin's theory of the Associative Imagination departs radically from such a model in two important ways. In the first place, any conceptual tenor to which its associated elements point is too elusive, too private or enigmatic, to be named. Instead of beginning with a concept like evil, then searching for an emblem to embody that concept, the Associative Imagination works the other way round, with images for which no conceptual equivalents yet exist. It operates the way Tennyson does in 'The Hesperides', whose myth Ruskin analyses in the concluding pages of *Modern Painters*, book V. From Tennyson's incantatory formula, 'Five links, a golden chain, are we,/Hesper, the dragon, and sisters three' ('The Hesperides', ll. 65–6), no single concept of greed or evil can be extracted. His words remain potent and alive, charged with magic and mystery, precisely because the elements they associate defy easy translation or paraphrase.

A second important link between Ruskin's theory of the Imagination Associative and a symbolist poetic is the trust each assumes in sensory objects. Ruskin never loses his faith in the material reality of the visible world. An allegorical imagination accepts the primacy of the concept, of the idea of evil, for example, and regards the figurative emblem of that concept, the serpent or the dragon, as a mere fiction or exemplum with no true existence of its own. By contrast, a student of Evangelical typology like Ruskin believes that the figurative exempla of Scripture are both real and symbolic. Trained in youth to accept the figures and emblems of the Bible as real events and people, Ruskin always trusts objects enough to be a symbolist. He is a 'literalist of the imagination', whose association of images, in escaping the logical controls of the allegorical poet, can inspire in the reader an aesthetic equivalent of awe. If Ruskin's own criticism is often as exciting as the art it analyses, it is because Ruskin recognizes that a central problem in aesthetics is to do justice to the fact that a great work of the Associative Imagination is an object of disinterested contemplation, a kind of surrogate god, that like Keats's Grecian urn never ceases to 'tease us out of thought/As doth eternity'.

Precisely because there are no rules that the Imagination Associative can follow, it must work independently of the conceptual understanding. But Ruskin is too verbal a critic to subside into speechlessness. Nor is he content with the kind of impressionistic commentary that limits itself to unintelligible outbursts about what clearly matters in art but cannot be explained. He believes that if the artist is associating his images imaginatively two effects can be observed. Removal of any part will immediately destroy the whole. And equally important will be the endless variety of the imagination's resulting combinations. 'As all its parts are imperfect, and as there is an unlimited supply of imperfection . . . the imagination is never at a loss,' Ruskin concludes, 'nor ever likely to repeat itself' (1903–12, vol. 4, p. 241).

Like the panels in successive versions of Tennyson's poem 'The Palace of Art', the images of the Associative Fancy can be shifted in and out, shuffled and reshuffled like a deck of playing cards, without much difference in the overall result. But instead of combining predictably similar perfections, the Associative Imagination combines imperfections that are unpredictably different. Because Ruskin presented all but the first and fourth volumes of *Modern Painters* to Browning and his wife, it is probably safe to assume that Browning had studied and even been influenced by Ruskin's theory of the Associative Imagination by the time he came to write 'Andrea del Sarto' in 1853. Separately imperfect, as Ruskin requires, all the items evoked in the painter's 'twilight-piece' – the passing of Andrea's youth and hope, the diminution of his early promise as a painter, the decline of the day and year – work together to modify Andrea's perception of 'A common grayness silver[ing] everything' in the onset of night.

You smile? why, there's my picture ready made,
There's what we painters call our harmony!
A common grayness silvers everything, –
All in a twilight, you and I alike
– You, at the point of your first pride in me
(That's gone you know), – but I, at every point;
My youth, my hope, my art, being all toned down
To yonder sober pleasant Fiesole.

There's the bell clinking from the chapel-top;
That length of convent-wall across the way
Holds the trees safer, huddled more inside;
That last monk leaves the garden; days decrease,
And autumn grows, autumn in everything.

('Andrea del Sarto', ll. 33–45)

It is as if, with an intuitive grasp of how his picture will compose, Andrea seizes and combines in a flash, in the single instant he exclaims, 'there's my picture ready made' (l. 33), all the important elements of the scene. For how else, as Ruskin asks, can the imagination identify in advance from among the infinity of ways in which any image may be imperfect the precise quality of imperfection that all the other images of refuge and fear, seclusion and death, which reach the eye through a strange veil of sight, can somehow render perfect and complete?

Out of dissimilar impressions of beauty and despair, hope and disenchantment, loveliness and death, Andrea creates a unity of membership, 'what we painters call our harmony!' (l. 34). He secures in each impression of vacuity, fatality, and sinking into death, the precise and grave mystery of 'autumn in everything' (l. 45). Around places far withdrawn the painter constructs a peculiar atmosphere of mixed gray-and-silver lights, a palpable illusion to be touched and seen on the dark air. In his solitary cultivation of beautiful things Andrea appears careless of 'what he was born to be and do' (l. 48). He seems weak as always with some inexplicable weakness. In composing the rest of his life into a 'twilight-piece', he has reached that turning-point after which 'every milestone on our road is a grave-stone, and the rest of life seems a continuance of our own funeral procession' (F. H. Bradley, 1930, aphorism 70). And yet out of the secret places of a unique temperament, Andrea has combined imperfect impressions to produce an exquisite effect. Every unpromising element of sententious plaintiveness and agitation in his speaker, of weak fatality and delay, Browning has converted instantly to some perfect end.

To grasp the mysterious arrangements of the Imagination Associative, Ruskin's critic has to leave the dictionary behind and follow certain novel chains. In 'Bishop Blougram's Apology', the elusive intimations of 'a sunset-touch,/A fancy from a flower-bell, some one's death,/A chorus-ending from Euripides' are designed to break down the conceptual stability of words, which is the mainstay of the sceptic's dogmatic 'unbelief'. To follow the play of Browning's Imagination Associative in such a passage is neither difficult nor easy to do. It is an activity that makes us uneasy.

> Just when we are safest, there's a sunset-touch,
> A fancy from a flower-bell, some one's death,
> A chorus-ending from Euripides, –
> And that's enough for fifty hopes and fears
> As old and new at once as nature's self,
> To rap and knock and enter in our soul,
> Take hands and dance there, a fantastic ring,
> Round the ancient idol, on his base again, –
> The grand Perhaps!
>
> ('Bishop Blougram's Apology', ll. 182–90)

Behind the fugitive impressions from nature that disquiet a rationalist confident in his scepticism, and behind the more disturbing fact of death and the solemn chorus-ending, Browning's Bishop intuits an attitude of flickering hesitation, wavering in emphasis between the death of day and the glory of nightfall, between Euripides' faith and disbelief in 'The grand Perhaps'. If any of the elements the Bishop combines were to be removed, his whole evocation would go 'to pieces', as Ruskin says, 'like a Prince Rupert's drop' (1903–12, vol. 4, p. 240). The removal of the third member, 'death', would annihilate a necessary element of terrible beauty in the scene, just as the removal of the 'sunset-touch' would destroy a desirable ambiguity in the dimming light, wavering in emphasis between 'a *glory* done' and 'a glory *done*', like Tennyson's 'buried sun' in *In Memoriam* (cxxi, 1–4). Each impression is indispensable to the synonymic chain which Browning links. Only the retreat from image to image, the play of all four terms together, allows Browning to define resemblances among four classes of impressions and hence a more complex and general fifth class. This fifth class, as Ruskin recognizes, is unnamed, because what it intuits 'is neither to be taught, nor by efforts to be attained, nor by an acuteness of discernment dissected or analysed' (1903–12, vol. 4, p. 233). Often poetry produced by the Imagination Associative becomes less analysable as its loveliness becomes more definite though more fugitive. Criticism of such poetry often culminates in commentary where, as Coleridge envisaged of an ideal language which would collapse all meaning back into a single unit of equivalence, there are no more words but only the silence which marks the amazed possession of all words.

3 The Comparison of Wholes to Wholes: Dallas's Test of Imaginative Composition

Ruskin's theory of the Imagination Associative puts the mystery of the holistic axiom into its sharpest focus. None of the individual words or images the poet associates can quite encompass the mystery of his subject. But when taken all together, these images intimate that mystery with an exactitude that astonishes Ruskin. Should the critic try to explain this uncanny power of intimation? Or should he reluctantly take Wittgenstein's advice: 'What we cannot speak about we must pass over in silence' (1961, p. 151)?

There is one Victorian theorist, E. S. Dallas, who believes he can explain what remains to Ruskin a mystery. Dallas maintains that if Ruskin is baffled by the operation of the Imagination Associative, it is because the conscious mind of the greatest artists can never fully control the success of what is really an unconscious operation. The imagination is not, strictly speaking, a faculty at all, but a mental operation. It is 'but another name' for 'the automatic action of the mind or any of its faculties'. Imagination is, in fact, 'the entire mind in its secret working' (Dallas, 1866, vol. 1, pp. 195–6).

Though Dallas concedes the difficulty of positing in poetry a consciousness of something which lies outside of consciousness, he believes that only the paradox of unconscious thought can explain the difference between the imagination of a Homer and the genius of an Aristotle. Both are automatic, but only the former is an involuntary or unconscious process. When poetry is composed in the unconscious, it often leads to fluctuations of mood, impelling a speaker like Arnold's Empedocles to revise his sense of what words can express. A depth of meanings, focused in 'the shock of mighty thoughts' revived (*Empedocles on Etna*, ii, 242), creates poetry that possesses the mind like some past we have relived for a moment, then lost from memory.

Dallas's theory of the unconscious has important antecedents in German criticism. In Schelling's *Transcendental Idealism*, for example, published in 1800, 'the opposition and reconciliation of the conscious and unconscious elements in the productive imagination is the key,' as one commentator observes, 'both of his theory of art and of his metaphysical system' (M. H. Abrams, 1961, p. 883). In England, however, the idea of unconscious and automatic mental processes, though applied by Carlyle in his essay 'Characteristics' to mental health in general, does not assume a crucial role in poetic theory until Dallas offers what he takes to be a new theory of imagination, 'that Proteus of the mind', which has been identified with all the human faculties – with memory, passion, reason – and which has proved as a result 'the despair of metaphysics' (1866, vol. 1, p. 179).

In practice Dallas believes there are two tests the critic can conduct to determine whether the poet's mind has indeed been operating imaginatively 'in the dusk of unconsciousness'. A poet who has been composing imaginatively will discern resemblances rather than differences. And he will also 'assert the resemblance of wholes to wholes' (1866, vol. 1, pp. 265, 269). When affirming that 'man is an animal', the logician compares the whole class man with a part of the class animal. But in affirming that 'man is a flower', the poet compares the whole class man with the whole class flower. In doing so the poet does not stop to analyse the process by which the anthropologist differentiates men from apes. But he does something just as remarkable. The poet who first intuits types, the whole class man and the whole class flower, and who then proceeds to perceive similarities among them, exhibits a complex process described by Dallas as the 'crux of reason'. Poetry illustrates this 'process' as it 'works automatically' (Dallas, 1866, vol. 1, p. 295), building out of countless details a recognizable class or type.

Dallas's second test of imaginative composition, the comparison of wholes to wholes, helps explain the power of Arnold's lyric, 'To Marguerite – Continued'. A sociologist like David Riesman would compare Arnold's 'mortal millions' (1.4), which comprise an imaginative whole, not to *all* masses or aggregates, but to a mere portion of such wholes, to what he memorably calls 'the lonely crowd'. But even when Arnold is describing the sharing of solitudes, he compares the separated lovers, one imaginative whole, to another whole, to an entire archipelago of sundered islands. The islands' 'longing like despair' (l.13) is the endless desire of the heart for a recovered wholeness, a desire which is always being simplified into love for specific people, then found wanting. In meeting Dallas's second test, these impressions of whole seas and archipelagoes revive the terror of our perishing each alone, and they do so with a force that a comparison of Arnold's 'mortal millions' to a 'lonely crowd', to the mere portion of another class, could never equal. That small and large wholes, shattered loves and broken continents, should be dissolved by similar forces is more harrowing, more 'shattering' in the figurative sense. As Dallas's theory helps explain, the constant comparison of broken wholes to broken wholes makes the isolation of sundered lives and broken continents more universal and devastating. It helps the reader feel Arnold's estrangement to the full.

4 The Whole Precedes the Part: John Grote and T. H. Green

Every holistic axiom about language presupposes a contextual theory of knowing. Ruskin's critic passes from imperfect parts to perfect wholes, and Dallas's critic compares wholes with wholes. As soon as we study the theories of knowledge advanced by the leading Victorian advocates of holism, we find the units of understanding expanding even further. In the writings of John Grote, T. H. Green, and F. H. Bradley, the search for contexts proves endless. There seems to be no conclusion that any of these idealist philosophers can reach about an ultimate context for meaning that would entitle any of them ever to conclude their search.

By offering a full and logical defence of the claim made by Ruskin and by his precursors Wordsworth and Coleridge when they assert not merely the centrality of the imagination but also the truth of its creations, John Grote in his unfinished *Exploratio Philosophica* (1865) achieves for a holistic theory of knowledge what Ruskin in his theory of the Imagination Associative achieves for a holistic theory of art. Unjustly neglected today, and largely eclipsed in reputation by his Utilitarian brother, George, the eminent historian of Greece, John Grote develops a holistic theory of the imagination, a faculty he places midway between passive sensation and active intellection. More active in its operations than mere knowledge of acquaintance, but less active than a fully developed knowledge of judgement, the imagination organizes the information it receives into intelligible wholes. Grote believes that when most philosophers talk about sensations they are really talking about what Locke calls 'ideas of sensation'. They are describing a partnership in sense perception, a 'constant self-correction arising mainly from our constantly rubbing against things' (John Grote, 1865, vol. 1, p. 152). By arguing that imagination is a rudimentary form of knowledge by judgement, Grote is trying to correct a confusion between two different theories of sensation, one atomistic and one holistic, and both originating in Locke.

In Locke's theory of knowledge an impression like yellow or white is a mere sensum, a patch of colour that has vanished almost as soon as it appears. But in order to explain how the 'white paper' of the mind, 'void of all characters' (Locke, 1924, p. 42), comes to be furnished with its own stock of ideas, Locke has to turn the patch of sensation into an 'idea', into something recurrent and permanent. If there exists a sensation of yellow not now being sensed, Grote would argue that such a patch of colour cannot, strictly speaking, be a sensation at all. And if the yellow is being perceived, but only fleetingly as a patch whose being is 'bare, uncharacterized', the sensation is certainly not written as an abiding character on any white paper inside the mind. On the contrary, such a perception is committed at once to oblivion, as if a picture were painted on the surface of a lake. If it were possible for the mind to experience a bare sensation of yellow, Grote believes that all the mind would know is that 'SOMETHING exists, but WHAT it is that exists, is what we have no means of knowing' (1865, vol. 2, p. 148).

Recognizing the futility of constructing a substantial world out of shadows, Grote follows Hume in distinguishing ideas of sensation from mere impressions. When philosophers and critics talk about a combination of sensory impressions or images, they are not talking about a combination of vanishing impressions. They are talking about a combination of sensations closely related to impressions, but connected to a network of other possible impressions. Energetically opposed to the building-block theories of the atomists, Grote insists that imagination, like knowledge of judgement, is a matter of apprehending a whole web of organized impressions. Sensations of yellow and white which we have perceived in the past and expect to see in the future are sensations which the imagination has already converted from impressions into ideas, as Hume had argued. Because all perceiving is an imaginative organization of impressions into intelligible wholes, Grote concludes that 'our so-called knowledge is a vast imagination which we take care to make self-consistent: and fresh imagination which possesses this consistency we call experience' (1865, vol. 2, p. 169).

As our ideas of sensation more nearly approximate the pure immediacy of Hume's impressions, they retain 'the smallest amount of reflection' consistent with their still 'being knowledge'. But since no one has ever seen an unmediated sensation, an impression of yellow before it has been converted by an educated eye into an idea of yellow, there can be no such thing as Ruskin's fiction of an innocent eye capable of seeing as a blind man would if suddenly granted the gift of sight (Ruskin, 1903–12, vol. 15, p. 27). For as soon as the imagination dockets, files, and groups its impressions, testing and transforming them into stable ideas of sensation, the mind is changed from Locke's 'unfigured tablet' into what Grote calls an enriched and 'figured' slate (1865, vol. 2, p. 206).

The great merit of Grote's theory is its clear acknowledgement that, beyond the margins of our knowledge by acquaintance, there lies the vast unmapped territory of unmediated sensation, a wilderness as yet undominated by the mind's imaginative acts. For Grote imagination is the 'atmosphere of judgement', the mental activity that turns a bare impression of jocund yellow into a stable whole of swaying colour and recurrent joy, impressions and feelings which the mind of the observer is then able to prolong, dominate, and value. When the sheer here-and-now of yellow patches moving in the breeze is transformed by Wordsworth into ideas of imagination, they reveal like all mastered feeling a double character. They are at once a sense experience and an evaluation. A swaying mass of yellow colour, which carries for Wordsworth a strong charge of sheer elation, is not sterilized of its affective life in 'I wandered lonely as a cloud'. Instead, it is stabilized so that the 'inward eye' of the imagination may revive and appraise it. No longer dominated by the brute violence of sensation, the poet enjoys an elementary freedom which allows him, in Grote's phrase, to feel 'at home' in the world. If nature herself is capable of 'composing with' the artist as Ruskin discovers when sketching the ivy and the aspen in *Praeterita* (1903–12, vol. 35, p. 314), it is because, as Grote and Ruskin both find, imagination is the antecedent condition of truth. Its antithesis is not falsehood but the sheer anarchy of unorganized sensation.

Grote accepts a holistic theory of knowledge because the alternative theory entails as its corollary an anarchic atomic world which, being a smaller unit of understanding than Ferrier's *minimum scibile per se* (Ferrier, 1854, p. 106), is not finally intelligible. The only world we can truly perceive has already been organized by imagination into meaningful wholes. Wordsworth does not first imagine individual daffodils. He perceives all at once, as an indivisible whole, 'a crowd, a host'. The 'ten thousand' visible at a glance are as multitudinous as a galaxy of stars. A reader is seldom puzzled by Ruskin's examples of how the Associative Imagination works. And yet everything Ruskin says about the subject eludes precise understanding. Grote helps explain how, in Ruskin's sense, the component parts of great art may be called 'imperfect'. Like any integral part when removed from an imaginatively organized whole, these parts are deficient not only in definiteness or in logical meaning but in something more primary, sheer intelligibility. Unlike Ruskin, Grote is no longer involved in the contradictory task of trying to draw definite conclusions about an imaginative activity that resists definition. To make sense of Ruskin's theory, Grote has only to formulate a holistic theory of knowledge. And to make sense of a holistic theory of knowledge, Grote has only to demonstrate why component items cannot be solitary. When we sunder such items from a living whole, we try to know less than can be known, as Ferrier had argued, and so we pass not into the concrete particularity that the sensory atomists envisage but into the most unintelligible abstraction.

A better-known advocate of holistic theories of knowledge is T. H. Green. Though Green is a less rigorous thinker than Grote, he is important to any student of Victorian poetics. As one of Hopkins' Oxford tutors, Green shaped the development of the nineteenth century's most original devotional poet. Like all the theorists and critics studied in this chapter, Green assumes that the whole precedes the parts and maintains the parts in living connection. When

Hopkins presents his impressions of Oxford in the sonnet 'Duns Scotus's Oxford', the unity of this city of the mind resides not in a successive awareness of particular images or even in a relation of these images. As Green would insist, the unity resides in a consciousness of simultaneity which takes place in the perceiving mind itself. The awareness of successive images is never itself a succession.

Just as John Grote takes Locke to task for isolating individual impressions or images, so Green attacks Hume for reducing perceptions to fleeting impressions of sense. In his *Introduction to Hume's Treatise on Human Nature* (1874), Green launches a sustained polemic against the premise that fact, a datum, is something given to us in experience as an isolated sensation. Hume pictures himself as a spectator in a 'theatre, where several perceptions successively make their appearance; pass, re-pass, glide away' (Hume, 1888, p. 253). But to speak of a 'sensation of white', Green argues, is already to relate it to similar sensations and to a background of many different sensations from which it is removed. Because to think of a 'sensation' is to think of it as related to an observing mind, Green concludes that all reality is mind-made.

In opposing the popular view that in 'poetry we feel, [in] science we understand', Green argues in his *Prolegomena to Ethics* that poetry cannot consist in mere feelings, for all poetry presupposes an organizing subject capable of relating its feelings. Like Hume's impressions of sense, no mere feeling unformed by thought can constitute a relation, and only relations are real. Feelings are successive, but the terms of a relation, 'even a relation of succession, are, just so far as related, not successive'. In order to constitute a relation they must be present together (Green, 1906, pp. 2, 36). The fiction of a mere feeling or sensation divorced from thought has led thinkers like Mill and Hume to weave webs of insubstantial atoms which they then pronounce real. But if reality does not depend on the fiction of fleeting impressions that we try to dignify with the name of things-in-themselves, then Green is surely right to conclude that once the atomist has sundered consciousness from the world it organizes, no reason exists 'why there should not be any number of [. . .] creations. We have asserted the unity of the world of our experience', built upon the power of the understanding 'to make nature', in Kant's phrase, 'only to transfer that world to a larger

chaos'. The error consists in a separation of Hume's impressions of
sense from his ideas of sense. Only a massive abstraction can div-
orce partners God has married. To divorce such elements an
atrocious act of violence must be committed. Because feeling and
thought are married, 'each in its full reality [always] includes the
other' (Green, 1906, pp. 45, 15, 55).

Effects of temporal and spatial simultaneity are as striking in
poems like Hopkins' 'Duns Scotus's Oxford' as they are in cubist
paintings by Braque and Picasso. Since Hopkins, a student of
Green, was surely familiar with his tutor's holistic theories of
knowledge, it is important for students of Victorian poetics to
understand the implications of these theories. To explain how suc-
cessive phenomena may become simultaneous and how the objects
of our own slowly attained knowledge may already exist as objects
of an eternal consciousness called God, Green introduces an import-
ant analogy:

> We often talk of reading the book of nature; and there is a real ana-
> logy between the process in which we apprehend the import of a
> sentence, and that by which we arrive at any piece of knowledge.
> In reading the sentence we see the words successively . . . But
> throughout that succession there must be present continuously
> the consciousness that the sentence has a meaning as a whole;
> otherwise the successive vision, attention and recollection would
> not end in a comprehension of what the meaning is.
>
> (*Prolegomena to Ethics*, 1906, p. 81)

Green argues that the analogy of reading sentences or phrases
implies the existence of an ideal reader, God, who can experience
the book of nature as a related whole. This argument seems con-
vincing only if we posit the pre-existing consciousness of God as a
first axiom. If we start with the fact of individual consciousness like
Ferrier or Kant, then try to determine what the fact of understand-
ing words implies, any inference from language to ontology seems
highly problematic. More logical is Green's attempt to account for
the paradox of simultaneity. A third event may follow a first and
second event. But to the extent that the three events are contem-
plated as successive, to that extent they become the 'constituents of a
knowledge of succession' (Green, 1906, p. 65). And to that extent all
three events must be simultaneously present.

Many of Hopkins' most original poems achieve cubist effects of instantaneous perception which illustrate the truth of Green's thesis that whenever we imagine or perceive, meaning is present to our consciousness not as a sequence of successive parts but as a simultaneous whole. The illusion of a three-dimensional perspective in the second of Hopkins' two earlier sonnets 'To Oxford' is due to the interaction of consistent clues. Such is not the case, however, in the later sonnet, 'Duns Scotus's Oxford', which produces a two-dimensional effect of overlap by deliberately wrenching out of shape the poet's rural, urban, and medieval notations.

> Towery city and branchy between towers;
> Cuckoo-echoing, bell-swarmèd, lark-charmèd, rook-racked,
>   river-rounded;
> The dapple-eared lily below thee; that country and town did
> Once encounter in, here coped and poisèd powers;
>
> Thou hast a base and brickish skirt there, sours
> That neighbour-nature thy grey beauty is grounded
> Best in; graceless growth, thou hast confounded
> Rural rural keeping – folk, flocks, and flowers.
>
> Yet ah! this air I gather and I release
> He lived on; these weeds and waters, these walls are what
> He haunted who of all men most sways my spirits to peace;
>
> Of realty the rarest-veinèd unraveller; a not
> Rivalled insight, be rival Italy or Greece;
> Who fired France for Mary without spot.
>   ('Duns Scotus's Oxford')

Hopkins compounds his pictorial impressions as freely as his Miltonic syntax rearranges word order in the first two lines, engulfing his subject in branching modifiers: 'Towery city and branchy between towers;/Cuckoo-echoing, bell-swarmèd, lark-charmèd' (ll. 1–2). In creating a blend of metaphor and fact, Hopkins' merging impressions quickly annihilate the familiar three-dimensional illusion found in his two earlier sonnets 'To Oxford'. Instead of viewing Oxford from a fixed point of view, 'underneath this chapel-side', Hopkins now teases the eye with ambiguities of perspective, shifting from aerial impressions of towers and trees to lower-angle 'shots' of their brickish base.

Finally, in the sestet of the sonnet, the voyage back into the medieval Oxford of Duns Scotus dislocates the observer in time as well as space. Though Scotus is praised as 'the rarest-veinèd unraveller' of contradictions in medieval ontology, Hopkins' own contradictions in perspective drive home the message that his sonnet is primarily an exercise in the fluid merging of parts into wholes. Thus branches flow into towers, which merge with larks and with 'coped and poisèd powers' (l. 4). According to Green, the world consists of mind-related wholes. Hopkins boasts of the mind's power to relate such wholes by boldly riveting his compounds with hyphens and as boldly rearranging the evidence of his senses. In his reversing impressions, for example, both 'branchy . . . towers' and 'towery city' (l. 1), 'cuckoo-echoing' country and 'bell-swarmèd' town (l. 2), become well confused, as light and sound, and images of rural and urban Oxford, flow easily together.

Hopkins' sonnet is a good match in words for a cubist painting by Braque or Picasso, in which the introduction of contradictory clues in the treatment of light, for example, resists all attempts to apply the test of three-dimensional consistency. In their appeal to the eye, the ear, and the historical imagination, Hopkins' shifts of perspective, both temporal and spatial, compensate like a cubist painting for the shortcomings of one-eyed vision. In the process of coaxing the eye out of its normal habits of stereotyped perception and three-dimensional viewing, Hopkins also illustrates Green's doctrine that the meaning of a city like Oxford is apprehended as an instantly perceived whole. Like the design informing a picture or the meaning informing the words of a sentence, this whole is present to our consciousness all at once, from the moment we begin to perceive or read.

5 Holistic Versus Atomic Theories: Bradley and Mill

The boldest Victorian defence of holistic theories of language and knowledge comes late in the period with the publication in 1883 of F. H. Bradley's *The Principles of Logic*. The principal target of Bradley's attack is the logical atomism of J. S. Mill, but behind Mill stands the atomism of Hume and Locke and the whole British empirical tradition. The aesthetic equivalent of an atomic theory of knowledge is Ruskin's doctrine of sensory atomism. Set forth most clearly in *The Elements of Drawing*, Ruskin's doctrine of the innocent eye continues to exercise an important influence on Pre-Raphaelite and impressionist aesthetics, even after it has been disavowed by Ruskin himself as a doctrine deserving theoretical respect.

Victorian poets love to dawdle with the painted shell of the universe, as Arnold irreverently says of Tennyson (1932, p. 63). Their fondness for sensory detail is the subject of exceptionally able monographs by Patricia Ball, by Herbert L. Sussman, and by Carol T. Christ, who argues that Victorian poets reflect 'a change of emphasis from classes to individuals' (Christ, 1975, p. 150). Citing the descriptions of physical nature in William Paley's *Natural Theology* (1802) and in such popular scientific books as Philip Gosse's *A Year at the Shore* (1865) and *Evenings at the Microscope* (1859), Herbert L. Sussman shows how Victorian scientists and theologians share the belief of the Pre-Raphaelites that 'acute observation [may] unveil spiritual truth' (1979, p. 4). But what kind of particularity do the poets and theologians have in mind? Is spiritual truth unveiled by the descriptive details of some Pre-Raphaelite and impressionist poets? Or is it unveiled by the sensory details of the symbolists? It is important to differentiate between the induced vivacity of two traditions that are easily confused. One use of detail originates in associationist psychology and in doctrines of atomism. The other use presupposes holistic theories which, turning objects into fields of force, place the reader at the centre of energy.

Merely descriptive uses of sensory detail hark back to the eighteenth-century associationist psychology of Hartley and Locke. This psychology is primarily an attempt to show how moral and theological belief can be reconciled with the empirical assumption of the scientists that all knowledge derives from sense experience. For this reason natural theologies like Paley's are often linked as closely as pre-Darwinian science to eighteenth-century psychology. But as associationism assumes a far more ambitious role in nineteenth-century thought, theology and the inductive sciences begin to part company. In his *System of Logic*, for example, as I showed in Chapter I, Mill defends associationism as that complete psychological and logical system, and as that ultimate arbiter of truth, which James Mill and Alexander Bain had laboured to make it. Unlike Locke and Hartley, Mill uses the combination of discrete sensory facts to classify and relate all departments of mental life. This triumph of associationism, as a scientific and a logical dogma, stands behind and illuminates the sensory atomism of much Pre-Raphaelite and descriptive verse.

The difference between the two forms of sensory detail is illustrated in many sections of *In Memoriam*. In section XI, for example, in his memorable evocation of autumnal landscapes, Tennyson's microscopic focus on the silvery gossamers and on the pattering sound of the chestnuts seems to commit him to a sensory atomism so extreme, so 'diatonic', as Hopkins would say, that the reader feels tricked by sleight of hand when the mourner at the end of this section begins to blur the differences between natural and psychological 'calm' by turning a finely nuanced landscape into a geography of the soul. The same conflict between atomistic detail and inscape obsesses Hopkins, who is often at a loss to make the extreme sensory atomism of his verse – the single, unrepeatable quality of whatever is 'counter, original, spare, strange' ('Pied Beauty', l. 7) – rhyme or chime in God.

As W. J. Fox showed as early as 1831 in his brilliant use of the new empirical psychology to analyse Tennyson's early poetry, the sensory atomism of associationist thought is an important influence on Victorian poetics. But it must not be forgotten that Tennyson's portrayal of the atomic philosophy in a monologue like 'Lucretius' is as much an attack upon associationist psychology as it is upon the atomic models of Newtonian and early nineteenth-century physics. For a more systematic critique of associationism than Tennyson or any other Victorian poet provides, we must turn to Bradley's *Principles of Logic*, where the atomism of Mill's *Logic* is subjected to its most devastating scrutiny. As. T. S. Eliot has observed, 'Bradley did not attempt to destroy Mill's logic. Anyone who reads his own *Principles* will see that his force is directed not against Mill's logic as a whole but only against certain limitations, imperfections and abuses. He left the structure of Mill's logic standing, and never meant to do anything else' (1932, p. 448). Bradley deplores only the caprice of Mill's 'psychological Atomism'. 'Destiny and chance', he decrees, 'are two names of one lord that sways the procession of fleeting units.' As Tennyson dramatizes in 'Lucretius', the accident of presentation or the fate of association 'in [the atoms'] short-lived occupation of that void which is the soul' consecrates a principle of randomness. Like the arbitrary swerving of the atoms in *De Rerum Natura*, the only rule in such a world is that there is no rule. As Bradley wryly observes, 'the "final inexplicability" of J. S. Mill may recall an echo of the "free will" of Epikurus' (1883, p. 276), the Greek philosopher whom Lucretius, we may recall, adopted as his model.

Bradley's main objection to Mill's theory of association is its premise that 'individual atoms are the units of association'. Maintaining that 'no particular ideas are ever associated or ever could be', Bradley opposes to Mill's Law of Contiguity the Law of Redintegration, a phrase he borrows from Sir William Hamilton. Superficially alike, the two laws 'are separated by the chasm that divides irreconcilable views of the world' (Bradley, 1883, p. 279). Whereas the Law of Contiguity combines atomic units, Redintegration associates universals. 'What operates in the first is an external relation *between* individuals. What works in the second is an ideal identity *within* the individuals' (Bradley, 1883, p. 280). The psychological atomism of Tennyson's 'Lucretius' dramatizes the folly of trying to endow fleeting impressions with permanence. Like one of the atoms streaming through the void in *De Rerum Natura*, these impressions are consigned to instant death. In Bradley's words, 'there is no Hades where they wait in disconsolate exile, till Association announces resurrection and recall'. When the fleeting sensory atoms recorded in such poetry are 'bodily buried in the past, no miracle opens the mouth of the grave and calls up to the light a perished reality'. Bradley concludes that Mill's 'touching beliefs' to the contrary 'may babble in the tradition of a senile psychology, or contort themselves in the metaphysics of some frantic dogma, but philosophy must register them and sigh and pass on' (1883, p. 280).

Like association by contiguity, association by similarity is dismissed by Bradley as 'a downright fiction'. Since similarity is a relation, it cannot exist 'unless both terms are before the mind'. In section XI of *In Memoriam*, for example, there would be no association by similarity between present sensations of calm in the high wold and great plain and of tranquillity in the faded leaf and gossamers unless all these sensory impressions, however atomic or discrete, were simultaneously present as part of the 'calm despair' of the mourner's mind (l. 16). Only an actual relation in the poet's

mind between the pattering chestnuts and the Turneresque sym-
phony of sweeping bowers and bounding main can 'shake the realm
of Hades', as Bradley says (1883, p. 294), and conjure from the dar-
kest recess of the mourner's soul an image of the 'dead calm' in
Hallam's corpse. In discounting the contribution of the poet's
memory and imagination to mental phenomena like the heaving
deep and the corpse on the ship, remote realities never actually seen
by Tennyson, Mill's Law of Similarity is asked to perform a 'mir-
acle of resurrection' it is unfit to perform. In a tone of solemn
banter, Bradley concludes that Mill's conviction that 'there can be
no reality but particular existences' is 'nothing but metaphysics . . .
and, what is more, . . . nothing but a dogma' (1883, p. 305).

Just as the error of atomism is to abstract sensory particulars from
a concrete whole, so the error of inference is to abstract particular
facts from a whole complex of facts in which they appear. In the
name of concreteness, each method breeds a progeny of abstract
particulars. For 'if we find that $a-b$ is true *within x*, on what ground
do we rest for our desperate leap to the assertion that $a-b$ is true
without condition?' (Bradley, 1883, p. 507). Mill's Method of Dif-
ference employs subtraction 'where arithmetic is not known to be
even possible' (Bradley, 1883, p. 509). The atomic assumption of
Mill's Method of Difference is that units are indifferent to their
junction in a whole and 'may', as Bradley notes, 'be freely treated as
independent elements'. 'From the given total $AB--df$, by removal
of $B-f$, we abstract $A-d$, and we argue that $A-d$ is true of reality'
(1883, pp. 508–9). But as Bradley objects in logical defence of the
distinction Ruskin makes when contrasting the Associative Imagin-
ation with the Associative Fancy, 'our reasoning depends on the
[sensory atomist's] unwarranted assumption that in $AB--df$ we
have nothing but units'. In fact, Mill's 'cutting may not merely
loose the string of a bundle. It may have utterly destroyed the con-
nection which maintains the parts in existence' (Bradley, 1883, p.
508).

Bradley's holistic critique of Mill's *System of Logic* is anticipated
by William Wallace's *Prolegomena* to *The Logic of Hegel*, first
published by the Clarendon Press at Oxford in 1874, nine years
before Bradley's own *Principles* appeared. Just as the scholastic theo-
logians had used Aristotle's logic to 'help them in the arrangement
of their religious beliefs' (Wallace, 1874, p. lxxvi), so nineteenth-

century scientists have 'looked upon the Inductive Logic of Mill in the light of a new revelation', Wallace observes. Like Bradley, Wallace attacks Mill's *Logic* for its failure to found its methodology of the sciences upon a comprehensive analysis of thought as a whole. 'A mere sense-world to the [Hegelian] philosopher is what an irreducible nebula is to the speculative astronomer.' Out of that nebula the theorist, like the true logician, 'expects that a solar system, a concrete unity, will one day spring. Even so from mere sense the concrete notion of reason will be evolved. But in the form of sense the matter of sense is not concrete, a unity of opposites: but a chaos' (Wallace, 1874, p. lxxviii).

This 'chaos' implicit in sensory atomism is apparent in poems like 'Lucretius', where Tennyson sets out to expose the enormous dogmatisms perpetuated in the name of associationist thought. But even in poems of detailed sensory notation like 'The Palace of Art', the failure of the panels to cohere in the soul's consciousness as parts of a meaningful whole abstracts from reality. It may sound paradoxical and perverse to speak of abstract particulars, but I believe that many poems of extreme particularity become abstract by destroying the unity which should maintain the parts in meaningful relation. If we take Bradley's argument seriously, the abstract particularity of these poems must radically qualify Carol Christ's equation of the 'finer optic' of Victorian poetry with an art of the concrete. As Christ seems tacitly to acknowledge, nothing could be less concrete than 'the artificiality of species and the [supposed] independence of the particular' (1975, p. 15).

If we are looking for a poetry of minute detail that is more genuinely concrete, we must turn from the blue vein on the breast of Browning's Madonna to new symbolist experiments by poets like Tennyson and Morris. When Tennyson describes Maud as a 'Passionless, pale, cold face, star-sweet on a gloom profound', his impressions cohere only in some northern nowhere, some region where the 'maddened beach dragged down by the wave', the 'shining daffodil', and the 'ghastly' auroral 'glimmer' in the nighttime sky, all fuse illogically like backgrounds in surrealist painting (*Maud*, 1, 99–101). The poet uses his apparition of terrifying beauty, heavenly splendour, the beautiful avenger transformed into ghostlike vision, not to count the whorls of the shell, as he does later in the poem, but to fashion a series of magnificent rhythmic curves that plunge downward and then upward before culminating in the half-stormy sweep of 'The shining daffodil dead, and Orion low in his grave' (I, 101). If Tennyson were to arrange his words more logically, the whole might fall asunder, as Bradley observes of that given total AB−−df, from which Mill's Method of Difference tries to abstract A−d. In an earlier symbolist experiment like 'Now sleeps the crimson petal', Tennyson's lover identifies so completely with the minutely focused objects that he and the woman, the stars and the earth, the lily and the lake, begin to fuse together in images that approximate in words a water-lily painting by Monet.

Sometimes when a poem is casually read, it seems to fall apart into a loosely linked chain of visual marvels like William Morris's 'The Chapel in Lyoness'. But on closer inspection we realize that no atoms of colour could be as visually absorbing as the interplay of wild rose and gilded screen, of silver and gold, all 'thinly outspread' 'against the jasper sea' (ll. 37, 46, 48, 53, 91–2) unless Morris had first shifted attention to the pattern in the plane by frustrating readers who expect to find a coherent picture of the three-dimensional world they normally perceive. The careful introduction of contradictory clues, as in a still life by Braque, keeps such a three-dimensional world safely out of view. Some details may be true, but others are clearly false. Ozana's lament that during his illness 'no man came a-near' (l. 4) is contradicted, for example, by the fact that 'a faint wild rose' has been placed upon his face by Sir Galahad, who claims to have watched Ozana 'All day long and every day' (l. 34). When Ozana's hallucination introduces a frame within a frame, and the knight protests, 'Ah! me, I cannot fathom it' (l. 33), Morris is deliberately withholding the clues that would enable a reader to try out various interpretations until he finds the one which best supports a coherent narrative. In the absence of such coherence, Morris's colourful succession of fragments, each as discontinuous as the panels of a medieval triptych, is not really repudiating a holistic approach to language and art. For a conventional narrative unity he is simply substituting a purely aesthetic whole, rich in colour and in visual appeal. By short-circuiting the normal passage of words through concepts, Morris is able to trace a pattern in the plane that allows his readers to delight, not merely in atoms of sensation, but in intricate arabesques of colour and form.

Despite Bradley's strictures, Mill's *System of Logic* is a comprehensive and admirable construction, setting forth with unequalled boldness an atomistic, building-block theory of knowledge and words. Its aesthetic equivalent is the doctrine of sensory atomism set forth in Ruskin's *The Elements of Drawing*, which is used to vindicate Pre-Raphaelite and impressionist theory and practice. Reviving the theory of Hume that Green demolishes, the teaching that perception consists in fleeting impressions of sense, Ruskin argues in *The Elements of Drawing*, as he had argued earlier in the first book of *Modern Painters*, that 'the whole technical power of painting depends on our recovery of what may be called the *innocence of the eye*' (1903–12, vol. 15, p. 27). Ruskin assumes that the painter or poet can deliberately forget what he 'knows', so as to transcribe only ' a sort of childish perception of . . . flat stains of colour, merely as such, without consciousness of what they signify' (vol. 15, p. 27). In trying, however, to become like Monet a disengaged eye, can an artist ever reproduce a pure patch of colour, a flat stain of sulphur yellow, to take Ruskin's example? Or in striving for what E. H. Gombrich calls a triumph of 'matching' over 'making' (1960, p. 296), does the artist who tries to abolish 'what we only know' about grass, recording what we actually see, not reduce the world to chaos? Almost any convention imposed by the perceiver would seem to suit art better than an unmediated natural subject taken 'straight from life'. To most mid-Victorians the 'innocent eye' is about as innocent as it is to the post-Gombrichian critic, for whom the least ingenuous art is that which pretends to be a candid snapshot. Even in *The Elements of Drawing* Ruskin insists that 'every hue throughout [an artist's] work is altered by every touch that [he] add[s] in other places' (1903–12, vol. 15, p. 134). For as Gombrich observes, the artist's 'mental act rests on knowledge of how colours will affect each other. In fact, it demands a willingness to use a pigment which in isolation still looks unlike the area to be matched in order that it may look like it in the end' (1960, p. 310).

Many of Browning's monologues support Bradley's argument that by sundering atoms of sense from the wholes to which they belong a doctrine like Ruskin's theory of the innocent eye robs these atoms of stability and permanence, consigning them to instant death. Browning's Spanish monk and Bishop of St Praxed's become photographic plates, negatives on which fleeting impressions are vividly printed. Reducing these perverted impression-

ists to disembodied eyes, tongues, and nerves, Browning can leave
them suspended in the void, as sheer sensibilities, artists without
imaginations or minds. In 'Caliban Upon Setebos' the speaker's
childish perception of flat stains of colour – 'meshes of fire', 'one
fire-eye in a ball of foam' (ll. 14, 47) – represents the point on the
spectrum where the necessary distinction between sensory atomism
and sensory wholes is hardest to maintain. But if the eye did not
build up its patches of sensation into intelligible wholes, the mind
would be bombarded by streams of atoms which would dissolve
objects in a hurtful swirl of mist, light, and dazzle, which not even a
Turner or a Monet in his most impressionist experiments could
conceive or paint. Even when Caliban, initiating his stammer from
the mud, seems most nearly a grotesque antenna and a naked
viscous eye, his colourful language is actively transforming into
stable and recurrent wholes the crude and fleeting impression of
sense that Hume identifies. For once a mere atom has assaulted the
eye it passes into nothingness. Despite its particularity, an atom of
sensation is less substantial than a shade and as bloodless as a passing
ghost.

6 *The Holistic Legacy and the Contextual Paradox*

Every theorist discussed in this chapter agrees that meaning is
bound to a context. But each also tacitly acknowledges that the con-
text of meaning is boundless. Even when meaning seems narrowly
bound to an individual word or phrase, philologists like Trench and
Müller show that the true context of interpretation reaches far back
into the fossilized history of the word. Meaning is bound only by
the limits of the philologist's historical understanding or by the
limits of a poet's power to restore forgotten etymologies. In
Ruskin's theory of the Imagination Associative, the context of
meaning is the perfect whole in which all the imperfect words in a
poem or all the imperfect images in a picture have to be interpreted.
In each subsequent theory that this chapter analyses, the context of
meaning widens. E. S. Dallas argues that when poets use metaphors
the true context of meaning is the unconscious association, not just
of words with words, but of whole classes of words with other
whole classes. In order to understand metaphor Dallas believes we

have to understand the nature of the mind's unconscious operations. The more John Grote and T. H. Green explore the contexts of meaning, the more boundless the contexts become. According to Grote, knowledge is 'a vast imagination', a true *terra incognita*, which we gradually chart and subdue by making it 'self-consistent'. For T. H. Green the context of meaning is nothing less than the mind of God, which sustains a mind-related world in much the same way as the meaning of a sentence sustains the relation of its grammatical parts. To confine the analysis to any narrower context is to reify those abstract particulars which every holistic theory of language and knowledge is pledged to break down. Unless we also understand F. H. Bradley's doctrine of undifferentiated wholes, it is difficult to make sense of his critique of solipsism in *Appearance and Reality*. And unless we understand that feeling is a 'non-relational unity' of many in one, we shall be unable to see how it furnishes Bradley with positive knowledge of the Absolute, which he defines as a Whole that is qualified 'non-relationally'. In each case meaning is bound to context, but as in Coleridge's dream of an undifferentiated language the units of equivalence prove boundless. Only this paradox of a boundless context makes intelligible Bradley's analysis of apagogic inferences, which allow his logician to affirm through a process of exhaustive negation. This same paradox also helps explain our sense that what Bradley does not say in *Appearance and Reality* is at least as important as what is said. If the Absolute is a 'non-relational whole', then outside the language of poetry it is not hard to see, in the words of Bradley's own aphorism, why '"One never tells more than half," and in the end perhaps one cannot' (1930, aphorism 44).

In Chapter 21 of *Appearance and Reality*, Bradley argues that solipsism is a necessary by-product of Idealism only if we believe that the original form of experience is always given as 'my experience' or as 'your experience'. But reflection shows that immediate experience is undifferentiated. As Richard Wollheim explains, 'the mind and the external world being concurrent products of a single process, we would be clearly wrong to attribute the existence of the latter to the agency of the former' (1973, p. 231). Immediate experience is a whole which predates the moment at which the classification of subject and object begins to apply. In his doctoral thesis on Bradley, T. S. Eliot even argues that when immediate feeling develops into subjects and objects there is nothing left over that would allow us to distinguish between the contents of the mind and its objects. Mental presentations have no meaning. Like the musical forms to which Pater says all art aspires, they are not intended to mean but to be. To approximate in words the experience of wholes which override the distinction between subject and object and which, like the mental presentations of Bradley's observer, are devoid of content, the poet may try to give his verse a musical organization. This is Eliot's own solution in *Four Quartets*, and it is something Tennyson tries to do in *Maud*, which 'has a musical structure which can easily be understood in musical terms' like Rousseau's *Pygmalion* (Culler, 1977, pp. 196–7). Tennyson even experiments with the popular polka measure, extending the music of 'flute, violin, bassoon' (*Maud*, I, 863) until the metre catches the whirling rise and fall of the lover's hopes. Because music abolishes the distinction between form and content, allowing Tennyson to skate on the thin ice of hallucination and nightmare, it can satisfy in art the same needs that Bradley's ideal of an undifferentiated whole satisfies in his metaphysical writing.

Bradley is compelled 'to believe', he says, 'in a Whole qualified, and qualified non-relationally, by every fraction of experience' (1893, p. 470). He also asserts that immediate experience provides him with a positive idea of this 'non-relational unity'. As Hugh Kenner has noted, '"non-relational" is the key phrase'. Its consequence for poetry is best studied in the verse of T. S. Eliot, which perfects a syntax of psychic totality capable of reproducing the quality of Bradley's non-relational wholes by using 'participles and relative clauses related to nothing, the gestures of verbs rather than their commitments, syntax not abolished but anesthetized' (Kenner, 1965, p. 43). Richard Wollheim warns that any attempt 'to trace the influence of Bradley's philosophy' upon a poem like *Four Quartets* is 'a most hazardous and uncertain undertaking' (1973, p. 248). But anyone who has tried to relate the images in *Four Quartets* will know what Bradley means by 'non-relational'. No sooner does a logical relation seem to establish itself than it is defied. 'Little Gidding' begins in winter, but the meeting with the phantom takes place in autumn. Shortly after the 'one Annunciation' in 'The Dry Salvages', a god appears. But he is not Christ but Krishna. Though 'Little Gidding' uses all four elements in part two, earth dominates part three, and fire becomes prominent again only in the last three lines of part five. We cannot expect the critic or the poet to show us only one logical way of looking at *Four Quartets*. Often it is touch and go with the metaphors. We never know how much meaning we can extract and when they will cease to yield. In 'Little Gidding', for example, the consolations of a language 'tongued with fire beyond the language of the living' seem to ebb away in the fire-gutted ruins 'of sanctuary and choir'. A moment later, however, in the 'dark dove with the flickering tongue' there bursts upon us another image of fire descending from heaven. While the destruction wrought by the dive-bomber pertains logically to the sanctuary's disintegration into four elements, it also returns us to the 'pentecostal fire' of both the human and divine word. 'The dark dove' does not simply rot and mar all monuments of the human spirit. Like 'the brief sun', flaming the ice 'when the short day is brightest', the concentration of light and dark, creation and destruction, helps us enlarge our vision and assimilate our dread. Because all these metaphors simultaneously adhere to and remain separate from each other, we are invited to participate in the difficult task of holding incompatible things simultaneously in our mind as part of a 'non-relational' unity or whole.

Because Bradley denies that relations are real, he substitutes for Green's mind-related whole a concept that seems much less amenable to logical analysis. It proves easier to say what Bradley's 'non-relational' whole is *not* like than to say what it resembles. Bradley is prepared to entertain any and every proposition about the real, then systematically subtract every proposition that is self-contradictory. Whatever remains is asserted to be real, even though it resembles nothing so much as the vacuum in a bell jar after all the air has been exhausted. This tendency to void all human allegiances reaches an extreme in Eliot's *Four Quartets*, and it is hard not to discern Bradley's influence in a poem which takes its 'bearings', as one critic says, 'from the idiom of cleansing, surgery, and "voiding"' (Donoghue, 1969, p. 232). Like 'The Vanity of Human Wishes' or Arnold's poem 'Resignation', Bradley's metaphysics is offered as a stay against our vanity. It drains the Absolute of its properties, as Bradley's psychology voids the mind of its contents. It is no wonder Bradley says 'the ghosts of Metaphysic accept no substitute. They reveal themselves only to that victim whose life they have drained' (1930, axiom 98).

Bradley takes the rhetorical trope *apophasis*, which affirms by denying, and turns it into a fresh specimen of logical inference. As he explains in his *Principles of Logic*, 'take any idea, no matter what it is, suggest of it the real and find it compatible; bring it into collision with other ideas which are disparate with itself, see that it defeats them in open competition, and then go on at once to assert its truth – this alarming process appears to have no limit' (1883, p. 386). This process may be alarming, but it is the very process Bradley uses to assert that the Absolute must be real, since 'its opposite is impossible'. The more that anything 'exhausts the field of possibility, the less possible becomes that which would essentially alter it' (Bradley, 1893, p. 477). Unless Arnold and Pater had first exhausted all the alternatives, it would be impossible for them to reach any conclusions in 'Resignation' and *Marius the Epicurean*, where 'truths' are finally embraced because they defeat all rivals in open competition. Bradley calls his criterion of truth 'inconceivability of the opposite' (1893, p. 476). Its presence in *In Memoriam* accounts for that poem's curious blend of scepticism and belief. Tennyson reaches the certitudes of his Prologue only because he finds himself forced into ever darker, more forbidding corners of a world where God and nature seem at strife. We could say of both Pater and Tennyson what Richard Wollheim says of Bradley. The position in which each writer finally rests is 'the last refuge of a sceptical and critical mind in its retreat from a series of positions, successively found untenable' (Wollheim, 1959, p. 233).

The wider and more coherent the context of meaning becomes, the less we may be able to say about it. In trying to give his concept of a non-relational whole some positive content, Bradley is usually reduced to unintelligible paradox: 'There can be no outside, because already what is inside is everything'; 'My experience and its states, in a sense, actually are the whole world . . . But it is less misleading to assert, conversely, that the total world is my experience' (1893, pp. 477, 466). We read Bradley, not because he has any aphorism to deliver about the whole, but because his books are full of what Hugh Kenner calls 'an exciting tautness of implication'. 'No quotation' in *Appearance and Reality* 'survives the whole.' Because his thoughts about the Absolute come from the other side of silence, like T. S. Eliot's or Christina Rossetti's, each time we want to see what Bradley means 'we must reread the book' (Kenner, 1965, p.

57). If a final word about the whole exists, writers like Bradley and Eliot know they can never hope to fix that word or speak it in their discourse. The Toa that can be spoken is not the real Toa, and as Tennyson's Ancient Sage knows, words are 'one part sound and three parts silence'. As one commentator says of T. S. Eliot, 'the words are never certain and are good only when they direct the listener to the silent meaning' (Donoghue, 1969, pp. 212–13).

In *Appearance and Reality* each wider context of meaning discloses a still wider context. The horizon of contexts is boundless – so boundless that not even the boundaries of a personal God can survive intact as a predicate of Bradley's Absolute. People who want God to be a finite person 'much like themselves' 'desire one conclusion, and, to reach it, they argue for another' (Bradley, 1893, p. 471). Even a poet like Christina Rossetti, who would recoil in horror from Bradley's conclusion that a personal God is bound to too finite a context, dramatizes a version of this same paradox. In her lyric 'In the bleak mid-winter', for example, there is a sudden shift into high celestial drama, then a return to the simplicities of the manger scene. Alternating between the wonders of angelic veneration and the lowly homage of 'The ox and ass and camel'(1. 23), it is as if Rossetti were trying to seal off the limits of 'bleak mid-winter' from the disturbing entry of a God whom 'Heaven cannot hold . . . / Nor earth sustain' (ll. 9–10). When infinitude finally moves down from heaven to earth, only the loving mother, Mary, is able to dispel all human nervousness at trying to put an undiminished truth, whose context is boundless, inside the comforting limits of a poem. God's downward mobility is a category for Incarnation, which cannot be categorized. But as Mary, like Rossetti, composes her simple art of the heart, whose words reach into silence, she can put the reader through an actual experience of the sufficiency of a finite, context-bound love to a universe whose horizons recede indefinitely and erode any boundaries we are tempted to impose.

THE DARKENED GLASS:
AGNOSTICISM AND THE PURIST TRADITION

Philosophers like Hamilton and Mansel make God less and less accessible to conceptual understanding. The more closely they approach the limits of the sayable, the more poetry may have to be used to define the indefinable or take the place of religion altogether. Both developments are part of an élitist, anti-democratic crusade to remove aesthetics and theology from the market-place. Reactionary in a political sense, the move from the market-place back into the sanctuary is associated with Tractarianism, with the High-Church scepticism of H. L. Mansel, and with later efforts of Pater and the aesthetes to restore to art a sense of purity and detachment.

The intellectual historian can identify two distinct strains in the agnostic and purist lines of theorizing which allow poetry to move into the sacred space vacated by God. Both strains can be found in Carlyle, who combines the reactionary thrust of Sir William Hamilton, wrapping the truth about God in veils of mystery, with the revolutionary thrust of Carlyle's hero, Friedrich Schiller. Like Schiller's Julius in *The Philosophical Letters*, Carlyle has been led into the moral and intellectual wilderness. The only alternative to perishing there is to become the author of a new sacred book. As an agnostic semiotician in *Sartor Resartus*, Carlyle denies that any symbols, including the central symbols of Christianity, are intrinsic. Since there are no real icons or indices (in Peirce's sense), the mystery of creation is entirely in human hands. Man must become the new god, the architect of his own humanity and values. A more conservative agnostic like Matthew Arnold seeks the comfort of Spinoza's ethical certitudes and the Brahmanic peace of the *Bhagavad Gita*, both of which allow a measure of detachment and withdrawal. Often the radical and conservative strains are combined in the same thinker. H. L. Mansel, J. H. Newman, and W. G. Ward, Clough's Oxford tutor, each combine the piety of a fideist with the mental agility and the scepticism of a logician who has been rigorously trained in the study of Aristotle at Oxford.

IV The Agnostic Imagination: Indeterminate and Absent Subjects

In the preceding chapters I examined three representational axioms: Mill's axiom of the mirror of nature, Ferrier's axiom of the framed event, and T. H. Green's holistic axiom that the truth is the whole. In all three cases the primary object of representation was Blake's 'vegetable glass of nature'. The next four chapters will widen the scope of the inquiry by examining Kantian, Tractarian, and finally Hegelian axioms of cognition which try to represent truths that lie on the far side of this 'glass'. But the truths of ethics and religion prove more elusive than the fugitive auroral light in 'The Holy Grail' or the dewy gossamers that 'twinkle into green and gold' in *In Memoriam*. New presentational axioms of the absent, the elided, or the indeterminate subject begin to replace the dominant representational axioms. If the subject of a poet's predications happens to be ineffable, like God, then agnostic theology teaches that the subject has either been removed altogether or has come to acquire contradictory qualities. When a poet's predications possess all the hallmarks of a conventional representation except a fixed or an assigned connotation, then its symbols are unconsummated, like the symbols of a musical composition. Such unconsummated symbolism is a feature of new presentational forms which in the agnostic theology of Mansel, in the Kantian aesthetic of Masson, and in the deconstructed Platonism of Pater and the aesthetes, replace the traditional representational axioms that dominate the philosophic and aesthetic thought of the earlier Victorian period.

By moving, in roughly chronological order, from the merely equivocal theories of knowledge enunciated by Mansel in the 1850s, to the analogical knowledge of Schleiermacher and Browning, and then to the univocal knowledge of the Victorian Hegelians, I shall be standing on its head the pyramid structure of knowledge analysed in Mill's univocal mirroring of sensory fact, in Tyndall's pictorial analogies of waves and ether, and in Huxley's and Pearson's merely equivocal knowledge of physical nature. The present chapter will serve as a hinge or pivot, for even in opening the door on supersensible truth, it will focus on philosophers like Mansel, for whom all proper knowledge must strictly conform to the scientist's conceptual understanding of physical nature. To qualify as knowledge, the strict Kantian insists, a concept must have some verifiable content in sense experience. No Victorian was clearer on this point than F. D. Maurice, who observes that Kant 'is as afraid of transgressing the boundaries of the understanding, and has at least as severe notions of what these boundaries are, as [Locke], or as any one who has walked most warily in [Locke's] steps' (1872, vol. 2, p. 621). Unable to encompass God in the net of their conceptual understanding, Victorian Kantians like Sir William Hamilton and his agnostic disciples begin to transform analogy from a *lucid* veil into a lucid *veil*, making both poetic and theological language increasingly opaque.

As Hamilton and Mansel begin to write their own critiques of Pure Reason, their contemporaries find they can no longer assume a stable language of analogy in which nature leads a double life as object and sign. Partly as a result of Tennyson's growing interest in oriental mysticism, for example, the analogical participation of the natural order in the divine continues to fade in his poems, until the world itself threatens to dissolve in the cold and imageless void, 'the Abysm of all Abysms' ('The Ancient Sage', l. 40). In Edwin Arnold's translation of *The Bhagavad Gita*, which he owned, Tennyson would have read that the real self or Atman remains forever beyond the 'double seeming' of the mind's antinomies. Because God's nature remains profoundly hidden, 'unconceivably' itself, as Tennyson affirms in 'De Profundis' (l. 48), his words about God remain mere 'shadows' or equivocations, the mere symbolic fictions of which *The Bhagavad Gita* speaks.

Some pages of William Brockie's *Indian Thought: A Popular Essay*, also in Tennyson's library, recall Kant's analysis of the antinomies in his first *Critique* and Mansel's demonstration in *The Limits of Religious Thought* that the attributes applied to God are in logical contradiction. 'The Supreme Being' of Hindu thought, explains Brockie, 'exists in the world, comprehending all things, but is comprehended by none . . . He is free from the influence of quality, yet possesses every quality' (1876, p. 15). In Tennyson's precarious inner awareness both of God's presence and withdrawal, as in the Vedanta's teaching that 'man can never know God until he is concious that it is impossible to know Him' (Brockie, 1876, p. 18), the crisis of the sceptical imagination is never fully resolved, nor is the trace of an earlier analogical tradition ever quite effaced. The 'presence-absence of the trace' (Derrida, 1976, p. 71), without which words for absent objects could not exist, carries in itself the difficulty of expressing the divine presence, a life without difference, in mere discursive signs.

Of the major Victorian poets, Matthew Arnold and Clough are the most uprooted. 'Wandering between two worlds, one dead, / The other powerless to be born' ('Stanzas from the Grande Chartreuse', ll. 85–6), Arnold is the quintessential displaced person, suffering from an utter personal, theological, and historical homelessness. Like his dead brother and sister-in-law in 'A Southern Night', who are buried in distant graves – the husband among 'the sandy spits' and 'shore-locked lakes' (l. 1) of the Mediterranean Ocean and his wife beneath the 'hoary Indian hills' (l. 73) – Arnold is displaced in time as well as space. For this restless agnostic, who loves to ponder like Mansel and Spencer 'God's . . . untold . . . mysteries' (l. 89), an inability to locate the unspeakable object of worship produces the anguish of a man born out of his time, the anguish of a religious man without religion.

Agnostic theology's development of the sceptical side of Kant's thought points the way to a simultaneous rediscovery of the neglected constructive side of Kant. This reconstruction will involve the recovery of analogies of authentic experience, often based on moral experience and love. These analogies prepare for a consideration of increasingly cognitive analogies, Platonic and Hegelian, in later chapters. Ranged at the opposite end of the spectrum from the scientific models studied in Chapter I, the last of these analogies, the Hegelian, will prove to be the most ambitious. The English Hegelian F. H. Bradley claims for the metaphysician and the poet the same degree of knowledge that empirical epistemology ascribes to physical science. But instead of studying the mere facts of physical nature, Bradley in the constructive second book of his *Appearance and Reality* claims all reality as his province.

1 Mansel and Kant: The Limits of Analogy

In his Bampton lectures for 1858, *The Limits of Religious Thought Examined in Eight Lectures*, H. L. Mansel, a lecturer on Kant, and Dean of St Paul's, contends that the divine nature can never be logically grasped by the mind's mutually exclusive concepts of a being that is at once absolute, infinite, and a First Cause. An absolute God is the negation of all relation, but the concept of a first cause is the absolute affirmation of a particular relation. If we try to escape from this apparent contradiction by introducing the idea of succession in time, Mansel finds we are checked by a third conception, the idea that God is infinite. Contradictions so thorough-going tell with equal force, Mansel believes, against all dogmatists and all atheists. Though they may teach us, in some instances, that it is 'our duty . . . to believe [what] we cannot conceive', the antinomies besetting all our ideas of the absolute and the infinite are one of the trouble spots of knowledge. They suggest it is impossible to enclose within logical schemes the inexhaustible dynamic life of God and His creation.

Brought face to face with the crisis of religious intellectualism, Mansel follows Kant in proclaiming that 'the highest principles of thought and action, to which we can attain, are regulative, not speculative' (Mansel, 1867, pp. 41–2, 100). The principles of our religion and morality 'do not serve to satisfy the reason, but to guide the conduct: they do not tell us what things are in themselves, but how we must conduct ourselves in relation to them'. Unlike Kant, however, Mansel rejects the idea of a law without a lawgiver. Such a regulative fiction he finds no more intelligible than the fiction of an absolute and infinite Creator. According to Kant, we know God's commands to be divine, not because they are commanded by God, but because we are in fact morally bound by them. Mansel believes that in building the moral sense into a kind of Jacob's ladder, Kant's fiction of a moral law binding 'upon all possible intelligences' allows divine traffic to flow again between heaven and earth at the inadmissible cost of elevating morality above the mind's capacity to understand it. Unable to share Kant's experience of a moral law which fills the 'mind with ever new and increasing admiration and awe' (Kant, 1923, p. 260), Mansel wants to acknowledge the mystery which really exists, and in the impotence of his reason to 'take refuge in faith' (1867, pp. 143, 86).

But how can it be our duty to have faith in a God who is not only unknowable but also inconceivable? Like Mansel's contemporary, F. D. Maurice, we may feel that we cannot be asked to have faith in nothing. Surprisingly, Mansel's most sustained efforts to resolve these difficulties originate, not in the Bampton lectures themselves, but in the eighth chapter of his earlier *Prolegomena Logica* (1851). Here Mansel is careful to distinguish between two kinds of negative thinking: one merely material or psychological, the other formal or logical. The material form of negative thought exists in a man born blind. He has a negative idea of colour in general. Such is the case, Mansel argues, with all our speculations concerning God. This material or psychological negation is not to be confused with the more radical logical negation which occurs whenever a grammatical subject is shown to possess contradictory predicates.

Sir William Hamilton's demonstration that the concepts of the absolute and the infinite are self-contradictory would appear to be an example of this second kind of deficiency. But in *The Limits of Religious Thought* Mansel argues that the contradictons that appear at first to be logical and formal are a result of a mere psychological condition. Because the condition of our consciousness is distinction and limitation, we are forced for psychological reasons to say that God is both limited and unlimited. He is 'actually something . . . and actually nothing' (Mansel, 1867, p. 51). If God were not something, He could not be an object of our consciousness. But if He were not also nothing, He could not remain absolute and unlimited. Merely to be 'unable to think of an object as existing' is not at all the same thing, he insists, as 'to be able to think of it as not existing' (1851, p. 252). The agnosticism that springs from the merely material or psychological form of negation is compatible with faith, for it asserts undogmatically only the absence of any knowledge of God, not any apodictic knowledge of God's absence. Because the inability to conceive of God's attributes is not, as we may first think, a logical defect, but a result of a psychological deficiency in ourselves, we cannot conclude that negative thoughts about God's attributes entail His non-existence as well.

When, like Aristotle and Cicero, we mistake 'a psychological deficiency for a logical impossibility' (Mansel, 1851, p. 253), the first kind of negative thought for the second, we pass from agnosticism to atheism. But to take this final step it is first necessary to 'pronounce how consciousness exists in beings of a different nature from ourselves'. To do so is manifestly impossible, since it would first be 'necessary that we should be capable of possessing their natures and faculties, as well as our own, and of comparing the two together, by the aid of a third power independent of either'. Mansel concludes, therefore, that as long as agnosticism confines itself to its proper sphere, to the merely material or psychological kind of negative thinking, it is powerless 'to limit the province of faith by that of reason' (1851, p. 255). There is only one way in which agnosticism can force the theist to deny that what he cannot compass in thought he may still believe to exist. And that is by passing, quite illegitimately, 'from criticism to dogmatism, a dogmatism resting its claim to dictation on a complete ignorance of the matter . . . it dictates' (Mansel, 1851, p. 255). An example of such an 'illegitimate passage' would be Feuerbach's theology, which in prying loose 'the essence of Christianity' from a mummified mythology tries to shackle it to man instead.

Apart from critiques by F. D. Maurice and J. S. Mill, the most sustained Victorian attack upon Mansel's thesis comes in Part I of *First Principles*, 'The Unknowable', the major theological contribution of Mansel's most influential disciple, Herbert Spencer. Against Mansel Spencer argues that the Absolute is more than a mere negation. For if the Absolute were merely an unknowable negation, how could we ever know it is unknowable? There is no reconciling our knowledge of the truth of this doctrine with the general condition which exists if it is true. In order to show how the Absolute escapes from conceptual thought but not from consciousness in general, Spencer develops his theory of 'symbolic conceptions'. To conceive of scientific and religious truth at all, we must use either a metonymy, a word that allows the more or less randomly chosen part to stand for the whole (the thunder for God), or else an abstract but univocal sign, a notation like π or x, 'utterly without resemblance' to its referent (Spencer, 1880, p. 94). Ultimate ideas of God, space, and time have to deal with entities whose attributes are too vast or numerous to be united in a single thought. 'We must either drop in thought part of their attributes, or else not think of them at all' (1880, p. 22).

Though Spencer's God is present to the human mind, not as a mere negation but as a kind of nebula out of which the solid nucleus of all later thought is formed, Spencer brings science and religion together only by demoting their symbols to the status of mere extrinsic signs. 'Utterly without resemblance to that for which it stands', the theological sign is condemned to the eternal silence of Milton's 'nethermost Abyss', the realms of 'Chaos and ancient Night' (*Paradise Lost*, II, 969–70). Spencer's 'altars to the unknown and unknowable God' (1880, p. 36) bear a disturbing resemblance to Schelling's altar. The gods of both thinkers are worshipped in an agnostic void, in that abyss of night where in Hegel's acid phrase 'all cows are black'.

2 *Agnostic Semioticians:*
Carlyle and Sir William Hamilton

The transformation of old-style natural theology like Paley's into the post-Kantian subject found in most Victorian poets and essayists can be dated from the publication in October 1829 of Sir William Hamilton's *Edinburgh Review* essay on Victor Cousin's *Course of Philosophy*. Instead of listing and elucidating the reasons we have for believing that God is both absolute and infinite, Hamilton argues, like Kant, that God *cannot* be an object of knowledge. Rational inquiry into the grounds for saying things about God usually assumes that God is knowable and known. Hamilton identifies such inquiry with Cousin and Schelling. As in the emanative pantheism of Plotinus, God is the generative principle of Cousin's whole system. Such a God is knowable, and is conceived by means of difference, plurality, and relation. A more immediate and mystic form of pantheism can be found in Schelling, whose God, though knowable, is not directly conceivable. Because Schelling's Absolute possesses contradictory qualities, Hamilton praises Schelling for his 'negative merit' in 'having clearly exposed the absurdity' of the view that God as an object of rational inquiry is ever really conceivable (1829, p. 208). The fullest exposition of this view prior to Hamilton is Kant's teaching that God is not an object of knowledge, but a mere regulative principle. Hamilton, however, goes one step beyond Kant. Any attempt to understand God, he argues, generates antinomies that are intrinsically unresolvable. A philosophy of religion must operate from – and demonstrate – the proposition that there is a way God is. He must be either absolute or infinite, for example. But to say He is both absolute and infinite is like saying matter is at once indivisible and endlessly divisible (1861, vol. 2, pp. 372–3). Only a fool or an idolator would say that the subject of such contradictory predicates is truly knowable or known.

The consequences for language of Hamilton's paradoxes are explored most imaginatively by Carlyle, who would surely be familiar with them, having published his own *Signs of the Times* just four months before Hamilton's essay on Cousin appeared in the same journal, the *Edinburgh Review*. The pathos of trying to name a God who is neither nameable nor known is most acute in Carlyle's chapter, 'Symbols', in *Sartor Resartus* (1833–4). If God is not a member of a class and if we can never say exactly what He is, all symbols of God would seem to be mere extrinsic signs. To raise an altar to Silence and Secrecy, as Teufelsdröckh exhorts (Carlyle, 1901, vol. 1, p. 174), is to hypostatize the void. Is the worship of such Silence and Secrecy not that 'intrepid' identification of 'God ... with zero' for which Hamilton condemns Schelling? Carlyle's professor lauds 'the benignant efficacies of Concealment'. Concealment may be benign, but how can it be useful? What Hamilton's God is to Hamilton's attempt to philosophize about God, silence is to thought and secrecy is to virtue. Carlyle tries to vindicate such oxymorons by assimilating the wisdom of silence to the virtue of shame in ethics and of humility and holiness in religion. But if the intuition of the invisible and the unspeakable is the product of an arbitrary abstraction, how does it differ from the 'self-delusive imagination' Hamilton derides in Schelling? To reach the unspeakable by subtracting speech, we 'annihilate the object, and we annihilate the subject, of consciousness. But what remains? – Nothing,' Hamilton concludes. 'We baptize [the zero] with the name of Absolute, and imagine that we contemplate absolute existence, when we only speculate absolute privation' (1829, p. 208).

We may speak, like Teufelsdröckh, of the uniqueness of the Peasants' symbol of the clouted Shoe or of the Wallet-and-staff chosen as a symbol by the Netherland Beggars. But the idiosyncrasy is precisely what these symbols share with other idiosyncratic things: it is not what makes them unique. A symbol that promises to reveal the whole truth is not what it purports to be. If it were not a lucid veil, an oxymoronic revelation through concealment, then the symbol would be that whole truth itself and not a mere symbol. To remove the concealment would destroy the very idea of a symbol. Teufelsdröckh finds himself 'everywhere . . . encompassed with Symbols'. But if everything is a symbol, then nothing is a symbol. There is only a network of symbolic relations, with no god-term at the centre in which all the satellite signs can be grounded. To avoid this subversive conclusion, which threatens to turn Carlyle into a Victorian Derrida, a second narrower definition of symbol is proposed. A symbol proper advertises itself as a symbol. As a 'visible record of invisible things', it gestures toward some referent. But does every symbol, in the narrower sense, including the Cross, do nothing more than gesture? Carlyle's conclusion is thoroughly agnostic. 'Nay the highest ensign that men ever met and embraced under, the Cross itself, had no meaning save an accidental extrinsic one' (1901, vol. 1, p. 178). In providing the comfort of a limit, not even the Cross can begin to contain the infinity that breaks through and erodes it.

If the Cross blurs rather than defines the nature of what it labels, is there any such thing as an intrinsic symbol? Carlyle seems to think that any symbol that is already solidly anchored in a referent is merely extrinsic. Any other anchor would have served as well. Only when a symbol floats free of any ground can it be made truly intrinsic through some unforeseen use of it in a great work of art or in the life of a great man, who makes his deeds symbolic by anchoring them in some undiscovered ground. In works of art and in heroic lives Carlyle's professor finds examples of the truly intrinsic. But what is truly intrinsic cannot be analysed. Only extrinsic symbols can be analysed, and they tend to trivialize their subjects. To the degree that symbols are intrinsic, they cease to be symbols: they become the thing-in-itself. And to the degree that they are symbols, they cease to be intrinsic. The fatal rift between the unnameable subject and its properties begins to reappear.

'Like Ixion, we embrace a cloud for a divinity' (Hamilton, 1829, p. 221). In the self-sufficient pedantry of our science, we conspire to shut up an unknowable God in signs which cancel each other out. Carlyle comes closest to Hamilton's disturbing insight in 'Natural Supernaturalism', where the more significant the experiences become, the more the unsayable aspect seems to dominate. The play on 'stupid', 'stupor', and 'the Stupendous' is Teufelsdröckh's way of suggesting that, instead of producing stupid indifference, the stupidity of what we say about the unsayable should induce in us the stupor of reverie and wonder, and through contemplation of our stupidities some renewed appreciation of the Stupendous. But to approach the Stupendous is like approaching the speed of light in Einstein's universe. It is not to have a vision of 'the star-domed City of God'. On the contrary, it is to be annihilated. For as Hamilton insists, we live within limits and boundaries. Any breaking down of symbols, and any exposure of their merely extrinsic status, is indistinguishable from death. Unmediated encounter with the divine is an encounter with Schelling's void. As Nietzsche saw, when he accused Carlyle of a constant passionate dishonesty toward himself, there is something almost comically precarious about the balance of Carlyle's psyche. If he is always running away from what he seems to be racing toward, it is because he is faced with knowledge that is both deeply desired and deeply terrifying. As agnostic semioticians who can neither know nor conceive of a God who is continually invading their boundaries and breaking down the comfort of their names and definitions, Hamilton and Carlyle must consign their subject to the limbo of Teufelsdröckh's 'signless Inane', a no man's land beyond tropes and signs altogether. It is no wonder Nietzsche thought Carlyle was an English atheist who made it a point of honour not to be one (Nietzsche, 1968, p. 75).

3 God Knowable and Unknowable: Tennyson and the Boundaries of Consciousness

The best glosses on Tennyson's exploration of the boundaries of consciousness are to be found in Kant's *Prolegomena to any Future Metaphysics* (1783), a treatise we know Tennyson owned.[1] The key passage is Kant's discourse on boundaries, where he insists that 'the setting of a boundary to the field of the understanding by something, which is otherwise unknown to it, is still a cognition'. A boundary itself 'is something positive', which 'reason only acquires by enlarging itself to this boundary, yet without attempting to pass it; because it there finds itself in the presence of an empty space, in which it can conceive forms of things, but not things themselves' (Kant, 1940, p. 877).

As the 'untravelled' world glimpsed through the arch of experience begins to stream away from Tennyson's Ulysses at alarming speed, the poet seems to be echoing one of the rare poetic passages in Kant's first *Critique*. The domain of 'pure understanding' is 'an island', Kant says:

> [an island] enclosed by nature itself within limits that can never be changed. It is the country of truth (a very attractive name), but surrounded by a wide and stormy ocean, the true home of illusion, where many a fog bank and ice that soon melts away tempt us to believe in new lands, while constantly deceiving the adventurous mariner with vain hopes, and involving him in adventures which he can never leave, and yet can never bring to an end.   (1881, p. 205)

Tennyson may also be echoing this well-known passage in Kant when he writes of sea-voyaging, of passing 'from the great deep to, the great deep', in *In Memoriam* and *Idylls of the King*. By the time these later poems were written, Tennyson would certainly have read G. H. Lewes's *Biographical History of Philosophy*, whose 1845 edition also appears in Tennyson's library. Lewes comments at length on Kant's arresting metaphor on the empire of truth, surrounded by the stormy and illimitable sea (1845–6, vol. 4, p. 99). And Tennyson may have discussed this image with his friend F. D. Maurice, who in his *Moral and Metaphysical Philosophy* analyses Kant's maritime metaphor even more extensively than Lewes (1872, vol. 2, pp. 620–1).

Tennyson's sceptical awareness of the boundaries of consciousness and knowledge accounts for the exacting honesty of *In Memoriam*. No sooner has a pattern of transformation seemed to establish itself than the pattern is defied. We can best grasp the shifting, unpredictable quality by comparing *In Memoriam* with Keble's cycle of devotional poems, *The Christian Year*. Each poem in Keble's cycle celebrates a specific day in the liturgical calendar, and it comments on a biblical text. Though Tennyson makes some use of Keble's seasonal symbolism, the frame around one section of his poem has a way of becoming the subject of the next section. Often a boundary will become central by virtue of its very status as a boundary. In section xxxvi, for example, the reader has to adapt to a new use of geological language: the 'Aeonian hills' (xxxv, 11) and 'homeless sea' (xxxv, 9) are now enclosed by a 'mystic frame'

(XXXVI, 2). But no sooner has the reader made the supernatural frame central, than he finds he has overadapted. The geological space inside the frame is no longer the primary meaning, but it has not been completely displaced either. The roaring waves 'round the coral reef' (XXXVI, 16) are just as incessant as 'the moanings of the homeless sea' (XXXV, 9). The only difference is that the watching eyes can now perceive a design and final cause in nature. From section to section, the reader never knows what will be picture and what will be frame. But in the midst of death, these outsides that are also insides are very much alive. Their unpredictable switches are like life itself.

To move from section CIII to CIV of *In Memoriam* is like waking from a dream in which one knows and still does not know that the dream is unreal. The rebirth of love, the experience that is framed in section CIII by the mourner's 'vision of the dead' (CIII, 3), moves outside the frame to become the actual subject of section CIV, a lyric on 'the birth of Christ'. If Keble were writing section CIII, its typology would be explicit. The three maidens would signify faith, hope, and charity. The dove would prefigure the Holy Spirit. The veiled statue might be a statue of the first Noah, and 'the man we loved' (CIII, 41) his antitype, Christ. But this is not the way Tennyson writes. The elements of his dream do not all admit of evaluation within a single system of values, but look two ways at once. If they demonstrate Keble's theory that there is a divine order and only fools forget what it is, they also demonstrate Kant's theory that a transcendent order exists, but only fools think they can describe it as it is.

Though truths of pure reason and empirical truths can 'subsist together', they can do so, Kant insists, 'only at the boundary of all lawful use of reason' (1940, p. 873). In section CIII of *In Memoriam* there are two such boundaries. One boundary divides the first and second quatrains, separating the frame of the mourner's waking experience from the dream vision that it frames. The second, more important boundary both divides and joins the two 'deeps' in the pivotal phrase, 'From deep to deep' (l. 39).

> Until the forward-creeping tides
>   Began to foam, and we to draw
>   From deep to deep, to where we saw
> A great ship lift her shining sides.
>
> (*In Memoriam*, CIII, 37–40)

After the second use of 'deep', the original frame and picture space are reversed. The maritime frame around the first picture, a surreal portrait of landscapes, statues, and manorial halls, is now the subject framed. And in the second picture the scenes on land are now a mere frame. As Kant had argued, however, the meaning of each picture depends on the intersection of the two 'deeps' and on the boundary space they share. Though Hallam and the maidens appear in both pictures, we come to accept remarkable transformations as we slip from one frame to another. The maidens weep in both pictures, but for different reasons. At first they weep because the dreamer dies and must leave them. Later they weep because they feel betrayed. 'I did them wrong,' the dreamer says (l. 46). In the first picture Hallam is a mere veiled statue. In the second picture he is larger than life, and he alone has power to solace the maidens. Kant warns that in crossing the divide that separates 'deep' from 'deep' we may be deceived into thinking that melting ice and fog banks are solid lands (1881, p. 205). Thus the farther shore in Tennyson's second voyage is merely 'landlike' (CIII, 56), and presents only the illusion of a goal. Unlike the landscape of distant hills and hidden summits that frames the first picture, the destination of the 'great ship' with 'shining sides' is not a real shore but an insubstantial 'crimson cloud' (l. 55). Tennyson combines the comfort of boundaries with an experience of something boundless and unsayable.

In dramatizing the transition from one side of nature to the other in his early prize poem, 'Timbuctoo', Tennyson twice refers to the image of a bounded circle. And he uses the word 'bound' in two different senses.

> ... my Spirit
> With supernatural excitation bound
> Within me, and my mental eye grew large
> With such a vast circumference of thought
> That in my vanity I seemed to stand
> Upon the outward verge and bound alone
> Of full beatitude.
>
> ('Timbuctoo', ll. 88–94)

The first use of 'bound' as a verb dramatizes the poet's excitement, as his heart bounds toward the 'bound alone / Of full beatitude'. In the second use of 'bound', the proximity of the adjective 'alone' to 'bound' suggests that this circumference is the only boundary line dividing two modes of consciousness. On this line alone an observer may inhabit two worlds at once. 'Alone', however, might also hark back to the preceding line, where it can modify the infinitive 'to stand'. Is the speaker, in his 'vanity', claiming to be the sole occupant of the point of intersection between 'beatitude' and 'thought'? Such vanity might be justified by Kant, who boasts that 'the setting of a boundary to the field of the understanding [thought] by something, which is otherwise unknown to it [beatitude], is still a cognition' (1940, p. 877). In driving a knife between the noun 'bound' and the preposition 'of' ('bound alone / Of full beatitude'), Tennyson's isolation of 'alone' does more than merely *mention* the idea of an extreme and limiting case. It also *uses* the idea of aloneness, giving it grammatical force in the poem.

Even on the boundary line between 'beatitude' and 'thought', the poet can never, in Kant's phrase, 'cognise . . . the Unknown . . . as it is in itself' (1940, p. 874). Even in using the boundaries of East and West, of life and death, to defy boundaries in section XCV of *In Memoriam*, Tennyson's vision of 'boundless day' (l. 64) is only what Kant would call a form of 'symbolical anthropomorphism', which 'in fact concerns language only, and not the object itself' (1940, p. 873). We are astonished, I think, that poetry of such breathtaking power can refuse to convert itself into simple consolations and assurances elsewhere in the poem. But this is because the surrealism of the northern landscape movingly reveals the paradox involved in the poet's sceptical removal of himself from his own vision. His assimilation of the landscape to a looking-glass world of talking breezes (l. 60) is subtle but conclusive. And it allows Tennyson to avoid what Kant calls 'objective anthropomorphism' (1940, p. 874). Tennyson's reluctance to force or falsify his vision of 'boundless day' seems to me a profound moral achievement. But 'like all such achievements in great art', as John Bayley observes of Shakespeare, 'it makes absolutely no parade of its own moral nature' (1981, p. 183).

In section XLVI of *In Memoriam*, the tomb is the frame through which Tennyson views 'The eternal landscape of the past'. To pass from one side of the tomb to the other is to pass from love to Love, from a person we love to a God of Love. Switching the position of the picture and the frame helps explain the paradox of the preceding lyric, 'the second birth of Death' (XLV, 16). But how can death be just an interchange of frames and pictures, or a mere enlargement of margins? The arch in 'Ulysses' frames an 'untravelled world' that beckons from the future. But the tomb in *In Memoriam* frames a landscape that is said to be both 'eternal' and 'past'. How precisely is this possible?

> We ranging down this lower track,
>   The path we came by, thorn and flower,
>   Is shadowed by the growing hour,
> Lest life should fail in looking back.
>
> So be it: there no shade can last
>   In that deep dawn behind the tomb,
>   But clear from marge to marge shall bloom
> The eternal landscape of the past;
>
> A lifelong tract of time revealed;
>   The fruitful hours of still increase;
>   Days ordered in a wealthy peace,
> And those five years its richest field.
>
> O Love, thy province were not large,
>   A bounded field, nor stretching far;
>   Look also, Love, a brooding star,
> A rosy warmth from marge to marge.
>
>   (*In Memoriam*, XLVI)

Though 'the eternal landscape' does not properly belong 'to this lower track', it nevertheless borders its 'path' and supplements it, like Kant's concept of the *parergon*. The repetition of the phrase 'from marge to marge' (ll. 7, 16) never allows us to forget that the marginal supplement, the *parergon*, is in some ways the essence of the picture. Even in Tennyson's 'eternal landscape', the margins, though greatly enlarged, are not erased. In the last two lines the larger Love that originally framed the 'province' of human love is now the bounded space of a second picture. In this other picture what was outside is now inside. The flowers and boundaries are still present, but now time is 'fruitful' and the past itself is said to 'bloom'.

In replacing the narrow 'path' of the specious present with whole tracts of eternity, Tennyson is not asking us to think of eternity as a privileged moment outside of time. Eternity is rather the way in which the mourner's memories of 'fruitful hours' and 'ordered' days, 'A lifelong tract of time revealed', compose themselves in his mind into an ideal 'landscape'. Of course, the experience of such an ideal 'landscape' is an experience the reader of *In Memoriam* is always expecting to have but can never fully attain. And yet as we read the poem, we begin to achieve what Kant says is not strictly possible. By analogy with what we experience on 'this lower tract', we begin to experience what cannot otherwise be known 'In that deep dawn behind the tomb'.

Death can be called a 'second birth' only because the portal of 'that deep dawn' provides an ever-expanding frame around the mourner's landscape of the past. The expanding frame may be only an accessory or supplement. But as one critic says, such a boundary space or *parergon* 'is not incidental; it is connected to and co-operates in its inside operation from the outside' (Derrida, 1978, p. 63). By placing himself at the boundaries of consciousness, Tennyson, like Kant, is trying to construct categories for what cannot otherwise be categorized. '*"Definition"* (from *finis*, a limit end)', as Stephen Booth observes, 'denies the essence of what it labels: an experience of the fact of indefinition' (1983, p. 85). Only by trying to frame a continually expanding landscape of the past, glimpsed through the portals of the tomb, can a poet like Tennyson who is unable to bear very much reality begin to cope with his fears of indefinition and death.

Like the mystery of St Paul's 'unspeakable words', which are 'not lawful for a man to utter', the mystery of *In Memoriam* is an attempt to make luminous a vision beyond faith which, if intelligible at all, is likely to outlast most forms of communication. Tennyson gives us hints of the conditions of framed viewing under which such a vision might be communicated at 'the outward verge and bound' of human thought. But even when Tennyson knows that his destiny has a destination, defeat is still a condition of every effort to reach it. Because the 'one far-off divine event' is never reached, every approximation to an 'end' is also an epitaph, a memorial to what has eluded Tennyson and escaped his understanding. Words initiate and sustain discourse. But only some vision outside of words, some vision beyond the boundaries of consciousness which confronts finite understanding with the fact of infinity, can end it. 'Philosophy', says Wittgenstein in his *Tractatus* (1961, p. 49), 'must set limits to what cannot be thought by working outwards through what can be thought. It will signify what cannot be said, by presenting clearly what can be said.' Tennyson, like Kant, cannot translate the 'unthinkable' into ordinary language. Only in poetry can 'the unsayable' be said.

4 Clough's Agnostic Imagination: The Uses of Uncertainty

Some of Clough's theological uncertainty can be traced to his reading of David Friedrich Strauss and to his early admiration of Friedrich Schiller, whose philosophic prose and aphorisms Clough eagerly absorbed as a student at Oxford (Mulhauser, 1957, vol. 1, pp. 98, 182). Nor should we underestimate the influence of Clough's friend and Oxford tutor, W. G. Ward, who barely conceals his scorn for the sermons of Clough's Rugby mentor, Dr Thomas Arnold (Ward, 1841, pp. 298–364). As an historian, Dr Arnold overrates the historical evidences of Christianity. 'History by itself, if we knew it ten times better than we do,' Ward asserts, 'could prove little or nothing' (1841, p. 318). Dr Arnold had argued that we should trust our private judgement in interpreting scripture, just as we accept it in reading Thucydides and Aristotle. But Ward exposes the folly of Arnold's assumption by drawing out hidden inferences and consequences. Arnold wrongly assumes that each interpreter is as spiritual as Christ or as St Paul. Playing Blougram to Arnold's Gigadibs, Ward displays a deeply sceptical habit of mind designed to remove any middle ground between his own Tractarian brand of Christianity and total unbelief. Clough, it seems to me, is also greatly indebted to the Carlyle who wrote 'Natural Supernaturalism'. Both writers inhabit worlds filled with unnameable facts. These worlds abound in ambiguities and fearful mysteries, where knowledge remains tentative and uncertain.

The uses of uncertainty are explored in one of Clough's most daring though familiar poems, 'Qui Laborat, Orat', which is a prayer to end prayer in the familiar sense. By substituting a religion of work for a religion of silence, Clough prays that future invocations of God will not be necessary. The best gloss on this redefinition is a comment in one of Clough's Oxford notebooks which identifies the new centrifugal force of positivism with a religion of work in which God equals zero, and the new centripetal force of scepticism with a religion of silence in which the world contracts to nothing (Bodleian MS. Eng. poet d. 133, folio 79). Clough's redefinition of prayer begins in the second quatrain, where the invoked 'Source of all our light and life', the apparent subject of the opening sentence, is turned unexpectedly from a grammatical subject into a grammatical object, in apposition to 'thy presence' (l. 6). Already Clough is shifting attention from an unknowable God to a worshipper in whose 'mortal moral strife' (l. 3) the real nature of God is revealed.

> O only Source of all our light and life . . .
>
> Mine inmost soul, before Thee inly brought,
>   Thy presence owns ineffable, divine;
> Chastised each rebel self-encentered thought,
>   My will adoreth Thine.
>
> ('Qui Laborat, Orat', ll. 1, 5–8)

In line 7 Clough could be using elliptical grammar ('my will having chastised') or he could, more logically, be using a nominative absolute construction. By detaching the line grammatically from the rest of the sentence and by sundering the participle 'having been chastised' from the noun it modifies, a nominative absolute would more effectively isolate and contain 'each rebel' and 'self-encentered thought' and it would also be more indeterminate in meaning than a mere ellipsis. It would allow either God or the soul to be the agent of chastisement.

Under the disguise of prayer, Clough seems actually to be telling God what to do by replacing the auxiliary verb of prophecy or prediction with the verb of command. 'Thou shalt unnamed forgive,' Clough decrees, and Thou 'shalt make . . . work be prayer' (ll. 17–20). The negatives also have unusual force: 'O not unowned, Thou shalt unnamed forgive' (l. 17). To affirm that God is 'not unowned' is to make a desperately minimal affirmation. And if God is 'unnamed', is it because He is not strictly nameable? Clough may be recalling Sir William Hamilton's philosophy of the unconditioned or Carlyle's theory of intrinsic signs. He may also have encountered a similar idea in James Douglas's book, *Errors Regarding Religion*, which Clough consulted when doing research on Buddhist and Hindu thought for his Newdigate Prize entry, 'Salsette and Elephanta'. Douglas vigorously defends the thesis that any attempt to know God as He is, or to be at one with God, is a religious heresy. If 'the only atonement we have need of is, an At-one-ment, or a mode of becoming one with the divine essence,' Douglas asserts, then there can be 'no atonement, in the Christian sense of the term', which always requires some divide of ignorance or sin to be crossed (1830, pp. 158–9). Douglas's preference for Buddhist transcendence to any form of Hindu idolatry may have predisposed Clough to prefer a religion of silence to any religion that tries to know God as well as God knows himself. If God is unnameable, and should not even be named the unnamed, then any prayer to such a God is a prayer that our understanding of God be made less idolatrous. Such a prayer fittingly culminates in Clough's hope that his persuasive re-definition of prayer as work will be acceptable in the sight of an unknowable God.

Clough's predilection for contradiction and uncertainty culminates in his astonishing 'Hymnos Ahymnos', 'A hymn, yet not a hymn'. Depending on the resolution of the indeterminate syntax, the opening refrain could proclaim either an orthodox belief in the ark of the covenant or a Feuerbachian faith in the divinity of man.

> O thou whose image in the shrine
> Of human spirits dwells divine –
>
>   ('Hymnos Ahymnos', ll. 1–2)

Does 'divine' modify 'human spirits' or 'thou'? Whether Clough is thinking of ancient Israel or of Feuerabach, in either case once God is turned into an object of philosophic reflection He disappears behind the mind's antinomies. Having been cleansed of idols by the critical philosophies of Hamilton and Kant, the understanding of the religious philosopher can operate only on the 'blank and void of empty mind' (l. 6), as totally devoid of sensory content as Kant's Ideas of the Pure Reason.

All confident definitions of God have a way of dissolving in Clough's hand. '"The light is here", "behold the way", / "The voice was thus", and "thus the word"' (ll. 12–13). The gesturing adverbs are too frantic and directionless to be trusted. We may be sure that whatever definition Clough intends, God himself has a different definition in mind. Even Clough's invocation of God in the second refrain can mean opposite things.

> O thou that in our bosoms' shrine
> Dost dwell, because unknown, divine!
>
> ('Hymnos Ahymnos', ll. 9–10)

Does the clause 'because unknown' modify the verb 'Dost dwell'? Or does it modify 'O thou'? If the former, the divinity of God depends on His unconsciously dwelling in 'our bosoms' shrine'. Though He may live in the human mind, it is 'the essence of Christianity', according to Feuerbach, that our knowledge of this truth should be subliminal or repressed. But if the clause 'because unknown' modifies 'O thou', then Clough is repeating Hamilton's argument that God is divine because unknowable. The only way an unknowable God can be known is to be brought to life in the heart and mind of His believers, as Ward and Mansel both argue.

Clough's third refrain is the most Hamiltonian and agnostic. Now God's divinity is equated with His mystery, or at least with His unintelligibility and lack of definition.

> O thou, in that mysterious shrine
> Enthroned, as we must say, divine!
>
> ('Hymnos Ahymnos', ll. 17–18)

God exists, not as a definable formula, but as a presence experienced in the soul and heart. Though there is ancient precedent for such rhetorical practice in the Hebrew names for God, the language of tautology is also used to render the thwarting of the intellect:

> Enough that in our soul and heart
> Thou, whatsoe'er thou may'st be, art.
>
> ('Hymnos Ahymnos', ll. 23–4)

Another alternative is developed in the last six lines. God can at least be worshipped as the god of moral theology, or as the Feuerbachian and Straussian god. If God is present in man, then God's death does not really matter. Clough's uncertainties extend even to the syntax of the final line: 'I will not ask to feel thou art' (l. 40). Is he 'asking' in the sense of petitioning or praying, or in the sense of seeking rational answers? In the first case, he will not seek to prove God's existence by feeling He exists. In the second case, in an exact reversal of the first use of 'ask', he will not search for rational proofs.

Because Clough refuses to commit himself, his hymn dramatizes the painful struggle of the mind to come to terms with a full consciousness of God – and thus to limit and define that knowledge, to hold it in check. A full consciousness of anything escapes definition. Like deity itself, it is illimitable. Therefore to be conscious of God at all Clough must keep marking limits to an ever-widening range of possibilities. The comfort of seeking and finding prematurely stable ideas about God is far removed from what actually happens to us when we read Clough's poetry. The satisfactions and frustrations of reading Clough are ultimately the pains and pleasures of consciousness itself. Evasions and lies give way to the fascination of what can and cannot be known about a subject.

The uncertainties of Clough's theological verse also flash light into the twists and turns of thought in poems like *Amours de Voyage* and *Dipsychus*. To pass from divine to human love in *Dipsychus*, for example, may be to set up an idol. Love, the Miltonic 'large repose / Restorative' (x, 30–1), should straddle the boundary between the known and unknowable, as the Miltonic phrase itself, framing the noun 'repose' between two adjectives, straddles successive lines. But, as we know from Clough's religious verse, the accomplished miracle of such a crossing is easier to achieve in poetry than life. In *Amours de Voyage* the acutely heightened consciousness of Claude keeps postponing closure by refusing to decide anything. Though uncertainty in a heightened consciousness is the great enemy of closure and death, in another sense it is closely allied to death. In seeking to expand indefinitely, consciousness becomes a synonym for the death of Claude's mind as it mystically fuses, like Nebuchadnezzar's, with oxen and grass (III, x, 212–13). As in Clough's religious verse, consciousness spreads like a disease. Claude, who is notoriously unmethodical in tracking Mary down, possesses, not the purposiveness of a successful lover, but the negative capability that Keats associates with the dramatic art of Shakespeare. As his consciousness keeps exposing him to every fresh sensation, breaking down then multiplying resolve, Claude even imagines outcomes for events that have not yet happened, and will probably never happen.

When Claude expands the end of a railway journey into the end of time and the intrusion upon him of some eternal tie (*Amours de Voyage*, III, vi, 111–12), we sense the peculiar force with which a half-dreaded, half-desired knowledge thrusts itself upon his mind. Like Carlyle in 'Natural Supernaturalism', Clough keeps running away from what he seems to be running toward. He even tries to run away from his knowledge that he is running away. As a poet of uncertainty, Clough reminds us that to answer questions is always to delimit arbitrarily a whole *terra incognita* of unknowables. An obsessive curiosity about what lies behind the veil is always matched by a fear of knowing too much. Like Carlyle's self-concealing rhetoric, with its endless inventories and appositions, the expansive, circling hexameters of *Amours de Voyage* roll over and over each other like huge ocean waves, but without actually seeming to move anywhere or to advance. They dramatize the anxiety of someone who is conscious of more than he can allow himself to know. The conflict is not between truth and deception. Both Clough and Carlyle pose other, more difficult choices. Some enigmas, they seem to be saying, must not be questioned too closely. As semioticians, we should not try to decipher or inscribe more of the signless inane than human kind can bear.

5 Agnostic Theories of the Word: Arnold's Deconstruction

An agnostic semiotician preserves God's priority by refusing to have Him named. His 'unknowable God' is a stable signifier, but totally devoid of any defining content. Like Browning's Prior, the agnostic starts with a concept so primary that there is no way to name it without betraying its primacy: 'Man's soul, and it's a fire, smoke ... no, it's not ... / It's ... well, what matters talking, it's the soul!' ('Fra Lippo Lippi', ll. 184–7). If God or the soul is not to remain just an empty space in the language, whatever is betrayed by words and hence left out, the sceptic may have to focus on some empty signifier like Matthew Arnold's 'stream of tendency' or his 'transcendence of the lower by the higher self', until a mere cipher-phrase or abstract concept begins to fill without ambiguity the holes that would otherwise be left gaping in his text.

Arnold's agnosticism may not derive directly from Mansel or
Spencer. It may have originated in the doctrine of learned ignorance
advocated by Arnold's seventeenth-century hero, Joseph Glanvill.
But it seems to have been reinforced by a study of one of Mansel's
and Spencer's chief nineteenth-century sources. In one of the
reading-lists found in his early diaries, Arnold makes mention of
Victor Cousin's lectures on modern philosophy (Allott, 1959, pp.
259–60). As I have already argued, Victorian agnosticism can be
said to begin with Sir William Hamilton's seminal review essay of
Cousin's course of philosophy, published in the *Edinburgh Review* in
October, 1829. Taking issue with Cousin's theory that God is com-
prehensible, Hamilton argues that 'the unconditioned is incognis-
able and inconceivable' (1829, p. 200). Drawing upon the writings
of the Indologian H. T. Colebrook, however, Cousin himself,
when expounding the inconceivability of the Hindu understanding
of God, anticipates Hamilton's own agnosticism. To resemble God,
Cousin explains, the yogi must 'reduce himself to pure being, by
the abolition of all thought' (1852, vol. 1, p. 397). The 'incognis-
able' God of Kantian thinkers like Hamilton and Mansel was criti-
cized by contemporaries like W. H. Smith for being too Asiatic, for
being 'one with the Brahm of Indian theology' (1859, p. 53). But the
sublime transcendence of the Hindu God apparently appealed to
Arnold, who was already familiar with the grandeur of that concept
from his study of Victor Cousin, from his knowledge of the
theology of the *Bhagavad Gita* (Allott, 1959, pp. 262–3), and, as
Professor S. Nagarajan has shown (1960, p. 341), from an aware-
ness of the striking affinities between the Vedantic apology for art
and his own critical ideal of disinterested objectivity.

Arnold's persuasive redefinition of God retains the venerable
emotive meaning of the word but changes its descriptive meaning.
The habit of using the word 'God' to signify ethical ideas takes pos-
session of Arnold's mind long before he starts to search in his theo-
logical prose for an abstract formula that will give peace to his soul
without insulting his intelligence. But by a painful paradox,
Arnold's need for belief increases as his capacity for containing God
in some concrete sign diminishes. In Arnold's struggle with
language, as in his struggle for religious faith, there is revealed the
loneliness of the quester who seeks univocal discourse with God, or
at least the grace of analogical understanding, but who is left in the

end with only blank counters and extrinsic signs. Arnold's plight is that of his own Stagirius, the fourth-century counterpart of Mansel and Spencer, who empties his language finally of all analogies and symbols, in order to keep his words open to some higher truth. The allegorist's tendency to assimilate to his own deductive arrangements a given metaphorical structure or mythology, like that of the Bible, is a recurrent feature of Arnold's poetry. In 'The Buried Life' and 'Rugby Chapel', for example, the urge to paraphrase his fictions, to pass prematurely from metaphor to exegesis, illuminates the *pons asinorum* of the poet who, unable profitably to avail himself of the ideas current at the time, devotes his energy to an exposure of the fictive structure of the prevailing dogmas and to the construction of a new set of doctrines. So anxious is Arnold in 'The Buried Life' to give his controlling sign – the 'unregarded river of our life' (l. 39) – an unambiguous meaning, that he keeps labouring this meaning, even after he has made it tediously transparent to every reader. From genuine insight Arnold passes into his implausible theory of why fate ordained that man should be unconscious of his buried life. The denunciation of man as a 'frivolous' child (l. 31), who would betray his true identity if it were once revealed to him, is hectoring and unpleasant. The tone betrays the anxiety of the discursive thinker to assimilate the metaphors of poetry to an inferior group of abstract arguments and theories. If Arnold and his reader finally arrive at salvation in 'The Buried Life', it is not through enunciating or embracing a doctrine of the hidden life. It is rather through experiencing a recovered wholeness by passing with Arnold into a world of Wordsworthian mountain-gods and seas, where a sense of healing powers in nature can both include and resolve complexity.

> And an unwonted calm pervades his breast.
> And then he thinks he knows
> The hills where his life rose,
> And the sea where it goes.
>   ('The Buried Life', ll. 95–8)

Combined with the muted volley of Arnold's concluding rhymes, the diminution of the metre from lines of twelve and ten syllables to three spondaically weighted trimeters has the effect of securing the conclusiveness of the triads, of making their resonant, almost sing-song descent at once stable and mysterious, fated but enigmatic, too. A poet more confident of his resources would have attached himself more closely to the river throughout. Instead of continuously paralleling metaphorical with conceptual language, he would have let his poem run 'a course of lucky events', as Frost says (1968, p. 18), trusting the sufficiency of what he finds.

For a more resourceful combining of a stable signifier with an expanded narrative commentary, we may turn to Arnold's famous elegy for his father, 'Rugby Chapel'. All exegesis, like allegory, tries to supply conceptual equivalents for the poet's fictions. But in doing so, it runs the danger of using abstract symbols which impoverish the fullness of these fictions. When Arnold in 'Rugby Chapel' abdicates imaginative vision for elaborate critical commentary on his father's steadfast purpose, he seems to be taking just such risks. The surmise that Dr Arnold, even in death, is still practising his moral callisthenics is meant to affirm a ritual link with deity, like the 'practised . . . strength' (l. 42) of Pindar's athletes. But the muscular theology of a Rabbi Ben Ezra leaves Arnold uneasy. He is not content to let his father bounce from his moral gymnasium into the silence of eternity. He wants that silence to speak, not just through the 'murmur' of a single signifier like the hidden river in 'The Buried Life', but through the voice of several signifiers. Arnold's original figure of the ocean wave, which 'swelled / Foamed for a moment', then is 'gone' (ll. 70–1), generates two much fuller narratives of life. In the first of these journeys, a mountain pilgrimage toward death, each traveller, in saving only himself, perishes alone. In the second journey, a desert pilgrimage, a dispirited band is exhorted to press the journey homeward like the children of Israel in Exodus. A poet who fully trusted his signifier would have told the stories of the two journeys, then let the reader guess the application of the second narrative to Arnold's father. On the other hand, an allegorical poet who translated his fictions directly into theory or concept would have told the story of the secular journey toward death, then added the story of the spiritual journey toward God by way of explicit commentary on the first narrative. But Arnold, neither a symbolic poet nor an allegorist, mixes narrative and gloss throughout. And in the figure of the 'beacons of hope' (l. 192) and the 'angels' (l. 190) he introduces still another signifier, a trope which has more to do with rugged prowess and athletic vigour. Though the figure of a military leader, marshalling his troops, may in some sense belong to the story of Moses in Exodus, the strength of a Miltonic 'angel', 'radiant with ardour divine' (l. 191), normally excludes the militancy of Arnold's final figure. An angel may be presented as a stern, a generous, or even an affable figure, but not as a celestial Duke of Wellington, as a champion of warring Christianity.

The journey figures of 'Rugby Chapel' are far less stable than the hidden river of 'The Buried Life'. But their very instability allows Arnold to glide, so to speak, from genre to genre, from allegorical pilgrimage to eulogy, from narrative to homily, refining his ideas as he goes. The poet of 'Dover Beach' and of 'Stanzas from the Grande Chartreuse' cannot with propriety write as a Victorian St Augustine. He cannot present life as an unambiguous spiritual pilgrimage, leading straight from the rocks of the wilderness to the City of God. But neither, in an elegy for his father, a leader in the Victorian Broad-Church movement, can he omit religion altogether. Arnold solves the problem, not by comparing his father directly with Moses, but by using the Mosaic 'servants of God' (l. 162) as a more capacious, less stable symbol. Signifying an heroic ideal, both biblical and secular, these 'servants' include Arnold's own prophets of culture, who recognize like Arnold himself in 'The Function of Criticism' that the 'promised land . . . will not be ours to enter . . . but to have desired to enter it, to have saluted it from afar, is already, perhaps, the best distinction among contemporaries; it will certainly be the best title to esteem with posterity' (1960–77 (1962), vol. 3, p. 285). If Arnold admires everything about Catholicism except its Christianity, he admires everything about biblical typology except its doctrinal content. Moses is no longer a type of Christ, as he is for Browning in 'One Word More' and in the Prologue to *Asolando*. He is now a type of Dr Thomas Arnold and his agnostic son, who uses the biblical type to prefigure a new religion of culture and man. Instead of focusing on an empty signifier, the conventional journey of life, then filling that cipher with a preconceived content, Arnold turns the journey into several rich but shifting symbols. These full, less stable, more provisional signs enable Arnold to discover that the City of God (l. 208) is not just some goal at the end of time. The City is the fullness of community, secular as well as biblical, as it is for Comte and Strauss, and it exists in the depths of time as a whole.

If Arnold is allowed to redefine the City of God or the Promised Land as a useful fiction, then he has no difficulty using concrete, intelligible language to describe it. Without such a fiction, human inquiry may have no goal. But the fiction may also subvert disinterested inquiry, because it can mean anything and everything Arnold wants it to mean. On the other hand, if the City of God is retained as Arnold's phrase for the indescribable ground or goal, it will stand for whatever is the case, whether or not anyone can understand or validate it. Though too empty of content to qualify as a metaphor, it will at least restore disinterested inquiry to Arnold's search. But what trope or fiction could ever encompass such an idea? An indescribable idea seems indistinguishable from the fictions it was designed to replace.

As a disciple of Herder, who insists that poetic discourse is reducible without residue to its words, Arnold is committed to a theory of fictions which greatly enriches the language of his essays and the appeal of Arnold's own criticism. But discourse which is only about its own fictions also subverts the authority Arnold wants to confer on the poet and the critic. As a successor of Joseph Glanvill, it is as if Arnold wanted to be a Cambridge Platonist and an agnostic both at once. For as Ruth apRoberts has shown, Glanvill is a kind of seventeenth-century Hamilton or Mansel:

> Glanvill has a strong sense of the limitations of reason. 'The knowledge I teach,' he says in his preface, 'is ignorance,' and he anatomizes the limits and untrustworthiness of our senses and intellects to demonstrate the absurdity of the dogmatists, anticipating Arnold's attacks on Arnold's own dogmatists and their 'insane license of affirmation.' ... Twentieth-century science has rediscovered the 'vanity of dogmatizing'; we know that the best we can manage are hypotheses, or 'convenient supposals,' as Glanvill calls them (apRoberts, 1983, pp. 10–11).

If Glanvill is an agnostic, however, he is agnostic in the tradition of Nicholas of Cusa. His Platonism is not to be confused with the nominalism of Vico and Herder. As a Cambridge Platonist, Glanvill still grounds his words for God in an unknowable goal or end that continues to function as the object of disinterested inquiry.

Arnold's problem is that, when his words are grounded, like

Glanvill's or Mansel's, they become thin and attenuated. When they become concrete and metaphoric, like Vico's or Herder's, they cease to be grounded. An authoritative grounded language is too impoverished to appeal. And an ungrounded language, fully performative and Viconian, lacks the authority Arnold wants to confer on the rich metaphorical language of his poets. Who can really give allegiance to an ungrounded fiction? If God is a supreme fiction, it is in our interest to know it? Despite recent attempts to rehabilitate Arnold as an original religious thinker, it seems to me that F. H. Bradley is not merely being uncivil, just more articulate than most commentators, when he takes Arnold to task for his inconsistencies (1876, pp. 316–19). Arnold is by turns a Platonic realist and a Viconian nominalist, and in both roles he keeps subverting the truths he wants to affirm. According to Vico and Herder, truth is a property of the mind's fictions. But if one of these fictions is the world we create, then a poem that is only a self-contained fiction is not fully true, because it fails to ground itself in the largest fiction. Arnold proves quite incapable of reconciling Vico's performative theory of language and truth with a constative theory like Glanvill's or Hamilton's. The theory of workable fictions, inherited from Herder and Vico, controverts its own pragmatism by confidently concluding that the beneficial consequence of a consensus is the *a priori* truth about truth. Conversely, Arnold's Brahmanic pronouncements about the truth of an ultimate goal or ground, a City of God which he embraces as a disinterested alternative to a merely partisan consensus about what qualifies as a useful fiction, is equally subversive of its own authority. For such a ground cannot be described. Like the Brahm of Indian thought or the God of agnostic theology, it must be accepted in the end as a mere regulative fiction in Kant's sense.

6 Feuerbach and Thomson: The Rending of the Veil

Though I have no evidence that James Thomson was directly influenced by Feuerbach's *The Essence of Christianity*, his vision of Melencolia in *The City of Dreadful Night* dramatizes as powerfully as any Victorian poem Feuerbach's teaching that theology is veiled anthropology, a repressed knowledge that man is divine or, more precisely, that god is man in alienation from himself. As Feuerbach says, 'that which in religion is the predicate', the new theology must now proclaim 'the subject, and that which in religion is a subject we must make a predicate, thus inverting the oracles of religion' (1841, p. 60). When we say God suffers, what is truly divine is the human predicate 'suffering', not the subject 'God'. The truth that theology has traditionally suppressed is the truth that 'he who suffers for others, who lays down his life for them, acts divinely, is a god to men' (1841, p. 60). Betraying a fear that there may be nothing behind the lifeless rind of nature for man to venerate, Thomson dramatizes the teaching of Feuerbach, also expounded by F. H. Bradley and Hegel, that in seeming to worship images of sacramental or daemonic nature, the poet is really worshipping the spirit in himself.

As the veils are drawn aside, Thomson discovers in Melencolia the departed spirit, brooding and introspective, of man, to whom he chants a great paean, at once destructive of the older theology and triumphantly sublime. Knowing its own worth, the mind knows the rapture of its freedom, happy and blessed in a new religion that allows man to live 'the life of genius', as Feuerbach says, keeping 'holiday' and 'theoretic festivals' (1841, pp. 5, 98). Like Keats's long-suffering Moneta in *The Fall of Hyperion*, Thomson's Melencolia concentrates in her gaze the transience of experience and the enduring truths of science and art. Though she seems to take upon herself the sorrows of the world, she has also experienced more of the boredom and the horror than Keats's Moneta.

Like Dürer's unforgettable engraving of Melencolia, Thomson's 'stupendous, superhuman ... bronze colossus' (ll. 1044–5) is one of those rare works of art which appeal immediately to every observer, and yet is clearly in its sombre Miltonic majesty a masterpiece of the highest order. The vision of Melencolia elevates the latent and still repressed knowledge of the mind's powers, which in primitive eastern art, according to Hegel, is merely a source of the grotesque or bizarre, into a self-conscious, introspective knowledge, the peculiar achievement of sublime Romantic art (Hegel, 1970, pp. 110–27). The difference between a repressed and a self-conscious knowledge of the mind's own powers is not only the difference between Hegel's primitive symbolical and culminating Romantic forms of art. It is also the gulf dividing introspective man from the rest of the animate creation. In representing the sad divinity of man, an attribute formerly repressed in consciousness but now exalted as the only refuge from atheism, the sublime immensity of Thomson's Melencolia is quite literally a boundlessness, a surpassing of measurable extension. As suffering, brooding mind, man's soul attains to an intensity of self-knowledge that is so boundless in its significance, so sublime in its value, that not even the immensity of nature's grandest objects can begin to measure it.

Denying the Creator–God in the name of self-activity, without which man is not truly human, Thomson wants to invert the oracles of religion by celebrating a repressed knowledge of man's own divinity. Such liberation of the self may end in 'Fichte's clever cut at God himself' ('Bishop Blougram's Apology', l. 744). But it also remains the most important goal of Browning's effort to gothicize despair in the grisly pilgrimage of Childe Roland, as it is of Thomson's difficult struggle to envisage Melencolia. By being in his own nightmare, grotesque and horrific as it is, Thomson makes it sublime. Because he acquires the double aspect of Melencolia, who retains a dual identity as muse and destroyer like Keats's Melancholy and Moneta, Thomson can share in the goddess's sublimity and be 'himself', in Pope's words, the 'great Sublime he draws' ('An Essay in Criticism', III, 680). In her struggle toward a vision that would comprehend all intellection, all suffering and all joy, Melencolia embodies the mind's repressed knowledge of its own supremacy. Vindicating Hegel's teaching that there is nothing behind the veil which is not already in front of it, Melencolia is an image of the new Feuerbachian god. She is the divine self-consciousness Thomson has been seeking.

7 Hopkins and Scotus: Univocal and Equivocal Signs

Like most devotional poets, Hopkins tries to avoid two opposed tendencies: the agnostic Hamiltonian focus on stable but wholly extrinsic signs which can merely gesture in the direction of an inconceivable God, and the idolatrous Feuerbachian focus on a full creation, but on a creation which substitutes anthropology for theology by replacing the Word of God with the words of man. The agnostic pull in some of Hopkins' poetry of despair, though largely

a predilection of his mind and temperament, is inadvertently re-
inforced by the study of Duns Scotus, Hopkins' favourite theo-
logian. Why should the analogical mirrors that glisten in 'God's
Grandeur', and that 'flame out, like shining from shook foil' in
many of Hopkins' sacramental lyrics, be of no avail in 'Nondum'?
Creation gapes in this poem as an immense and 'empty hall' (l. 10),
as an ancestral ruin, the estate of some indifferent host who has
abandoned hearth and home. All Hopkins can do is await a miracle,
a restoration of the hierarchical character of the first creation, which
will allow him to track the 'abysses infinite' (l. 25), recovering the
clue to God's 'dread and vacant maze' (l. 30). Like Duns Scotus,
Hopkins aspires to a knowledge of God that is more than analogical.
But, paradoxically, in striving for unmediated vision, Hopkins in
his darkest poems ends by seeing much less than Scotus. His efforts
to harness the divine energy has the unforeseen effect of knocking
down the scaffold of analogy, producing a knowledge of God that is
not univocal, as he had hoped, but incurably equivocal.

If Aquinas's theory of knowledge were true and the object of the
mind's knowledge were merely the forms of material things, then
Scotus believes that knowledge of God would be limited to sense
experience. No genuine theology, or science of God, would be
possible. Though Scotus and Aquinas both agree that God is
generally seen through a glass darkly, they offer different explana-
tions of this mystery. For Aquinas the shadows that dim the analogi-
cal mirrors are a result of the soul's constitution. As long as the soul
is united to a body, it can have knowledge only of forms that are
realized in matter. According to Scotus, Aquinas' doctrine of the
soul's hylomorphic composition degrades the soul beneath its natu-
ral dignity. The mind's darkened understanding of God is not,
Scotus argues, a result of any defect inherent in the body or soul.
There is no crack or flaw in the reflecting mirror itself. The obscurity
is rather the result of a hindrance, of an intercepting veil placed be-
tween the mirror and its object. The veil is placed there *forte ex pec-
cato*, as a result of sin, as Augustine had tried to explain. And just as
there is no material impediment or flaw that would distort the
mind's knowledge of God, so there is nothing in the mind, Scotus
concludes, to hinder its apprehension and intellection of individual
things. Instead of moving slowly upward, from all the phenomena
of the visible and invisible kingdoms, through choiring angels, to

successively higher beings, as in the endlessly graduated analogical firmament of Aquinas and Aristotle, Scotus' idea of univocity may disclose in each created thing a total image of God. As a Scotist celebrant of the urgent univocity of being, Hopkins may leap at once to God. But what are the consequences of such a leap for Hopkins' patient Thomist concern for analogy and causality? I suspect that a similar question may have occurred to Aquinas himself. In the light of his blinding vision of God while celebrating Mass in 1273, would everything Aquinas had written about causality and analogical understanding not seem suddenly trivial and unimportant? Perhaps this is why Aquinas decided not to proceed with the third part of his *Summa*.

Hopkins is temperamentally a Scotist in his belief that each singular thing is intelligible as a fixed vortex of God's ubiquitous stress or force. In seeking a bulwark in specific detail, however, it is as if Hopkins were aspiring to be more 'Scotist' than Scotus. So obsessed does he become with idiosyncratic detail that he involuntarily resists the notion that God can truly be what Scotus calls a *universale concretum*, a deity who 'is "fetched" or "pitched" or "selved" in every other self' (Hopkins, 1959a, p. 128). In 'No worst, there is none', for example, Hopkins is so totally obsessed by each exquisite and refined torture he thinks peculiar to himself that he loses sight of what connects him with Orestes and King Lear. In celebrating the *concrete* universal at the expense of the concrete *universal*, Hopkins loosens the communal bond.

There is another explanation of Hopkins' loss of analogical grip. So overpowering is Hopkins' fear of being annihilated by the pantheistic idols of the world, which his Scotist veneration of each unique item threatens to enshrine, that at times he veers too far in the opposite direction. Hopkins never tires of denouncing a promiscuous 'chromatic' merging of the individual self in the 'Intellectus Agens' of the Averroists or in the Hegelian Absolute. But in straining against their centripetal pull in a bleakly gnostic testament like 'Spelt from Sibyl's Leaves', he swings so far out from every concrete signifier, beyond the last orbit of analogy, that he seems to drift forever in dark unpeopled space, like a stranded astronaut or one of Dante's lost souls. As Hopkins moves toward the 'womb-of-all', the 'hearse-of-all' (l. 2), he shows how gnostic dualities of black and white, body and soul, eviscerate the Aristotelian doctrine of the soul's hylomorphic composition, until the body of language itself becomes a mere lifeless tomb.

Like Scotus, Hopkins is also in danger of gravely attenuating his theology by decreeing that the Incarnation is prior to the creation of angels and of men. Though Hopkins dislikes Hegel and disavows any influence, his doctrine of a double Trinity recalls Hegel's teaching that the trinitarian God is both wholly real *apart* from his worldly manifestation and wholly real *in* that manifestation. Hopkins sees all things as created, not only by the Christ of history, but also by a pre-human and Plotinian Christ, a Son who descends into an unhistoric world of 'aeonian' or angelic time, the scholastic *aevum*. Without such a pre-worldly existence, Hegel argues that the Trinity's worldly manifestation would be incomplete. In Hopkins' shadowy conception of an 'extrinsic and less than eternal' procession of the Son from the Father, however, in some invisible manner aeons 'before the Incarnation and "before Abraham was"' (1959a, pp. 197, 113–14), the concrete, historic, temporal character of the Incarnation is already fading into a Platonic mist which God himself would think twice before penetrating.

In losing all fixed compass points, the tortured plaintiff of a sonnet like 'Thou art indeed just, Lord' finds that all stability has gone out of religion and all assurance out of the petitioner's words. What were once intrinsic signs are now the mere extrinsic husks of language. Once the umbilical cord between words and the Word is cut, language is powerless to reach out and touch things. Contracted to the shrunken testament of a eunuch, unable to 'breed one work that wakes' ('Thou art indeed just, Lord', l. 13), Hopkins' words are lifeless and emasculated. When they become more animated, they are subject to a helter-skelter freedom, like the frenzy of the Furies in 'No worst, there is none'. And they waste no time in driving from Hopkins' firmament the last saving vestige of inscaped form. At the centre of the new dark firmament of agnostic poetry, which is too often Hopkins' firmament, stands the suffering poet, the victim of an *ultima solitudo*, isolated like Arnold by an utter personal, theological, and historical aloneness. Tortured at the centre of his faith, the Hopkins of the dark sonnets abandons any pretence to analogy. He improvises instead in a language of circling metaphors and dark equivocations, which change the whole direction of devotional poetry.

8 Victorian Agnostics and the Rise of Formalism

For agnostic thinkers like Sir William Hamilton and H. L. Mansel most theology lacks verifiable content in sense experience, and is therefore beyond the power of representational language to define. One of two consequences may ensue. Words for God may become increasingly abstract, until they resemble Spencer's π or some other mathematical fiction. Alternatively, they may abandon representational for presentational language, as I show in the next chapter. A presentational predication makes no attempt to *re*-present a dead or departed grammatical subject. It is content instead to present images lacking any determinate meaning. The most radical form of indeterminate predication is found in Sir William Hamilton's philosophy of the unconditioned and in H. L. Mansel's *The Limits of Religious Thought*. According to Kant, from whom Hamilton and Mansel derive their theories, a presentation with some content in sensuous intuition, like a storm or shipwreck, may be used to represent the concept power. But what happens when a representation, like our words for God, who is 'past all / Grasp God' (Hopkins, 'The Wreck of the Deutschland', stanza 32, ll. 6–7), lacks a corresponding presentation in sense experience? And what happens, conversely, when a pure presentation, like the image of being bound to a Tarpeian cliff of destruction, lacks a corresponding representation in some determinate object or idea, like 'the storm' of Christ's 'strides' or the mighty 'thunder-throne' of his grace ('The Wreck of the Deutschland', stanza 33, l. 8; stanza 34, l. 5)?

Though Mansel shows in his *Prolegomena Logica* that it is possible to have an immediate sensory *presentation* of moral and aesthetic qualities without any determinate conceptual *representation*, he also shows in his later Bampton lectures, *The Limits of Religious Thought*, that the proposition cannot be reversed. There can be no determinate representation of an infinite and absolute God, not even of Hopkins' 'double-naturèd' God, without a corresponding sensory presentation. Because the concepts of the infinite and the absolute, like the concepts of an infinitely divisible substance and of an indivisible atomic particle in physics, are in logical contradiction, Mansel asserts that a God who is simultaneously infinite and absolute is not only unknown but also in principle unknowable. Victorian agnosticism reaches its logical culmination in the first book of F. H. Bradley's *Appearance and Reality* (1893), where the mind-made relations which T. H. Green had defined as the hallmark of the real are shown to be as incurably contradictory as Kant's paralogisms, hence indeterminate and unreal. All appearances, Bradley argues, are relational, and the relational is unreal. Most theories of knowledge grant primacy to the object signified. They treat the relational forms that signify as mere notations, as a mere convention which must be mastered to arrive at truth. Any other system of signs would do as well. But if Bradley is right, then there exists only an unreal network of differential relations with nothing at the centre. No privileged concept or ideology survives that would allow the interpreter to remain comfortably outside the play of forms. By altering and displacing the centre of truth during the analysis of the formal system itself, Bradley in the first book of *Appearance and Reality* anticipates, without in any way influencing, Jacques Derrida's notion of a 'système décentré'. Like Pater, whose eloquent nominalism disintegrates the stability of the mind, no less than the stability of nature, Bradley in his sceptical moments turns the world itself into a flux of relations. He provides an epistemological equivalent of de Saussure's linguistic system, according to which there is only a network of infinite relations without a centre, 'only differences with no positive terms' (de Saussure, 1969, p. 166). T. S. Eliot compares Bradley's finite centres to the windowless monads of Leibniz (Eliot, 1964, pp. 198–207). Each replaces the representational mirror of nature with a more autotelic model. The full agnostic implications of Bradley's critique are apparent only in his concluding chapter of *Appearance and Reality*. In a confession of his 'Ultimate Doubts', Bradley announces that God's justice and personality cannot be preserved as ultimate attributes of the Absolute, which in his own austere words 'is not personal, nor . . . moral, nor . . . beautiful or true' (1893, p. 472). This denial of ultimate reality to God shocked Bradley's contemporaries, and the Clarendon Press threatened to stop publication.

It is only a short step from the inquiring, critical, agnostic side of F. H. Bradley to the scepticism of Pater, Swinburne, and Arthur

Symons. The flux of sensations that extinguishes the light of the mind and that relentlessly dissolves the stable forms of nature impels Pater to take refuge in art. The more Pater's critic, like his poet, aspires 'to burn always with [a] hard, gemlike flame' (1900, vol. 1, p. 326), the more he seems through some occult trick of optics to revive the impression and image, the unique item of apprehension, in some particular of his own chosen style. Salvation lies in turning things into forms of one's own sensibility. It lies in liberating both the critic's and the poet's medium. With the same pathos that Pater conveys, Arthur Symons acknowledges that 'it is with a kind of terror that we wake up, every now and then, to the whole knowledge of our ignorance' (1919, p. 325). The void in nature is a defect art alone can moderate. The uncertainty remains. But art helps domesticate the mystery, taming the terror into new decorum. By offering a kaleidoscope to divert the eye, to amuse it with its many-coloured glass, art yields the cognitive pleasure of seeing ever-changing shapes and forms emerge.

Only when 'the unknowable God' of Sir William Hamilton and his agnostic Victorian successors is allowed to dwindle to the status of a supreme fiction, can art be viewed as the new sacred centre. The purist doctrine of art for art's sake segregates the spiritual territory of art from the everyday world. It replaces Kant's transcendent deity, the impersonal Absolute of F. H. Bradley, and the inviolable Brahm of Hindu thought, in flight from a profane world of mere appearances, with a secular substitute. If it is 'intellectually dishonest' to speak of 'the personality of God' (Bradley, 1893, p. 471), then the question of whether God stands above or below his internal distinctions may seem intellectually unimportant, because it is no longer possible to take any practical interest in such a God. Once God and metaphysics have finally receded into the twilight, along with Nietzsche's other idols, then poetry need no longer be celebrated as the mere handmaiden of some higher truth. It can be enjoyed instead as an end in itself, like liberal education or the attainment of virtue, which are often said to be their own reward. Poetry becomes a form of disinterested play that allows people to take delight in the disengaged use of their cognitive faculties. Aristotle would hasten to add that for free, rational beings there is no higher activity than this, and therefore no standard by which it can appropriately be justified or judged.

V From Representation to Presentation: The Limits of the Sayable

With the ascendancy of scientific thought, Victorian philosophy divides itself in two. One branch, the Utilitarian, subordinates itself to scientific method. The other stream, the Idealist, condemns the Utilitarians for being arid and trivial, and seeks an ally in the poets. As the representational axioms of empirical philosophy and earlier descriptive genres give way to new axioms, poetry may even assume more and more of the philosopher's burden. A representational genre like Tennyson's English idylls mirrors facts in the external world. A re-presentational genre like *Maud* duplicates an action in a medium of the poet's choice. A presentational genre like 'The Vision of Sin' makes no pretence of duplicating anything. But the purer its kaleidoscope of self-contained forms becomes, the more its poetry can approach the limits of the sayable and continue the inquiry of the idealist philosophers by other means. In such poetry it is simply not true that one must either speak of the unspeakable or be silent. In riddles, parables, and dream visions the poet can drop hints. Outside of poetry, the ineffable heights and unplumbable depths the idealist tries to reach may not be strictly sayable.

One measure of the oblique and intractable quality of these presentative genres is their inaccessibility to logical understanding. As I showed in Chapter II, the inaccessibility to logic of subliminal awareness is already an important concern of Carlyle and Keble in the 1830s. The mystery of the unconscious is an even more important subject for Ruskin when he comes to formulate his theories of imagination ten years later. The most comprehensive treatment comes only in 1866, however, with E. S. Dallas' publication of *The Gay Science*, which argues that, just as imagination is not a faculty as such, but the unconscious *manner* of the mind's operations, so poetry is not so much a *representation* of the unconscious as a *presentation* of its subject in an unconscious manner. The representational axiom of the mirror of nature presupposes that a poet knows and *re-*

presents the unconscious, as an object of imitation. Rejecting the paradox of a conscious knowledge of the unconscious, which by definition lies outside of consciousness, theorists like E. S. Dallas, H. L. Mansel, Walter Pater, and Robert Louis Stevenson substitute for the poet's *re-presentation* of the unconscious an unconscious act of *presentation*. In a remarkably original essay 'On Some Technical Elements of Style and Literature', R. L. Stevenson distinguishes between representative arts like sculpture and painting, and 'self-sufficient', 'merely presentative' genres like music, literature, and the dance (1885, p. 1502). H. L. Mansel, who uses the same distinction in his *Prolegomena Logica*, seems to have influenced Pater, a confessed admirer of Mansel's book. As the representational mirror grows darker and more opaque, it comes to present nothing but itself. When combined with Kant's teaching in his *Critique of Judgement* that art preserves a principle of purposiveness devoid of any extrinsic purpose, or a form of purposiveness for its own sake, it is not hard to see how the substitution of presentation for representation leads to late-Victorian theories of art for art's sake.

1 Browning and Bradley on Re-Presentation

To say that language is representational is to say that it mirrors nature and pictures facts. But when belief in a world of facts ceases to exist, or when historical facts have been lost with the passage of time, this representational mirror of nature has to be replaced with some pictorial analogy which re-presents the facts in a medium of the artist's choice. In Victorian poetry the most exhaustive study of this process of substituting a re-presentation for a photograph or a Xerox copy of an historical original is Browning's poem *The Ring and the Book*. And the best prose gloss on the process is F. H. Bradley's parable of the fresco painter who is asked in *The Presuppositions of Critical History* to portray 'in a continual progress the figures and the actions of generations' (1874, p. 130). Bradley's painter is assigned an impossible task. Like Browning's historical painter, he is asked to 'Correct the portrait by the living face' (*The Ring and the Book*, x, 1873), to compare copies with originals, and somehow come clean. But how are we to step outside our portraits to compare them with lost originals? In painting a historical picture, Browning and Bradley can compare only portraits with other portraits. Even if it were possible to compare copies with originals, how would Browning and Bradley analyse the results? What Andromeda or Christ pictures have in common is that they are recognizable pictures of Andromeda or Christ. Such characteristics cannot be specified. We instantly recognize that Caponsacchi is like Perseus or Christ, or we do not recognize it. No further analysis seems helpful. A portrait is not a direct transcript or photograph. It presumably finds in the medium of paint or words some analogy or likeness between its own formal patterns and a real-life original. But the more such analogizing resists analysis, the purer the portrait's representation becomes. If the medium itself is allowed to supplant the original that is being analogized, then re-presentation turns into a form of pure presentation in which the medium becomes the message. Such a presentation meets Archibald Macleish's requirement that a poem should not mean but merely be.

As a kind of fresco painted by many artists, *The Ring and the Book* is partly a reproduction of events by witnesses who borrow their facts on hearsay or who paint from defective copies or from models that have since been lost. In fact, reference back to a real-life original may be just an aberration in the history of thought, designed to satisfy Plato's obsession with an ideal reality. But without such a real-life original, how is it possible to know if a picture is a photograph or a portrait, if it is a representation or a re-presentation? If we are convinced that Browning, like Bradley's fresco painter, has been given an impossible task, then we might be tempted to conclude that all such a painter can hope to produce is a presentation or re-presentation that abandons all pretence to faithful transcription. As a 'Maker-see', Browning is asked to produce an original that cannot be recognized in any of its surviving portraits, and so cannot be copied. He is asked to paint an original that no one has seen.

'*How* do you know that as it stands the picture cannot be a copy of the real? Because', Bradley answers, 'you know *both* original *and* copy, and you compare the two together' (1874, p. 131). If there is no way to hold the original in one hand, however, and our representations of it in the other, then there is no way of comparing the two that would allow us to arrive at truer copies. 'Nothing can be like an idea except an idea', argues Bishop Berkeley. And perhaps nothing can be like a poem except another poem, and nothing can resemble a mere potrait of some dead model or lost original except another portrait. 'Making up' distinctions between good or bad copies and good or bad re-presentations is a vaguely boundaried activity. Do poets, painters, historians, and theologians 'make up' such distinctions in recognizably similar ways? Or is the activity Browning studies as many-sided as the interpreters who do it and as the distinctions they 'make up'? The very phrase 'make up' is teasing and puzzling. Like the word 'invention', it looks two ways at once. Representation seems to be a simple, self-evident process. But the more closely we examine it, the more complicated it becomes.

Both Browning and Bradley try to distinguish between the way we 'make up' historical representations and the way we 'make up' literary re-presentations. The latter are to the former what a myth like Perseus and Andromeda or a kerygmatic document like the Gospels is to a historical narrative. A pictorial or literary re-presentation portrays something like heroic deliverance and redemption. But such deliverance and redemption are possible if and only if there could be real-life individuals like Caponsacchi and Pompilia such that if these individuals actually existed Browning's poem would portray them and their actions as representative. It is important that these characters exist in the historical record, in the Old Yellow Book, just as it is important that the Bible be a representation of historical characters. What is portrayed must be actual and individual. What is re-presented in a myth of deliverance and redemption, however, is not individual but generic. It is a kind or class of action, not limited to what may be done by specific individuals. Historical representations are of the actual and the individual. Mythic re-presentations are of the possible and the generic, and of events that may not actually have happened.

Though there can be historical portraits only of real people like Elizabeth Barrett, there can be literary re-presentations of persons who are both real and imaginary. A character like Pompilia is partly a real historical portrait, representing someone in the source book. But Pompilia is also a fictional re-presentation, because her portrait is also a picture of earlier pictures. Her monologue is recognizable as the speech of a character we meet in the opening book of Browning's poem. Pompilia is a person Browning has read about in the Old Yellow Book. But she is also a person Browning remembers from his own writing. Every re-presentation projects a person from the mind of the historian or artist. In a historical portrait the projection purports to be referential. But the reality behind a mythical person like Andromeda is the actual writing of the Greek myths and the creation of all those paintings and poems, including *The Ring and the Book*, in which Andromeda appears. We cannot say, however, that a portrait of Pompilia or Christ is like what it re-presents because of analogies or likenesses we can then proceed to analyse and understand. For this reason it is not always easy to decide whether a picture of Christ or Pompilia is meant to be a historical portrait or a literary re-presentation. Even if the picture was meant to represent a real-life original, we may prefer like Strauss to take the picture as projecting rather than referring. What is antecedently known about Elizabeth and Pompilia becomes part of the poet's alloy, and as a fiction it works as well as real knowledge or belief. When the writers of the Gospels depict Christ or when Browning depicts Pompilia, they are referring not just to the portraits of these characters to be found in historical sources or in eyewitness reports. They are referring as well to the personages projected by their own writings. If the projections succeed, we should be able to envisage the depicted persons and recognize them if we were to meet them, whether or not the depictions purport to be referential.

Grammar, says Nietzsche, is the philosophy of the people. Browning wants to free the poet from the shackles of that philosophy, which too often turns out to be the empiricist's uncritical faith in the mirror of nature or the positivist's assumption of a world of pictured facts. By using verbs instead of nouns, and unusually large syntactic units, Browning hopes to combat the tendency to isolate objects arbitrarily, then to call what we say about them a representation of the facts. He shows how even the simplest assumptions of the mirror theory of language are problematic and enormously complex. Scientific historiographers like von Ranke and Buckle had failed to see that it is no objection to a theory of representation that it does not sharply divide the gold from the alloy, the fact from the fictions. Nor need such a theory sharply divide the metaphorical projection of meaning from its non-metaphorical depiction. Each representation is really a 're-presentation', a mental creation, into which many habits and prejudices unconsciously enter. A literal representation of events in the Old Yellow Book is uninteresting, merely anecdotal, unless we can construe them as a re-presentation of events in the Gospels, in which Browning and his readers have a more authentic interest.

2 *Presentational Forms: Unconsummated Symbols in Kant, Masson, Mansel*

Kant is often celebrated as a herald of art for art's sake, because his theory of aesthetic judgements supplements the *ad hoc* and open-ended orderliness of nature with an orderliness that is closed, repeatable, and intensive. Ideas of the Pure Reason bear the same relation to ordinary concepts as the presentations of Kant's poet bear to an ordinary representation. Unlike the second item in each ratio, the first item lacks a verifiable content in a world outside itself, and so cannot be defined or understood in the usual conceptual terms. An idea like God is too exalted for the conceptual understanding to organize according to casual and other scientific laws. It is the theological equivalent of the poet's presentational forms, which are, so to speak, the architects of a second nature, more lofty and visionary than the brazen world of nature. Though a person who was incapable of aesthetic judgement would be incapable of perceiving any world at all, the poet's judgements do not merely duplicate or 're-present' nature. They present a self-contained formal world with its own autonomous laws. It is a world with a destiny but no specific destination.

In order to understand how the representational mirror of nature is turned into a kaleidoscope of presentational shapes and forms, I shall first explore the influence of Kant's *Critique of Judgement* on a Victorian critic, David Masson. Then, in order to understand the logic of presentational forms themselves, I shall briefly examine H. L. Mansel's neglected *Prolegomena Logica*. This treatise has long been out of favour with professional logicians. But it deserves to be resurrected by students of aesthetic theory, for it seems to have directly influenced the leading theorist of late-Victorian formalism, Walter Pater.

David Masson is the Victorian theorist who most consistently reflects Kant's aesthetic teachings. Though indebted to an idealizing Baconian theory of the imagination, which tends to dismiss poetry as mere feigned history, Masson's idea that the poet possesses a special intellectual habit, distinct from the habit of the scientist, owes most to Kant. Distinguishing poetical ideas from scientific ideas, Masson repeats Kant's teaching that whereas the scientific understanding translates sensory fact into concepts, the poet's imagination, which is said 'to be nothing more than the ghosts of his senses wandering in an unseen world' (Masson, 1856, p. 429), is very effective, not in duplicating nature, but in creating a second and stronger nature. Masson's arresting phrase for this process is the imagination's capacity to 'secrete' fictitious circumstance (1856, p. 430).

Like Kant, Masson believes that the poet's ability to 'connect one concrete phantasy of the dreaming mind with another' is a 'particular mode of intellectual exercise' which may assume one of two forms. It may generate what Kant calls an 'idea' of imagination (1951, p. 157), an idea like God and His 'awful rose of dawn' in Tennyson's poem 'The Vision of Sin', which Masson analyses. Alternatively, the poetry may produce an aesthetic idea of a concept's attributes. An example of an aesthetic idea is Tennyson's use of the gap-toothed man and the orgiastic dance to present, not a concept of sin, but some of sin's possible causes or results.

If we consider Kant's 'idea' of imagination first, we can see how Tennyson uses his vision of God 'on the glimmering limit far withdrawn' ('The Vision of Sin', l. 223) to present an idea of supersensible reality for which there is no example in nature. Because such an imaginative idea 'enlarges ... the concept [of God] ... in an unbounded fashion' (Kant, 1951, p. 158), its presentation of mountain peaks and dawns allows the mind to reach a purely aesthetic estimate of magnitude which cannot be reached by any merely 'mathematical estimation' (1951, p. 89). Scientific measurements present 'relative magnitude by means of a comparison with others of the same kind'. But Tennyson's sublime idea of a God who makes both *out of* himself and *for* himself 'an awful rose of dawn' ('The Vision of Sin', ll. 223–4) surpasses every standard of sense by presenting 'magnitude absolutely, so far as the mind can grasp it in an intuition' (Kant, 1951, p. 90).

More common than a use of the imagination to present a sublime idea like God is its presentation of what Kant calls 'the aesthetic attributes' of an idea. Masson perceives that in 'The Vision of Sin' Tennyson's 'continued phantasmagory of scene and incident [is] representative of a meaning' (1856, p. 430) which is identified with the effects of hedonism in much the same way as in Kant's own example of an 'aesthetic attribute', 'Jupiter's eagle with the lightning in its claw is an attribute of the mighty king of heaven, as the peacock is of its magnificent queen' (Kant, 1951, p. 158). Masson develops Kant's idea that the aesthetic attributes of a subject actually quicken the poet's rational powers by exciting a number of sensations and secondary representations for which no existing expression can be found. As soon as the reader's thought tries to catch up with Tennyson's apparition of the music and the dance, for example, the whole passage becomes opaque, an orgy of controlled incoherence. The tempestuous abandon of the music breeds a thought about executing, as in a dance, the 'liquid mazes' of the rainbow. Almost at the same instant the metaphor in 'liquid' generates a second idea, the comparison of light to water. When both ideas reappear a moment later in the 'torrent rainbow ('The Vision of Sin', l. 32) and in the synaesthetic frenzy of the dancers' being 'dashed together in blinding dew' (l. 42), it becomes impossible to tell what is subject matter and what is metaphor. In trying to define the inscrutable quality of hedonistic ecstasy and abandon, Tennyson furnishes what Kant would call an 'aesthetical idea' of sin, 'which takes the place of a logical presentation' (Kant, 1951, p. 158). Because the weirdly literal images in such poetry seem merely to impinge, leaving the speaker queerly detached from the pictures that keep opening in his head, the total effect is not photographic, not representational at all, but magical or preternatural.

Tennyson himself seems to have been influenced in 'The Vision of Sin' by Arthur Hallam's theory that poets use images to project meanings too elusive for conceptual language to express. In an influential review essay, published in 1831 in *The Englishman's Magazine*, Hallam praises poets of sensation like Shelley, Keats, and Tennyson for their ability to find in 'the colours . . . sounds, and movements' of external nature the signature of many feelings the poet could not otherwise express (1831, pp. 850, 856). The orgiastic whirl that catches the sound and flings it in circles, performing a dance with the rainbow ('The Vision of Sin', ll. 26–32), suggests mysterious affinities between Hallam's world of sense and those unsayable elements of experience for which no grammar exists, but which Hallam's poet of sensation, like Kant's poet, is uncannily able to express. Hallam's *Remains in Verse and Prose*, privately printed in 1834 with a memoir by Hallam's father, is included in Tennyson's library. And I think it highly probable that an experiment in surrealism like 'The Vision of Sin', which Tennyson did not complete until after 1839, bears the imprint of Hallam's theory.

So far in this section I have been establishing a link between Kant's *Critique of Judgement* and the formalist aesthetics of David Masson and Arthur Hallam. I should now like to argue that a similar link is discernible in the line of descent that can be traced from Kant down to H. L. Mansel, whose *Prolegomena Logica: An Inquiry into the Psychological Character of Logical Processes* (1851) was admired by formalists like Pater. Because Mansel's *Prolegomena* studies the difference between 'presentative' and 'representative' forms, it retains an interest for students of poetic theory that it has ceased to retain for professional logicians, most of whom would deny that Mansel's inquiry into the psychological character of logical processes is, strictly speaking, a logical inquiry at all. Anticipating the efforts of later Victorian formalists to detach words from their referents, merely enjoying colour, sound, and syntax for their own sake, Mansel argues that 'all intuition is direct and presentative: all thought . . . indirect and representative' (1851, p. 11).

Under 'intuition' Mansel includes moral presentations of right and wrong as well as such presentations of self and volition as lead, he believes, to concepts of substance and cause, respectively. Mansel is the Victorian ancestor of ethical philosophers like G. E. Moore. He implies that some observers are morally blind, just as some are colour-blind. We either have an immediate intuition that an action is virtuous or vicious or we do not. No further analysis seems relevant. To qualify as an intuition only one condition is necessary: the object must be 'immediately related to the conscious mind' (Mansel, 1851, p. 9). By contrast, in representational thinking 'the object is mediately related through a concept gained by comparison' (1851, p. 10). In the representational thought of Newtonian physics, for example, a concept of gravity mediates between Newton and his consciousness of the falling apple. Most poetic images are representative and presentative simultaneously. But the purer art becomes, the less trace it retains of any external referents which the mind can compare with its own presentations. Presentational forms remove the mediating concepts, leaving 'two elements only', as Mansel says, 'the subject and the object [of its direct and present consciousness]' (1851, p. 10). The presentations to which Kant refers the concepts of physical science are sensory intuitions. Because metaphysical, aesthetic, and moral ideas have no direct content in sensuous intuition, they are denied the cognitive primacy of a concept. Though Mansel retains Kant's test of sensory intuition, he alters Kant's definition of the word 'presentation' by arguing that a presentation is by no means confined to the senses. 'Individualize your concepts does not mean sensationalize them, unless the senses are the only sources of presentation' (Mansel, 1851, p. 33). Unlike Kant, for whom sensory presentations are privileged, Mansel believes that moral presentations of right and wrong, for example, are as direct and intuitive as perceptions of colour or as the irreplaceable impressions we receive from a painting or a poem. If right and wrong express agreeable and disagreeable qualities, which according to Mansel it is 'the province [not] of reason but of feeling to perceive' (1851, p. 312), then we can understand why an impressionist critic like Walter Pater should want to choose a moral term, 'virtue', to describe the unanalysable quality of a 'picture', a 'landscape', or 'an engaging personality in life or in a book', each of which has the property 'of affecting one with a special, a unique, impression of pleasure' (Pater, 1900, vol. 1, p. ix). Because each virtue consists of a distinct presentation, capable of being disengaged and noted as a chemist notes some natural element, Pater believes that the intuitions of ethics can be assimilated to the intuitions of art. He can insist that each is valuable for 'its virtues, as we say, in speaking of a herb, a wine, a gem' (1900, vol. 1, p. ix).

Mansel's *Prolegomena Logica* is of twofold importance to late-Victorian theorists like Pater. It psychologizes Kant in ways that make him more accessible and useful to formalist criticism. And in elaborating some important distinctions between representational and presentational forms, Mansel prefigures symbolist attempts to replace the representational mirror of nature with a kaleidoscope of self-contained shapes and forms. From Mansel Pater may have learned that, even in observing 'abundant and often recondite laws' (Pater, 1901, vol. 5, p. 12), art must still be 'intuitive, direct, and presentational', as Mansel says. The second, more important, source of Mansel's appeal and influence lies in his theory of how the apparently ineffable 'presentative' qualities of art possess a logic and coherence of their own. Mansel can logically defend Masson's axiom that it is as wrong to extol poetic genius above scientific talent as it is to assume that, simply because its laws are more accessible to the critic's intellect, conceptual understanding is a nobler faculty than Kant's productive imagination. 'In certain exercises of the mind,' Masson is quick to observe, James Mill 'could probably have crushed Keats, who certainly was no weakling, as easily as a giant could crush a babe... Or, to make the case still more decisive, suppose the two men to have been Keats and Aristotle; Keats, a consumptive poetic boy, and Aristotle the intellect of half a world' (1856, p. 351). Masson argues that the distinction between poetic genius and conceptual understanding is meant to be descriptive, not evaluative. But until Mansel can offer a more logical explanation of the difference between representation and presentation, the aesthetic ideas of the poetic genius are likely to be exalted above the mere intelligence of men of talent.

Unlike a conceptual representation, Mansel says, the presentative images of the poet can be immediately 'depicted to sense or imagination'. They do not 'require to be fixed in a representative sign', but possess a significance which is implicit rather than conventionally defined. Whereas representative or discursive signs 'fix the concept in understanding, freeing its attributes from the condition of locality, and hence from all resemblance to an object of sense' (Mansel, 1851, p. 14), the presentative images of the poet are examples of what Susanne Langer calls 'unconsummated symbols'. In one of Mansel's presentative forms, 'the actual function of meaning', as Langer explains, 'is not fulfilled; for the *assignment* of one rather than another possible meaning to each form is never explicitly made' (1960, p. 240).

As in music, to which Pater says all art aspires, the presentative images of Mansel's poet possess all 'the earmarks of a true symbolism except one: the existence of an *assigned connotation*'. Because symbolist and surrealist poems abound in presentative images which possess the outward form of representative signs without their conventionally assigned significance, they approximate music's 'unconsummated' form of symbolism. For 'music at its highest, though clearly a symbolic form, is', as Susanne Langer says, 'an unconsummated symbol' (1960, p. 240). In a surrealist poetry of nightmare like James Thomson's *The City of Dreadful Night* (1874), the omnipresence of such symbols makes the poetry difficult in the High Modernist manner. Like *The Waste Land*, the poem is demanding, not because its thought is difficult but because it is largely non-existent. In using a flow of heterogeneous fragments to present the schizoid inner life of his speaker, Thomson may seem at first to be using a discursive style of writing. But the etymological meaning of 'discursive' (*discurrere*, 'to run about', 'to run in different directions') is radically at odds with Thomson's uncanny ability to compress into a single impression disparate pictures of the burning hillock, the bleeding eyeless socket, the red lamp and eyes of fire. No unit short of the total presentation seems capable of expressing opposite meanings of torment and purgation simultaneously.

A more representational symbolism would have used concepts with an assigned connotation, as Mansel explains, to mediate and mute the intensity of Thomson's impressions. But such representations could never have equalled the immediacy Thomson achieves. The sudden descent of the moon, which falls 'south-west' in section four (l. 259), as if sick and declining, recalls vivid nightmare impressions out of *The Ancient Mariner* and Wordsworth's 'Lucy' poems. Thomson is not representing an ordinary Sahara. He is presenting instead a desert of the soul. The self that swoons away, cleansed in the redemptive tide, has acquaintance with saving grace. Its 'corpse-like me' (l. 302) dies into life. But the knowledge of the recording self that remains behind is too vile to utter.

> They love; their doom is drear,
> Yet they nor hope nor fear;
> But I, what do I here?
>
> (*The City of Dreadful Night*, IV, 306–8)

In the words of Eliot's Gerontion, 'After such knowledge, what forgiveness?' Thomson does not merely use the introspective method of a confessional poet to develop a stream-of-consciousness technique. But neither does he present the impression of a hallucinatory world, broken all in pieces, by using methods that are wholly objective. It is more accurate to say that Thomson, in embracing the symbolist faith that 'even our dreams and hallucinations are somehow bound up with reality' (Edmund Wilson, 1931, p. 11), uses both methods at once, but not quite either by itself. By casting the flow of his inner life into unconsummated symbols and presentative images of the kind Mansel distinguishes from representative signs, Thomson has allowed primitive forces far below the level of the conscious mind, and 'innumerable shades of fine emotion' far beyond the capacity of concepts to define, to take on an irreplaceable power and precision of their own.

3 Pater and the Aesthetes:
Platonism Deconstructed

The Victorian dismantling of Plato's metaphysics begins with George Grote, who in his *Plato, and the Other Companions of Sokrates* (1865) distinguishes between dialogues of 'search' and dialogues of 'exposition'. In anticipation of Pater's *Plato and Platonism* (1893), Grote approves the dialogues of search, which exhibit those negative features of Socratic dialectic which Hegel had already analysed and praised. It is only a short step from Grote's conclusion that Plato's Socratic *method* is his true *message* to Pater's conclusion that Plato's importance lies, not in any system he may dogmatically expound in treatise form, but rather in his invention of a new literary form, the dialogue. This new genre is so well adapted to Plato's analytic thought and to his ironic temper that, in Pater's view, Plato's medium is his real message.

In the last chapter I shall have something to say about Hegel's influence on Pater's formalism. But the Utilitarian and nominalist George Grote exercises a far more pervasive influence. For Grote, like Pater, is a vigorous deconstructionist. As Frank Turner has argued, 'Nietzsche's understanding of Socrates in no small way depended on [Grote's] work' (1981, p. 309). Both Grote and Pater expose the purely formal and logical structure of Plato's metaphysics, then proceed to denounce, like Nietzsche, the errors on which the metaphysics is based. Only by following Grote's lead in criticizing Plato's search for a Parmenidean 'One' or 'Absolute', which 'to the majority of acute peoples is after all but zero, and a mere algebraic symbol for nothingness' (Pater, 1893, p. 32), can Pater disengage from the Plato of 'ontological science' a second Plato, a 'tentative thinker of suspended judgements', more worthy, he believes, of respect and imitation.

Pater carefully distinguishes between Plato the metaphysician, who enunciates his doctrine of being, and Plato the tentative inquirer, the inculcator of a habit of mind rather than the propounder of a doctrine. Pater is clearly in love with the second Plato, for whom 'a survival of query [is] still the salt of truth' (Pater, 193, p. 176). Pater's Plato is a probative, richly sensuous philosopher, an artist who loves to tell a story for its own sake. Enthralled by the Plato who transforms the colourless One of Parmenides into a world of 'delightfully multiple' ideas, Pater is just as strongly repelled by the monotheism into which Plato relentlessly absorbs the 'old Greek polytheism'. The Greek philosopher's appeal no longer lies in his metaphysical teaching that truth itself is a formal principle. The only form that concerns Pater is aesthetic form, the poetry of Plato's dialogues. And the only Platonic precept Pater seems to have retained is the teaching that aesthetic 'form, in the full signification of that word, is everything, and the mere matter ... nothing' (1893, p. 4).

Using his innovative anlaysis of the dialogue's 'essayist mode', which he finds well suited to the genius of a 'representative doubter', to support his formalist premise that 'philosophic truth consists in the philosophic temper' (1893, p. 168), Pater is led to the problematic conclusion that art, like philosophy, seeks only its own formal ends. Pater's praise of perfect proportioning and form is a defence not only of Greek practice but also of the practice of such Victorian aesthetes as D. G. Rossetti and William Morris, for whom art, like the Platonic philosophy, has no purpose but its own perfection. Instead of distracting themselves with external ideals, objects, and moral sentiments, these poets are often prepared to sever their bond with whatever has, in Santayana's phrase, 'dragged sensibility into a slavery to things and stifled and degraded it'. For Rossetti and Pater, as for Santayana, 'salvation' lies 'in emancipating the medium' (Santayana, 1968, vol. 1, p. 272).

In his poem 'The Portrait', for example, which belongs like Pater's essays on Giorgione and Leonardo to the genre of art criticism, D. G. Rossetti uses the portrait of his dead wife to commemorate a memory, and he uses the poem about the portrait to commemorate the mere memory of a memory. For a poet who 'could paint the whole world and had lost his own soul,' as Santayana says, 'it is always the play of sensibility, and nothing else, that lends interest to external themes' (1968, vol. 1, p. 272). Intuiting, as Pater says of Plato, that the artist increases his power by reserve, Rossetti does not try to be exhaustive. He gives instead a mere pregnant hint of loss, some single gesture that is also a profound caricature of that loss. He seems to know that 'the implicit is alone important where life is concerned'. When Santayana repeats the Greek proverb that 'the half . . . is better than the whole' (1968, vol. 1, p. 272), he is also repeating an observation Pater makes about Thucydides' 'stringent shorthand art' and Greek 'economy of means' (1893, p. 255).

Pater's temperamental attachment to a richly sensuous Plato, to a philosopher more in love with the visible world than with its invisible counterpart in an ideal world, is clearly a predilection D. G. Rossetti shares in a sonnet like 'The Love-Letter', which strips away all the conceited drapery of Petrarcan convention. Instead of making cosmic maps or Platonic emblems out of his visual impressions, Rossetti turns the physical properties of the love-letter into an object of immediate devotion. Gestures become more important than words, and physical qualities of the ink and penmanship more important than any ideas the script conveys.

The Plato both Pater and D. G. Rossetti admire is a Plato who has helped redeem matter and vindicate the dignity of sense impressions. Their deconstruction of Plato's ontology is nowhere more evident than in a sonnet like Rossetti's 'Silent Noon', where the Platonic ladder of love, mounting in a joyful ascent toward a more perfect beauty, survives only marginally in the fragile threadwork of an entomological Jacob's ladder 'loosened from the sky'. 'Deep in the sun-searched growths the dragon-fly / Hangs like a blue thread loosened from the sky' ('Silent Noon', 11, 9–10). Subject and verb hang suspended across lines, as the spacious run-over ('dragon-fly / Hangs') prepares the lowering from heaven of a 'blue thread' on which the soul, seen now as a hovering insect, rotates in space like a tiny helicopter. Devoid of Plato's ardour for the infinite, which Pater criticizes as a 'mind trying to feed on its own emptiness', Rossetti is in love with sensory forms alone.

Just as Pater is reluctant to distinguish between a Platonic model and its copy, so poets like Browning, Morris, and Swinburne are reluctant to assume that art represents some original that stands apart from their creations like a God who has withdrawn from the world. In his early monologues, instead of positing such a God, Browning prefers to assume the role of a clever but malicious god himself, not unlike the deity of Caliban, who is constantly playing practical jokes and tricks. It is a puzzling role, one for which Browning and his eccentric artists in crime seem oddly suited. Puzzle poems like 'Count Gismond' and 'The Statue and the Bust' function like a whiplash, inviting the reader to see what is there yet not seen. The narrator in 'The Statue and the Bust' repudiates his role as a judgemental god. He refuses to comment upon his story or even to draw a moral: '*De te, fabula*' (l. 250). What Browning has in mind in telling the story of an adultery not committed is a question that contains its own answer. One cannot elaborate. Browning's best poems are often his shortest. Their marvellous economy is part of their power. Some revelation has taken place in a flash, even when the reader cannot say exactly what has been revealed.

Other poets like Swinburne and Morris mystify in different ways. To blur Plato's distinction between a model and its copies, these poets either thicken the verbal medium or so attenuate its content that reading their verse is like the experience of proof-reading. I mean that the reader is forced to pay such exclusive attention to the details of spacing, typography, punctuation, and syntax that the meaning itself begins to disappear. It is rather like trying to concentrate on inflection and sound to the point that one begins to hear the English language as one would hear a foreign language one does not understand. Because Browning and Hopkins allow a tumbling in of images and a congestion of ideas to express their impatience with sequential thought, they often seem to be saying nothing about everything. By contrast, Swinburne and Morris have a way of saying everything about nothing. Mention the sea or a garden or a lost love and Swinburne can talk forever. He is inexhaustible. But even when the reticent Hopkins opens a poem in a stammer of ecstasy, he wants to stop almost as soon as he begins. It is as if he can imply more than he can say. The voluble Swinburne, however, seems to say more than he means. Instead of writing 'I know what your throat and hair *look like*', for example, Swinburne turns the verb and preposition into two weightily alliterative nouns: 'The likeness and look of your throat and hair' ('The Triumph of Time',

l. 192). In using a very self-conscious appositional grammar, full of
syntactical equivalents and alliterating parallelisms, Swinburne is
no more inclined than Pater to give 'an air of illusive reality' to some
Platonic original that stands apart from his verbal forms. For Swin-
burne, as for Pater, the music of syntax ceases to represent a world
external to itself. It presents instead a self-contained kaleidoscope of
repeating forms that diffuse as well as concentrate Swinburne's
meanings. Swinburne retains only that side of Victorian Platonism
which redeems the world of sense by dethroning the archetypes.
Nature is no longer an emblem book whose characters trace the
moving shadows of eternity. Blake's 'vegetable glass' of nature is
now only a nominalist scripture. The Platonist's bible of types and
antitypes has been overthrown, leaving in its place a mirror of idols,
a mere picture-book of ravishing forms. This 'golden book of spirit
and sense', as Swinburne calls it in his 'Sonnet: With a Copy of
"Mademoiselle de Maupin"' (l. 1), is the aesthete's bible, not
because it records the best that has been thought and said in the
world, but because its pictures replace God as the new focus of dis-
interested contemplation.

Just as Mansel's negative theology culminates in an agnostic
theory of language, so the deconstruction of Platonism culminates
in the nominalism of Pater and in the aestheticism of poets like Wil-
liam Morris and D. G. Rossetti. By Pater's nominalism I mean his
notion that words no longer refer to Platonic universals. They do
not even denote an abiding sensory referent. They evoke at best a
pattern of sounds, a self-contained verbal music. We can study such
a disappearance of the referent in Rossetti's sonnet 'The Hill
Summit', where dazzling visual sensations of 'this feast-day of the
sun' turn the blazing 'altar' spread 'for vesper-song' (ll. 1–2) into a
visual marvel. The summit Rossetti climbs is clearly a Pisgah-
height, a hill of contemplation on which he might expect to receive
some supernatural vision. But he enjoys elevated geographical
vistas without the anticipated visions. By the end of the sestet as he
watches 'the last bird fly into the last light' (l. 14), intimations of
revelation have so darkened that we are unable to decipher any ex-
plicit meaning behind the absorbing visual impressions.

A similar removal of meaning darkens Christina Rossetti's vision
in her poem 'I See That All Things Come to an End'. What voice,
she wonders, will speak to her from the far side of nature, when all

voices on this side have ceased to speak?

> Nevertheless old ocean's roar
> And wide earth's multitudinous cry
> And echo's pent reverberant store
> Shall hush to silence by and by . . .
> ('I See That All Things Come to an End', ll. 5–8)

Like an expansive echo, the adjectives preceding the nouns in the central stanza swell from two to three. But a momentary bellows-like expansion is followed by a final contraction. In the last lines, 'Man opes *no more* a *mor*tal eye, / *No more*' (ll. 10–11), the echoing elements come hard and fast upon each other, then die away. They are not answered by any Platonic presence beyond nature, by any God who manages to outlast His physical attributes, or are they? In the silence that follows the echoes we are confronted by a speechless and untimely event. It is the sort of hiatus in which Wordsworth's Boy of Winander ciphers death, but in which he also hears the sound of mighty water torrents and a blast of the eternal.

The logical culmination of Pater's nominalism is an impressionist experiment like Arthur Symons' poem 'Colour Studies: At Dieppe', which educates the eye, not by offering it a Platonic vision, but by scrupulously discriminating among white and grey-green colours before they are allowed to blend.

> The grey-green stretch of sandy grass,
> Indefinitely desolate;
> A sea of lead, a sky of slate;
> Already autumn in the air, alas!
>
> One stark monotony of stone
> The long hotel, acutely white,
> Against the after-sunset light
> Withers grey-green, and takes the grass's tone.
> ('Colour Studies: At Dieppe', ll. 1–8)

As an array of visual sensations, the quoted stanzas compose themselves into syntactic fragments, with no principal verb until the final line. They define emotions that might have attended one of Wordsworth's experiences of 'visionary dreariness'. But in the absence of any such vision, these detached sensations evoke only a mood of indefinite desolation. Colour assumes a comparable function in Morris's poem 'The Defence of Guenevere'. Instead of defining some Platonic universal, the words that ascend through the 'long throat' dissolve into a sequence of visual marvels, into a picture of waves rising in ripples to the mouth and into patterns of colour and liquid light.

> See through my long throat how the words go up
> In ripples to my mouth; how in my hand
>
> The shadow lies like wine within a cup
> Of marvellously colour'd gold
>
> ('The Defence of Guenevere', ll. 230–3)

In Morris's world blue is no longer 'blue of larkspur, blue of Mary's colour' (T. S. Eliot, *Ash-Wednesday*, IV, 10), but a visual sensation drained, like Guenevere's 'green hope' (l. 255), of all intelligible meaning. Uncontaminated by any emblematic values which might attenuate the visual impact, the meaning of the red and blue cloths that Guenevere must choose (ll. 34–8) is precisely that they have no meaning. The substitution of Pater's nominalism for a doctrine of Platonic universals allows Morris to create the kind of two-dimensional poetry happily characterized by Ian Fletcher as 'pure surface over void'. Like sensory deposits left on a photographic plate after the celestial bodies which emitted them have vanished, the colours in Morris's poem are the only remaining imprint of a conceptual meaning with which these colours were once emblematically linked, but from which they are now completely dissociated.

4 Ruskin on the Ineffable: The Imagination Contemplative and the Limits of Allegory

In order to understand the transformation of representational theories of art into the presentational theories of the formalists, few Victorian commentaries are more instructive than the discussion in the second book of *Modern Painters* where Ruskin sets forth his theory of the Imagination Contemplative. The visionary poetry he is analysing seems at first to be representational, even allegorical. But the more closely we examine Ruskin's examples, the less representational they seem. He is really identifying the productions of the Imagination Contemplative with presentational symbols which, because they are 'unconsummated' and not fixed in meaning by any assigned connotation, are not as conventionally allegorical as some critics have assumed.

When Ruskin praises the allegorical art of Dante and Milton, he is less impressed by a predictable translation of Satan into evil, for example, than by ineffable qualities in the allegory that defy translation. George Landow has shown that Ruskin's 'praise of allegorical art and the arguments he summons to its defence reveal . . . that Ruskin borrows widely' from Christian sources (1971, pp. 398–9). But the allegorical examples Ruskin uses also reveal that he is critical of conventional allegory for the same reason Northrop Frye believes most modern critics are averse to it. 'Commentary, we remember, is allegorization.' And, as Frye says, 'the commenting critic is often prejudiced against allegory without knowing the real reason, which is that continuous allegory prescribes the direction of his commentary, and so restricts its freedom' (1957, pp. 341, 90). Both Ruskin and the modern critic, even when discussing art whose outward form seems representational and allegorical, prefer more presentative modes.

Though Ruskin cites examples of Miltonic allegory when discussing the operation of the Imagination Contemplative, its productions are to Spenserian allegory what a kaleidoscope of presentational forms is to the representational mirror of nature. The art Ruskin has in mind is allegorical only in the generalized Coleridgean sense. In his influential *Aids to Reflection* Coleridge distinguishes between two uses of language. In tautegorical discourse, the words and their referents are used to express 'the *same* subject . . . with a *difference*'. In allegorical discourse, they are used to express 'a *different* subject . . . with a resemblance' (1905, p. 182). Coleridge affirms that all analogies are more 'tautegorical' than metaphors. In biblical typology, for example, the historical analogies on which the figures are based are strongly 'tautegorical': Israel's temptation in the desert and Christ's temptation in the wilderness express the *same* principle with a difference. Metaphor, by contrast, is more 'allegorical' than analogy, because the gap between the sign and its referent is wider. According to Coleridge, the biblical language of ransoming or discharging a debt is a mere metaphor. It tells us as much about St Paul as it does about the subject of his discourse.

The more allegorical a work becomes in Coleridge's sense, the *more* presentative and untranslatable it becomes. And the *less* allegorical it will be in the assigned or merely conventional way in which the goat always represents lechery, the tiger wrath, and so on. Coleridge speaks of this latter process as a translation into picture language of concepts like the seven deadly sins, which are already abstractions from the language of sense. But Newman's *Dream of Gerontius*, which is one of the few Victorian poems that is allegorical in this conventional sense, is hardly 'allegorical' in the sense Ruskin has in mind when he praises Milton and Dante for their genius in putting into words an ineffable meaning which comes to the reader from the other side of silence. Because such language directs attention to the silent *meanings*, it uses analogies that are *less* allegorical than the unstable analogies of Mansel's agnostic theology, which Coleridge would call mere metaphors. But because the language of prophecy is one part sound to four parts *silence*, its analogies tend to be *more* allegorical than the historical analogies of biblical typology, which are the only genuine analogies according to Coleridge's definition of that term.

In tracing the theological origins of Ruskin's theories, George Landow makes Ruskin more medieval than he is. Contrary to what Landow says, Ruskin does not find 'himself within the medieval Christian universe which founded [allegorical] conceptions of art' (1971, p. 399). As a Victorian who has more in common with Pater than with Keble, Ruskin is far more aware than Dante, Bunyan, or Augustine that the mystery of life and its arts does not allow the poet to fix or assign one meaning only to each visible type of the spiritual world. The Contemplative Imagination of Ruskin's poet has all the hallmarks of a true allegorical symbolism except one. Its symbols are untranslatable, because they lack an assigned connotation. Like the music to which Mansel's and Pater's presentational forms aspire, the symbols of even a Milton or Dante, Ruskin believes, imply far more than they say. Unlike the goat or the wolf of conventional allegory, the symbols of a great visionary poet are unconsummated.

Ruskin develops his theory of the Imagination Contemplative, not to explain conventional allegory, but to show how visionary artists can define with remarkable precision experiences that are generally thought to be indefinite, ungraspable, and therefore unsayable. Not surprisingly, Ruskin's theory is less applicable to a genuine allegory like *The Faerie Queene* than to a curiously indeterminate poem like *Idylls of the King*, in which most uses of Spenser turn out to be mock-epic rather than seriously allegorical. The complete collapse of Gareth's last adversary, Night, who as a 'blooming boy' proves to be the least dangerous, makes mock-heroic use of Artegall's misdirected attack on the armed Britomart (*The Faerie Queene*, IV, vi, 19). Few passages better illustrate Walter Benjamin's phrase: 'Allegory exists empty-handed.' Tennyson's Night uses the bare derisive mask of allegory – skeletal and grimacing. It is as if Tennyson were using allegory to subvert allegory. As he more directly identifies each successive adversary with a psychological reaction in the mind of Gareth and the reader, these parody Malegers and Britomarts come less and less to resemble the characters of medieval and Renaissance allegory. They become instead familiar and untamed potentialities of every heart and mind.

In order to discuss sublime art at all, Ruskin believes we must study the way the Imagination Contemplative allows a prophet-seer like Dante or Milton to find bodily equivalents for subjects outside of nature. Depriving a subject like Death or Satan 'of material and bodily shape', the Imagination Contemplative of a great visionary poet like Milton forges 'qualities together in such groups and forms as it desires' (Ruskin, 1903–12, vol. 4, p. 291). As a prophet who sees 'in a sort untruly, because what [he] see[s] is inconceivably above [him]' (Ruskin, 1903–12, vol. 5, p. 209), Milton stamps Satan's power of evil 'with the image of a comet', in order to give 'one fearful and abstract conception ... distinctness and permanence' (Ruskin, 1903–12, vol. 4, p. 291).

Because a prophet or a seer writes in haste, under the urgency of inspiration, the first distinguishing feature of his Imagination Contemplative is a tendency to drop connectives. Sometimes he will use temporal and syntactical shifts to encourage readers to construct meanings for themselves. Whenever in the poetry of Browning, Meredith, and Hopkins, the full understanding of a passage is deliberately thrown ahead of the reader, the discrepancy between the speed of the presentation and the time required to overtake the onrush of syntax and thought 'directly mimes', as Robert Preyer has said (1965, p. 75), 'the disorder, incompleteness, and puzzlement' of a poet composing in haste.

A second hallmark of the Imagination Contemplative is its use of dreamlike condensation, narrative deletions and dissolving syntax to fuse disparate images into one fearful ideogram, like the montage of cinema. We seldom think of Tennyson's style as difficult to follow because of its incessant rapidity and dislocation. And yet when trying to define the inscrutable quality of elation and despair that animates the lover's vision of the 'cold and clear-cut face' in *Maud* (I, 88–101), Tennyson is able to sink a shaft straight down to the mind's unconscious depths, where the lover finds it difficult to keep emotions like love and hate separate. The provisional quality of *Maud*'s presentational symbolism is nowhere more evident than in the ability of its images to fuse opposite impressions. The corpse's 'blossom[ing] in purple and red' (I, 923), for example, combines half-formed thoughts of the blood-dripping 'passion-flower' and of the 'red-ribbed' hollow to create out of two depictable objects the representation of a third thing that is graphically undepictable.

A third hallmark of the poet's Imagination Contemplative is an aptitude for calculated indistinctness. In D. G. Rossetti's sonnet 'Lost on Both Sides', the imperfect matching of the rhymes 'since' and 'inns', 'long' and 'among', 'wooed' and 'brotherhood' helps sustain a movement of stunned wandering and confusion.

> So separate hopes, which in a soul had wooed
> 　　The one same Peace, strove with each other long,
> 　　And Peace before their faces perished since:
> So through that soul, in restless brotherhood,
> 　　They roam together now, and wind among
> 　　Its bye-streets, knocking at the dusty inns.
> 　　　　　　　　　　　　　('Lost on Both Sides', ll. 9–14)

We should hardly have arrived at the grim astonishment of the rivals' roaming 'together now . . . in restless brotherhood' (ll. 12–13) unless the poet's Imagination Contemplative had made the sestet's little allegory of Peace and desolation much more inscrutable and riddling than the octave's straightforward narrative of the former rivals, reconciled by the death of the woman each has loved.

The poverty of words is the motive for metaphor. The poet of

Contemplative Imagination recognizes that only the indigence of language makes his presentational symbolism necessary. If there were a word in the dictionary or in the lexicon of science for every new idea, then language would indeed be an unclouded mirror of nature. The world would be intelligible as an object of immediate knowledge, and neither poetry nor science, as modern physics conceives science, would be possible. But language is not Bacon's *abecedarium naturae*. It is not a representational mirror of nature but a lucid veil of presentational forms that hold meaning in reserve. And it makes the world intelligible only as a mystery.

Even if it were possible for a latter-day poet of Contemplative Imagination to consummate his presentational forms in the allegorical or figural types of an Augustine or Dante, Patmore wonders in his poem 'Dead Language' whether modern readers would be able to decipher such types. He is afraid these types might be misunderstood as a 'language dead', as another example of what Arnold, in speaking of the medieval faith of St Bruno, calls 'a dead time's exploded dream' ('Stanzas from the Grande Chartreuse', l. 98). Patmore's constant struggle with these problems imparts immense honesty and precision to his prayerful efforts in 'the Child's Purchase' to say what is unsayable. If the ineffable is truly ineffable, how can he even *say* it is ineffable? Instead of allowing the human forms to eclipse the divine form, producing another version of his Psyche odes, Patmore addresses his poem to an 'Unknown Eros', whose consummation in a specific connotation, the Virgin Mary, is delayed till the last moment. Poetry becomes an object of disinterested contemplation when poets like Patmore and critics like Ruskin begin to assimilate art to religion. To preserve the mystery and keep his art contemplative and pure, Patmore makes the representational mirror as clouded as he can. He supplants the ecstasies of erotic love with celestial reticences, with what he calls 'raptures of refusal' ('The Child's Purchase', l. 96). By diffusing the figural analogies between Eve and Mary and by expanding other less consummated symbols into armies of Jacob's angels, shuttling back and forth across the firmament, Patmore shows how Ruskin's poet of Contemplative Imagination is able to pass up and down a great chain of being, moving between thought and vision in a progressive enrichment. When we study them in a poem like 'The Child's Purchase', we can see how the unconsummated symbols of Ruskin's visionary poet provide a link between the untranslatable presentations of Kant's, Masson's, and Mansel's poet, which are purely disinterested, and the more accessible representations of a poet like Keble, who subordinates art to doctrine.

5 Generic Criticism and the Limits of the Sayable

The shift away from representation toward new presentational axioms coincides with the decline of allegorical language and the ascendancy of new symbolist techniques. It also coincides with a growing indeterminacy in Victorian poetic genres. By indeterminacy I do not mean simply that a poem like *In Memoriam* is simultaneously an elegy and a confession. Most poems of all historical periods are instances of more than one genre. By generic indeterminacy I mean the radical failure of a poem to satisfy the expectations it seems to raise. In 'The Lady of Shalott', for example, Tennyson seems to be writing a highly elliptical ballad or narrative poem. But what story is he trying to tell? Is he narrating a pathetic love-story like 'Lancelot and Elaine'? Is he writing about an artist in her ivory tower? If he is writing a riddle poem or parable, it is a parable to which no single meaning can be confidently assigned.

Unreeling before the eye like a giant microfilm preserved in the archive of some Italian museum, even *The Ring and the Book* is generically indeterminate. To try to read this newspaper epic as if it were as imaginatively ordered or organized as *Paradise Lost* or the *Aeneid* is to make a category mistake about its genre. The final speeches of Pompilia and Guido, for example, are preoccupied with the subject of concluding. Yet few endings are more inconclusive. No sooner has Pompilia asserted 'No more now' than she contradicts herself by saying 'Well, and there is more!' (VII, 1769, 1771). And just as Guido is about to conclude the second of his two long monologues, he protests that he has not yet 'spoken one word' 'out of the world of words' he 'had to say' (XI, 2417–18). In each case there is a failure to conclude, a failure to reach an expected ending. The large-scale inconclusiveness of *The Ring and the Book* is reflected in even the smallest grammatical elements. Guido's wordplay on 'unmanned, remanned' (XI, 2393) is not exactly a form of punning like the earlier 'new-manned / By Newman' (I, 444–5). But even in recalling that pun, it offers something more indeterminate and more disquieting to the reader's equilibrium than the sudden collision of separate meanings that takes place in a pun. Nothing would seem at first to be more rhetorically conclusive than Guido's chiastic inversions: 'On earth I never took the Pope for God, / In heaven I shall scarce take God for the Pope' (XI, 2391–2). The reversal claims to have a special pertinence. But what precisely is it? Does Guido mean that he will refuse to accept God's authority in heaven as he has refused to accept papal authority on earth? Or does he mean that he will accept God as a kind of Pope beyond the Popes? The chiasmus has a special imprecision. It fails, for all its specificity, to set limits to its meaning. Like the sentences which divert the monologues from proceeding to their generically signalled conclusions – 'Well, and there is more' (VII, 1771), 'Sirs, have I spoken one word all this while?' (XI, 2417), such figures give a sense of the inconclusive and the concluded simultaneously. We are reminded that neither Browning nor his readers can keep themselves comfortably inside the categories dictated by Browning's quest for historical certainty and prophetic truth. The future, like the past, is something incomprehensible, a mystery unlimited and undiminished by anything that can be said about it.

Browning is fond of Zen-like understatement, even to the point of being frustrating and provoking to critics who want to extract a single meaning from the last lines of poems like 'Porphyria's Lover' – 'And yet God has not said a word!' (l. 60) – and 'Bishop Blougram's Apology' – 'By this time he has tested his first plough / And studied his last chapter of Saint John' (ll. 1013–14). Browning often deepens the indeterminacy and sense of mystery by turning monologues like 'My Last Duchess' and 'The Bishop Orders His Tomb' into puzzle poems or riddles. The flash of illumination sent from the beggar to the proud patrician speaker in 'Imperante Augusto Natus Est' is a permanent possibility in all such poems, where vision comes with a flash of insight, like the clean brush-stroke of a Zen artist. One either sees or does not see. There is no rule to be learned for bringing into focus an ambiguous picture or an indeterminate meaning. Like the problem of choosing between conflicting wave and particle theories of light, the problem of choosing between the incompatible virtues of Arthur and Galahad in 'The Holy Grail' is also unresolvable. We are not permitted a choice, but are invited to apprehend and keep in poise the two perspectives.

To experience comparable indeterminacy in Victorian poetry we have to turn to Clough's *Dipsychus*, where instead of affirming, unequivocally, that one of the two dramatized minds is right, Clough can sometimes be felt behind the seeing eye of Dipsychus, and sometimes behind the seeing eye of his tempter, the ubiquitous Spirit. Unwilling to set a good angel against a bad, Clough turns from the debate poem's simplistic faith in logic to a more indeterminate mode which first internalizes the action, then passes it through equally privileged minds. For Clough and Tennyson the unambiguous conclusions of the medieval *psychomachia* and morality play tell at most consoling lies. The poems they prefer to write tell many difficult truths. And to tell such truths, Clough and Tennyson must substitute for the certitudes of an allegory like *Pilgrim's Progress* the pleasures of uncertainty. In place of proud and knowing irony, they present the hesitations and the doubts of pure negativity, of indeterminacy itself.

But is it possible for a genre to be indeterminate, or to fix an idea that is genuinely indeterminate? Does indeterminacy not annihilate the very condition of generic study? As Victorian poetry turns from representation to pure presentation, it tries to chart and even cross the boundaries of the sayable. Is the meaning of such poetry not too indeterminate for generic critics to classify? Generic criticism is by definition a labelling and naming. If new poetic genres try to name the unnameable, then the generic critic would seem to be in the indefensible position of denying the essence of what he names.

The *reductio ad absurdum* of this line of argument is the conclusion that each poem is unique, *sui generis*, unlike any other poem that was ever written. The most recent advocate of this theory is E. D. Hirsch, who calls every attempt to relate a poem to other members of its generic family 'a wrong guess'. If one danger of using 'master keys to unlock large numbers of texts' is the 'fitting of the lock to the key rather than vice versa' (Hirsch, 1967, p. 89), it seems to me that Hirsch's own theory of 'intrinsic genres' poses the opposite danger of offering no keys at all. Hirsch consigns generic study to analytic judgements, to true but meaningless tautologies: 'this lyric is this lyric', which is the one kind of judgement no generic theorist wants to make. A poem like *Idylls of the King* may veil or destroy, to the point of contradiction, its own generic category, with the result that in the last idyll the reader is momentarily as lost or bewildered as King Arthur. But such uncertainty does not entitle us to plant an epitaph on generic study as such. Unless we study poems as generic instances of some class or category larger than themselves, we are condemned to an extreme form of solipsism.

The full subversive potential of idealist thought reaches a climax only in the assault against the theory of genres launched by such twentieth-century idealists as Benedetto Croce and R. G. Collingwood.[1] But that assault is already implicit in the growing indeterminacy of Victorian poetic genres. The attack has been continued more recently by Jacques Derrida, who admits we need to make use of genres but who argues that we are plunged into contradiction the moment we do so (1980, p. 213),[2] and by Geoffrey Hartman, who is impatient with generic criticism for failing to keep in mind the strangeness of what it studies. He is clearly out of sympathy with what he calls 'Frye's sophisticated armature of categories' and with 'all emphasis on forms and genres in conservative criticism, which tends to be – let us admit it – Aristotelian' (Hartman, 1980, p. 184). Since the evolution of genres is a continuous historical process, doubts about the validity of generic study tend to coincide with discontinuities in modern literature and with doubts about the concept of historical cause. The best antidote to these doubts may be a keener sense of what literary history properly entails.

It seems to me that each poem and reader are different, but not intrinsically different. A poem is always a generic instance of *something*. To identify a poem's genre may not require the wit or agility of a metaphysical poet. But because no computer can be programmed to produce a metaphor, it can never be taught to take the place of a good generic critic. The classification of poems is not a mindless taxonomy. But neither is it an inductive science with covering laws, capable of being stored in a computer's data bank or memory. At its best, generic criticism is a metaphoric invention. Such an invention is Arnold's 'dialogue of the mind with itself', the new mimesis of Browning's 'Maker-see' in *Sordello*, and the *imitatio Christi* of Dallas's dramatic poet. The invention of new and more inclusive norms and categories invites the meaningful comparison of poems with both the immediate and more remote members of their own generic families.

Generic criticism must chart transitions from exploring within the limits of the familiar and the sayable to the much stranger quest experiences Tennyson presents in 'Ulysses' or 'Lucretius'. In these poems the questers stand at the frontiers of language, poised ready to hurl outward into the uncharted and unknown. Like the language of the idealists when they challenge the ascendancy of science by trying to crash the sense-barrier, the more the unsayable aspects of experience come to dominate a genre like the pilgrimage or the quest poem, the less reducible that genre becomes to any norms or rules. It may not, for example, tell us much about 'The Lady of Shalott' to call it a Victorian 'Book of Thel'. Nor is it more discerning, perhaps, to say that transition poems like 'The Book of Thel' and Romantic quest or journey poems like 'Alastor' are the sonata-allegro forms out of which Wordsworth and Tennyson build such large-scale symphonies of 'the way of a soul' as *The Prelude* and *In Memoriam*. Such classifications, however, illustrate the kind of transhistorical taxonomy that generic criticism properly entails. I am not denying that poems that try to say the unsayable, like 'Childe Roland' and 'The Holy Grail', may be so untranslatable that they seem to defeat the whole purpose of generic criticism by being *sui generis*, or the only members of their class. And it will not do to say that the untranslatable poem is simply another poetic kind, because each untranslatable poem tends to resist translation in a different way. The generic critic's task is not how to say the unsayable – a task which may safely be left to the poets themselves – but what to do about it. When the most pervasive and interesting features of poetry escape our understanding, we should not conclude that genre is somehow intrinsic to each poem we read. We should try instead to invent categories that make sense of what we find. By studying the shift away from representational axioms to new presentational forms, the generic critic of Victorian poetry can relate the unknown to the known without making either the poetry or the mysterious trouble spots of knowledge any *stranger* or *less* strange than they really are.

THE LUCID VEIL:
PROPHECY AND THE ORACULAR TRADITION

Many Victorians regarded Tennyson and Keble as oracular poets. Poems like *In Memoriam* and *The Christian Year* were read as sacred books. Only with the gradual erosion of belief in Keble's biblical types, in Arnold's Platonic archetypes, or in the Absolute of the Hegelian seer, are the oracular powers of these high Victorians finally replaced by more purist modes of theorizing. The truths of the oracular poet are lucidly veiled. They are lucid to the degree that they are partly a creation of the prophet who proclaims them. And they are veiled to the degree that the prophet's contribution to the truth is disguised or repressed, with the result that he seems unable to exercise any voluntary control over the god or daemon who speaks through him.

The oracular line of theorizing tries to do justice to two sides of truth. It accepts the conservative theological precept that the models of creation are established by God. But it also inherits from Romanticism and from the expressive line of theorizing the Viconian precept that man makes his own civilization and that at the centre of man's creation are the poets. There appears in both Platonic and Hegelian thought, which are often combined in a scholar like Jowett, the conception of a model world superior to the existing world. But this higher world is no longer associated with the Garden of Eden or with a Golden Age. It is now brought into being by the poet's own creative power. The truly oracular poet creates his own truth. Unlike Keble, he does not merely receive it from a divine source. The power of the prophetic poet is derived partly from the oracle on whose behalf he speaks, and partly from the oracular power of his own imagination, a power which was formerly ascribed to God's revelation.

In the short paratactic stanzas of oracular poems like *In Memoriam* and *The Christian Year*, the aphoristic style is both the language of unquestioned authority and the language of personal probation and inquiry. Bacon uses aphorisms when the state of knowledge is still tentative, and where a formal Euclidean format would imply more knowledge than is yet attained. But unlike the discursive statements of the scientist, the oracular pronouncements of the prophetic poet cannot be refuted. Oracular poetry treats everything it encounters as undeveloped forms of itself. It never attacks, only includes.

Both the Platonic and Hegelian strains within the Victorian oracular tradition are in danger of reverting to one of the two purist modes of theorizing I examined in Part Two. The purist side of Platonism resides in Plato's teaching that truth itself is a formal principle. And the purist side of Hegelian thought resides in Hegel's doctrine of self-making. This doctrine is a logical extension of Vico's teaching that truth is literally a fiction, something we 'make up'. If poetry presents oracular truths capable of being glimpsed only through a darkened glass like the God of the agnostics, then the reflecting medium of art may eventually become so obscure that any end external to itself ceases to exist. The progressive attenuation of material forms in Hegel's theory of the arts may lead to Pater's conclusion that art is all spiritual content. But this conclusion easily converts itself into what seems at first to be the counter-proposition that the material content of art is nothing and the spiritual form is all. Wilde in the 1880s speaks in the same vein. But in *De Profundis* he elaborates a different thesis. Absolute Idealism is to the Personal Idealism of a Pringle-Pattison or F. C. S. Schiller what the moral absolutes of an earlier aesthetic tradition are to the existential postulates of Wilde's new Humanism. Christ in *De Profundis* is the supreme artist, because (instead of evolving the world from an Idea, like the absolute idealist) he patiently evolves his ideas from his experience of the world and from his willingness to take upon himself, like a true humanitarian, the suffering of mankind. Wilde, like Keats, discovers there are no frontiers between suffering people, and he must pray for them all.

Frank Turner has shown that behind Victorian interpretations of a prophetic Socrates and an oracular Plato lie ideological battles between Utilitarian philosophers and liberal Anglican historians. According to Hegel and George Grote, Socrates is a subversive prophet, the greatest of the sophists. Their notion that Socrates' attack on Greek custom is a prophetic moment in a necessary evolution of Greek morality is a radical teaching, opposed by Victorian advocates of a more conservative Socrates. In his prophetic conclusion to *Idylls of the King*, where it is said that even one good custom may corrupt the world, Tennyson seems to have been influenced by Hegel's attack on custom in his radical interpretation of Socrates. Even Browning seems to have accepted George Grote's account of Socrates, the revolutionary prophet, in writing *Aristophanes' Apology*. In Browning's poem the adversaries of Aristophanes, the reactionary comic dramatist, are Euripides and Socrates, whose radical prophetic role in Greek culture is grasped only by Hegel and by such radical Victorian interpreters as G. H. Lewes and George Grote.

VI The Victorian Reconstruction:
The Recovery of Analogy

In order to recover more constructive methods of representation, Victorians try to rehabilitate doctrines of analogy. The idea of historical analogy has a theological source in both Tractarian and Evangelical typology, which discerns a resemblance between an Old Testament type and a New Testament antitype. The same idea has a secular source in cyclical theories of history pioneered by Vico and Herder and adapted both by Comte and by the liberal Anglican historians. Thomas Arnold uses the doctrine to draw parallels between fifth-century Athens and Victorian Britain, for example, or between Britain and imperial Rome. The idea is later used by Pater, whose faith in historical analogy allows him to turn *Marius the Epicurean*, his own version of Hegel's *Phenomenology of the Spirit*, into a *Bildungsroman*, not just of a first-century Roman, but of the consciousness of western man.

There is both a conservative and a liberal tradition of biblical interpretation with which Victorian poets and critics are familiar. And each exercises an important influence on criticism. The public, clearly communicable meanings discerned by a liberal critic like Jowett appeal to Browning. But they would seem to have little in common with the elusive, often hidden analogies decoded by a conservative critic like Keble, who appeals more to Hopkins and Christina Rossetti. And yet in trying to decipher the Bible's 'great code of art', both the liberal and conservative hermeneutical critics share at least one assumption. They profess to discover meaning rather than create it. Their constructive doctrines are not to be confused with the hermeneutics of the German Higher Critic, David Friedrich Strauss, who expounds meanings that are created rather than found, and whose theories also appeal to Carlyle and Browning. Very seldom does the interplay between conservative and liberal hermeneutical traditions or between moderate and left-wing Hegelian thought result in mere intransigence or deadlock. Each tradition is complex and displays some flexibility in manoeuvre.

Another method of reconstruction is more narrowly theological. It uses Schleiermacher's analogy of dependence, developed most resourcefully by Browning, but also superseded by Browning when it threatens to make his theology too ideal and not sufficiently historical. The two most ambitious blueprints for reconstruction are the Platonic and the Hegelian. For Hopkins, the Platonic realist of the undergraduate essays, the universe is conceived as a diatonic scale of nature. Hierarchically fixed intervals prevent any promiscuous merging or blending. The universe is ordered and fixed, and proceeds downward from the whole to the parts. All this is changed in the Hegelian model, which I consider in the final chapter. Hegel turns the static scale of nature into a moving altar-stair. The God who stands at the top of the stair is not completely real until he is toppled from his perch. He must be made to build new altars to the divine at each successive station of a descending stair that slopes through darkness before climbing back to its original height. Hopkins's diatonic scale becomes a chromatic scale, since sudden fusions of one type into another are now possible and God in the world becomes the perpetual vision of downward mobility.

1 Conservative Hermeneutics: Keble's Tractarian Typology

A conservative hermeneutics assumes *a priori*, on God's authority, both what must have happened and what must be going to happen in the course of history. Most liberal interpreters make use of moral argument and human analogies. When Browning, like Schleiermacher, asserts that feelings of dependence entail belief in God, he is affirming that what is humanly prior is also logically prior. Without authentic human experience, we would have no logical ground for affirming God exists. But when a conservative interpreter like Keble asserts that Noah and Moses are both types of Christ, he is reversing this process by claiming dogmatically that what is theologically prior precedes and presupposes what is humanly and historically prior. If the antitype in the New Testament did not exist, then there would *be* no type.

Analogies between an imperfect order in the past and a perfect order it prefigures allow a conservative hermeneutical critic like

Keble to substitute a future-directed typology, based on final causes, for a past-directed science of logical entailment and efficient causes. Similarly, the analogies assumed by Matthew Arnold between the classes in society and the powers of the human person ascribe to a controlling analogy in Plato's *Republic* an authority that is related less to observation and knowledge than to faith, prophecy, and vision. In a typological system, as in a Platonic theory of knowledge as *anamnesis* or recollection, the normal relation of cause and effect is reversed. The type is related to its antitype, not as cause to effect, but as effect to cause. Figural and Platonic analogies are held to be true because they are quasi-divine or sanctioned by faith. They are not affirmed to be authoritative or godlike because they are logically entailed by feelings of dependence or by moral arguments.

The key to Keble's conservative hermeneutics is the typological symbolism expounded in his *Tract 89*, 'On the Mysticism Attributed to the Early Fathers of the Church'. Like Irenaeus, the Church Father he translated, Keble is eager to defend the historicity of each analogy between the two covenants against the gnostic assaults of theologians like Origen and Philo, who want to substitute for historical typology fanciful allegories that turn Adam and Eve into types of the soul and body, respectively. By adhering to a strict historical interpretation of Scripture, Keble believes it is possible to interpret the Gospel as a revelation of the same God who created man in his original state. Because a typological use of historical analogy claims to be proleptic, it allows interpreters like Keble to determine what the future will be like in advance of its actually happening. It is no wonder that a philosopher of history like R. G. Collingwood objects that typological history makes the error of splitting up 'the single reality of [history] into two separate things: one which determines and one which is determined' (1946, p. 54). Any teleological form of historical explanation commits a form of what Maurice Mandelbaum calls the 'retrospective fallacy'. This fallacy consists in assuming that if we read the past backwards 'we shall arrive at exactly the same view of this series of events as if we had been observing it in the order in which it occurred' (Mandelbaum, 1971, p. 135). But teleological interpretations that would be out of place in contemporary theories of history simply confirm Keble's axiom that, though the two stages of God's plan remain distinct, analogies between Old Testament history and the Christian events they prefigure confer 'as it were the signature of God on his work . . . guaranteeing', as one commentator says, 'the authenticity of Scripture' (Daniélou, 1960, p. 30). Typological theories of history are really forms of *Heilsgeschichte*, or what Northrop Frye has called 'the history of God's actions in the world.'. . .

> *Weltgeschichte* uses the criteria of ordinary history, and attempts to answer the question, What should I have seen if I had been there? *Heilsgeschichte*, as we have it for instance in the Gospels, may say to us rather, 'This may not be what you would have seen if you had been there, but what you would have seen would have missed the whole point of what was really going on' (Frye, 1982, pp. 47–8).

In his cycle of devotional poems, *The Christian Year*, Keble not only celebrates in the Old Covenant the types of the historical events which occur in the New Covenant. As a future Tractarian, interested in liturgical renewal, he also celebrates the types of the *sacramenta*, the signs which constitute a system of 'correspondences' between the two covenants, allowing Keble to recognize the theological unity of Scripture. Able to mount 'in tides against the stream / Of ages gone and past', the 'ocean vast' in 'The Circumcision of Christ' (ll. 23–4) recalls the mystery of Noah's deliverance from the Flood, which in the rite of baptism is also the mystery of each believer's deliverance. In the epigraph to his poem for 'The First Sunday After Christmas', Keble's allusion to Joshua introduces another Old Testament type, whose baptism in sweet and drinkable waters balances the harsh and bitter initiations of the Israelites in the waters of the Red Sea. By combining allusions to Noah and Joshua with references to God's turning back the Red Sea for Moses, Keble shows that when interpreted typologically 'the waves of Time' (l. 15) become the symbol and sign of Christ, the true Noah on whom the dove of the Spirit permanently descends. The name 'nouah' means 'remnant' or 'survivor'. Christ is a Noah who undergoes death himself in order that he may rise as the head of another race, restored by a covenant he alone could make.

One of Keble's most inventive uses of typology occurs in his poem for the 'Fourth Sunday in Lent', where the 'truest image of the Christ' is said to be Joseph, 'Old Israel's long-lost son' (ll. 51–2). So far as I can tell, this particular use of Joseph is original with Keble,

the advocate of reserve, who sees in Joseph's reticent affection for
his brothers a typically Tractarian figure of Christ's love for man.
Equally original is Keble's typological use of Andromache's love
for Hector in his poem for 'Monday Before Easter'. The comfort
available from a faith in kinds is ironically eroded by a God who
blends and overrides, and so extends into infinity, a whole spectrum
of loves that Andromache turns over in her mind with fond but
exact scrutiny.

> 'Father to me Thou art, and Mother dear,
>   And brother too, kind husband of my heart' –
> So speaks Andromache . . .
> So evermore, by Faith's undying glow,
> We own the Crucified in weal and woe.
>
> ('Monday Before Easter', ll. 1–3, 5–6)

This pagan typology is characteristic of Keble, who in his Oxford
Lectures on Poetry argues that even a Roman atheist like Lucretius un-
knowingly foreshadows the Christian revelation.

In *Tract 89* Keble observes that the biblical commentators were
invited to supplement *interpretatio*, the art of deciphering an author's
meaning, with *applicatio*, the art of keeping that meaning alive and
valuable. In perfecting his own *ars explicandi*, Keble perceives, as in
his youthful Chancellor's Prize essay of 1812, 'On Translation from
the Dead Languages', that an interpretation of a text is all the more
spirited for the obstacles each translator has to overcome. Instead of
inhibiting invention, fidelity to a difficult original often spurs the
interpreter's imagination. For 'completeness and correctness' are
both 'parts of Fidelity', and if the translator is 'to lose no part of his
original', he must often supplement the correctness of a word-for-
word translation with the completeness of a paraphrase. To be faith-
fully complete as well as correct the translator may have to 'be
content with resemblance of [an] analogy', which enables him 'to
produce on the whole the same effect', though his 'happiest touches
may not exactly coincide with' the original (Keble, 1812, MS. Don.
d. 67, folios 44, 48). Though the proper balance between literal
translation and the creative, participatory activity of readers is a
major concern of *Tract 89*, Keble is no precursor of a reader-
response theorist like Wolfgang Iser. He insists in *Tract 89*, for
example, that even heretical thinkers like Origen who pushed alle-

gorical and symbolical readings as far as they could go were also as faithful as possible to literal meanings, without which an author's intentions could never be agreed upon or known.

A minor example of such literal interpretation in Keble's own hermeneutical poetry is the concluding line of his lyric for 'The Twenty-Fourth Sunday After Trinity': 'the Lord who dwells on high / Knows all, yet loves us better than He knows' (ll. 55–6). A loose interpretation of the concluding phrase would be hackneyed. It would translate flatly as 'God loves us better than he realizes'. But by being literal, Keble is able to reinvent the idiom. The unexpected precision of the final phrase is a result of Keble's restoring two meanings of the verb: knowledge of acquaintance, the French *connaître*, and conceptual knowledge, the French *savoir*. The multiple meanings of the phrase 'He knows' tighten the line and put the needed note of mystery into God's unmerited love, which is in excess of what his knowledge of man, his acquaintance with him, would warrant.

To produce a spirited as well as an accurate translation, however, the interpreter must be of a kindred nature with his author. This perception leads Keble to formulate his theory that the 'grace of original composition' consists 'in transforming ourselves, as nearly as possible, into the semblance of the author' (1812, MS. Don. d. 67, folio 53). Thus in the poem for 'St Bartholomew's Day', nature and the Bible, though both are sacred scriptures, are also registers in which the soul can to its astonishment find its own story written.

'What word is this? Whence know'st Thou me?'
    All wondering cries the humbled heart,
To hear Thee that deep mystery,
    The knowledge of itself, impart.
                            ('St Bartholomew's Day', ll. 25–8)

If the phrase 'deep mystery' (l. 27) is in apposition to 'Thee', then the 'mystery' Keble deciphers in both volumes is primarily the nature of God. But as befits the mystery of his subject, Keble keeps the syntax open. Because the pivotal phrase 'deep mystery' can also reach back to modify the 'humbled heart' (l. 26), the knowledge God imparts can also be a deciphering, not of God himself, but of 'the mystic heaven ... within', a phrase Keble uses in 'Septuagesima Sunday' (l. 43). It is only a short step from Keble to a later hermeneutical critic like Karl Barth, who asserts that the biblical interpreter cannot be satisfied until 'the document seems hardly to exist as a document; till I have almost forgotten I am not its author' (1933, p. 8). Only by earnestly wrestling with the meaning of God's two scriptures, as they address the deepest problems of his life, can Keble's interpreter reaffirm, in Irenaeus' great aphorism, that 'The glory of God is man alive'. Of the one hundred and nine poems in *The Christian Year*, some forty rely exclusively on biblical typology. But many of these innate typologies are supplemented by species of inferred typology. By requiring completion in the life of each interpreter, inferred typology defies poetic closure. In 'The First Sunday After Christmas', for example, the antitype of the miracles performed by Joshua and Hezekiah is the unfolding in each reader of a long and complex process of appropriation. Every book in the Bible, like every lyric in *The Christian Year*, is also the type of its own ideal reading.

In *Tract 89* Keble argues that biblical typology, as God's grammar, is more than a mere set of 'poetical associations' chosen at will by individual interpreters. But this is not to say that hermeneutics, properly conceived and practised, is a univocal decoding of God's meaning either. Failure always to translate the analogies in identical ways suggests that the Author of nature does not permit a full deciphering of the code. Univocal translations would 'convey more knowledge than the rule of the Church allowed' (Keble, 1840, vol. 8, p. 31). In Keble's theology of reserve, God's mysteries are withheld from the human mind and are not strictly sayable. Analogies may try to focus and define. But because every definition of God denies the unnameable essence of what it tries to name, Keble uses his doctrine of reserve to keep intact the mystery of indefinition. By combining theories of analogy and reserve, Keble avoids both idolatry and atheism. Using reserve to oppose the nominalism which would allow words to replace the Word as sacred centre, Keble also uses analogy to focus, limit, and define. He minimizes neither our sense of the limitless nor our sense of the comforting limitation afforded by the familiar biblical types and by the repeating landmarks of the Christian year.

Closest in temper and inspiration to the conservative hermeneutics of Keble are the typological lyrics of Hopkins and Christina Rossetti. Though Hopkins seems to realize that the only safeguard of the interpreter's 'inquisitive mind' is a willingness to proceed, in Keble's phrase, 'on some principle' of *interpretatio*, some convention of an author-based hermeneutic, not 'merely pleasing' to himself (Keble, 1840, vol. 8, p. 152), he is more inventive than Keble in his use of scriptural types. In his hermeneutical poem 'New Readings', 'Although the letter said', Hopkins develops a contrast within the Gospels themselves between two covenants typified by two kinds of food. He is doing for the new covenant what Origen did for the old when he distinguished between the manna, a food for the imperfect, and the unleavened bread of the Promised Land, a type of the Eucharist. Since grapes cannot normally be expected to grow on flinty soil, the parable of the sower would seem to express a natural truth. Yet it is possible to find in it a new *applicatio* that strikingly reverses the logic of Christ's own parable: 'I read the story rather / How soldiers platting thorns around CHRIST'S HEAD / Grapes grew and drops of wine were shed' ('Although the letter said', ll. 3–5). The eucharistic figures of the wine and of the 'grains' shed 'from His drooping Head' (ll. 12–13) are left 'swinging; poised, but on the quiver', as Hopkins says in a letter to Robert Bridges dated 24 October 1883. For what he has to express is not 'an interesting uncertainty' but an 'incomprehensible certainty'. Without the certainty there would be no interest. At the same time, the 'unknown', the 'reserve of truth' beyond which the poet's inventions reach, and which the mind 'still feels to be behind', imparts 'an ecstasy of interest' to Hopkins' use of types. Unless some meaning is held in reserve, suggesting the possibility of a better and fuller understanding of typology, spiritual advance is blocked. By refusing to consolidate traditional readings of the parables in Matthew 13, Mark 4, and Luke 8, Hopkins transforms the 'dull algebra' of 'schoolmen' into a lyric of riddling elegance and power. The 'new reading' which he offers is not merely 'a curiosity satisfied', with the result that the 'trick found out ... the answer heard', the interest in the parable suddenly vanishes. On the contrary, the surprise of Hopkins' hermeneutical lyrics is more akin to 'some solutions to, say, chess problems so beautifully ingenious' or to 'some resolutions of suspensions so lovely in music that even the feeling of interest is keenest when they are known and over' (Hopkins, 1935, pp. 187–8).

The conservative hermeneutical tradition of Keble is nowhere more evident in Hopkins' canon than in a strictly typological sonnet like 'Andromeda', which turns Perseus into a type of the true Noah, who has been delivered by God from the waters of death so that he might deliver every true believer from a similar fate. Without ever explicitly alluding to the sacrament of the church, Hopkins develops a potent baptismal typology, according to which Perseus-Noah is also the newly baptized warrior who goes down into the font to attack the sea dragon, coming forth victorious like Christ as the firstborn of a new creation.

While usually less daring than Hopkins in her reinvention of figural types, Christina Rossetti displays greater empathy. Though I have no evidence that Rossetti was familiar with the theological aesthetics of E. S. Dallas, the astonishing empathy of her verse seems to result from a wedding of Dallas's Christian existentialism (Dallas, 1852, p. 255) to Tractarianism's staider, more conservative doctrines of typology and reserve as set forth in the two tracts on reserve by Isaac Williams (tracts 80 and 87) and in Keble's *Tract 89*. These doctrines hover over her lyric, 'Echo', for example, intimating parallels between Eden and Calvary. As in typologies of Eden and the Christian paradise, there are hints that 'in the speaking silence of [her] dream', Rossetti may be able to retrace the course of the first creation, turning it into a paradise happier far than that which she has lost.

As God had placed man in Eden, so Rossetti, like Israel, must wait to be brought into the new Paradise in her lyric 'Somewhere or Other'. All that now sets Rossetti apart is the thin partition of 'just a wall, a hedge, between' (l. 10). Her intimation of happiness is suddenly as familiar though elusive as T. S. Eliot's fleeting glimpse of 'the pool . . . filled with water out of sunlight' (*Burnt Norton*, l. 37). Hope breaks out in the discovery that 'the last leaves of the dying year' have 'fallen on a turf grown green' (ll. 11–12). Even if the green turf of autumn is only a freshly sodded grave, its greening of the dying year seems to reaffirm the paradox of Adam's happy fall and perhaps even the victory over death of the second Adam. Like the children's laughter in Eliot's *Burnt Norton* (ll. 42–3), the 'turf grown green' comes as a lovely surprise. It happens without warning, as grace, without the poet's making any effort or conscious straining for effect.

The keystone of Keble's conservative hermeneutics is the saving

faith of each interpreter. Sometimes Christina Rossetti's best de-
votional lyrics dramatize the affective life of Keble's Christian in-
terpreter and his power to empathize with a setting until the objects
he perceives turn before his eyes into scriptural types. Rossetti's
lyric 'Good Friday', for example, opening in a tone of bare notation,
presents in the poet's 'stony' heart a type that seems at first to be
utterly devoid of figural meaning.

> Am I a stone, and not a sheep,
>   That I can stand, O Christ, beneath Thy cross,
>   To number drop by drop Thy Blood's slow loss,
> And yet not weep?
>
> ('Good Friday,' ll. 1–4)

Recovery comes only at the end of the poem in Rossetti's rediscov-
ery and confident reinvention of the typological meanings buried in
her opening metaphor. Now she finds she is a stone in the sheepfold
of the Shepherd; and smitten by his staff, she celebrates in Moses'
power to bring water out of stone a type of Christ's much greater
miracle in shedding blood for the cure of stony hearts like her own.

In her poem 'A Better Resurrection' the same metaphor of the
stony heart is combined with Ecclesiastes' figure of the 'broken
bowl' (12:6) to furnish Rossetti with two essential elements of a
eucharistic typology. As Rossetti, in Keble's and Dallas' sense,
'appropriates' Christ, or rather Christ appropriates her, the earlier
similes of despair are confidently transformed into the greater as-
similating power of the poem's single typological metaphor, which
is now strenuously empathic: 'Melt and remould it, till it be / A
royal cup for Him my King: / O Jesus, drink of me!' (ll. 22–4). No
poem in *The Christian Year* is more intensely personal. And since it
is no longer decorous or civil at such a banquet to keep insisting on
one's unworthiness, no poem better illustrates Keble's doctrine of
God as a reticently affectionate host who has expressly honoured
this guest, singling her out for special favour.

Keble's insistence on the personality of God and on the holiness of
the heart's affections is the subject of another devotional lyric by
Rossetti, 'I have not sought Thee, I have not found Thee'. As Christ
thirsted on the cross and submitted to the 'buffeting billows of
death' (l. 4) as a true and greater Noah, so Rossetti goes down into
the 'cold billows' that 'surround' her, confident of victory over the

'darkness' of death (l. 11). The protracted 'darkness' is a result of using the spacious participial form 'Thy perishing me' (l. 6) to separate out the two elements, human and divine, that the pronominal forms seek to join. But so appropriate is the second stanza's implicit Noah typology to both the transformed soul and to God that by the end of the lyric, locked together by three binding verbs – 'look and see / And clasp' (ll. 11–12), the thirsting soul and the Christ who thirsted on the cross slip into each other. Lost in a coupling of pronouns, the new Noah and the drowning soul are no longer divided, as they were at the end of the first stanza: 'Thy perishing me'. Now their union is celebrated by a grammatical convergence, by a fusing of 'thee . . . Me' (l. 12) in an empathic merging of persons.

2 *Liberal Hermeneutics: Browning, Jowett, Strauss*

Jowett's theory of biblical interpretation exercises an important influence on Browning, who tries to forge out of Jowett's and Strauss's theories a more liberal hermeneutical tradition than the one available to Keble and Newman. Without insisting that Jowett's essay 'On the Interpretation of Scripture' (1860) is an explicit source of *Balaustion's Adventure* (1871), the most hermeneutical Greek poem in Browning's canon, I want to suggest that Jowett's attempt to establish five criteria of a genuine 'science of Hermeneutics' provides the best gloss on Balaustion's own method of interpreting Euripides. Browning was a good friend of Jowett, and as a student of Broad Church theology Browning would certainly be familiar with his friend's essay. We know that they discussed Euripides' *Alkestis* together, and that Browning owned a presentation copy of Jowett's *Dialogues* (*The Browning Collections*, 1913, item 991). As a classical scholar, Jowett wants to interpret the Bible with the same scholarly rigour and critical good sense that he brings to the study of Plato's *Dialogues* or that Browning's Balaustion brings to her recitation and interpretation of Euripides' play. Jowett and Balaustion both contend that, far from being an arid scholarly enterprise, hermeneutics can actually be a life-and-death issue. Balaustion's appropriation of Euripides is an act of 'saving faith', as E. S. Dallas would say, not just in the theological sense but also in the literal sense that it 'saves'

Balaustion and her Athenian comrades from death at the pirates' hands.

The first criterion of any 'science of Hermeneutics', Jowett contends, is the canon of determinate meaning. By approaching the Bible without preconceptions, Jowett believes we should be able to gauge an author's original intentions and the effects his meaning had on the 'hearers or readers who first received it' (1861, p. 378). He might be hard pressed to show how an interpreter can pass from a mere inference about an original meaning to that meaning itself. What counts as an original meaning would seem to depend upon what the interpreter is able to infer from his own experience. We know the past by an inferential judgement, as Bradley says, and its meaning 'can be nothing to us but parts of our experience' (1874, p. 94). But Jowett is determined to break out of this hermeneutic circle. He wants the Old Testament to have the same single, ascertainable meaning for the authors of the New Testament that it had for its own Old Testament authors. In no other way can he turn hermeneutics into an inductive science. If the New Testament authors had applied Jowett's own canon, however, the New Testament would never have been written. Browning exposes this contradiction in *The Ring and the Book*. But in *Balaustion's Adventure* the difficulty is less acute. In 'Teaching Euripides to Syracuse' (*Balaustion's Adventure*, l. 170) Balaustion finds she can renew last year's miracle by placing herself, in Jowett's words, 'as nearly as possible in the position of . . . the writer' and his original audience. Because she is interpreting Euripides' play to a Greek audience shortly after it was originally performed, she finds she can follow Jowett's first canon without involving herself in the same logical contradiction.

A second hermeneutical requirement specified by Jowett is a measure of empathy in each interpreter. In *Balaustion's Adventure* such sympathy is notoriously lacking in the Athenians who ridicule the Syracusans' 'exorbitant' praise of Euripides. They patronize their fellow Athenian as a social outcast, 'A man that never kept good company' (l. 286). A play about rescue like *Alkestis* can become itself the means of rescue only when Balaustion comes to share the inmost thoughts of the play's Christ-like heroine, the wife who is prepared to die in Admetos' place.

Having granted the 'greatness or sublimity' of Scripture, however, Jowett is quick to remind the reader of a third hermeneutical principle. The meanings of Scripture are intelligible and plain. The Bible's 'greatness is of a simple kind; it is not increased by double senses . . . elaborate structure, or design' (Jowett, 1861, p. 382). Jowett assails as anachronistic and dangerous the typological methods of biblical interpretation revived by Newman and by fellow Tractarians like Keble in *Tract 89*. Though typology is a quasi-scientific machine into which any text can be fed with fairly predictable results, Jowett asserts that it distorts the original meaning of Scripture by 'accommodat[ing] . . . it to the thoughts of other times' (1861, p. 370). When typological critics assert that the Ten Commandments are a type of the Sermon on the Mount, are they not committing the fallacy *post hoc propter hoc*? Instead of setting in motion some ponderous machine that would deprive the Bible of ordinary meaning, Jowett's interpreter is advised to look for no other design in Scripture than he could find in a text by Plato or Homer. Such indeed is Balaustion's practice of finding in her secular scripture only such meanings as belong to the contagious influence of magnanimity or to the paradox of dying into life. As a classical scholar, Jowett would not presume to reconcile the tragic fatalism of *The Agamemnon*, say, with Euripides' psychological reduction of a totally different action in *The Bacchae*. Why should he apply different criteria to the Bible? Why should one part of 'this huge, sprawling, tactless book', as one commentator calls it, be expected to coincide with a later part? Sitting 'there inscrutably in the middle of our cultural heritage . . . [and] frustrating all our efforts to walk around it' (Frye, 1982, pp. xviii–xix), the Bible's narrative of spiritual evolution is more often obscured than clarified by commentators' efforts to unify it typologically.

A fourth hermeneutical principle, which Browning's Balaustion follows just as scrupulously as Jowett, is the principle of 'interpret[ing] Scripture from itself' (Jowett, 1861, p. 382). If undiscriminating interpreters rely excessively on historical scholarship or on a close knowledge of other texts, they may find in the Bible only what they want to find. Though Jowett's appeal for unprejudiced reading assumes a zero–degree of literacy that is illusory in theory and unattainable in practice, his real plea is for each interpreter to read the Bible as a self-contained work. By reciting the *Alkestis* by day and meditating it by night, Browning's Balaustion clearly honours Jowett's ideal. Instead of studying Greek mythology or commentaries on religion, she finds there is no substitute for immersing herself in Euripides' play.

Jowett's canon '*Non nisi ex Scripturâ Scripturam potes interpretari*'[1] (1861, p. 384) is not quite as trivial as it first sounds. The issue being joined here is between critics like Jowett who believe familiarity with a work allows an interpreter to resolve many apparent contradictions and a critic like Strauss who ascribes many of the same contradictions to a corrupt text, to an error in transcription, or most likely to the unhistorical character of the biblical narrative. A similar debate took place a hundred years earlier between the distinguished biblical scholar Benjamin Kennicott, a collator of many Hebrew texts, and an obscure reviewer of Dr Kennicott's *Critica Sacra*, a Hebrew scholar named Raphael Baruh.[2] Their debate is of great interest to Browning scholars because a copy of Baruh's *Critica Sacra Examined* was given to Browning by his father, who esteemed the work highly. Instead of concluding like Kennicott that apparent inconsistencies in the Bible are proof of an unhistorical or corrupt text, Baruh plays Jowett to Kennicott's Strauss. Once we grant the different rhetorical purposes of the authors of Genesis and Chronicles, Baruh believes that the contradictory genealogies for Shem's children can easily be explained (1775, p. 12). Drawing attention to authors' different aims and audiences, Baruh tries to resolve discrepancies by becoming, like Browning's Balaustion, a literary critic. If Balaustion were to rewrite Euripides' play, she would write a Greek version of Chaucer's *The Franklin's Tale*. Admetos' willingness to die in Alkestis' place would make magnanimity contagious. But Browning realizes that the different story Euripides tells does not make his tragedy unhistorical or spurious. Admetos is a sadder and a wiser king at the end of the story than he was at the beginning. The change in his character, far from impugning the play's historicity, attests to its genuineness. It embodies that principle of development which Jowett is trying to expound in the Bible and which sets apart the evolutionary theology of the *Oresteia*, say, from standard accounts of biblical theology.

Jowett's fifth and last hermeneutical principle is that a commentator who uses Scripture to comment on itself will gradually become aware of a natural design 'best expressed under some notion of progress or growth'. Such an evolutionary assumption, Jowett argues, 'is no mere *a priori* notion, but one to which [the Bible itself] is . . . a witness' (1861, pp. 385, 347). It is as absurd to reject the Ten Commandments as inauthentic and legalistic, merely because they differ from the precepts formulated in the Sermon on the Mount, as it would be for a classical scholar like Jowett to reject Homer's celebration of Achilles' heroism simply because it differs from Virgil's understanding of what makes Aeneas an heroic embodiment of *pietas*. In *Balaustion's Adventure*, the gradual awakening of Admetos' conscience, his growing hatred of those qualities in his father which he comes to despise in himself, and especially his capacity for self-reform, all confirm Jowett's principle of growth and development.

On only one important matter of critical interpretation, which I have saved till last, do Browning and Jowett begin to part company. Ivy-strippers like Jowett may be tempted to hack away all commentary as rank excrescence. But like the serpentining ivy that twines round the stone, entering chinks in the wall, the commentator should be welcomed, Balaustion urges, as one of 'God's parasites'. Unlike Browning's ring-maker, however, whose reconstruction of what is creative in his source is itself creative, Balaustion's ivy-climber is content, like Jowett, to assign to commentary a secondary function. Because 'The column', not the ivy, 'holds the cornice up' (*Balaustion's Adventure*, l. 357), the literary critic, though writing within literature and not outside it, is demoted to the lowly office of expounding what Hopkins would call mere rhetoric, or the communicable part of literature.

The main problem with Jowett's hermeneutics is its attempt to assess an author's original intention. An intention which has not already been realized and made accessible to an intelligent reader can never in practice be recovered. In what sense, then, can it qualify as an intention at all? If Jowett wants to call an unrealized intention an intention, he is free to do so. But it seems to me to be of doubtful authority and of no interpretive use.

According to Jowett, hermeneutics is an interpretive science with a critical function. According to David Friedrich Strauss, a commentator Browning knew well, hermeneutics is a critical exercise with no interpretive function. Or if hermeneutics has an interpretive role, it is one in which intentions are no longer accepted as the standard of one uniquely valid reading. A close inspection of *The Life of Jesus* reveals that, instead of carefully considering the historical evidence, Strauss unhistorically assumes that the biblical authors were trying to write scientific history. Because their narratives were unhistorical by Strauss's positivist criteria, he concludes that the Bible was trying to project a myth of racial community which possesses both the infinite and finite qualities that contradict each other only when ascribed to an individual like Christ. To the degree that such a putative historical critic is free to impose on his materials any ingenious meaning of his choice, hermeneutics becomes indistinguishable from novel-writing. To the degree that such a misreader disguises his misreading, insisting that he is restoring an original meaning, he is really a critic in the guise of an interpreter, though a critic in whom the normal laws of evidence and argument have ceased to apply. Once Strauss has shown that the Bible belongs to the genre of *unconscious* invention or myth, there seems to be nothing to impede his assimilation of criticism to fable, or the art of *conscious* invention. If the Bible is no longer thought to be grounded in historical events, however, why should its interpreters be bothered by such questions as 'Is that what the Bible really says?'

Browning is deeply concerned with these questions in his poem 'Development'. If we assume that myths are adapted only to the infancy of the race, then we shall tolerate and indulge them as we tolerate and indulge the child's pretence in 'Development' that the furniture is Trojan architecture, that the cat is Helen, and that the child himself is hoary Priam. As we grow older, however, we reject such myth-making as what Strauss would call an 'unconscious invention'. And yet the fables or intentional inventions of adulthood are not substitutes for myth for the simple reason that once we redefine myth as an unconscious fiction, its imaginative adequacy is lost. The failure of acknowledged fictions to command belief is exactly analogous, as Browning understood, to the failure of a God conceived as a mere postulate of the Practical Reason, as a mere regulative principle, to govern morally or regulate. 'Be Kant crowned king o' the castle in the air!' Browning's Hohenstiel-Schwangau jeers. Once God is turned from a constitutive principle into a mere regulative one, He cannot even regulate in the moral sphere where Kant wanted Him to govern. Hans Slouch wants meat and moral sustenance, 'nor chews / "The Critique of Pure Reason" in exchange' ('Prince Hohenstiel-Schwangau', ll. 1108, 1110–11).

In his poem 'Development' Browning explores what happens when a critic like Wolf or Strauss tries to ground Homeric epics in ancient Near Eastern history, in the biography of Homer, or in moral allegory. Any critic who tries to read literature in these ways is doing his best to imitate science. He wants a method of grounding criticism, and he wants other critics to accept his chosen ground. The attempt to ground the *Iliad* in one of Strauss's historical mythi, in an actual history that has been imaginatively interpreted, fails to reckon with the fact 'there was never any Troy at all, / Neither Besiegers nor Besieged' ('Development', ll. 69–70). And efforts to ground interpretation in the biography of the author fare no better. The epics may be works of many authors, and Homer may never have lived. If there is 'No Homer, no authentic text, / No warrant for the fiction' (ll. 71–2), perhaps the interpreter should allegorize the fiction. But is the translation of fictions into ethical concepts, for example, a loss or a gain? In Aristotle's *Ethics* experiences which the reader of epic poetry believes unique to himself are expressed in the common run of concepts. In great biblical or classical literature, by contrast, a St John or a Homer seems to speak to each of us alone.

Browning's father, we are told, wisely withheld Aristotle's *Ethics* from his son. But what was his purpose? Was he using Homer as a bait to trap the imagination before disengaging the boy's mature intelligence as the only faculty capable of apprehending the true function of myth? Browning is sceptical. Even in later life, as he 'grows double over' the Stagirite, he questions the value of moral treatises. Are they genuine improvements on poetry and myth, or only impoverished substitutes? Are we to read Homer in our youth and Aristotle as we grow older? Or is the only advantage of reading moral philosophy in old age rather than in youth the advantage of keeping the pages of the book undefaced by bread and milk, uncrumpled and without 'dogsear' (l. 115)? The negative thinking of Strauss can be felt behind these subversive questions, which begin to erode the very concept of 'development'. Historical, biographical, and allegorical translations of any scripture, secular or sacred, are going to be as incommensurable and as unamenable to 'development' as every attempt to reconcile the wave's motion with the scientist's acoustical charts of the sound in *The Ring and the Book* (x, 1402) or the architect's blueprint with the finished house in 'The Parleying with Bernard de Mandeville' (ll. 170–97).

In an informative discussion linking Browning's concept of development to Herder's *Entwicklung*, Ruth apRoberts calls Browning's poem 'Development' 'a miniature allegorized *Literature and Dogma*' (1983, p. 25). Browning may have assimilated Herder's influence from Carlyle. But I think his attitude to Herder and to the Higher Criticism of both Homer and the Bible is much more ambivalent than Arnold's. Homeric criticism is inseparable in the Victorian mind from biblical criticism. Like Herder, Arnold may rejoice unambiguously in the Viconian formula: 'Verum factum'. But for Browning truth is never simply a name by which we dignify our own constructs and fictions. Poems like 'A Death in the Desert' and 'Fears and Scruples' suggest that Browning is deeply disturbed by theories of the Bible's acknowledged fictionality. I doubt if Browning is really saying in 'Development' that 'we still turn to our great fictions, rightly understood as such and all the more valuable for that' (apRoberts, 1983, p. 26). The tone of Browning's poem is admittedly playful and elusive. But Browning often jokes about matters that trouble him, and an easy Arnoldian acceptance of the Bible's fictions seems to me quite as alien to the temper of Browning's hermeneutical verse as an uncritical literalism.

Contrary to what Max Müller had argued, myth is not a 'disease of language' (Müller, 1869, vol. 2, p. 74). It is not a concealed form of descriptive discourse grounded in some forgotten conceptual use of words, which scholars can now recover. Like George Grote in *A History of Greece* (1846), Browning believes that Strauss is right to argue that myths are the product of an age of faith and only communal loyalties can validate them. If Grote and Strauss make an error, it is not in arguing that myths are historically ungrounded utterances which, in Grote's memorable phrase, evoke 'a past which never was present' (1869, vol. 1, p. 43). Their mistake is to assume that all discourse aspires to the grounded descriptive discourse of science. It is to forget that science supersedes 'only the accidents of mythology and not real mythology', which, as Northrop Frye reminds us, is 're-created by the poets' (1982, p. 66). Because a myth, contrary to Müller, cannot be compared to any alternative use of words, it cannot be grounded. Myths are neither figurative nor literal, since as the only name for the divine ground they cannot be compared to any alternative name, either figurative or literal. For this reason, as Strauss says, myths are to be carefully distinguished from such ungrounded uses of performative language as 'fables, premeditated fictions and wilful falsehoods'. Instead of expressing a prior state of affairs, legends and myths are ways of doing things with words. To create a legend, Strauss insists, is to make and celebrate an idea that arises from a set of facts. A myth is the reverse: it creates a fact out of an idea (Strauss, 1846, vol. 1, pp. 25, 42). But since Strauss also insists that Christ is only one among many exemplars of the divine ground, it becomes difficult to distinguish Christ from such latter-day exemplars as Caponsacchi, say, or the believing prophet or reader, who may fashion new types of an ongoing testament.

In borrowing from both Jowett and Strauss, Browning seems to be saying that each theorist is right about what he affirms and wrong about what he denies. Surely no poet has ever tried harder to discover the truth about a murder case than Browning carefully studying the documents in the Old Yellow Book. Jowett is surely right to demand painstaking study and research. And yet Strauss, with his disquieting insights about the freedom of poets and critics to impose a vocabulary of their own choosing, is right too. There is no way Browning can affirm Jowett's doctrine of the decidability of meaning without at the same time affirming Strauss's disturbing counter-truth that the language of criticism is performative. In trying to enter the mind of a dead author to discover what he meant, there is no reason why an interpreter should have to become a living anachronism. The dead are dead, whereas every new interpreter is alive and owes something to himself.

Browning assumes that interpretations can be grounded in authorial intentions, and like Jowett he seeks the comfort of consensus. But unless interpretation is redefined as a form of translation, in which a dialect or an obsolete iconography is deciphered, it is hard to see how interpretation can be as strictly scientific as Jowett tries to make it. Jowett's straightforward, demystifying view of interpretation seems flawed, because it suggests that there can be no more than one correct reading of a work. It also implies that no critical understanding of a work could hope to prove illuminating. Jowett never fully realizes that the kind of knowledge Balaustion brings to Euripides' *Alkestis* is not just knowledge of the kind she can look up in a glossary or a handbook, but knowledge of the interpreter herself in an ideal meeting of type and antitype, of the poem and its beholder. The best interpretations cease to be mere descriptive inventories. They become instead an invention, a 'coming upon' or a 'finding', in both the constative and performative senses of that word.

3 Browning and Schleiermacher: The Analogy of Dependence

Keble's conservative theories of biblical interpretation are assumed to be true because they have God's warrant. Browning's more liberal theories are assumed to be true because they restore the logical arguments of the philosophers and the natural theologians. Of these arguments none is more important in Browning's early hermeneutical verse than the analogy of dependence developed by the German philosopher, Friedrich Schleiermacher. Connop Thirlwall's translation of Schleiermacher's 'Critical Essay on the Gospel of St Luke' was published as early as 1825. But unlike Matthew and Thomas Arnold, Browning may not have known it. Browning did, however, own W. Dobson's 1836 translation of *Schleiermacher's Introduction to the Dialogues of Plato*, and he was probably familiar as well with Strauss's discussion of the Christology of Schleiermacher in the third volume of *The Life of Jesus* (1846, vol. 3, pp. 417–25).

Anticipating the faculty psychology of Browning's *Paracelsus*, where an important distinction among power, knowledge, love provides a psychological base for the trinitarian analogies in 'A Death in the Desert', 'Saul', and 'The Parleying with Bernard de Mandeville', Schleiermacher differentiates feeling from two other forms of consciousness – knowledge and doing. He then argues that piety is a province of feeling alone. According to Schleiermacher, 'two forms of consciousness (Knowing and Feeling) constitute the abiding-in-self, while Doing proper is the passing-beyond-self' (1928, p. 8). But in one important respect feeling 'stands alone in antithesis to the other two'. For whereas the act of knowing, as opposed to the mere possessing of knowledge, is a form of doing, feeling 'belongs altogether to the realm of receptivity, it is entirely an abiding-in-self' (1928, p. 8).

Though feeling by itself is not necessarily religious, Schleiermacher believes it becomes religious by acquiring consciousness of its own dependence. In 'self-consciousness', he explains, 'there are only two elements: the one expresses the existence of the subject for itself, the other its co-existence with an Other' (1928, p. 13). Without the second element, the co-existence with an Other, the soul would be pure activity. But receptivity is precisely that feeling of dependence which Schleiermacher isolates as the specifically religious quality. It is the quality, for example, that characterizes Browning's use of the passive voice: 'God is seen God', 'A Man . . . / Thou shalt love and be loved by' ('Saul', ll. 249, 310–11), where the verb form has the same receptive force as the locution: 'Then the truth came upon me' ('Saul', l. 237). Like Schleiermacher, Browning believes that the feeling of dependence characterizes religion. It transforms the self-reliance and aggression of a Byronic overreacher like Paracelsus into the dependence of a biblical hero like David, who confesses the insufficiency of his power and knowledge. Unlike Paracelsus, David is not just a source of spontaneous activity and ferment. Because he is also a passive recipient of vision, the oracle in whom vision happens to take place, David is absolutely dependent, as Schleiermacher would say, on a power outside himself.

Browning's Paracelsus finally acknowledges that in adding love to knowledge he must add, not the voracious Romantic love which Aprile equates with loving infinitely, but a love which Schleiermacher would call pre-eminently religious, because it embodies a feeling of imperfection and dependence. Qualifying the indefinite shape of any purely active or spontaneous quest for the infinite, the feeling of dependence brings the discovery that receptivity may be elevating, whereas a feeling of the pure unchartered freedom Wordsworth renounces in his 'Ode to Duty' may merely enervate the soul and drain it of energy. When Browning's David momentarily entertains the subversive hypothesis that he may actually surpass God in his capacity to love, he is trying to imagine what a feeling of total freedom, of love without restraint, would be like. But it is impossible to imagine such freedom, because as Schleiermacher explains it is impossible to eliminate the consciousness of self. And as long as we retain any trace of self-consciousness, we retain 'a consciousness of absolute dependence'. For 'spontaneous activity comes from a source outside of us in just the same sense in which anything towards which we should have a feeling of absolute freedom must have proceeded entirely from ourselves' (Schleiermacher, 1928, p. 16). Browning's assertion in *La Saisiaz* that the existence of the self and the existence of God are the two facts on which all theological surmise must be based (l. 222) owes as much to Schleiermacher as to the Cartesian *cogito* or to the moral arguments of Kant. The first fact entails the second. Once we affirm our consciousness of self, we also affirm our dependence on God. His existence is implicit in that abiding consciousness of self which, because it 'is never zero' but 'accompanies our whole existence, and negatives absolute freedom', as Schleiermacher says, 'is itself precisely a consciousness of absolute dependence' (1928, p. 16).

Though W. C. DeVane (1955, pp. 201–2) and W. O. Raymond (1950, pp. 29–30) both acknowledge Strauss's influence on Browning's poem 'Christmas-Eve', the specific influence of Strauss's commentary on 'The Eclectic Christology of Schleiermacher' has not to my knowledge been identified or explored. In the third volume of *The Life of Jesus* Strauss praises Schleiermacher for saving 'many in these days from the narrowness of Supernaturalism, and the emptiness of Rationalism' (1846, vol. 3, p. 417). These are the two extremes Browning dramatizes in 'Christmas-Eve', as he moves from the swarming hollow of St Peter's hive to the lecture room of the 'hawk-nosed' Göttingen professor. Like Schleiermacher, Browning finds more piety in the Nonconformist chapel among believers who, as Strauss explains, set out 'from that internal experience resulting to the individual from his connexion with the Christian community' (1846, vol. 3, p. 417). And like Schleiermacher, he is openly sceptical about God's ability to materialize among the 'incense-gaspings' and 'taper-fires' of the Roman liturgy. In Schleiermacher's words, 'the transference of the idea of God to any perceptible object, unless one is all the time conscious that it is a piece of purely arbitrary symbolism, is always a corruption, whether it be a temporary transference, i.e. a theophany [as in the Roman rituals of 'Christmas-Eve'] or a constitutive transference'. An example of 'constitutive transference' would be the representation of God as 'permanently a particular perceptible existence' (Schleiermacher, 1928, p. 18), like the deity who materializes in the Bishop of St Praxed's demonic parody of the Mass, and who is said to be 'made and eaten all day long' ('The Bishop Orders His Tomb', l. 82).

The more radical side of Schleiermacher's thought, which is also expounded by Strauss, can be found in poems like 'A Death in the Desert' and 'Saul'. Because all dogma must be based on the feeling of dependence, we must infer Christ's nature solely on that ground. 'Whatever in the dogma of the church goes beyond [analogical inference from the feeling of dependence] – as, for example, the supernatural conception of Jesus, and his miracles . . . – ought not to be brought forward as integral parts of the doctrine of the Christ' (Strauss, vol. 3, p. 420). In 'A Death in the Desert', where the logic of a 'love' behind 'the will and might' (ll. 500–1) reflects the influence of Schleiermacher's faculty psychology and of his attempt to infer all dogmatic truths from a feeling of dependence, St John is careful to distinguish this dogmatic core of Christology from less essential facts like miracles. For Browning's St John, as for Schleiermacher, miracles are believed, 'not because they are involved in our internal experience, but only because they are stated in Scripture; not so much, therefore, in a religious and dogmatical, as in an historical manner' (Strauss, 1846, vol. 3, p. 420).

Strauss praises as 'a beautiful effort of thought' Schleiermacher's effort to keep the faith unmutilated and 'science unoffended' by limiting Christian doctrine to what can be inferred from a feeling of absolute dependence. But Schleiermacher's theology suffers, he believes, from one fatal fault. There is no logical way in which Schleiermacher can pass from a Christ who may never have existed except as an idea in his own consciousness to a Christ who really lived. The analogical argument in Browning's 'Saul' rests on just such 'a backward inference', as Strauss calls it. From the inward experience of dependence as an effect, David argues to the person of Christ as a cause. But how, as Strauss asks, can it be proved 'that that inward experience is not to be explained without the actual existence of . . . Christ' (1846, vol. 3, p. 424)? Using an analogy of dependence, is it possible for Browning or Schleiermacher to reach an idea of Christ that is more than just ideal?

To put the question another way: if no historical Christ ever existed, how could Browning or Schleiermacher hope to know this fact? A sceptic could argue that our feelings of dependence might be delusively stimulated by a mad scientist or wizard in such a way that we merely think our lives depend on a Christ who actually existed. So Browning and Schleiermacher do not know that Christ existed, even though they feel absolutely dependent on His having done so.

A possible reply to such scepticism is that, though Browning and Schleiermacher do not know that their feelings of dependence are not deceiving them, they do know that if the feeling of dependence were in fact delusive they would have no experience of depending on a Christ who is historical and not just an idea in their minds. Because they *do* have such an experience, the denial of the consequent means that the hypothetical premise of the sceptic is invalid. This argument against scepticism may admittedly prove more than is wanted. For it can be used, not just against Strauss's criticism of Schleiermacher, but against all the more radical sceptical arguments.

Though diverse by meaning and definition, God's sacrificial love for man and David's love for Saul are made to converge upon a common meaning. Each love is strong from its very incapacity to achieve what it desires, and so from its dependence on a power greater than itself. David finds that objects like the palm-wine can be used analogically. The soul after death is to the body what the palm-wine is to the tree. But the wine is only an analogy of proper proportion. The absent tree is to the wine which sustains life what the illustrious Saul is to the fame which survives him after death. Because there is no intrinsic similarity between a dead man and a tree, David must try to develop a more participationist theology. What is unspeakable, because blasphemous, about David's own capacity to surpass God in his love for Saul forces him to re-invent his picture of God. His analogy of dependence, grounded on the normative value of love, an emotion all men ought to cultivate and live by, entails the existence not just of any God but of Schleiermacher's suffering God-in-man, who is constrained through love to die for all humanity. For Browning's David it is a great initial advantage that the fact in history, the Incarnation, which is the equivalent of his love, is still unrevealed and necessarily remains ahead of him in time. To find in history the otherwise unspeakable facts of his own imagination, David must show how the analogies of attribution gone dead in the theological creeds were once a speculation of great breadth and daring. He must show how their very formulation was once a poem.

But has David actually established Christ's historical existence? As in ontological arguments for God's existence, all he seems to have proved is that if we think of God we must think of Him as necessarily existing in history as a God who assumed human form. A backward inference from a feeling of dependence can establish only the existence of an ideal Christ. Though David himself illustrates that a feeling of dependence can take place apart from and prior to Christ's historical Incarnation, Strauss insists that, according to the premises of an orthodox doctrine, an historical Christ is 'both possible and necessary' (1846, vol. 3, p. 425). Anyone like Schleiermacher who defines myth as 'the historical presentation of what is supra-historical' (1928, p. 722) has a much feebler sense of history than Browning. There is only one way in 'Saul' in which Browning can escape from Strauss's trenchant critique of Schleiermacher's analogy of dependence. He can cross Schleiermacher's psychological analogy, which is grounded on a feeling of dependence, with a figural analogy, which makes David a type of Christ. Because it is the essence of biblical typology to show how past events are indeed a figure of historical events to come, Browning can combine the imaginative power of David's inductions from inward experience with a Christology that is figural and typological, hence more solidly historical than Schleiermacher's more 'ideal' theology can ever hope to become.

4 Beyond Schleiermacher: Browning and the Double Trinity

In the last two sections I have been analysing affinities between Browning's poetry and two influential traditions: Schleiermacher's theology of dependence and the liberal hermeneutics of Jowett and Strauss. I would be leaving a distorted impression of Browning, however, if I were to end the discussion here. Though I am inclined to take Browning at his word when he protests to Furnivall that he had no first-hand knowledge of either Kant or Hegel (Irvine and Honan, 1974, pp. 502, 582), I am also convinced that in trying to remove some of the difficulties that are posed by a merely ideal Christology like Schleiermacher's, Browning arrives independently at a solution that strikingly resembles Hegel's answer to the same problem. I am referring to his doctrine of a double Trinity.

Browning's dilemma in 'Saul' is part of a larger question: how can religion be made to include the believer's self-activity without jeopardizing Christian doctrines of dependence on God? In trying to reconcile a philosophic understanding of religion with a unique historical event, a hermeneutical poet like Browning is being asked to act as glue and solvent, as flour and yeast, simultaneously. Even when the striving for the infinite in Browning's Paracelsus is replaced in a speaker like David by a feeling of dependence, this feeling is still too ideal unless it can be focused on an historical individual. If David's feeling of dependence establishes Christ's existence, it is still only Schleiermacher's ideal Christ, a God-man who exists only in David's mind. In other poems Browning seems to accept the truth of Hegel's cruel remark that, if Schleiermacher were correct in his attempt to make the feeling of dependence specifically religious, then the best Christian would be a dog. Such speculation may terminate in the theological confusions of a drudge like Browning's Caliban. In trying to envisage in the Quiet a deity that is totally other than himself and on whom he is absolutely dependent, Caliban can picture only a form of emptiness with no historical content.

Browning's solution is to adjudicate the claims of cult and thought. Without the cultic side of religion disclosed in the Roman and the Nonconformist liturgies of 'Christmas-Eve', religion would be confined to a sphere of thought beyond time, leaving history unredeemed. But without a philosophy of religion, which is represented by the German professor's lecture in the same poem, the cultic side of religion would lack an intelligible explanation of who God truly is. It is important to transfigure historical faith into philosophic understanding. But how can this transfiguring take place unless the cultic and historical forms of religion, which Browning wants to retain, are in fact unessential to the religious content?

To understand this hermeneutical dilemma we must clearly distinguish between two concepts of history which are often confused. To speak of the historicity of faith is to speak of the historically revealed and given. But to speak of historicity as a self-constituting process is to speak of something man himself must make. One concept of history assumes that the past is over and God's entrance into history has already been achieved. The other theory argues that God and the self are still to be brought into being through faith, argument, and deed. Hegel had said that men should 'honour' the divine 'as *their* deed, their product, and their existence' (Brazill, 1970, p.

149). But he had also said that men 'honour the divine in and for itself'. In other words, God's self-activity is manifest in man. But man's faith is also receptive of the divine. In a very real sense, it *depends* upon God.

Is the difference between God and man, then, like the clash between two concepts of history, illusory or real? Browning's constant meditation upon a trinitarian interplay of power, knowledge, love, represents his most resourceful answer to this question. If 'saving faith' in God is not to be reduced to mere 'epic faith' in an historical document or chronicle, then speakers as dissimilar as Browning's Francis Furini, David, Paracelsus, and St John must each proclaim the logic of a pre-worldly trinitarian play that is eternally complete apart from any Christian revelation. And yet without an actual trinitarian incursion of God into history, Christianity would offer no improvement upon Plato. As Browning's Pope recognizes, it would be unable to make eminently real what Plato made derivatively real. Even if the historical events which St John has witnessed in 'A Death in the Desert' never actually took place, he believes that the trinitarian logic of a 'love' behind 'the will and might' (ll. 500–1) would require the invention of the Gospel story. But such a gnostic view of history re-enacts Shelley's flight from the world. Browning seeks a middle way that will overreach history without allowing history to disappear in the intense inane. He is looking for a version of Hegel's double Trinity (Hegel, 1895, vol. 3, pp. 33 ff; Fackenheim, 1967, pp. 149–54, 204–6, 218–19).

Neither Strauss nor Feuerbach, whom Browning read in translation, discusses Hegel's doctrine of a double Trinity. And Browning did not have enough command of German to read Hegel in the original. But the many similarities between Hegel's double Trinity and the interplay in Browning's poetry between historical Christianity and a timeless trinitarian logic are too striking to ignore. Like Hegel, Browning discerns behind the Persons in the Trinity an interaction of Idea, Spirit, Nature. Only the middle term, Love, unites the abiding truth of the second or pre-worldly Trinity with the incursion into history of the first Trinity. As Browning's Pope argues, there is evidence in nature of divine power and knowledge, but no evidence of a good or veracious God: 'Is there strength there? – enough: intelligence? / Ample: but goodness in a like degree?' (*The Ring and the Book*, x, 1363–4). As soon as he adds to 'intelligence' and 'strength' the missing middle term, which Hegel calls 'Spirit' and which Browning's Pope calls 'love without a limit', then the sacrificial quality of this love requires an incursion of the Trinity into history. As the second Person of the Trinity, Love 'supplies' the 'tale' of historical religion. But as the middle term of a timeless dialectic 'beyond the tale', Love or Spirit also overreaches history.

Christ is the Hegelian Spirit (Love). God is the Hegelian Idea (Power). And the world is the Hegelian Nature, which Browning associates with Knowledge. If Christ is to unite these two Trinities, he cannot be described as a mere moral teacher. To venerate Christ as a Jewish Kant, who instructed man in the 'simple work' of moral 'nomenclature', is like praising, 'not nature, / But Harvey, for the circulation' of the blood ('Christmas-Eve', ll. 971–3). But Christ overreaches the law he expounds. Browning's assertion that the actual world is overreached by Love or Spirit rests on the assumption that it is overreached by God (or the Hegelian Idea). And this Idea can overreach the world only if the Spirit or Love which recognizes this truth is not a mere finite spirit, a mere good man, but an infinite spirit that forms the middle term of a double Trinity, directing Browning, as it directs Hegel, 'from the cistern to the river' ('Christmas-Eve', l. 1015).

To live in a world that is doubly overreached by Spirit and Idea, Christ and God, is already to be where Browning wants to be. Since he leaps from the finite to the infinite all at once or not at all, Browning finds that his task is to disclose the infinite as an absent presence. An impossible goal is a goal which not only does *not* exist but *cannot* exist. The infinite is not such a goal, for as Browning shows in 'Two in the Campagna' even when we seek the finite we intend the infinite: 'Only I discern – / Infinite passion, and the pain / Of finite hearts that yearn' (ll. 58–60). Unlike Paracelsus, whose quest for infinite knowledge is an indefinite quest which tends to lose itself in what Hegel calls the bad or spurious infinite, Browning's speaker rejects the concept of limits as such, and not just this or that limit. Being aware of the finite, he is already beyond it.

To reach God through history Browning refines the argument Bishop Blougram uses against Gigadibs. He shows that anyone who denies the possibility of reaching 'love without a limit' is contradicting himself in his very denial. Gigadibs the empiricist asserts that he cannot believe 'In any revelation called divine' ('Bishop Blougram's Apology', l. 153). But he contradicts himself because his assumption cannot be empirically established. Browning's speakers usually perceive the infinite out of the corner of their eye, the way Browning's dreamer catches a glimpse of the elusive white-robed figure in 'Christmas-Eve' (ll. 437–9) or his Roman patrician catches the eye of Augustus Caesar behind the mask of a beggar: 'And I had a glimpse – just one! / One was enough' ('Imperante Augusto Natus Est – ', ll. 118–19). St John and Abt Vogler may assert that there are points rather than stars, partial arcs rather than complete rounds. But these very denials of the infinite implicitly affirm it.

Browning's God is not really an object of historical knowledge but the precondition of it. Whereas the fictive judgements of Kant's moral theology resolve the actual into the virtual, Browning's hypotheses about God submit to the test and demand verification. The difference between Kant's God and Browning's is the difference between what Hans Vaihinger calls a merely 'fictional' and a 'hypothetical' entity (Vaihinger, 1924, p. 128). Blougram's final taunt to Gigadibs is that, as an atheist who acts morally, Gigadibs believes practically in God and immortality, since he acts as if God and immortality existed. For Kant this is all any believer really does. ' "I believe in God" means simply that "I act as if a God really existed" ' (Vaihinger, 1924, p. 306). But Browning seeks a less fictive mode of belief. Kant's God is only a useful surmise, like the virtual focus of an optical image in which the rays of light merely seem to converge. There is a subjective but no objective necessity in affirming that a virtual image exists. By submitting to the test Browning means the test of each believer's unconscious affirmation. He is thinking of nothing so scientific or empirical as an archaeological discovery. Like a more recent commentator, Browning knows that even the alleged 'discovery of a large boat-shaped structure on Mount Ararat with animal cages in it' would merely shift the 'criterion of truth' from the Bible 'to something else' (Northrop Frye, 1982, pp. 44–5). The scientific tendency to convert theology into archaeology by excavating 'some mummy-scrap' or some marine fossil that will prove Moses lived or that Jonah's whale actually existed ('Easter-Day', ll. 177–84) is just as dangerous as Kant's opposite practice of fashioning a fictional God that will minister to our 'hopes and fears' ('Easter-Day', l. 181).

Browning's God is neither a supreme fiction nor a grammatical subject, but a verb implying a process of development, a process of accomplishing itself. Like Hegel's double Trinity, Browning's constant rotation of Power, Wisdom, Love, describes a circle. By assuming in his premise what a logician would hope to prove in his conclusion, Browning commits a form of *petitio principii*. But his circle is not a vicious circle, because Browning shows how sceptics like Karshish and Cleon are groping for a God whom they already worship unconsciously. Their *unconscious* affirmation of the infinite is necessary. All they are free to grant or withhold is their *conscious* affirmation. When Browning's speakers choose or decide, they are really excluding all possible avenues of choice except one. This is what Paracelsus fails to see. Reluctant to say 'No' to anything, he cannot grasp that only God can say 'Yes' to more than one alternative at a time. For this reason Browning's final challenge to his critics is also Bishop Blougram's challenge to Gigadibs. Try to deny the principles that the believer cannot strictly speaking demonstrate, and the believer can show the sceptic that he himself unconsciously affirms these principles in seeming to deny them. Like Hegel and other God-builders of the nineteenth century, Browning believes that though 'God may have lost his function as the subject . . . of a predicate', He 'may not be so much dead as entombed in a dead language'. Browning is continually trying to bring God alive in a world which recognizes that the divine creation, as traditionally conceived, 'was an illusion projected from the evolutionary operations within nature' (Northrop Frye, 1982, pp. 14, 18). Each historian and critic, like every interpreter of the Bible, has to project the eternal, and he has to empathize with what he is given. The two functions have to be seen as reciprocal activities, as inseparably entwined as Hegel's two Trinities or as Browning's knowledge *of* God and his self-knowledge *in* God. Neither can be allowed to obscure or dissipate the other.

5 Arnold's Platonism:
Analogies of Self and State

Arnold's poetry and criticism look two ways at once. As a Victorian Hans Vaihinger, Arnold belongs in a purist agnostic tradition. He is

the Victorian apologist of art for art's sake and a precursor of
modern formalism. But like Keble and all the other writers studied
in this chapter, Arnold also belongs in an oracular hermeneutical
tradition. He is an Orphic as well as a hermetic figure. Having stud-
ied the hermetic Arnold in Chapter IV, I now turn to the Orphic
Arnold, whose use of Plato has less in common with the Plato of
Grote and Pater than with the Plato of liberal Anglicans like R. D.
Hampden, Connop Thirlwall, and F. D. Maurice.

It is important to state at the beginning that Keble is Arnold's
godfather in spirit as well as name. Though Arnold's hermeneutical
writings are far more radical than Keble's, Arnold does not merely
jettison the principle of authority enshrined in Keble's conservative
theory and practice. Authority undergoes a sea-change in Arnold. It
re-emerges in the cultural and literary criticism in Arnold's appeal
to an authoritarian Platonic tradition quite alien to the Plato of
Grote, Jowett, and Pater.

Jowett applies to Scripture the same interpretative methods he
later refines in his commentary on Plato's *Dialogues*. Arnold's pro-
cedure is precisely the reverse. Instead of treating the Bible like a
Greek text, he turns literature into a bible. Arnold transfers to
poetry the same value-making function that his godfather Keble
restricts to Scripture alone. Though Arnold is as critical of typologi-
cal interpretations as is Jowett, he uses Platonic analogies between
powers of the human person and social classes to establish spiritual
principles that will enjoy, he hopes, the same authority as the his-
torical analogies that are used in typological criticism of the Bible.

Any account of Arnold's Platonism must also recognize some of
its equally important affinities with Jowett's theories. The oc-
casional similarities between these two Hellenists deserve to be
better known. In 1841 Arnold won a classical scholarship to Balliol
College, Oxford, where he became a close friend of Jowett, later
Balliol's most famous Master. As undergraduates Arnold and
Jowett were both members of a small discussion club called the
Decade, an Oxford version of the Cambridge Apostles. And in later
life each championed the central importance to culture of a classical
education. As a professional educator and critic of culture, Arnold
must have been struck to the heart by Jowett's stirring explanation of
why Plato's theory of education is far in advance of Victorian
views. Though Arnold in *Culture and Anarchy* is still partly

entranced by the sentimental view of Greece promoted by such pre-Victorian Germans as Winckelmann, Schiller, and A. W. Schlegel, his Hellenism has far more in common with Jowett's systematic study and application of Plato, including an advocacy of Plato's *Republic* as an educational model. Arnold's reading-lists suggest that he finished reading Plato's *Republic* either before March 1845, in preparation for the Oriel fellowship examination, or else during the early part of that summer (Allott, 1959, vol. 2, pp. 258–9). In his later social and cultural criticism, it is almost as if Arnold were taking up Jowett's challenge to some contemporary Socrates to become a 'schoolmaster abroad', a tutelary genius like the scholar-gipsy 'who will tell [men] of their faults, or inspire them with the higher sense of duty'. Like Arnold, Jowett in his commentary on *The Republic* is all too aware that 'the destination of most men is what Plato would call "the cave" for the whole of life' (1871, vol. 2, p. 161). Jowett's 'schoolmaster abroad' must be as implacable as Arnold's Oxford student in 'The Scholar-Gipsy'. He must be as relentless, as disturbing, and as dangerous to ignore, as a conscience.

Just as Arnold in *Culture and Anarchy* attacks the Utilitarian fallacy of making happiness, the mere satisfaction of 'doing as one likes', the measure of what ought to be, so Jowett in his commentary on *The Republic* criticizes J. S. Mill for making the self-love and happiness of the individual the basis of morality (1871, vol. 2, p. 48). Like Plato, Jowett and Arnold both advocate some centre of political and spiritual authority in society, analogous to the moral authority which Plato accords to justice and which Arnold ascribes to the individual's ability to live according to all his aspirations and powers. *Culture and Anarchy* envisages a harmonious development of the power of knowledge, the powers of beauty and manners, and the power of conduct, which are the special attainments of the upper middle class, the aristocracy, and the Philistines, respectively. The obvious model is Plato's ideal Republic, which celebrates the harmony of four virtues. Wisdom, courage, temperance are the virtues of Plato's rulers, soldiers, and common citizens, respectively. And the fourth virtue, justice, rules over all the others as a philosopher-king, ruthlessly prosecuting every wayward impulse. As powerful allegories of rational morality, neither *Culture and Anarchy* nor Plato's *Republic* is a blueprint for social reform. There is hardly a passage in *Culture and Anarchy* that can be directly translated into a particular action, and except for the *Laws*, which are a practical scheme for the establishment of small city-states and a blueprint for tyranny, the conclusions of *The Republic* will work only in heaven.

My own findings support David Newsome's conclusion that 'Arnold's Plato was the Plato of the *Republic*. He had not time for the purely metaphysical dialogues; although he had read the *Phaedrus* and the *Symposium* he rarely quoted from them' (1974, p. 130). Like Plato, Arnold often implies that his ideals are, in Jowett's words, 'none the worse because they cannot be realized in fact'. Analogies between the self and the state may be mere 'noble lies', like Plato's fiction of the earth-born men. As a supreme fiction, it may 'in some sense . . . have reality', as Jowett concludes, 'but not in the vulgar one of a reign of philosophers upon earth' (1871, vol. 2, pp. 151–2). Though fictions that cannot be proved to be useful and necessary must be eliminated, the renunciation of all fictive judgements would be a renunciation of life. The falsest judgements may be the most indispensable ones for us. From the inscription on the presentation copy he gave to Browning, for example (*The Browning Collections*, 1913, item 705), it appears that Arnold wanted to make gifts of Glanvill's book *The Vanity of Dogmatizing*, rather as if he were a one-man Gideon Society dispensing bibles to his unconverted friends. Far from being the esoteric concern of an Oxford professor of poetry, an apostle of culture, the status of Glanvill's fiction about the scholar-gipsy is the status of literature itself. To give validity to fictions is a life-and-death issue. No one knew better than Glanvill, a sort of seventeenth-century Sir William Hamilton, that 'man cannot live', as Hans Vaihinger says, 'without measuring reality by [that] purely imaginary world of the unconditioned, the "self-identical"' (1924, pp. 352–3) which Arnold presents in his fiction of the scholar's 'immortal lot, / . . . exempt from age / And living [as he liveth] on Glanvil's page' ('The Scholar-Gipsy', ll. 157–9).

Arnold's Platonism bears striking affinities, despite its scepticism, with Keble's doctrine of reserve. The truth abides, but it remains as self-concealing and evasive as the shy, reclusive hero of 'The Scholar-Gipsy'. Arnold's real promised land is the harmonious life of the individual, of which the well-ordered, classless society envisaged in 'Equality' and *Culture and Anarchy* is but the representative fiction. Such indeed is the status of the Greek gods and heroes, who died that they might live in the beauty of acknowledged myth.

Nowhere is this idea more beautifully and honestly expressed than in Arnold's classical poem 'Palladium'. Just as each reader's renewing the battle in the plain is an important part of the Gospel's meaning, so by shifting from a past to future verb tense – 'We shall renew the battle in the plain / Tomorrow' ('Palladium', ll. 13–14) – Arnold links an heroic achievement in Homer to another action placed in future time, in which the reader as Everyman is now the hero. To some readers Athene's statue in 'Palladium', like the Greek ideal it stands for, may seem too remote, too withdrawn from the world we actually inhabit, to be a source of real authority. But Frank Turner's claim that Arnold's Hellenism denies the darker side of ancient Greek culture, which is rediscovered only later in the century by anthropologists like Andrew Lang and James G. Frazer, seems radically untrue of Arnold's poetry. In dramatizing the surge of chaos on the darkling plain, Arnold seems fully conscious of the 'nonrational, aggressive, and self-destructive impulses' which Professor Turner believes his Hellenism effectively denies (1981, p. 36). In 'Palladium' the renewal of the battle on the darkling plain recalls the dark side of Hellenism recounted by Thucydides, and it powerfully dramatizes the saying of Goethe quoted by Arnold in his first Homeric lecture: 'From Homer and Polygnotus I every day learn more clearly that in our life here above ground we have, properly speaking, to enact Hell' (1960, vol. 1, p. 102).

In Arnold's thought the Platonic analogies I have been tracing between powers in the human person and classes in society are combined with a historical, Viconian use of analogy designed to establish ties between Victorian Britain and fifth-century Athens. This Viconian argument is adapted by liberal Anglican historians like Arnold's father, who concludes that Thucydides is an historian of events that are more properly described as modern than ancient. According to this Viconian view of history, all nations develop through a series of stages that resemble the stages of individual growth and decay. Though nations in one phase of growth may share few characteristics with neighbouring nations in a different phase, Arnold and his father both believe that once similarities between analogous historical periods are discerned, the true contemporaneousness of societies as temporally remote as Periclean Athens and Victorian Britain can be convincingly established and explored. Given the analogous positions within the cycle of historical development of fifth-century Greece and nineteenth-century Britain, Arnold feels confident in drawing parallels between Pericles or Socrates and contemporaries like Goethe or Newman who seem to him to embody traditional humanist values. Though Arnold's Hellenic ideal may owe more to the aesthetic theories of Sir Joshua Reynolds's *Discourses* than to Plato or Aristotle, I cannot see what Frank Turner means when, having clearly explained the Viconian theory of historical analogy on which Arnold's judgements are based, he proceeds to berate Arnold for allowing 'double meanings and an almost disengenuous concealment of purpose' to characterize his entire discussion of Hellenism and Hebraism (Turner, 1981, p. 21). Arnold's interpretation of the Greeks is not, after all, a personal idiosyncrasy or aberration. It is based on a widely accepted theory of analogous ages, and it claims a venerable ancestry which includes Shaftesbury, Cudworth, and earlier Renaissance humanists in whom the gleams of 'intellectual fire and spiritual enthusiasm . . . brought the Platonic light to Britain' (Turner, 1981, p. 321).

Like most Victorians, Arnold believes the poet has an educational function. But he has both a radical and conservative answer to the question: how can the Victorian poet educate without necessarily becoming, like Arnold, a school inspector? In *Culture and Anarchy* Arnold sets forth the conservative ideal of an inner elect group. As the spokesman for this saving remnant, Arnold writes as a kind of secular Keble, drawing upon the educational model of Plato's *Republic* to defend the principle of spiritual authority. In a more radical essay like 'The Study of Poetry', however, which attacks religion for materializing itself in the fact, Arnold rejects Keble's conservative teaching that the models of creation are established by God. As a student of Vico and Herder, Arnold believes that man makes his own civilization and culture. In celebrating his discovery that 'the strongest part of our religion today is its unconscious poetry', Arnold is reaffirming his conviction that poetry expresses man's creation of his own culture, rather than his reception of culture from a divine source. 'For poetry the [created] idea is everything; the rest is a world of illusion, of divine illusion' (Arnold, 1960–77 (1973), vol. 9, p. 161). From his reading of Glanvill, Victor Cousin, and Kant's first *Critique*, Arnold would have learned that arguments about God collapse into antinomies. The philosophy of religion consists of half-truths implying their own opposites. The works of imaginative reason, by contrast, cannot be refuted. As Arnold discovers in the *Bhagavad Gita* and in the joyful Stoicism of his beloved Spinoza, poetry is the language of a higher truth which treats everything it meets as another version of itself. The higher dialectic of imagination and love never demolishes: it only includes. Arnold's imaginative recovery of what was formerly projected into religious creeds separates the acknowledged fictions of the poet from the supposed facts of the historian to which religion has mistakenly attached itself. The poet's authority and right to educate derive from a power in the mind that no longer depends on the prior educational claim of religion, morality, or law. By placing the analytic operations of understanding in a lower category, Arnold claims for the creative activity of his poet an educational value which Keble and earlier humanist critics like Sidney reserve for religion and ethics alone.

If Arnold is the most representative Victorian critic, it is because like Plato's criticism his theory of poetry faces two ways at once. A Platonic theory of ideas threatens to deprive art either of archetypal meaning or of independent value. If art is merely an embodiment of Plato's ideas, then it has no independent value. If it describes only the visible world, it cannot have archetypal meaning. Pater chooses the second alternative and Keble the first. Only Arnold, like Plato, is an Orphic and hermetic thinker simultaneously. Arnold is able to avoid both Keble's tendency to minimize play and disinterestedness and Pater's tendency to minimize ideas. Unlike Pater, Arnold and Plato value art because it is essentially related to the rest of the world. And unlike Keble, they insist that art's connection with the world is more than a replication of models established by God.

As an advocate of liberal education, Arnold commends studies whose products are useless but not trivial. The classical model of such advocacy is Plato's defence of the arts. In studying art, Arnold studies one paradigm for the relation between the intelligible and the visible worlds. Nature is God's poetry, as Keble says, because it is the book in which we can best decipher the divine alphabet. In art's adaptation of spiritual content to material form it is also possible to study the emergence of the visible world from the higher and more real spiritual world that Arnold fictionalizes in the 'immortal lot' of his scholar-gipsy. By contrast with Keble and Arnold, Pater argues that art can provide a liberal education only by freeing the mind from the contagion of content and ideas. Arnold agrees with Pater that to understand art is to understand something as unique and irreplaceable as the Mona Lisa's smile. But for Arnold and Plato the play of art is non-serious, not in the sense that art banishes ideas, but only in the sense that, like the pursuit of virtue or a liberal education, it is not immediately useful. The chief educative function of poetry is its free or disengaged presentation of the means of communication and the ways of knowing. Because poetry is playful or non-serious, hence pleasing, imitation that yields worthwhile cognitive experience, its study lies at the heart of Arnold's carefully reasoned defence of liberal education.

6 Hopkins, Plato, and the New Realism

As a hermeneutical poet, Hopkins belongs in the same conservative tradition as Keble and Christina Rossetti. But few of Hopkins' best-known poems are as narrowly hermeneutical as his sonnets from 'New Readings'. Most of his poems testify to a higher power that uses Hopkins as its prophet and oracle. As bearers of transcendent meaning, these poems are as luminous as crystal. At the same time Hopkins' use of inversion and apposition isolates words and obscures their syntactical function. By shifting attention from the oracular presence glimpsed through the words to the words themselves, Hopkins makes his language not only as luminous as crystal but also as hard and impenetrable. Hopkins' Janus-like ability to re-create a spiritual world while focusing attention on the physical properties of words can best be explained by his adaptation of Platonism. Each word is fixed in a Platonic scale of nature which, like the diatonic scale in music, preserves the difference of the sounds while establishing ratios among them. Valued not only as an end in itself but also as one rung in a Platonic ladder, each word may function simultaneously as a crystal-hard thing-in-itself and as a crystal-clear power of formation, a capacity of the oracular poet to refashion the world as an *ascensio mentis*.

Like the Cambridge Platonists of the seventeenth century, the young Hopkins hopes to preside over a true and lawful marriage of theological aesthetics and Platonism. In several prophetic essays he wrote as an Oxford undergraduate, Hopkins shares the renewed in-

terest in Plato and Hegel that dominates the philosophic life of
Oxford from the mid 1860s until the end of the nineteenth century.
In a paper written in 1865 for T. H. Green on 'The Position of Plato
to the Greek World', Hopkins praises the 'exhaustive and unhurried
demonstration, digressions and objections' and the 'files of parallels
used as proof' which characterize Plato's dialogues. Like all his aes-
thetic speculations, the tentative groping of Hopkins' essay is an
example of that search for 'a few first principles' which Hopkins,
like Grote and Lewes, values in Plato (Hopkins, 1959b, p. 116). The
same flexibility of intellect that Hopkins praises in Plato is a quality
of Hopkins' own dialogue 'On the Origin of Beauty' (1959b, pp.
86–114). Of most aesthetic and philosophic interest is Hopkins'
essay on 'The Probable Future of Metaphysics', where Plato is
linked with Aristotle and the Schoolmen as an example of the first of
'three great seasons in the history of philosophy'. The Victorian age
suffers, Hopkins believes, from the debilitating effects of the second
and third epochs in that 'history', the second being 'that of Bacon
and physical science and Positivism, the third that of Hegel and the
philosophy of development in time' (1959b, p. 119). To combat
both the positivist's veneration of fact and Hegel's 'philosophy of
flux', Hopkins urges a return to a version of Platonism based on the
idea of form and matter and on the doctrine of fixed species or types.

The Platonism Hopkins envisages is designed to oppose the
dominant atomism of the age, which 'like a stiffness or sprain seems
to hang upon and hamper our speculation'. By atomism Hopkins
means the 'over-powering, ... disproportioned sense of person-
ality' and egoism. He also means the glorification of that unique
sense of identity which he himself will later celebrate as *haecceitas*,
but which sometimes seems at odds with his own doctrine of
inscape. Atomism culminates in the nightmares of Hume and Pater,
and in the chaos foreseen by Tennyson's Lucretius, as each sundered
particle 'disintegrates and drops toward' the void (Hopkins, 1959b,
pp. 119–20). Ironically, atomism is the logical outcome of one
dominant impulse in Hopkins' own theory of language. In antici-
pation of de Saussure, Hopkins grasps that language provides him
with differences according to which one word or unit of discourse
cannot be anything but itself. If Hopkins uses alliteration, hyper-
baton, and dislocated syntax to divide experience into small separate
units for the mind to manage, it is simply because he is carrying to a

new extreme one important function of all language. Words differentiate experience because they are themselves a system of difference. Most poets form equivalences among the separate identities they have created. But because Hopkins' atomic parts function primarily as units of identity rather than as units of meaning, the purely formal differences among the separate identities may be too extreme for any inscape to organize. If atomism is one danger, promiscuous merging is another. In philosophies like Spinoza's, Hopkins attacks the opposite error of trying to sink all defining differences in an undifferentiated unity. Such a philosophy of fixed and absolute types is too monistic, 'too abstract, unpregnant, and inefficient – Spinoza as they point out *laudatur et alget*, has no disciples' (Hopkins, 1959b, p. 121). 'The new school of metaphysics' Hopkins foresees will try to avoid two dangers. To meet the challenge posed by atomism and by all philosophies of flux Hopkins will revive 'some shape of the Platonic Ideas'. But even in restoring a doctrine of fixed types, in which the Idea descends 'from the whole downwards to the parts', Hopkins' new Platonism – or 'to speak more correctly', his new 'Realism' – will defend the uniqueness of each created item against any promiscuous merging in the Absolute. Paradoxically, Hegel seems to pose a double threat to Hopkins. As the leading philosopher of 'Historical Development', he propounds a doctrine of pure atomic flux like Hume and Pater. But as the philosopher of Absolute Spirit, Hegel is also the great advocate of indiscriminate merging. He threatens to dismantle the fixed points of Hopkins' new 'Realism' and merge all its diatonic intervals in the chromatic blur of an Absolute that, like Spinoza's Substance, is too 'abstract, unpregnant, and inefficient' to win either the poet's or the philosopher's allegiance.

No matter which direction language faces, toward the isolated atoms of discourse or toward the undifferentiated kind of utterance which contains within itself all that can be said, Hopkins finds he confronts two different forms of emptiness. On the one hand, the more Hopkins uses alliteration and parallelisms to focus attention on a complex network of differences, the more unique and untranslatable each word or phrase becomes. In such usage, word-coinages like 'leafmeal' are no longer marginal but central functions of language. This is because Hopkins' words are now operating primarily as units of formal equivalence rather than as units of meaning. In ordinary discourse 'leafmeal' could not mean 'pieces of leaf' but only 'leaf food'. But in Hopkins line, 'Though worlds of wanwood leafmeal lie' ('Spring and Fall', l. 8), the difference between 'leafmeal' and 'piecemeal' is not so secure. As in any form of punning or word-coinage, the difference is indeterminate. It is only a short step from such indeterminacy to the kind of nonsense verse that asserts an equivalence whose meaning remains entirely within the enclosure of an artificial language: ' 'Twas brillig, and the slithy toves / Did gyre and gimble in the wabe' (Lewis Carroll, 'Jabberwocky', ll. 1–2). In 'desynonymizing' language, as Coleridge calls it, Hopkins may make each word so different from every other word that it cannot resemble anything but itself. In composing a *Te Deum Laudamus* like 'Pied Beauty', for example, a paean to God for 'dappled things', Hopkins' jubilation in the sheer diversity of creation, in 'Whatever is fickle, freckled (who knows how?)' (l. 8), gorges him with language. Intoxicated with the sound of his alliterations – 'swift, slow; sweet, sour; adazzle, dim' (l. 9) – Hopkins invites all words, in Roland Barthes' phrase, 'to perch, to flock, to fly off again' in a 'marbled, iridescent' hymn of praise (Barthes, 1975, p. 8). Hopkins is so exaggerating the pied beauty of his world, the principle of difference presupposed by any language, that in such lines he seems to be composing a page in Flaubert's 'imaginary book about nothing'. Because such a book is 'dependent on nothing external', as Flaubert reminds us, it is 'held together by the strength of its style, just as the earth, suspended in the void, depends on nothing external for its support'. Like nonsense poetry, it is 'a book which would have almost no subject, or at least in which the subject would be almost invisible' (Flaubert, 1953, pp. 127–8).

When Hopkins, fearful of being swallowed up in Flaubert's void, takes the opposite tack by trying to establish unifying connections among equivalent units of discourse, there is always a danger of abolishing too many differences. The movement to collapse all words into a synonym is an effort to return to an original, undifferentiated language and world. But once this process begins, there is nothing to arrest the skid into emptiness. The unravelling of the spool of 'véined variety' leaves the imageless mind 'selfstrung, sheathe-and shelterless', as Hopkins shows in one of his darkest sonnets, 'Spelt from Sibyl's Leaves', l. 14. In seeking to encompass all that is, as one commentator says, Hopkins shows that any attempt to abolish differences 'destroys what it seeks in the very process by which its quest is conducted. For what is undifferentiated exceeds comprehension; indeed, it remains inaccessible to experience, quite as though it were nothing at all' (Bruns, 1974, p. 163).

In order to achieve plenitude rather than emptiness, Hopkins must be both a hermetic poet who makes self-contained works and an oracular poet whose energy extends beyond the making of poems toward the creation of the world. In this task Hopkins makes use of the Platonist's 'new Realism' to posit a scale of fixed intervals, of '*saltus*' or 'breaks'. In his sonnet 'As Kingfishers Catch Fire', for example, Hopkins advocates the use of a diatonic scale, whose 'chords, to use technical wording, are mathematically fixed and give a standard by which to fix all the notes of the appropriate scale' (Hopkins, 1959b, p. 120). 'As tumbled over rim in roundy wells / Stones ring; like each tucked string tells, each hung bell's / Bow swung finds tongue to fling out broad its name; / Each mortal thing does one thing and the same' (ll. 2–5). We are not meant to sort out string and percussion instruments, nor to trace a temporal sequence. We receive instead in a single mounting impression a parataxis of distinct sensations: a plucked-string-resonating; a bow-struck-clapper-on-a-hung-bell-flinging-out-its-sound. Despite the simultaneous apprehension, these sounds are not allowed to blur chromatically, because Hopkins uses the Platonic-Christian model of a great ordered pyramid, sustained by the instress binding together the appropriately spaced inscapes and intervals of all objects and all sounds. 'Christ plays in ten thousand places, / Lovely in limbs, and lovely in eyes not his / To the Father through the features of men's faces' (ll. 12–14). Is Christ 'lovely in eyes not his' (l. 13) because Christ's loveliness lies in the eyes of his beholders? Or is he 'lovely' as the incarnate God, as a deity literally present in 'eyes not his'? While still preserving the intervals, such two-way meaning sustains a reversing flow, a movement back and forth, that keeps furling Christ in man and man in Christ. When syntax looks different ways at once, formal devices of equivalence like apposition and alliteration become at least as important as the meaning. But because the matching forms ('lovely in limbs', 'lovely in eyes') also assert genuine identities, the poetry is intelligible and capable of being understood by any persevering reader.

Whereas Plato appeals to Pater because he transforms the abstract unity of Parmenides into a 'delightfully multiple ... world of ideas', Hopkins wants to collapse all words into the Word. Pater is appalled by the thought that in Plato the colourful 'old Greek polytheism had found [its] way back after all into a repellent monotheism' (Pater, 1893, p. 39). But Hopkins wants to press language back into a primal word that supersedes all speech because it contains all speech. He wants all things to rhyme or chime in Christ. And to differentiate his richly coloured monotheism from the 'colourless One' of Spinoza and Hegel, Hopkins wants every note of his diatonic scale to make his world finely nuanced and varied. To preserve this variety and distinctness, the notes of the Christian poet must not be allowed to blur chromatically. The best way to produce the poetic equivalent of sanctity and detachment is to invert word order and dislocate meaning. The purer language becomes, the more it will draw attention to its own formal properties. Like Pater's aesthetic poetry, which satisfies a thirst for escape, as for the silence of a shrine or a museum, Hopkins' poems are woven out of ungrounded echoes and repetitions. As the alliterating sounds and assonances are modulated in a restless zigzag through the quoted lines, sudden fleeting affinities of joy and surprise define an inscape that becomes less analysable as the loveliness that binds Christ to man wavers unsteadily, uncertain which grammatical route to take. In an exacting but rapturous exercise of perception and thought, Hopkins seems to recognize that these verbal echoes are not a part, nor yet a copy, of the real world, and so are strangely different from any Platonic archetype or Christian presence they may seem to invoke. At the same time, to prevent a hierarchically ordered universe with Christ at its summit from disintegrating into an anarchy of sundered things 'in throngs', Hopkins must retain in his doctrine of fixed types or species 'some shape of the Platonic ideas'. In combining the playful overflow of his verbal high spirits with the intelligibility of a prayer, Hopkins is being faithful to the paradoxical status of language as a 'lucid veil'. His words function simultaneously as crystal-clear bearers of theological meaning and as crystal-hard verbal entities, dense and material in their own right like the sounding clapper or the stones that ring in roundy wells.

Platonism's focus on formal patterning encourages Hopkins to define his poems as a system of internal relations. But the Platonist's faith in the creative power of speech also encourages Hopkins to treat the poem as an utterance as well as an object, as an event as well as a self-enclosing harmony of forms. Against the prevalent evolutionary principle 'that knowledge is from the birth upwards . . . and mounts from the part to the whole', Hopkins staunchly champions the contrary assumption of Plato, Aristotle, and the Schoolmen. In learning to take into account the ontology as well as the formal properties of his words, Hopkins comes to view the world as a vast ordered pyramid, as a diatonic scale of nature. The intervals between the notes of this scale are fixed and absolute, and 'the Idea is only given – whatever may be the actual form education takes – from the whole downwards to the parts' (Hopkins, 1959b, p. 120).

VII Hegelian Aesthetics
and the Revolt Against the Absolute

In this concluding chapter I shall briefly consider the influence of
Hegel's aesthetics and theory of knowledge upon Victorian critics
like Sydney Dobell, E. S. Dallas, Walter Pater, and W. P. Ker. I
shall also show how Hegel's holistic axiom that the truth is the
whole helps differentiate the dialectical form of Browning's mature
dramatic monologues from the genres of framed narration that I ex-
amined in Chapter II. Like the authoritarian Tractarian and Platonic
traditions that were studied in Chapter VI, Hegelian aesthetics tends
to subordinate art to truth. But the revolt against the Hegelian
Absolute during the closing years of the nineteenth century has the
effect of transferring to the poet and the critic properties of self-
making that a conservative Hegelian like Bradley ascribes to the
Absolute alone. Like Pringle-Pattison, poets and critics know that
in art as in morals there is no way of avoiding uncertainty and risk.
Oscar Wilde celebrates the critic's seeing of the object as in itself it
really is not, because he believes that a passively received truth is
precisely what human beings cannot have and should not want.

Given some superficial affinity between Aristotle and Hegel, it is
perhaps no surprise that Victorian Oxford, the traditional centre of
Aristotelian studies in England, should also become a home after
1870 to the British Hegelians. Even the Hegelian Bradley is rightly
praised by T. S. Eliot, in his fine essay on Bradley (1932, p. 455), for
his Aristotelian respect for words and for his efforts to bring British
philosophy closer to the Aristotelian tradition. Like Aristotle's
formal causes, Hegel's concrete universals bring the abstract univer-
sals of Plato and Kant down to earth: according to J. H. Stirling,
herein lies 'the secret of Hegel' (1898, p. xxii). Aristotle and Hegel
both further agree that knowledge is not to be confused with scien-
tific classifications and inductions. For such inductive labelling they
substitute a doctrine of immanent teleology, which asserts that the
knower has no right to boast of any knowledge of an object until he
has penetrated to its inmost nature. The common doctrine of Spen-

cer, Mansel, Hamilton, and Mill is to banish God 'to an inscrutable region beyond the scope of scientific inquiry, where statements may be made at will', as the Oxford Hegel scholar William Wallace wryly notes, 'but where we have no power of verifying any statement whatever' (1874, xxvi, xxvii). By contrast, Aristotle and Hegel place God 'in the actuality and plenitude of the world' and not 'in the solitude of a world beyond'.

I do not wish to obscure, however, an equally important *difference* between Aristotle and Hegel. Unlike Aristotle's Unmoved Mover, who is never in process, Hegel's God is always in motion, always becoming. As Wallace says, Hegel penetrates 'the apparent fixity of a . . . term', even of a term like God. He sees 'through it into the process which bears it into being'. The mind of God, like man's mind, is not a substance but a subject. 'In this rather tersely put formula Hegel emphasizes his opposition to [Aristotelian] metaphysics' (Wallace, 1874, pp. liv, lv). Hegel wants to explain how God, for example, *makes* or *constitutes* Himself by becoming first a grotesque animal god in ancient Egypt, then a beautiful human god in classical Greece, and finally the sublimely transcendent 'I am that I am' of Genesis – or the equally sublime God-man of Christian faith. By contrast, Aristotle's final causes are immutable and fixed. One might formulate the difference this way: all Hegelian theories of self-making entail a belief in immanent form, but no Aristotelian doctrine of immanent form entails Hegel's more dynamic belief in growing and becoming, which is really a belief in self-making.

In the last three chapters, I have been analysing forms of analogical thought used by Victorian poets and philosophers to reach a knowledge of supersensible truth. I showed in Chapter IV how Victorian efforts to compass the divine nature in concepts that have a content in sensuous intuition, like the concepts of the physical scientist, lead in H. L. Mansel's philosophy of religion and in the religious poetry of Arnold and Clough to more and more equivocal forms of predication. Less equivocal are the analogies of authentic experience, often based on moral behaviour and love, which enable Broad Church theologians like F. D. Maurice and poets like Browning and Tennyson to see God through increasingly lucid veils. Though half concealing what they shadow forth, the authoritarian analogies of Tractarians and Platonists provide even more direct access to God. A truly cognitive analogy, however, should finally be able to close the gap between Tractarian typology's order of perfection and an imperfect order which merely prepares for and prefigures the higher order. If an analogy is truly cognitive, it should also be capable of building a bridge between the Platonic Ideas and their inferior copies – between what is eminently real and what is only derivatively real.

This concluding chapter examines two such analogies: an Aristotelian analogy of being, which I align with a fixed scale of nature, and a Hegelian analogy of self-making and becoming. In Aristotle's and Aquinas' ontology, God is Pure Being: in Hegel's *Logic*, He is pure Freedom or Becoming. Whereas Aristotle's God creates *ex nihilo*, Hegel's God passes out of the nothingness of sheer possibility into the differentiation of the actual. Aristotle's God of Being, for whom *operatio sequitur esse*, is also the God of Aquinas, Ruskin, Hopkins. But in Swinburne's Hertha we find traces of a radically different ontology, 'which asserts that, at least in the case of God, *esse sequitur operationem*' (Emil L. Fackenheim, 1961, p. 29). The God of this minor tradition, which is the tradition of John Scotus Eriugena, Jacob Boehme, Schelling, and Blake, is capable of generating a logic of His own which, however unintelligible in terms of a logic 'consisting of a simple forward movement' that 'leaves its terms static and unchanged', can be explained in terms of a 'self-constituting process which, in moving forward, integrates and re-integrates its own past into the forward movement'. As E. L. Fackenheim observes, 'the greatest attempt to explicate' this second kind of logic, which is the logic a God of Becoming generates, 'is beyond all doubt Hegel's work by that name' (1961, pp. 32–4). Such a God is Swinburne's Hertha, who in creating out of nothing (like Hegel's Absolute Spirit) passes into actuality before returning upon herself in a giant spiral.

All Victorian readers of *Essays and Reviews* (1860) would be indirectly familiar with Hegel's doctrine that, in order to complete His original creation, a God of Becoming requires His worshippers to actualize the freedom that is His gift to man. They would also have encountered a version of this doctrine in Jowett's influential essay 'On the Interpretation of Scripture'. Jowett's developmental principle is carried to its furthest extreme in the substitution of human self-making for divine activity in left-wing Hegelians like Strauss and Feuerbach, whose influence leaves its dissolving trace on Browning's 'Development' and his 'Epilogue' to *Dramatis Personae*.

1 Hegel among the Poets: The Victorian Legacy

When Jowett introduced Hegel's philosophy to Oxford in the late 1840s, Hegel had already been studied in England for at least a decade. He was already known to some of the liberal Anglican historians who had been exposed to German influences by Julius Hare's and Connop Thirlwall's translation of Barthold Niebuhr's *History of Rome*. The first Victorian review of Hegel's thought comes from G. H. Lewes, who in 1842 writes appreciatively of Hegel's *Lectures on Aesthetics*. In his essay for the *British and Foreign Review*, Hegel's ardent disciple avers that 'four years' constant study' of the master's *Lectures* 'has only served the more to impress [him] with its depth and usefulness' (Lewes, 1842, p. 44). Hegel's praise of the theological component in the third and culminating Romantic phase of art seems to inform Lewes's own assertion that poetry is the 'phasis of a religious idea'. Two years later in his *Biographical History of Philosophy* Lewes has become disenchanted with Hegel. He gives a sharply critical account of Hegel in volume 4 (pp. 198–230), and seems indebted to his mentor only when he adopts a Hegelian defence of the sophists (1845, vol. 1, pp. 158, 173). In the second edition of his *History of Greece*, published two years later, Thirlwall launches the next major Victorian attack upon Hegel's ideas (1847, vol. 4, pp. 529–56). Thirlwall's vigorous dissent from Hegel's theory that Socrates was the greatest of the sophists would be well known to Thirlwall's friend Tennyson, who owned a translation of Hegel's *Lectures on the Philosophy of History*, where Hegel develops his theory.[1] The hazards of combining Hegel's thought with positivism are the object of a spirited attack by James Hutchinson Stirling, who in his notes to Albert Schwegler's *Handbook of the History of Philosophy* attacks George Grote – and by implication Lewes – for making Hegel more radical than he is (Schwegler, 1871, pp. 381–2).

The appeal of Hegel to positivists like Lewes as well as to liberal churchmen like Jowett suggests that there are as many different

Hegels as there are disciples to expound him. Obviously, Hegel's influence on poetics will vary according to how much or how little of his thought a critic is prepared to use. If Hegel's crusade of dialectic against art is fully endorsed, then Hegel can be used to foster a theory of art in which the poet becomes a mere vassal, happy to sacrifice himself on the altar of the Absolute, as art is consecrated to the service of some higher power. In a late-Victorian, W. P. Ker, we can study this legacy of Hegelian aesthetics as it contends against a contrary impulse, culminating in Walter Pater's criticism, to formalize Hegel.

Among the major Victorian poets neither Browning nor Arnold seems to have been as familiar with Hegel as Tennyson, whose portrayal of Arthur in *Idylls of the King* may be modelled on Hegel's portrait of Socrates. In 1882 Browning assures Furnivall that he 'never read a line, original or translated, by Kant, Schelling, or Hegel in [his] whole life'.[2] But Browning's comments to overly keen admirers in the Browning Societies are seldom ingenuous, and in discouraging the notion that he is merely a versifier of other men's ideas Browning seems to me to be seriously minimizing his idealist heritage. In Carlyle's *Life of Schiller* (1899, vol. 25, pp. 108–14) and the 'State of German Literature' (1899, vol. 26, pp. 74–85), Browning must have assimilated Kantian ideas at an early age. And since George Grote, in 1865, quotes extensively from Hegel in *Plato, and the Other Companions of Sokrates* (1888, vol. 1, p. 383; vol. 2, pp. 403–4, 414), it seems to me inconceivable that when Browning published *Aristophanes' Apology* in 1875, a full decade after Grote first disseminated explicitly Hegelian ideas, he was not consciously indebted to the interpretation of Socrates made popular by both Hegel and Grote.

Scholars have recognized that A. W. Schlegel's attack on Euripides in his *Lectures on Art* (1846, pp. 111–44) prompted Browning to defend Euripides in *Balaustion's Adventure*. It is tempting, therefore, to interpret *Aristophanes' Apology* as a second defence of Euripides, in which Browning exposes the casuistry of Euripides' main detractor, Aristophanes, a kind of Greek Schlegel. I think it more probable, however, that in this poem Browning is producing his own version of the continuing debate between Christian apologists like Thirlwall, who praises Socrates as a staunch advocate of Platonic and later Christian values, and disciples of Hegel like G. H. Lewes and George Grote, who heralds Socrates as the greatest of the sophists (George Grote, 1869 (1850), vol. 8, p. 155). In Hegel's view, Socrates' attack upon *Sittlichkeit* and custom had to precede any genuine reconstruction of Greek morality (Hegel, 1857, pp. 281–2; 1892, vol. 1, pp. 384–448). Such is the role that both Euripides and his friend Socrates play in Browning's poem. They are both sceptics, dissolvers of custom, devoted to restoring a knowledge of our ignorance. Aristophanes, by contrast, is a Greek precursor of Thirlwall and the advocates of a Christian or Platonic Socrates. He insists, like every comic genius, that there is a way things are, and only fools like Socrates and Euripides forget what it is. Browning shows that it takes a great ironist or tragedian to remind us, in Stephen Booth's phrase, 'that there is a way things are' and only 'fools assume it is knowable and known' (1983, p. 78).

Browning's denial that he ever read Hegel masks his real affinity of temper with Hegel. Matthew Arnold, on the other hand, is quite prepared to quote Hegel, but he gives little evidence of understanding or even of reading him. Even in 'Spinoza and the Bible', where Arnold talks about Hegel in some detail, his observation that Hegel 'seized a single pregnant sentence of Heraclitus, and cast it . . . into the world of modern thought' (1960–77 (1962), vol. 3, p. 181), is a commonplace of philosophic observation requiring no original research. Arnold may have stumbled on this idea in Lewes's *Biographical History of Philosophy*, where readers are reminded that Hegel himself 'declares . . . there is not a single point in the Logic of Heraclitus which he, Hegel, has not developed in his own Logic' (1857, p. 67). Whereas Kant, Humboldt, Schelling, Herder, all appear on Arnold's reading-lists, Hegel is never mentioned (Allott, 1959, pp. 258–64). Just as Herder attacks Kant for separating the mental processes instead of proclaiming their essential unity, so Arnold attacks Hegel for substituting dialectical formulas for the bracing ethical certitudes of Goethe and Spinoza.

Unlike Arnold, however, Pater is deeply influenced by Hegel, and manages to formalize Hegel's thought in subtler but no less radical ways than he had formalized Plato's. Scholars can safely assume that, as a student of Jowett, who knew Hegel well, Pater was familiar with the Hegelian commentary of Sir Alexander Grant in his influential edition of Aristotle's *Ethics* (1857–8). Grant's was the first commentary to assimilate Aristotle's thought to the stages of historical development traced by Hegel in his *Lectures on the Philosophy of History*. Adapting the Hegelian terms, 'in itself' and 'for itself', Grant argues that, if regarded objectively, as something 'for the mind', Aristotle's term *energeia* can be translated in the normal way as 'an activity', an action that is desirable 'for its own sake'. But he also suggests the possibility of a second, more subjective translation, which renders *energeia* as 'consciousness', as some activity 'in the mind'. If we translate *energeia* as 'consciousness', then we can see how, in his influential 'Conclusion' to *The Renaissance* (1868), Pater's injunction to 'be present always at the focus where the greatest number of vital forces unite in their purest energy' (1900, vol. 1, p. 236) follows logically from Grant's Hegelian interpretation of Aristotle. Like *energeia*, art offers the kind of heightened consciousness that, in Grant's phrase, 'springs out of the mind and ends in the mind. It is not only life, but the sense of life' (1857–8, vol. 1, pp. 181–201, particularly 193).[3]

In the most Hegelian of his critical writings, the essay on Winckelmann (1867), Pater draws upon Hegel's theory of a Symbolical, a Classical, and a Romantic cycle of art, each phase aligned with a particular form. 'As the mind itself has had an historical development,' Pater observes, 'one form of art, by the very limitations of its material, may be more adequate than another for the expression of any one phase of its experience' (1900, vol. 1, p. 210). Few pronouncements could be more Hegelian. And yet there is nothing in Pater's statement to rule out a relativism that is quite foreign to Hegel's theory that aesthetic change is progressive. According to Hegel, painting, music, and poetry, the distinctively modern arts, are superior to both the Greek sculpture of the Classical phase and the ancient Egyptian architecture of the Symbolical phase. Pater acknowledges this evolutionary principle when he says that 'the art of Egypt, with its supreme architectural effects, is, according to Hegel's beautiful comparison, a Memnon waiting for the day, the day of the Greek spirit, the humanistic spirit, with its power of speech' (1900, vol. 1, p. 211). But there is a subtle shift of emphasis in Pater. Unlike Hegel, who sees in the progress of the arts a secure evolution toward an eventual victory of Absolute Spirit, when art will consummate itself by turning into dialectic, Pater sees a progressive attenuation or thinning-out of spirit. He actually reverses Hegel's strategy. Instead of freeing a spiritual *content* from a material *form*, which is the process Hegel analyses, Pater praises art for freeing a highly refined and attenuated *form* from the bondage of any impure *content* or contaminating *message*.

The change becomes self-evident when we compare Pater's famous statement that all art 'aspires towards the condition of music' with Hegel's view of music. Of the three Romantic arts, it is poetry, not music, that is pre-eminent for Hegel, because (as Hegel says) only poetry 'unites in itself, within the province of the spiritual inner life and on a higher level, the two extremes, i.e. the visual arts and music' (1975, vol. 2, p. 960). The subtle way in which Pater formalizes Hegel by promoting form over content is even more apparent in his odd verdict that Browning is a poet of situations, whose characters 'are always of secondary importance'. In his Preface to *Strafford*, Browning says exactly the reverse. His aim, we are told, is to show 'Action in Character' rather than 'Character in Action'. It is hard to make sense of Pater's reversal until we recognize that by 'choice situation' Pater means attenuated spiritual content, 'language in its most purged form, its remote associations and suggestions, its double and treble lights' (1900, vol. 1, p. 215). For 'situation' we must read, not the external actions of a play like *Strafford*, but Hegelian 'spirit', the discriminated moment that is already freed of 'the commonness of the world', and from which Pater can receive 'the impression of one imaginative tone'. In a final attempt to formalize Hegel, Pater quotes a passage from the master that allows him to revel in the purist paradox, beloved of Wilde, that life imitates art. The great Greeks, Pater quotes Hegel as saying, 'are ideal artists of themselves, cast each in one flawless mould, works of art, which stand before us as an immortal presentment of the gods' (1900, vol. 1, p. 219). Removed from its context, this quotation abets Pater's predilection to alter the teleological drift of Hegel's aesthetic doctrines by assimilating life to art, subordinating the spiritual content of Romantic art to the subtleties and refinements of the art form itself.

The more carefully a critic has read Hegel, the more scruples he will have in turning Hegel into Pater's champion of formalism. In his essay on 'The Philosophy of Art' (1883), for example, W. P. Ker, a more scholarly interpreter than Pater, is torn between conflicting reactions to Hegel's theories. Should the critic use poems for their educative value, subordinating art to the claims of some Absolute Spirit which is asserted to be the ground of art's efficacy? Or must each poem be studied as an end in itself? To the strict Hegelian, the work of art is not endotelic: it is merely a means to some external end. Ker, like Pater, wants to honour the integrity of each work of art. But he does not see how Hegel authorizes such a project.

Since Jowett's publication of his edition of Plato's *Dialogues* in the previous decade, many Victorians had viewed Plato through a Hegelian lens. This is especially true of Ker, for whom Hegel is the chief advocate of a theory of art which begins, Ker believes, with Plato. A chief tenet of this theory is that art is an 'education'. It exists, in Ker's phrase, 'for the sake of something higher, namely enlightenment, accurate and self-conscious insight' (1883, p. 163). This recalls Hegel's teaching that once a poet like Browning has arrived at David's plateau of vision in 'Saul', poetry can go no further: it can only die into a higher form of life. According to Hegel, such a change occurs when the dialectic of the poet is absorbed at last into philosophic vision. Poetry 'is not so fine a thing as philosophy,' says Keats, 'for the same reason that an eagle is not so fine a thing as a truth' (1958, vol. 2, p. 81). When Hegel's owl of Minerva takes wing at dusk, she soars high above the shadow of the eagle, looking down upon Apollo's realms of gold from sublimer heights of vision.

Another of Ker's Hegelian insights, which also seems to operate *against* Pater's theory of poetic autonomy, is his observation that the self-sufficiency of art is *less* applicable to some art forms than to others. Greek sculpture may not be 'symbolic of anything', he concedes, but 'in the art of Christianity there is no need, no possibility, that the image should accurately represent the reality. They are incommensurate from the first' (1883, pp. 183, 185). Ker's contrast between the beauty of ancient Greek art and the sublimity of modern art is indebted to Hegel's argument about the incapacity of sublime forms to compass the grandeur of their subject. Of more originality is Ker's criticism of Hegel for failing to see that though art is educational, it is not necessarily 'an education for some end different from art'. In a poem 'the particular thing exists with a being of its own' that 'cannot be exhausted by a formula or expressed in words' (1883, pp. 166, 169). Ker's essay shows how in 1883 criticism stands at a crossroads. Does poetry exist for the sake of a truth higher than itself? Is its transformation into science or philosophy a

consummation devoutly to be wished? Or does poetry educate in a
wholly different way? Perhaps it educates by a non-utilitarian but
valuable deployment of the cognitive faculties, in abstraction from
any practical context. This last possibility is the answer preferred by
a new formalism that is also as ancient as Aristotle and that is associ-
ated in the Victorian period with the revival of Aristotelian studies
at Oxford and with the work of two Oxford graduates, Ruskin and
Hopkins.

2 Aristotle among the Victorians: Ruskin, Hopkins, and the Oxford Tradition

In Victorian poetics the Aristotelian tradition is expounded most lu-
cidly by John Ruskin, especially in his influential theory of the Im-
agination Penetrative. Ruskin's Aristotelianism is best exemplified,
I believe, in devotional poems by Hopkins, who is directly
influenced by Ruskin. According to Aquinas, that medieval Aristo-
telian whom Ruskin as well as Hopkins read with care, God is sheer
existence.[4] He is irrevocably the being that He is, pre-existing like
the Logos by a finality deeper than any creation. As unique as a scent
or as a musical note, the imagination of a Homer or a Shakespeare
'never stops at crusts or ashes, or outward images of any kind; it
ploughs them all aside,' says Ruskin, 'and plunges into the very cen-
tral fiery heart' (1903–12, vol. 4, p. 250). What the Penetrative Im-
agination must seize in the object is an indivisible unity that defies
analysis. It is an actuality, an essence, something of which we can
say nothing with literal truth except that it exists.

Just as Ruskin's paternalistic economic theories in *Unto This Last*
are indebted to the political theories of Xenophon and Aristotle,
which are modelled on the economy of the Greek household, so
Ruskin's theory of the Imagination Penetrative is indebted to the
doctrine of immanent teleology set forth in Aristotle's *Metaphysics*.
Because Aristotle, the metaphysician, has brought Plato's Ideas
down to earth, he believes that when his poet imitates nature he can
penetrate to the final and formal causes that are now immanent in
the material cause. In presenting a landscape's inmost qualities, a
poet is portraying, not a more ideal, but a more essential nature.
Though Ruskin first works out the problem of the Penetrative Im-

agination in his drawings and sketches, he seems to have followed the suggestion of H. G. Liddell, one of his former tutors at Christ Church, Oxford, who, in response to Ruskin's question, 'Who is the best metaphysician who has treated the subject of imagination generally?' (Ruskin, 1903–12, vol. 3, p. 670), recommended Aristotle.

In Aristotle's *Posterior Analytics* (II, 7), Ruskin would have found the important distinction between what things are (the object of the descriptive sciences and of expository criticism) and the sheer fact of their existence, the mystery of their being this unique item and not that item. The question that has intrigued many philosophers from Leibniz to Wittgenstein – 'Why is there something rather than nothing?' – seems to be the source of Ruskin's constant wonder in the presence of art. Hopkins may have assimilated this wonder either through the medieval Aristotelianism of Aquinas, who seems like Ruskin to have been a thinker overcome with awe by the reality of things, or else more directly through Ruskin himself. The Aristotelian poet who can use his imagination to perceive and commemorate immanent forms will celebrate, not Sidney's 'golden world', and not the self-contained world of the symbolists, but the essential forms of the universe which God himself has fashioned. One source of this poet's wonder will be the discovery in himself of a greater power – and, despite his destitution, a greater dignity – than any possessed by the rest of creation.

Mediated through Thomistic interpretations of Aristotle as well as through Ruskin's own interpretations, Hopkins' doctrine of inscape is the Victorian poetic theory most directly influenced by Ruskin. This debt of Hopkins to Ruskin is a well-documented fact of literary history, most recently analysed in the last two sections of Patricia Ball's fine study, *The Science of Aspects* (1974). All salient features of a Penetrative Imagination are present in great intensity and fusion, for example, in Hopkins' curtal sonnet, 'Pied Beauty'. Every detail of this exuberant *Te Deum Laudamus* proclaims a relation of sameness and difference that is cosmic in scope. The echoing and chiming of groups of dappled things – of brinded cows, 'couple-colour' skies, and stippled 'trout' (ll. 2–3) – turn the rhyme-like relation, the *concordia discors* of nature, into a perfect analogy, a perfect reflecting mirror, of God's ability to unify diverse impressions. Microscopic impressions of rose-moles on a trout, 'fresh-firecoal chestnut-falls', and of 'finches' wings' (ll. 3–4), are joined to impressions that are vast in scope. Thus 'dappled' is coupled with the vague noun 'things' (l. 1), and the variegated colours of the brinded cow are stretched into a Turneresque blending of the cattle with the clouds and skyscape. Just when the variety of creation is fixed most definitely in the unique identity of what is 'counter, original, spare, strange' (l. 7), the rapid multiplication of antonyms begins to override distinction, celebrating the reversing flow of all beauty back again to God.

Using the abbreviated octave and sestet of the curtal sonnet to concentrate his energies, Hopkins composes at a level of intensity that allows him to reach through special qualifications of sense to the pied beauty, the unifying of diversity, that is the best earthly analogue of God's perfection. Thus 'couple-colour' (l. 2) becomes not just 'two-coloured,' but also, because of its association with the brinded cows, a form of cosmic conjoining – a coitus of sky and earth, a potential act of God's procreating or 'fathering-forth'. Hopkins' groupings are potent, not merely as sets of observed facts, but as alliances of analogy between fickle, freckled things and God. Hopkins may not be able to explain how he, like the fathering God, can progress from a tumult of diverse images, each unique, to the unity of an inscaped world. 'Who knows how?' he asks in wonder (l. 8). But what is most godlike about his poetry is its all-but-unanalysable ability to group together words and objects, through analogies of sound and muscular sensation, until the procreative God and the dappled, brinded things He fathers forth seem to conjoin, uniting physically as a single life-force.

Because Aristotle's *Poetics*, *Rhetoric*, and *Ethics* were required reading for all Oxford undergraduates until mid-century, it is not surprising that Aristotle's influence should reach far beyond Ruskin and Hopkins to shape the thought of Oxford graduates like Keble, Newman, and Matthew Arnold. Though Aristotle is sometimes venerated in such circles as the fourth Person of the Trinity, there is seldom any consensus about what Aristotle means by imitation, and his authority is invoked in contradictory ways. If Aristotle means that the object of the poet's imitation is *natura naturata* – a created order, then it is easy to see why critics like Henry Taylor, Aubrey de Vere, and Matthew Arnold (in his Preface to the *Poems* of 1853) should interpret imitation as the mere replication of a pre-existing order. But Aristotle may mean that the poet imitates *natura naturans* – a system of causes that generate an order of their own. If Aristotle is interpreted in this second way, it is easier to understand why Keble and Newman should try to use Aristotle's authority to defend more expressive and idealizing theories of art. In his review of Lockhart's *Life of Scott*, for example, Keble asserts that his own theory of poetry coincides 'well enough with Aristotle's notion of it, as consisting chiefly in Imitation or Expression' (1838, p. 435). In this astonishing sentence, doctrines that are usually regarded as antithetical are blithely equated. In his essay 'Poetry, with Reference to Aristotle's *Poetics*' (1829), Newman, like his friend Keble, casually appropriates Aristotle's mimetic label, but totally changes its traditional meaning. Newman contends that poetry should become to representational genres like history and biography what mathematical laws in physics are to natural phenomena. It should operate as their Platonic model or type. In arguing that perception is to the real what poetic imagination is to the possible, Newman's essay is clearly drawing more on Plato's thought than on Aristotle's. And yet if nature is defined as *natura naturans*, there are grounds even in Aristotle for holding Newman's view. Aristotle's poet is never merely reacting to a stimulus. Acting as opposed to reacting requires the observer to imagine. And this imagination is itself an action which Aristotle's poet, like Newman's, tries to imitate in an austere but liberating exercise of the mind's cognitive powers.

Paradoxically, Aristotle's theory of imitation is used both to consolidate and to subvert the representational axioms of Victorian poetic theory. To imitate nature, Aristotle argues, is to imitate an organized world that has been modelled on the arts. If art is man's nature, a second and better nature, it is because nature itself has been organized into substances and their properties, which are the very categories Aristotle uses to explain the nature of art. It is usually said that Aristotle's poet imitates nature. But it would be just as accurate to reverse the proposition and say, like Oscar Wilde, that nature imitates art. As I showed in Chapter I, however, the priority of an external nature cannot be permanently reversed until the mathematical physics of Faraday and Clerk Maxwell has allowed fields of energy and force to replace Aristotle's world of substances, each organized upon some single principle. One aesthetic equivalent of the new physics is the nonsense poetry of Lear and Carroll. For vanished substances and qualities Carroll substitutes new forms of order like numbers, logics, and mathematical games. The Aristotle whose authority is invoked by E. S. Dallas is not the Aristotle of the *Poetics*, but the Aristotle who extols the intellectual virtue of practical wisdom in the *Ethics*. Dallas's and Ruskin's poets must have the educated but immediate grasp of life that Aristotle associates with *phronesis*, which is best understood as a half-intuitive wisdom of ready application in emergencies, when the mind is trying to grasp a complex problem. Other Victorians, like Arnold and Newman, who advocate education by poetry, find in Aristotle a persuasive defence of the formalist propostion that art promotes delight in the free and disengaged use of the mind's cognitive powers. Resolving the split between pleasure and knowledge, Aristotle argues that the arts are specifically cognitive. The pleasure of knowing is the precise pleasure that reading a poem like *In Memoriam* provides. Such a poem produces objects of knowledge that are pleasurable to contemplate. And it also generates experiences that are truly cognitive, not in the sense that it teaches us about geology or evolution, but in the sense that it allows us to know (despite absorbing grief) life-giving instants of illumination and insight.

3 Types and Homotypes:
Dobell's New Mythus

In his essay on 'The Nature of Poetry' (1857), which only Robert Preyer has tried to rescue from oblivion, Sydney Dobell puts into critical currency a new term, 'homotype', which he wants to distinguish from the types and antitypes of more conservative hermeneutical criticism. Dobell seems at first to be writing as another Tractarian. He argues that in all 'essential metaphor' we 'find a recognition of something more than a phenomenal similarity'. We find 'a type' and an 'antitype', which Dobell compares to 'two lines that meet somewhere but not here' (1876, p. 53). The ultimate convergence of the sign and its referent entails a relation, however, that is more 'tautegorical', as Coleridge would say, more concerned to assert an identity, than any typological scheme that Keble or the Fathers had envisaged. Dobell is the critical herald of symbolist poets like Swinburne, who in poems like 'Hertha' mythologizes the Hegelian Absolute as a nineteenth-century version of the Stoic or Neoplatonic One. Such a deity, who is immanent in nature and in the process of becoming, is the successor of 'the pale Galilean'. Like the 'unknown . . . spirit' of 'A Nympholept' (l. 255), she is the 'agnostos theos' whom the gods of organized religion unconsciously worship.

To avoid an idolatry of the sensory sign, Dobell must honour the substitutive function of all metaphor. But to keep his signs iconic, he must turn mere types into 'homotypes'. The examples of 'essential metaphor' or 'homotype' that Dobell cites establish a much closer bond between Ceres' sheaves of wheat and the goddess, for instance, than the bond uniting a biblical type like Moses with his New Testament antitype. Astutely noting that there is often a phenomenal difference between an aesthetic idea or feeling and its metaphoric equivalent, Dobell criticizes the many-breasted Hindu goddess for being too similar to the fertility she is meant to represent. By contrast, Thorwaldsen's famous statue of night, which makes the observer feel he is actually confronting a black and shapeless void, is sculpted out of white marble. To explain the paradox Dobell develops his theory of substitution. Instead of saying 'I love', a poet will call up in his imagination some beautiful object like a rose, then find for that object some equivalent in words. A metaphor like 'rose' may be a better equivalent of love than a metonymy like 'kiss', simply because the metaphor is a genuine substitution whereas the metonymy is a mere contraction of a sensory referent, 'ardent lover'. But in avoiding an idolatry of the sensory sign, the poet must not embrace the opposite error of perpetuating a form of symbolism that too closely resembles algebraic equations or mere mechanical *sorites* in logic.

feelings = unspeakable facts of the imagination = metaphors in facts that have corresponding words = verbal equivalents

The poet's metaphoric equivalents, his 'homotypes', are related to each other, not in the way types are related to their biblical antitypes, and not in the way an algebraic sign is related to an unknown quantity, but in the way atoms are joined together to form the beautiful structure of a crystal.

If Browning ever read Dobell's lecture, delivered two years after the completion of 'Saul', he would have been struck by the remarkable similarities between Dobell's theory of homotypes and the many metaphorical equivalences he himself establishes when trying to create his 'new Mythus' of divine and human love in 'Saul'. In Chapter VI I analysed 'Saul' at some length when showing how Browning's use of the feeling of dependence reflects the influence of Schleiermacher's Christology as expounded by Strauss in the third volume of *The Life of Jesus*. I must briefly touch on 'Saul' again, because the four attributes Dobell ascribes to the perfect mind – knowing, loving, worshipping and ordering – correspond to the stages of David's argument in Browning's poem. The impulse to love the beautiful, which Dobell identifies with the mind of the poet and his feelings, Browing associates with David the lyric celebrant. In sections 9 to 13 David develops the third of Dobell's four attributes, the worship or veneration of sublimity. Only in sections 13 to 15 does David, as sage, discover in the palm-wine an analogy of proper proportion that allows him to perfect the first faculty Dobell cites, the power of knowledge. The fourth attribute of ordering is found in an Incarnational principle, discerned by David in Christ and described by Dobell himself as a principle of 'homotypy', whereby the Word in being made flesh allows the same life that animates the single sentence to circulate through a whole poem.

Dobell's audacious claim that even a short poem can be read as a 'congruous passage in that Poem of the Universe which is the ordered expression of [God's] Wisdom and His Love' (1876, p. 65) anticipates the Hegelianized Christianity of Charles Gore and other High Church contributors to the volume of essays entitled *Lux Mundi*, which Gore edited and published in 1889. Gore's volume stands in the same relation to the spiritualized nature Swinburne presents in a late poem like 'A Nympholept' (1894)[5] as *Essays and Reviews*, published by Broad Churchmen like Mark Pattison and Benjamin Jowett in 1860, bears to poems like Browning's 'A Death in the Desert' (1864) and *The Ring and the Book* (1868–9). Whether or not Swinburne and Browning were directly reacting to these landmark publications, their poems embody the theological concerns of each volume in an effective 'new Mythus'.

4 Hegel on Self-Making: Swinburne and Tennyson

Though Swinburne may have known nothing of Hegel's thought directly, he seems to have encountered in Blake, Jacob Boehme, and perhaps even in Indian thought, a form of Hegel's spiral journey out of Being into Non-Being, then back into Becoming. Such is the trajectory of Hegel's Idea, which at the end of the *Logic* returns to a higher form of its original unity. When Swinburne asserts that 'each man of all men is God' ('Hymn of Man', l. 49), he is not simply asserting that each man is already godlike. Like Blake and Feuerbach, he is claiming that each 'soul that labours and lives', that makes itself temporally by moving through distinguishable moments, has the power to 'recreate' the god 'of whom [all souls] are creatures' ('Hymn of Man', ll. 55, 48). Here is where the apocalyptic humanism of Swinburne and Blake, the doctrine that God is the eternal self,[6] connects with Hegel's doctrine of self-making. Man is not to make an idol of his present self, but is invited to worship a truly godlike self which is still in the process of being made.

Swinburne's fullest exploration of self-making is his difficult poem 'Hertha'. 'The truth is the whole,' Hegel says. But 'of the absolute it should be said that it is essentially result, that it is only in the end what it is in truth, and precisely in this consists its nature' (1965, p. 390). The closest theological equivalent is the Hindu doctrine that the cosmos undergoes an infinite number of deaths and rebirths. Swinburne's Hertha combines the spiral journey of Hegel's Absolute with the deep and appealing Hindu thought that the universe 'is but the dream of the god who, after a hundred Brahma years, dissolves himself into a dreamless sleep'. As Carl Sagan explains, 'the universe dissolves with him – until, after another Brahma century, he stirs, recomposes himself and begins again to dream the great cosmic dream' (1980, p. 258).

To differentiate such Hindu and Hegelian notions from the master-slave duality of biblical tradition, Swinburne parodies two sayings that St John ascribes to Christ: 'I am the way, the truth, and the life' (John 14 : 6), which Swinburne renders 'I am the search [the way], and the sought [the truth], and the seeker [the life]' ('Hertha', l. 25), and 'Before Abraham was, I am' (John 8 : 58), which he renders 'before God was, I am' ('Hertha', l. 15). The Christian God antedates only Abraham, who is a mere patriarch. But Swinburne's deity antedates God himself. As Omega, or 'the Deus explicitus', He is not what He is as Alpha, as the merely 'undeveloped God'. Hertha's making and doing do not merely proceed from what she *is*. Instead, her actions *constitute* what she is. Hertha is the deity 'which began' (l. 1), not only in the sense that she originated life, but also in the sense that she herself has originated. Until she passes into nature, she is only the indifference of sheer possibility: 'Out of me man and woman, and wild-beast and bird; before God was, I am' (l. 15).

One Hegel scholar, J. Loewenberg, has noted that Hertha is Hegel's Absolute Spirit, 'glorified through his power to transcend everything imaginable and everything thinkable' (1929, p. xxx). In allowing 'the laughing countenance' of this deity to become suddenly visible behind 'All death and all life, and all reigns and all ruins' ('Hertha', l. 35), Swinburne has done nothing to attenuate a reader's shock or outrage. A study of his revisions shows how the interchange of lines 36 and 38, for example, by separating out the elements that logically belong together – the 'grain', 'germ' and 'sod', the 'ploughshare' and the 'plough-cloven clod'[7] – makes the subversion resonate more strangely: 'I the grain and the furrow, / The plough-cloven clod / And the ploughshare drawn thorough, / The germ and the sod' ('Hertha', ll. 36–9). Instead of giving the past participle 'drawn' a direct object in the 'plough-cloven clod', Swinburne now turns the 'clod' into another nominative absolute in apposition to 'I'. In the revised version the 'clod' functions both nominatively, as an appositive, and accusatively as a noun supplied to fill the ellipsis after 'thorough'. As the grammar becomes more appositional, it increases the two-way flow between Hertha and the world: 'In my darkness the thunder / Makes utterance of me' (ll. 113–14). The final prepositional phrase, 'of me', may function as either a subjective or objective genitive. The thunder is *Hertha*'s voice, but it also *proclaims* her.

As the antitheses of tautology, 'I am I, thou art thou' (l. 33), yield to the perfect interchanges of first and second persons, Swinburne uses chiasmus, 'I am thou . . . thou art I' (l. 35), to frame a final identity of persons. Dramatizing the ease with which Hertha passes in and out of nature, Swinburne also has her bring into 'sight', not merely 'the sun and the soul', as in the original version of line 95, but 'the *shadowless* soul' (my italics). The buried reference to the sun turns natural description into metaphor. By making explicit the Feuerbachian irony of 'the shadow called God' set in the 'skies to give [man] light' (ll. 93–4), Swinburne's revision allows him to bring out boldly the unsettling contradictions that overthrow the static Alpha concept of God. In becoming both the arrow and the mark, the quester and the way, Hertha runs the whole gamut of creation from Alpha to Omega.

In his exuberant parody of Tennyson, 'The Higher Pantheism in a Nutshell', Swinburne makes fun of an oracular Hegelian seer who tries to say everything about nothing. His discourse contains no nouns, only pronouns, prepositions, and connectives, which can relate but not name: 'for under is over and under' (l. 3). A moment later he betrays the opposite disorder. He can name and equate doubt and faith, but because he cannot relate them in any further way he appears to be saying nothing about everything: 'Doubt is faith in the main: but faith, on the whole, is doubt' (l. 5). To parody a rationalism that has lost direction, Swinburne keeps exploring the logical consequences of converting hypotheses that are contrary to fact: 'If thunder could be without lightning, lightning could be without thunder' (l. 4). One could say of these inanities, as Dr Johnson says of *Cymbeline*, that 'to remark the folly of the fiction . . . were to waste criticism upon unresisting imbecility'. Truist reductions of Hegelian axioms, 'More is the whole than a part' (l. 15), combine with absurd misstatements of these axioms, 'but half is more than the whole' (l. 15), to produce outrageous violations of the law of contradiction, 'Doubt is faith', 'faith . . . is doubt' (l. 5), and the tritest truisms: 'One and two are not one' (l. 17). Swinburne's own myths of self-making, poems like 'Hertha' and 'Genesis', verge continually on such inanities. But because they usually manage to veer between the kind of solemn tautology which aspires to say nothing about everything, and the kind of empty relating which says everything about nothing, Swinburne's oracular lyrics are seldom in danger of stretching paradox to the breaking-point, as does this parody of Tennyson.

Whereas Swinburne would have encountered a doctrine of self-making in Blake, Tennyson would have been directly familiar with the idea in Hegel himself. At Jowett's urging, Tennyson read Hegel's *Lectures on the Philosophy of History* in the 1857 translation from the third German edition by J. Sibree, which is the only work by Hegel actually to appear in Tennyson's library. Of all Hegel's major works, these lectures may do most to foster a flight of philosophy from the world and a Brahmanic absorption of the individual in the nothingness or void. It seems to me that the dissolving trace of this side of Hegel's thought is clearly evident in *Idylls of the King*. The world of the *Idylls* is the world of Chronos before his conquest by the Olympians. Arthur should be the medieval Apollo, 'the Political god, who produced', in Hegel's words, 'a moral work – the State' (1857, p. 79). But the only traces of Camelot that survive Arthur are wreckage and ruin. As a mythical kingdom, it is still a Utopia 'without moral products; and what was produced – the offspring of ... Chronos – was devoured by it'. *Idylls of the King* remains a poem of disillusion and uncertainty because it is a poem in which time is still unfilled by meaning.

Hegel's paradoxes about 'World-Historical Individuals' like Caesar and Napoleon are always in danger of flying apart: it is difficult to hold together in the mind apparently contradictory propositions. Hegel says that the motives of a historical hero must spring from an unconscious inner spirit. But how can a hero like Arthur have knowledge of something that by definition lies beyond the pale of knowledge? 'Such individuals', Hegel argues, 'had no consciousness of the general Idea they were unfolding' (1857, p. 31). In a profound sense, Arthur did not know what he was doing. Self-knowledge is usually confined to the Hegelian seer, who in Tennyson's poem is sometimes Arthur but more often the narrator who writes the closing verse paragraph of 'The Passing of Arthur' or 'To the Queen'. World heroes discover and promote the truth, Hegel says. But in his next breath he speaks of these apparently free agents as instruments of truths that are 'already formed in the womb of time'. They are free only in the sense that they are free to know and promote what is necessary.

When Arthur laments that he makes war upon himself by fighting his own people, he seems to be recalling Hegel's words about the suicide of the spirit. 'It certainly makes war upon itself – consumes its own existence; but in this very destruction it works that existence into a new form' (1857, p. 76). That last clause explains why Arthur, at the very moment he seems to be dying by his own hand, killed 'by this people which I made', is also able to lecture

Bedivere authoritatively, telling him (rather oddly) what a king should be. Arthur's reminder that 'God fulfils himself in many ways, / Lest one good custom should corrupt the world' ('The Passing of Arthur', ll. 409–10) repeats Hegel's denunciation of custom. When Tennyson originally wrote these lines for his 'Morte d'Arthur', Hegel's *Lectures* had not been translated and Tennyson was probably unfamiliar with them. But in the later 1869 context of the poem, as a comment on all the *Idylls*, these lines take on a prophetic power peculiar to Hegel's seer. For now they command an impressive overview of Hegel's teaching that only a 'spiritual, generic life' (Hegel, 1857, p. 78), challenged by opposition, and continually overreaching itself, can escape the natural death by which individuals and whole cultures perish. Tennyson's jumps in perspective may lead us to assume that our own intellects are at fault. But like the reader of Hegel's *Lectures*, we learn to pull ourselves together and to go on to another crisis of our understanding. Tennyson's poem, like Hegel's spirit of history, has always been fulfilling itself, even when we, like Arthur, are unable to perceive it.

Tennyson was an avid reader of histories. In addition to Hegel's *Lectures on the Philosophy of History*, he owned a copy of Thomas Arnold's *History of Rome*, and he would certainly be familiar with his friend Connop Thirlwall's *History of Greece* (1847), which contains an important essay attacking Hegel's interpretation of Socrates. Thirlwall's liberal Anglican idea of the unity of truth cannot, it seems, be reconciled with Hegel's teaching that Socrates embodies a new reflective morality which requires the overthrow of unreflective custom and received opinion. And yet Hegel's idea that equally valid ways of conceiving truth could clash as the mind of God and the human spirit develop is deeply appealing to Tennyson, who explores just such a clash in *Idylls of the King*. In Hegel's view, Socrates is a tragic figure, caught like Antigone between conflicting loyalties. So is Tennyson's Arthur, who has to be faithful both to his sense of what he owes the state and what he owes the new morality. To Dagonet, Arthur seems 'the king of fools'. And to Vivien, he is a moral child who lacks the craft to rule. But if Arthur looks foolish, it is because he is also like the Socrates of Grote and Nietzsche the advocate of a higher self-critical awareness. Even in enforcing the rule of King Nomos, he is sworn to destroy that authority. Though Arthur could have prevented Guinevere's adultery by coercing her, he relies on persuasion rather than force. To be loyal to Arthur, as Tennyson says, is to be loyal to more than the authority of a sovereign. It is to be 'loyal to the royal' in oneself.

When 'Socrates wishes to induce his friends to reflection,' says Hegel, 'the discourse has always a negative tone' (1857, p. 281). Arthur's role in Tennyson's poem is comparably negative. In His 'ways with man' God seems more absent than present. There is more present despair than distant hope. In 'The Passing of Arthur' the old morality has to be accompanied to its grave 'Lest one good custom should corrupt the world', blocking the advance from mere *Sittlichkeit* to a higher reflective consciousness. Tennyson would no doubt have known George Grote's incisive Hegelian account of Plato's 'dialogues of search' in *Plato, and the Other Companions of Sokrates* (1865). Grote's account offers one of the best descriptions of the self-critical quest on which Tennyson himself is launched in *Idylls of the King*. Like any challenge to the authority of received opinion, which is always 'peremptory in exacting belief, but neither furnishes nor requires proof', *Idylls of the King* is a poetry of testing, analysing, refuting, 'which gives free play and . . . prominence to the negative arm' (George Grote, 1888, vol. 1, pp. 387–8).

A man who is created in the image of an unchanging God is committed in advance to a definition of who and what man is. But in a late and unjustly neglected poem, 'The Making of Man', Tennyson prefers to experiment and innovate. Until the experiment is complete and the poet with his 'prophet-eyes' has earned the right to say, in a final hymn of praise to man, the co-maker with God of his own beliefs: 'Hallelujah to the Maker "It is finished. Man is made"' (l. 8), humanity has only a negative identity. In accepting Hegel's conclusion that thought about God is an all-encompassing *self*-activity, Tennyson also repeats Hegel's idea that the end of any self-constituting process is immeasurably greater than its beginning.

5 Dallas and Hegel:
The Evolution of the Word

E. S. Dallas's intermittently original but perverse monograph, *Poetics: An Essay on Poetry* (1852), may seem at first to be merely wrongheaded. Why should lyrical genres, which seem to form the keystone of the arch in Romantic poetic theory, be identified with primitive eastern art? And why should the drama, scarcely the crowning achievement of nineteenth-century English poetry, be heralded as the culminating genre of modern literature? Dallas is hard to understand until we grasp the connection between his own generic theory and the evolution of Symbolical, Classical, and Romantic genres in Hegel's posthumously published *Lectures on Aesthetics*. When Dallas calls the lyric and visionary genres of poetry the dominant mode of eastern, primitive art, he is alluding like Hegel to the lyric art of the Psalmist. Hegel equates the highest form of Symbolical art with the sublime lyric poetry of the Hebrew Bible. Such poetry confesses the inadequacy of all created things to the nameless God of Israel, who stands sublimely transcendent above and beyond all words about Him. Having used the genres of lyric poetry to describe the divine poetry of the ancients, Dallas must equate the dominantly religious art of the nineteenth century, which he finds comparably sublime, with a different genre. When he speaks of dramatic art as a religious, Romantic form, embodying hope and the impulse to worship, Dallas is thinking, not of Shakespeare or Greek drama, but of Browning's dramatic monologues and of lyrics of 'saving faith' written by intensely personal devotional poets like Christina Rossetti.

Unfortunately, some of Dallas's associations – his connection, for example, of dramatic, epic, and lyrical genres with hope, faith, and love, respectively (1852, p. 119) – seem merely fanciful. Too many of his tables are woven out of his own imagination like the scholastic web of Bacon's spider. They betray that distemper of learning which Bacon calls 'fantastical'. Other ideas, however, are surprisingly innovative. One of his most original insights is that the transformation of classical epic into Hebrew lyric and then into modern Romantic and Christian forms of art is accompanied by a corresponding change in the poet's use of pronouns. In classical literature the poet describes persons and things: the third-person pronoun dominates. In Hebrew literature, by contrast, 'a lofty egoism runs through almost every page'. The sublime lyric poetry of the psalms is a poetry of first-person pronouns. Only in modern poetry, which is a literature of dramatic intimacy and empathy, does the 'you' enter. 'The gentle reader, *candidus lector*, is . . . often addressed', and

'the familiar you-and-me style ... is kept up from first to last'
(Dallas, 1852, p. 99).

Anticipating T. S. Eliot's argument in 'The Three Voices of
Poetry', Dallas distinguishes the first-person voice of lyric and the
third-person voice of drama proper from 'the familiar you-and-me
style' of genres like the monologue, which uses first- and second-
person pronouns to dramatize Fra Lippo Lippi's efforts to em-
pathize with his auditor: 'Tell you, I liked your looks at very
first. / Let's sit and set things straight now, hip to haunch' ('Fra
Lippo Lippi', ll. 43–4). The same pronouns dominate a devotional
lyric like Christina Rossetti's 'Twice', which establishes a very pre-
carious but potent relation between the 'You' of the first half of the
lyric and the 'Thou' of the second. Is God going to be any more gen-
erous or loving than the contemptuous 'You' who coldly studied
and then rejected the proffered heart as he might have studied, then dis-
carded, a flawed work of art? The last three stanzas repeat the drama
for a second time. Two of the agents, Rossetti and her preferred
heart, are the same. But now God is substituted for the critical lover.

> I take my heart in my hand –
> I shall not die, but live –
> Before Thy face I stand:
> I, for Thou callest such:
> All that I have I bring,
> All that I am I give;
> Smile Thou and I shall sing,
> But shall not question much.
>
> ('Twice', ll. 41–8)

The altered refrain, the new form of scanning and criticizing (which
is now refining, not dismissive), the smile of God, which replaces
the cold stare of the friend, and the poet's singing instead of
questioning, all show how Dallas's familiar I-and-thou style helps
Rossetti make the remote familiar, an art of the heart. Originally,
Rossetti had lacked the heart to examine her own heart. She had not
enough courage to be critical of others. Now she will 'not question
much', not because she is afraid of any divine injustice she may
expose in a dismissive 'You', but because she is confident that the
'Thou' she invokes in a blend of intimacy and reverence will treat
her with justice and compassion.

A similar 'I-thou' grammar of love and 'saving faith' is evident in Rossetti's poem 'Up-Hill'.

> Shall I meet other wayfarers at night?
> Those who have gone before.
> Then must I knock, or call when just in sight?
> They will not keep you standing at that door.
>
> ('Up-Hill', ll. 9–12)

Line 12 presumably refers to the host of the inn. But he is described, somewhat oddly, in the third person plural, as if he were another wayfarer, one of 'Those who have gone before' (l. 10). Perhaps the host is even the speaker himself. Some readers will resist such a suggestion because it upsets their generic expectations. What is appropriate in a riddle, they think, is out of place in a devotional poem. They may argue that if there *is* a host at the inn, as in Herbert's 'Love (III)', and if the host is the fellow-traveller, he has disguised his secret too well. But such a disguise accounts for the poignant brevity of the poem. Once the identity is guessed, the discourse is over, and the pilgrim can do nothing more than fall silent. In the meantime the temporary wandering of the answerer's true identity can be described in terms of a game with two players and three pronouns: 'I', 'you', and the enigmatic 'They'. The power of the familiar 'I-thou' style to humanize the conventions, making them more personal and interior, accounts, I think, for Dallas's otherwise puzzling complaint that English lyric poets are too dramatic, too willing to make a virtue of reticence and reserve (1852, pp. 147–8). Combining the enigmatic features of a lyric of disguise with the more conventional features of the dialogue and pilgrimage poem, Rossetti writes a poem of 'saving faith', and illustrates what Dallas means by a 'truly dramatic' as opposed to a merely 'epic' or narrative 'reception of the Gospel'.

According to both Dallas and Browning, the creations of the true dramatic poet are to the imitation or memory of the epical poet what resurrection is to death. What God is to the pantheist, the entire round of creation is to Browning's 'Maker-see', the dramatic impersonator who imparts to the soul of the believer a 'Divine life'. Just as Dallas's poet turns epic into drama, and Strauss purifies faith of its historical content, so Browning's St John keeps turning from history to the timeless logic of a 'love' behind 'the will and might'. He absorbs the shadow of history into the substance of 'what Is', into a vision which 'Is, here and now: I apprehend naught else' ('A Death in the Desert', l. 210).

The 'making present' of Dallas's dramatic poet has less in common with Aristotelian mimesis than with the kind of re-enactment or memorial suggested by the theological term *anamnesis*, the word used to express the Eucharist's ritual bearing into present time of Christ's Passion and Resurrection. As Jonathan Bishop observes, 'the term [*anamnesis*] incorporates the element of memory, as "imitation" at least in English will not do' (1972, p. 253).´ There may be an Oedipal relation in commemoration, an anxiety of influence that weighed heavily on Emerson when he protested that the imitation of Christ was not good enough for *him*. But the commemoration of Dallas's dramatic poet, like the deathbed memorial of Browning's St John, is Christian rather than Oedipal. It makes no more sense to speak of Browning and St John as rivals than to speak of a rivalry among the different persons of the Trinity. The relation of Dallas's poet to the events he imitates is like the relation of the Eucharist to the sacrifice it celebrates, or like the relation of liberty to law – of 'dramatic' as opposed to merely 'historical faith' – at the centre of the Bible.

6 Browning and F. H. Bradley: The Progress of Ethics

Like Sir Henry Jones, the author of the best Victorian study of Browning's moral and religious thought, many Victorians seem to have recognized affinities between Browning and the influential Hegelian movement which dominated English logic, ethics, and metaphysical thought from 1865 to the end of the century.[8] Though many of Browning's monologues were written well before *Ethical Studies* was published in 1876, Browning would have been familiar with many of Bradley's doctrines from William Whewell's frequent anticipation of these doctrines in his two-volume study, *Elements of Morality*, first published in 1845. Whatever the line of influence, no account of Hegel's legacy to the Victorians would be complete without some comparison of Browning's monologues and Bradley's book on ethics, which remains the most Hegelian writing of the ablest Victorian Hegelian.

Constantly correcting and refining each moral theory he examines, Bradley argues that morality is a drama of self-realization that cannot be terminated and still remain moral. Many of Browning's early monologues and love poems show why hedonism, the ethic of 'pleasure for pleasure's sake', is bankrupt. In seeking the sum of all pleasures, the lover in Browning's 'Two in the Campagna', for example, soon discovers, like Bradley, that the idea of an 'infinite passion' is self-contradictory. 'Infinite passion' must always include the irony of 'finite hearts that yearn' (ll. 59–60), the lostness of the unfinished man and his pain. The hedonist's 'infinite passion' is what Bradley calls a 'false universal'. It is infinite only in the sense of being a process *ad indefinitum*, a series of pleasures 'which has no beginning, or, if a beginning, yet no end', and which 'can not' therefore 'be summed till we are dead' (Bradley, 1876, p. 97).

Browning's hedonists speak a language of sensory denotation, devoid of any enduring concepts. By contrast, his gnostics and rationalists speak a language of empty concepts, deficient in sensory content. When Browning's ascetic Prior tells Fra Lippo Lippi to paint 'pure soul', he is telling him to realize a form which possesses no sensory content. But something that has no content cannot be willed. In effect, the Prior is telling the monk *not* to do as a monk what he is asked to do as a painter: he is simultaneously to realize and *not* realize. This contradiction dramatizes the paradox of all purely formal moralities like 'Duty for Duty's Sake'. For in Bradley's words, ' "realize" *means* materialize, it *means* particularize. "Realize" *asserts* the concrete identity of matter and form which "formal will" denies' (1876, p. 150).

The strictly ethical consequences of Bradley's paradox are explored in poems like 'The Statue and the Bust'. Because a will which does not act is no will but a 'psychological monster', as Bradley says, the Duke's observance of the mere moral forms, his deference to the bare ethical precept that we should turn 'The earthly gift to an end divine' ('The Statue and the Bust', l. 185), leads him to waste his life instead of use it. Unlike the true ascetic, Caponsacchi, the Duke fails to see that morality both negates and presupposes the pleasures of sense. If everyone were to negate adultery like the Duke and his lady, the very possibility of being moral would disappear. Browning's Duke forgets that 'every duty which presupposes something to be negated is no duty: it is an immoral rule, because self-contradictory' (Bradley, 1876, pp. 153, 155).

In *The Ring and the Book* Browning shows how Caponsacchi and Pompilia resolve in a higher unity the bare and empty concepts of the gnostic, which develop only the formal or internal side of the good will, and the blind sensations of the hedonist, which develop only the external side. As two contracting parties, Caponsacchi and Pompilia are both, in Bradley's words, 'already beyond and above the sphere of mere contract' (1876, p. 174). Andrea del Sarto's marriage, by contrast, has collapsed into mere economic bargaining. He has to bribe his wife to fulfil her part of the marriage contract ('Andrea del Sarto', ll. 205–43). A moral hero like Caponsacchi learns to particularize the generalized laws of duty for duty's sake, not by seducing a beautiful woman (as the lover in 'Two in the Campagna' tries to do), but by willing his priestly station and its duties. Without the personal morality of its adherents, institutions like the church would be mere empty forms. But apart from the church, heroes like Caponsacchi and Pompilia would be souls without a body. Caponsacchi discovers that only when he is faithful to his clerical vocation can the body of the world and its soul come together.

Like F. H. Bradley, Browning quickly loses patience with speakers who betray contempt for their station and its duties. He parodies the shrill self-conceit of Johannes Agricola, whose frantic theories of election are the mere vanity of an egotist who presumes to know better than God or the world. And he has little sympathy for geniuses like Paracelsus, too clever in general to achieve anything particular. Browning approves, instead, of unglamorous but dedicated characters like the plodding scholar in 'The Grammarian's Funeral' or the court lady in 'The Glove'. Though despised by many at the court, the lady has sacrificed something spurious and romantic for 'work to the best of her lights'. As Bradley would say, hers is a sacrifice the Romantic poets would have despised 'because [to them] it is stupid, and uninteresting, and altogether unsentimental' (1876, p. 202).

Like Bradley's teaching that moral ends are unattainable, and that if they ever were attained morality would abolish itself, Browning's doctrine of imperfection sets a limit to knowledge. Observing that 'the essence of morality [is a] contradiction', and that 'Hegel pushes this [premise] ruthlessly even against the postulate of immortality' (1876, p. 155), Bradley argues that 'if you are to love your enemies, you must never be without them; and yet you try to get rid of them. Is that consistent?' (1876, p. 155). When Browning's Abt Vogler proclaims, 'On the earth the broken arcs; in the heaven, a perfect round' ('Abt Vogler', l. 72), he accepts just such a contradiction. He knows that every attempt to close the broken arcs is immoral, since it removes the possibility of further closures. A moral command to connect the arcs contradicts itself. For once the arcs are closed they cease to be arcs, and man can no longer perfect his moral nature by connecting them.

According to Bradley, dialectic 'starts from a single *datum*, and without the help of any other premise it brings out a fresh result' (1883, p. 379). It would seem to be a form of analytic judgement. But unlike the *a priori* analytic judgements of the solipsist or seer, 'the result is not got by mere analysis of the starting-point, but is got by the action of a mental function which extends the *datum* through an ideal synthesis' (1883, p. 379). Experience furnishes a single conception. Because the whole mind then operates on that conception to produce a new result, 'the point in dispute', Bradley argues, 'is not whether the product is *a posteriori*, but whether, being *a posteriori* it is not *a priori* also and as well' (1883, p. 380). Though it seems contradictory to me to call a judgement *a priori* and *a posteriori* at one and the same time, I think we can be true to Bradley's paradox if we say that the logical form of a dialectical inference is analytic *a posteriori*. Dialectic depends upon experience for its minor meaning. But because its major meaning is the whole mind which operates upon that *datum* of experience, the conclusion of any dialectical process is necessarily present from the start. The form is analytic rather than synthetic. Such, in any case, is the logical form of Browning's mature dramatic monologues. Their minor meaning is furnished by some *datum* of experience like Fra Lippo's arrest by the police officers, which dramatizes his embarrassment at being both a sensualist and a monk. But the near-zeugma of always 'seeing' God with the same immediacy as the pagan garden of love, where the power of Venus seems inseparable from the great tenderness of Adam for his newly created wife (ll. 266–7), does more than merely repeat Fra Lippo's sensuality, which is felt to be an insufficient key to his character. The minor meaning of any dramatic monologue is always 'the real, in that fragmentary character in which the mind possesses it'. The major meaning is 'the true reality felt within the mind'. And as Bradley explains, the opposition between the fragmentary and the whole, between the minor and the major meaning, 'is the moving cause of that unrest which sets up the dialectical process' (1883, p. 381).

This odd form of inference, which is unfamiliar to the inductive scientist, differentiates a monologue like 'Fra Lippo Lippi', in which there are no conversions, from an autobiographical poem like *In Memoriam*, where the end is implicit in the beginning only because for the retrospective poet the experiences recorded are already over. So strange is this new dialectical form that even Bradley's analysis of odd specimens of inference can barely digest it. As he struggles to explain in his exposition of dialectic in *The Principles of Logic*, certain forms of judgement 'call out' or develop in their predicates what is given in their subject. Unless one reads Bradley with a live sense of what actually happens in a dialectical genre like the Victorian monologue, one may be unable to make any sense of his discussion at all. Here Browning's poetry may make intelligible what Bradley's logic can barely bring within the range of philosophical analysis. The more closely the idealist philosophies approach the limits of the sayable, the more they depend on poetry to continue philosophy by other means.

The function of Browning's dialectic is to narrow the gap between the fragmentary character of the real, as it is present from the start of a monologue, and that fullness of truth which can be brought into view only by an activity of the speaker's whole mind. But there must always be some disparity between the fragmentary truth now possessed by the speaker and the whole which eludes him. We might go further and say that, like morality itself, the art of the dramatic monologue as Browning perfects it 'aims at the cessation of that which makes it possible' (Bradley, 1876, p. 234). Morality, in Bradley's phrase, 'is the effort after non-morality' (1876, pp. 234–5). To prevent 'progress to an end which is completeness and the end of progress and morality' (Bradley, 1876, p. 235), Browning imposes strict limits on what can be known and reached. The words of a monologue initiate and sustain discourse. But only some vision outside of the monologue, some vision like David's or Abt Vogler's, which confronts finite understanding with the fact of infinity, can hope to end the self-contradiction of the ought, without which no moral education, no pilgrimage of self-realization, would be possible. If such a vision exists, it belongs only to the Word. Browning can seldom fix that Word or speak it in his poems.

7 The Revolt Against the Absolute: Pringle-Pattison and Schiller

If Pater is the father of twentieth-century formalism, Pringle-Pattison and Schiller are the fathers of modern existentialism and pragmatism. When Pringle-Pattison turns Hegel's doctrine of absolute or eternal self-making from a statement about God into a statement about man, he fosters the existential notion that Victorian man is not just a maker but a self-maker. Man is the architect of what Arnold calls a best or highest self. Such a notion pervades the verse of Browning and Clough. And it anticipates the poetics of pragmatism, especially as that tradition is expounded and practised by Robert Frost, who amply acknowledges his debt to William James, the pragmatist to whom F. C. S. Schiller dedicates his philosophical essays on humanism (Thompson and Winnick, 1971, p. 643).

In *Hegelianism and Personality* Pringle-Pattison criticizes Hegel for expounding his logic, his philosophy of nature, and his philosophy of spirit in an order which is the precise reverse of the order in which he obtains them. 'The forward movement is in reality a progress backwards: it is a retracing of our steps to the world as we know it in the fullness of its real determinations' (1887, p. 92). Just as Jowett criticizes Plato for making the beginning the end, for venerating as the 'crowning achievement of the dialectical art' a process of abstraction 'which is the most familiar process of our own minds' (1871, vol. 4, p. 187), so Pringle-Pattison criticizes Hegel for making 'the dialectical advance really depend upon the fuller knowledge which the subject brings with him from his experience' (1887, p. 95). Pringle-Pattison's main objection to absolute idealists like Hegel and Bradley is that their concrete universals are really abstract. Bradley and Hegel unite the Absolute with man only by attenuating the real content of both. God and man disappear, not indeed into the pantheistic substance of Spinoza, but into a logical concept. The spirit of the Absolute does duty at one time for God and at another time for man. But when we have hold of the divine end we have lost our grasp of the human end, and vice versa.

To turn man's temporal self-making into the eternal self-making of the Absolute, Pringle-Pattison believes that Hegel subtly confuses two concepts of development. He confuses development as a logical implication, as an ideal or timeless evolution, with development as a real process in time. Though it seems to me that Pringle-Pattison is prejudging the issue by attempting a persuasive redefinition of the word 'development', conferring the value-term 'real' only upon development in time, he argues convincingly that Hegel's fundamental error is to identify human with divine self-consciousness. Like Averroës, the medieval Aristotelian who teaches that man is absorbed at death into a general soul, Hegelians who try to construct the universe out of mere universals degrade the individual self-consciousness by allowing it to be swallowed up in the Absolute. If immortality is to be claimed by our moral instinct as in any sense a reward, then Pringle-Pattison believes, like Tennyson, that 'Eternal form [must] still divide / The eternal soul from all beside' (*In Memoriam*, XLVII, 6–7).

In his book entitled *Humanism*, the chief target of F. C. S. Schiller's spirited critique of Absolute Idealism is Bradley's *Appearance and Reality*. Schiller complains that Bradley's Absolute is to metaphysics what the figure *hysteron proteron* is to rhetoric, a reversal of the true sequence of events. 'The abstractions of metaphysics . . . exist as explanations of the concrete facts of life, and not the latter as illustrations of the former.' 'The Absolute Idea', Schiller concludes, 'is not exempt from this rule' (1903, p. 102). 'The Aristotelian conception of *Energeia*', he says, is 'our best starting-point', because such a conception 'affords no foothold for an unknowable substratum . . . The truth therefore is that *the activity is the substance*: a thing *is* only in so far as active' (1903, pp. 224–5). Proclaiming man to be the architect of a humanized universe, interpreted and self-made, Schiller bequeaths 'the bow of Odysseus' to the man who can 'bend it, and, if need be, use it upon' such enemies of truth as Bradley, who in ascending 'from the sphere of Appearances' and being received 'into the bosom of the Absolute reminds [Schiller] of nothing so much as of the fabled "rope-trick" of the Indian jugglers' (1903, pp. 190, 198).

In a less intemperate attack on Bradley in *Riddles of the Sphinx* (1891), Schiller criticizes Bradley's Absolute for the same reason that Bradley himself in his *Ethical Studies* criticizes a Kantian ethic of 'duty for duty's sake'. Each evades the test of application, and 'becomes useless and unmeaning' (Schiller, 1912, p. 155). In claiming universality, Bradley's Absolute, like Kant's categorical imperative, is 'only disclaiming the duty of meaning anything in particular'. By escaping 'the risk of being proved false', Schiller argues, Kant and Bradley 'forfeit the chance of being proved true' (1912, pp. 155–6). Invoking a pragmatic criterion of truth, Schiller insists that an assertion is never fully true until it has been tested.

The real revolutions in a culture take place first in literature. Only later do these revolutions find full expression in some philosophic movement or political manifesto. If we are looking for a poetic of Personal Idealism in Victorian culture, we must turn back from Pringle-Pattison and Schiller to poems by Browning, Clough, and even Christina Rossetti, all of whom use language, not to describe a prior state of affairs, but to shape and change their world. In anticipating Pringle-Pattison's 'anti-essentialist' notion of language and truth, these poets share three defining features of an existential poetic. Because Personal Idealism is a philosophy of self-making, the poetry of a personal idealist cannot be grounded in any pre-existing category or essence. It is committed to a performative rather than a descriptive mode of discourse. The grammar of Personal Idealism also tends to be a pragmatic grammar, which by translating nouns into blueprints for future action shows why we cannot entertain a philosophically or critically interesting theory about the 'essential' or dictionary meaning of a word. In being dissolved into verbal chains, nouns are made to point toward their consequence in practice. A third feature of Personal Idealism is its espousal of pragmatic theism. Because the universe of the personal idealist is open, plural, and subject to human control, it opposes the idea of any determining Absolute. The god in such a world may be vague and indeterminate, like Browning's 'the Quiet'. Or it may be subject to evolutionary transformation, like Hardy's Immanent Will or like the God of Clough's Adam in *Adam and Eve*. Under other circumstances, the personal idealist will be unable to 'create' his deity, freely deciding what God's attributes will be. The language of Personal Idealism is, in the first place, performative. All its doctrines must be shaped and believed into being. If religion merely described what exists, the believer would have nothing to do. Like Strauss, Browning's Pope foresees that if faith is to be professed in words that are truly performative, then new prophets like Caponsacchi will have to bring something new into the world, a form of Christianity that did not exist before. To the degree that Christianity is historically grounded, however, it cannot be fully performative. A 'grounded' performative is a misnomer, a contradiction in terms. Perhaps only in some form of 'process' theology like Caliban's, where words are no longer grounded in a god who is all-powerful as well as good, can every evil or delinquent act of Caliban strengthen that 'shadow-side' of God called Setebos and every virtuous act confirm His day-side.

Influenced perhaps by I. A. Richards' teaching that poetic statements are only 'pseudo-statements', J. L. Austin restricts the term 'performative' to non-poetic utterances like marriage vows, which have observable consequences in real life. Once we remove Austin's own restriction, however, we can see how the antinomian theology of Browning's Johannes Agricola, for example, in making a fetish of God's unmerited love, commits a form of the descriptive fallacy: it uses the constatives of an achieved salvation where performatives are required. And yet such mistakes in philosophical grammar are difficult to avoid. In a poem like 'Saul', Browning wants to discover how far a worshipper can be humanly receptive of God's gifts while still rising above mere receptivity. The speaker, David, must work at the height of his imaginative and intellectual powers. But he must also celebrate the otherness of God by remaining the seer in whom revelation takes place. To explore this paradox Browning keeps his speaker fluctuating between the performatives of self-making and the constatives of inspired seeing. A good example is David's use of *hyperbaton*, or inversion of predicate and subject, and of the auxiliary verb 'shall' instead of 'will': 'So wouldst thou – so wilt thou! / So shall crown thee the topmost, ineffablest, uttermost crown' ('Saul', ll. 300–1).

'So wilt thou' may sound at first like a simple future tense. It is more probable, however, that David is wavering between an auxiliary of volition (God 'wants' or 'desires') and an auxiliary of command. But if Browning is using the imperative of command, is David ordering God? Is he saying, in effect, 'so [shalt] thou'? Or is God Himself decreeing that His will shall be law? In either case, the transition from surmise to prophecy enacts a movement from the optatives of volition to God's future action on man's behalf. The transition is made possible by the grammatical ambiguity of the auxiliary verb, which allows David to hover over three different meanings ('God will', 'God wills', 'I will that God wills or that God will'), all focused in a single word. There seems to be no way Browning can bring dogma to life without turning constatives into performatives. But are such performatives merely the unaided power of creation, the prophetic genius of a David plunging blindly ahead in 'Saul' to create meaning out of chaos? Or is it possible to ground the performatives of self-making in an infinite that already exists, in a Christ that already 'stands'? If God's gift is freely given before prophets and poets dare grasp or even name it, how can they then exercise faith by finding the right names for God? If performatives are grounded, they annihilate the conditions of religious faith. If they are ungrounded, they destroy the specifically religious character of man's self-making, which according to both Browning and Schleiermacher is a feeling of dependence on God. Strictly speaking, there is no such thing as a grounded performative. Only God's performatives are grounded. And that is not because God is a master electrician who has wired his universe in advance of decreeing 'Let there be light', but because God is God. The dangerous, mysterious power of performative positing, which tends to erode the believer's knowledge of a gift God has already bestowed, appears to be one of the paradoxes of religion. Like Hegel, Browning speaks as if God's gift both *is* and is *not* fully real until a believer like Browning's David works at the height of his powers to bring that gift into focus and receive it.

Any performative use of words makes something happen. Though only an extreme form of process theology like Caliban's or Hardy's is fully performative, the deeds of even a Caponsacchi or a David are not the result of knowledge. Like any risk or wager, they are groundless positings, thrown out in advance of any known result to change the world. As Blougram tries to explain to Gigadibs, faith is a form of conduct, not the result of speculation. 'How

one acts / Is both of us agree, our chief concern' ('Bishop Blou-
gram's Apology', ll. 812–13). Action and conduct must precede
knowledge of what antecedently exists, not the other way round.

On to the rack with faith! – is my advice.
Will not that hurry us upon our knees,
Knocking our breasts, 'It can't be – yet it shall!'
                        ('Bishop Blougram's Apology', ll. 705–7)

Browning's 'shall!' is a performative, what Austin would call an
'exercitive', an auxiliary verb of fiat or decree (1962, pp. 119, 141,
150–61). Schiller's faith that man 'has no other and no better key to the
mystery of being' (1912, p. 164) than his own heroic energy and his
will to believe applies even to Christina Rossetti's poetry. In her
lyric 'A Birthday', for example, Rossetti 'believe[s] her future in', as
Frost would say, anticipating a grand adornment that is now at
hand. With the shift from descriptive to performative verbs in
stanza two, the heart in its ecstasy begins to give orders, demanding
homage worthy of an empress.

Raise me a daïs of silk and down;
  Hang it with vair and purple dyes;
Carve it in doves and pomegranates,
  And peacocks with a hundred eyes;
Work it in gold and silver grapes,
  In leaves and silver fleurs-de-lys;
Because the birthday of my life
  Is come, my love is come to me.
                        ('A Birthday', ll. 9–16)

This poetry is born of longing, ennobled by piety, and transmuted
by biblical and literary tradition into a triumph of constructive will.
Rossetti affirms that the birthday of her life is at hand, not because
she can prove that her lover's coming will inwardly adorn and
aggrandize her, but because the grandeur is necessary if such splen-
dour of the heart as she is seeking is ever to be found. Rossetti's
adornment of her passion, linked to the reverent solemnizations of
the Song of Songs, seems equally suited to the celebration of erotic
and religious love. Perhaps in the end the two are inseparable. 'Faith
is practical', as Bradley says, 'and it is . . . a making-believe' (1893,

p. 392). From such a pronouncement it is only a short step to the pragmatism of Robert Frost, who observes in an aside that sums up the legacy of the personal idealists, and that may well reflect the influence of his beloved William James, a much greater pragmatist than Schiller: 'Now I think – I happen to think – that those three beliefs that I speak of, the self-belief, the love-belief, and the art-belief, are all closely related to the God-belief, that the belief in God is a relationship you enter into with Him to bring about the future' (1968, p. 45).

A second feature of Personal Idealism is its grammar of pragmatic definition, which identifies meaning with use. Browning's Bishop Blougram defines the concept 'faith', for example, by translating that concept into a chain of predictable actions. If St Michael has faith, he will remain calm just because he feels the snake writhe beneath his foot. And if Blougram has faith, it means he can take a pinch of snuff that threatens 'the torpor' of his 'inside-nose' without making the sneeze actually come ('Bishop Blougram's Apology', ll. 667–72). Such definitions do not require real experiments to be made with snakes or snuffboxes. All they require is a prediction of results which could then be verified if the conditions were met. Many of the most idiosyncratic qualities of Blougram's speech stem from his pragmatic distrust of nouns. Substantives petrify into blank counters that block thought. They must be translated into chains of verbs, which can then serve as blueprints for action. Words like 'faith' and 'doubt' are not inscribed for stability and definiteness, only for reinscription. 'Faith' has to be reinscribed in order to accommodate the Bishop's joke that Gigadibs, like his wine, is 'cool i' faith' (l. 2), or the novel fact that 'faith means perpetual unbelief' (l. 666). Like Bishop Blougram, Ernest Pontifex in *The Way of All Flesh* retains the favourable emotive meaning of 'faith', while altering its descriptive meaning to identify the concept with its use. 'The just shall live by faith, that is to say that sensible people will get through life by rule of thumb' (Butler, 1967, p. 311). For Butler's Ernest, as for Browning's Bishop, what works is made the measure of what ought to be. What ought to be is not appealed to as the sanction of what works.

Because of his disconcerting honesty and wit, Clough is the acknowledged Victorian master of pragmatic definition. Though definitions are usually thought to be the special domain of the intel-

lect, where the conscious mind retains control, Clough shows that
this control is more precarious than we like to think. As nouns are
dissolved into chains of verbs, there is always a danger that fossil-
ized definitions will slip away into mere indefiniteness. And to fall
into indefinition is to risk a loss of control. It is to allow suppressed
knowledge or feeling to come irresistibly into view. If marriage
were indeed an 'eternal tie' 'made in heaven' (*Amours de Voyage*, III,
vi, 112), what would be the consequence of seriously entertaining
the idea? The prospect of definite ends, Claude muses, is what
makes tolerable the uncertainties of commitment, the risks of enlist-
ment, whether in the ranks of husbands or soldiers. If we felt knowl-
edge could survive our actions, all would be well. But Claude's
pragmatic definitions remind him that action unstabilizes what
might otherwise seem definite and secure. Lines 117–18 are framed
by carefully juxtaposed images of ends and beginnings: 'But for his
funeral train which the bridegroom sees in the distance, / Would he
so joyfully, think you, fall in with the marriage-procession?' Only
the distant prospect of the funeral train allows Claude to contem-
plate with equanimity the joys of the wedding contract. Marriage
may still be a great beginning, as it was for Adam and Eve. But it is
also a kind of fall. When death, with its certainty of an ending,
seems more definite than the uncertainties of service, marriage is
already being redefined as military enlistment and war. Does death
cancel the perilous marriage contract, or does it simply extend it
into infinity? Marriage is either an entry into the indefinite, or an
ultimate limit, a new entrapment. Perhaps the two alternatives are
reconciled in an 'Actual Abstract' (l. 132), which seems a kind of
definite Indefinite. But oxymorons are beyond Claude's compre-
hension. Only God can understand them.

  In the poem 'To Spend Uncounted Years of Pain', the usual order
of nouns and verbs in Clough's poetry of definition is reversed.
Now the chain of infinitives precedes the subject Clough tries to
define, although when that subject is finally introduced at the end of
the poem it turns out not to be a subject at all but a question. 'To
spend uncounted years of pain / . . . To gather facts . . . / Upon
the mind to hold them clear / . . . Unto one's latest breath to fear /
The premature result to draw – / Is this the object, end and law, /
And purpose of our being here?' (ll. 1, 5, 6, 8–11). Clough's triple
rhymes seem to prolong the indefiniteness of his pragmatic defi-

nitions. Even the rhyme word repeats without variation in the
second line: 'Again, again, and yet again.' In lines 7–9, the indefini-
tion of this definition poem extends even to Clough's indeterminate
grammar: 'And, knowing more may yet appear, / Unto one's latest
breath to fear.' Does the clause 'Unto one's latest breath' modify
'fear' or 'appear'? Does something more appear to Clough when he
draws his latest breath? Or is Clough afraid to conclude anything
until that hour arrives? Definition comes only with the syntactical
completion of the chain of infinitives in the last two lines. But even
here the terminal position gives only a muted sense of closure, since
for the first time in the poem Clough uses no couplet or triplet, and
we end not with the expected statement but with a question.

In 'Duty – That's to Say Complying', Clough explains what duty
really means by translating the concept into a chain of meaningless
gerunds: 'Duty – that's to say complying / . . . Upon etiquette rely-
ing, / Unto usage nought denying' (ll. 1, 5–6). The volley of femi-
nine rhymes turns the exercise of matching sounds into a mocking
imitation of mindless conformity. They are the echoing walls of a
merely polite civility. The satiric potential of pragmatic definition
is also resourcefully deployed in 'The Latest Decalogue', where
simple variations in the run-overs mock the authority of the Law,
while using the couplets to give the redefinitions their own auth-
ority and power.

A third feature of Personal Idealism is the pragmatic theism of a
poetic experiment like Clough's *Adam and Eve*, a precursor of
Frost's *Masque of Reason* and *Masque of Mercy*. In Adam's reductive
version of Eve's theology, 'the mighty mythus of the Fall' (*Adam
and Eve*, i, 80) is only dreamwork originating in two trivial events,
the death of a lamb and the chance appearance of a snake. For Eve,
the orthodox theist, whom one critic calls 'the Tractarian of the
family' (Biswas, 1972, p. 259), history is still a theological drama in
which God's finger guides her destiny. Adam, by contrast, is a fore-
runner of Pringle-Pattison and Schiller. He is a humanist and proto-
existentialist. The 'Word' that Adam hears is the prophetic voice of
a new experiment in theology, a new pragmatic theism. In celebrat-
ing the dynamics of flux, Adam is worshipping the soul's perpetual
falling away from the 'moist provocative vernal mould' (i, 14).
Though no orthodox First Cause is involved, Adam's attitude is in a
refined sense religious, an attitude of reverence he feels for the life

process itself. 'Live and grow,' the Word exhorts him, 'Look still / Upward, spread outward, Trust, be patient, live' (i, 117–18).

In combining a biblical fable in the manner of Milton with a satiric transformation of that mode in the manner of the Higher Critics, Clough has perfected a dramatic form able to entertain and push to the limit his own religious enterprise, his own 'experiment's sum' (i, 30). Like F. C. S. Schiller and William James, Clough believes that all attempts to ground theology in traditional metaphysics is an attempt to make a god-term of some wheel that plays no part in the actual cosmic mechanism. In renouncing scepticism, whose watchword is silence, for 'another religion miscalled irreligion whose watchword . . . is action' (Bodleian MS. Eng. poet d. 133, folio 82), Clough is trying to show why any workable theism must possess three qualities. It must be open and free rather than closed and determined. It must be plural rather than monistic. And it must be purposive and at least partly intelligible. Like Hardy's God, who has to be tutored by his pupils in 'God's Education', where the genitive in the title switches without warning from the subjective to objective form, Clough's God has to be 'created' by man in his own best image. Absolute Idealism, like any form of monism, is the great enemy, because it is the single most powerful means of forcing premature closure, of absorbing novelty and difference, and of giving licence to Eve's visionary vagrancy. It fosters the dangerous delusion that a determining God or Absolute has grounded our present vocabulary and world picture, and has mechanized man by designing him as a computer capable of writing and reading only one program.

The personal idealist, by contrast, seeks a fully human world whose intelligibility cannot be worried into being, but must unfold by surprise, like the risky and imperfect art of writing poetry or, as Clough's Claude would add, of making love. In traditional philosophies of religion, the statement 'God exists' has the same philosophical grammar as the proposition $2 + 2 = 4$, where truth or falsity is unaffected by anyone's believing it. But for personal idealists, as for pragmatic theists like Clough and Browning's Blougram, the truth of the statement 'God exists' has the same philosophical grammar as the statement 'my poem has a design' or as the proposition 'you like me', where belief in the design or in the liking may make the statements true. Like love-making, the proposition 'God exists' is performative. Instead of describing a prior state of affairs, it allows the pragmatic theist to create rather than discover. It translates as 'let God exist' or 'make something happen'. If Clough's darkness and despair are the necessary corollary of his optimism, it is because he understands better than most personal idealists the self-contradiction which pragmatism involves. The truth about truth, the personal idealist cheerfully argues, is that truth is whatever works within a known context or given framework. But this axiom contradicts the pragmatist's other depressing axiom that truth is unattainable because we can never get outside our frameworks and beliefs to evaluate them. The moment Claude tries to evaluate his beliefs, the framework grows indefinitely large. A railway tie turns into the eternal tie of the marriage contract, and the prospect of a train terminus into the terminus of life itself. Such expansion of the context is deeply subversive of the pragmatist's optimistic assumption that truth is what can be demonstrated within a single accepted framework. The mind possesses truth only when it is contemplating its own artefacts and fictions. But these fictions are bound to man-made contexts, and the real context is boundless and unknowable. We live in the best of all possible worlds. And everything which exists – everything which is given and not made, which simply is the case, whether anyone could understand or use it – is a necessary evil that makes despair as inevitable as the optimism that generates it.

Conclusion
Poetic Truth in the Victorian Age

'It is not by philosophy', said St Ambrose, 'that it pleased God to save His people.' 'This was a piece of luck for Ambrose,' one commentator has quipped, since Ambrose 'was no philosopher' (F. E. Sparshott, 1972, p. 3). I suspect we might say the same for most poets and critics. Yet many Victorian poets are drawn to philosophic subjects. Obvious affinities of method bind together the scientific theory of induction enshrined in Mill's *System of Logic*, for example, and the conviction of many Pre-Raphaelite poets that words are exact and descriptive, capable of being clear without ceasing to imply. Less easy to document, though more pervasive, is a habit of mind or temper common to a philosophic movement and a poetic tradition. In his essay 'Spinoza and the Bible' Arnold asserts that 'a philosopher's real power over mankind resides not in his metaphysical formulas, but in the spirit and tendencies which have led him to adopt those formulas' (1960–77, vol. 3, p. 175). Like Arnold, Pater believes that metaphysics derives from emotion and temperament, and that in order to understand a philosopher we have to understand his philosophy's psychological roots. But because language as well as feeling plays a part in philosophical and poetic speculation, it is important to expose a philosopher's axioms of cognition and the metaphors or figures he uses to expound these axioms and explore their consequences. Metaphors of the mirror, the framed picture, the kaleidoscope of presentational forms, provide the very principles of a theory's construction.

Like Pater, I believe that metaphysics is at once futile and fascinating, because like poetry it is mainly a projection of idiosyncratic ways of feeling and talking about the world. An empiricist like Bentham, Clough, or Samuel Butler reflects one type of mind, and an idealist like Ferrier or Tennyson another. Affinities between philosophers and poets are less a matter of conscious influence than of temperamental preference. Butler's and Clough's desire to be brutally honest, exposing what we do feel, not what we want or pretend to feel, is in keeping with Bentham's desire to show that something is good because it is useful rather than the other way round. Clough's exacting honesty springs from the same psychological need as Darwin's desire to explain what happens, not what we want to happen. Instead of explaining like theorists of creative evolution what nature would like to happen, Darwin explains how nature evolves by describing what accidental variations have in fact occurred.

'Metaphysical formulae', Pater maintains in *Plato and Platonism*, 'have always their practical equivalents' (1893, p. 40). A pragmatic theory like Butler's, Clough's or Bentham's reminds us of what is true of all metaphysical formulas. They point toward their consequence in practice. Their meaning is partly a matter of how they can be used. A metaphysical theory arises out of temperamental needs, and it confirms the poet or philosopher in his existing habits of feeling and need. The poet's needs usually seem to bear a closer resemblance to the idealist's needs than to the needs of the empiricist. Philosophers like Green and Bradley, for example, start, not with an axiom about utility like Mill and Bentham, but with a need to be satisfied that is shared by many poets, a theoretical need to abolish contradiction and to unify experience. Victorian Idealism is a full-time occupation, leading not to Utilitarian maxims about the greatest good of the greatest number or even to Hegel's axiom that the truth is the whole, but to what one critic in speaking of Bradley calls 'a decantation of verbal substances that will satisfactorily fill up the voids in mental existence, though with a different filler than the poet's' (Kenner, 1965, p. 58).

I have argued that Hopkins' arrangement of his syntax into sensory wholes satisfies the same need of simultaneous perception in the poet as is satisfied in the philosopher T. H. Green, Hopkins' Oxford tutor, by the metaphysical formula that the world is a mind-related whole sustained by God as the consciousness of a reader sustains the meaning of words in a sentence. But for either Hopkins or Green to borrow the other's methods would be 'to avail himself', as Kenner says, 'of an illegitimate short cut' (1965, p. 58). When Tennyson in *In Memoriam* and Arnold in *Empedocles on Etna* use philosophical ideas, they display little aptitude or need to think these ideas. Poets do not borrow the philosophers' methods but find different ways of satisfying the same needs. As Richard Wollheim says, 'the lesson, to be learnt only very slowly, is that philosophy has virtually nothing to offer those who would rifle it' (1973, p. ix). But if poets cannot learn directly from philosophers, perhaps the reverse is not true. R. G. Collingwood has said that 'the philosopher must go to school with the poets in order to learn the use of language' (1933, p. 213). I have shown how many visionary poems in the Victorian period provide a useful supplement to philosophy when each mode of discourse is approaching the boundaries of cognition and the limits of the sayable. An absolute idealist like Hegel seems in constant danger of crashing the sense-barrier. He and his disciples talk about such intractable entities as a self-constituting God or an Absolute that has taken flight from the world. Poets may not be able to teach the philosopher how to speak more intelligibly of these difficult ideas. But by writing poems about the mysterious trouble spots of knowledge, about what most needs saying but cannot be said, the poets I have studied may give the idealist philosopher a much more vivid grasp of the kind of experience to which mystery words like 'Absolute' and 'concrete universal' may actually refer, and without which it is difficult to make sense of them at all.

A literary reading of a philosophical work can be most philosophical, and a philosophical reading of a poem most literary. By a truly philosophical reading of works like Mill's *System of Logic* or Ferrier's *Institutes of Metaphysics*, I mean a reading that exposes the work's first principles and axioms. Such a reading studies these treatises as rhetorical fictions which deploy, either consciously or unconsciously, metaphors like the mirror of nature or the frame around a picture. Conversely, the most literary readings of Browning's monologues or Tennyson's *In Memoriam* may be readings which chart the progress of ethics in Browning's poetry or Tennyson's arrival at the margins of discourse. Usually the strategy of the idealist poets and critics is to reverse the order favoured by the empiricists. Mill, for example, is puzzled by the poet's specialized 'performative' use of words. What Mill sees as an aberration from the descriptive norms of scientific language, Coleridge, Edward Caird, and later champions of poetic discourse see as a norm. As J. L. Austin comes to concede, the primary function of language is performative. The mere descriptive *mention* of a word in a dictionary is a specialized instance of the word's fully performative *use* in a myth or a poem, rather than the other way round. Instead of treating myth as a deviation from the normal discourse of science, as a 'disease of language', Coleridge, Green, and Edward Caird all treat as primary the undifferentiated language of myth, in which all discourse is contained. Even philosophers of science like T. H. Huxley and Karl Pearson help sanction this reversal by arguing that it is merely more convenient, not more accurate, to say that scientific discourse is descriptive. According to Huxley, the scientific premise that the world is reducible to material description is a fiction. But it is a fiction that provides a good background for stories about changes among objects made up of material parts. In Richard Rorty's words, 'physics is the paradigm of "finding" simply because it is hard (at least in the West) to tell a story of changing physical universes against the background of an unchanging Moral Law or poetic canon, but very easy to tell the reverse sort of story' (1979, pp. 344–5).

1 Philosophy among the Poets

When examining an expressive tradition in Victorian poetics in the first three chapters, I argue that most poetry written in the period 1830–1870 draws upon three axioms. Poets, like philosophers, may use the empirical axiom of the mirror of nature, the axiom of the framed or lucidly veiled event, or the holistic axiom that the fragmentary character of the truth as we now possess it presupposes a fullness of truth that can be brought into clearer view only by an activity of the whole mind. The subject of the next two chapters is an agnostic and purist line in Victorian poetics. I show that after 1870 Victorian poetry becomes increasingly a poetry of symbolic fictions, formalist and self-contained. Instead of representing a subject in a mirror, the poet re-presents it in a medium of his choice, or else offers in place of a picture a pure presentation. The more purist poetry becomes, the more it tends to use three further axioms of cognition. It may draw upon Masson's assumption that the poet's language possesses all the hallmarks of conventional symbolism except one, the existence of an assigned connotation. It may alternatively assume like the agnostics that the poet's predications preserve the attributes of a divine subject that never really existed or that has now disappeared. A final possibility is the sceptical assumption that the poet's predications are in logical contradiction with each other, like conflicting wave and particle theories of light. The poet defines a subject that is not strictly knowable. In the last two chapters I examine an oracular and prophetic tradition in Victorian poetics. This tradition receives its most comprehensive treatment in Hegelian theories of art and knowledge, which I discuss in the final chapter. Hegel has to explain how his Absolute Idea at the end of his *Logic* is a return to Being, which is at its beginning. The end both *is* and is *not* present from the start. The classic embodiment of this doctrine is the dialectical axiom. We can study it in the dialectical form of Browning's monologues, in which there are no conversions. Instead of adding new information, a dramatic monologue, like a dialectical inference, simply 'calls out' or develops a truth that is already given. The form is curiously circular and repetitive. In Hegelian aesthetics we have travelled as far away as possible from the representational axioms of Mill. What Mill takes to be concrete in the sense data of the scientist, Oxford Hegelians like William Wallace and F. H. Bradley rightly perceive as abstractions drawn out of the chaotic mass of sense experience by the scientist's intelligence. If 'reality and concreteness as estimated by' Mill's *Logic* and by Hegel's 'are the very reverse' of each other as Wallace argues, then an important function of the poet's associative imagination and of his metaphors is to show how a single image or idea 'owns and emphasizes its solidarity with' other images and ideas (1874, pp. lxxviii, lxxix).

The representational axiom of the mirror of nature is the axiom of the empiricists, enshrined for the Victorians in Mill's classic account of induction in his *System of Logic* (1843). According to Mill, a judgemental inference is true because it pictures some fact of sense experience. And it is a source of knowledge because its predicate provides information not given in the subject. At first Mill excludes the poet's intuitive inferences from this representational norm. If all poetry aspires toward the condition of soliloquy, then its sentences merely repeat in the predicate what is given in the subject. Like any form of reverie, the soliloquies of Mill's poet are really only inspired tautologies. But to make poetry true, Mill later revises this theory by showing how many of the poet's intuitive inferences are judgemental inferences in disguise. They correspond to sensory facts which had either been forgotten or repressed in the poet's memory.

As early as the 1830s, in Ferrier's philosophy of consciousness and in the poetic theories of John Keble, Mill's representational axiom of the mirror is already being challenged by axioms of the subjectively framed picture or event. In Tennyson's 'Morte d'Arthur' the prologue and epilogue merely distance the reader from the narrative they frame. They make dramatic irony and critical detachment possible. In other poems like *Sordello* the narrator's intrusive commentary is at least as important as the medieval Italian history it frames. By the time we reach *In Memoriam* (1850) the relative importance of frame and picture is reversed. The mind is now lord and master over outward sense, and the human subject furnishes essential ingredients of his own knowledge. Like most autobiographical poems, *In Memoriam* frames experience twice. Hallam's life, death and afterlife are first framed by the immediate reactions of the mourner whose sorrow is recorded, and then by the retrospective experience and aesthetic commentary of the recording self. In Chapter III I trace the holistic axiom that truth resides in wholes back to the mid 1840s, where I analyse one early version of this doctrine in Ruskin's theory of the Imagination Associative. Full-scale development of this axiom comes only later in the Victorian period, in the speculations of Trench, Müller, Green, and F. H. Bradley.

In later Victorian thought increasing use is made of presentational axioms that place 'no entry' or detour signs on the route that leads from the poem to the world or from the world back to the poem. The effects of these axioms, which I examine in the second section of the book, is to re-present the world in a pictorial medium of the artist's choice by blocking the normal communicative function of words. When we begin a poem like 'The Chapel in Lyoness', for example, we assume we are dealing with some version of the representational axioms I discuss in the first three chapters. But the more of the poem we read, the more we sense that Morris is substituting a two-dimensional pictorial pattern for a coherent Arthurian story. The holistic axiom posited by Ruskin's theory of the Imagination Associative identifies the true subject of a poem as that unnameable whole to which each fragmentary image merely gestures or points. But an unconsummated symbolism, such as we find in Ruskin's theory of the Imagination Contemplative, assumes that though the subject has not exactly disappeared it is now too ineffable to be named. Keble's theory of the lucid veil, developed during the 1830s, had assumed that poets like Virgil and Lucretius were unconscious of their true subject. But that subject could finally be identified when the veil was removed. In 1866 E. S. Dallas goes one step further. The unconscious is no longer a subject to be veiled and then 're-presented'. It becomes instead an unconscious *manner* of presentation. As the meaning of the word 'unconscious' changes, the subject that Keble had veiled and that Ruskin made too mysterious to be named begins to disappear. The difference between Keble's axiom of the lucid veil in the 1830s and Dallas's axiom of the involuntary presentation in the 1860s is really the difference between two theories of the unconscious.

Increasingly important in late-Victorian poetics is the agnostic's axiom of the darkening glass and the dead or departed subject. In Pater's *Plato and Platonism* we find the Platonic sense of mystery, the veneration of form, and the sense of unifying design, without Plato's doctrine of ideas. An emphasis on secrecy and on the critic's need to cultivate occult impressions, without Arnold's anxiety to see the object as in itself it really is, turns Pater into a 'weak textualist', a decoder of abstruse forms and hidden values. Pater asserts that there are creative as well as critical virtues, which invite the observer to cultivate his own impression of the object. And yet moral critics like Arnold and aesthetic critics like Pater share at least one assumption: they profess to discover meaning rather than create it. Their interpretations are not to be confused with the 'strong textualism' of Oscar Wilde, who prefers to see the object as in itself it really is not. To cultivate one's impression of what is excluded or missing from art is to join ranks with Pringle-Pattison or F. C. S. Schiller who, in exalting human self-activity at the expense of receptivity, expound meanings that are frankly created rather than found.

Equally subversive and increasingly influential is the sceptic's axiom that, because the poet's predications are in logical contradiction with each other, a truth in art is one whose opposite is also true. Poets, like theologians and physicists, are trying to define a subject too mysterious to be defined. This axiom of the darkening glass originates at the beginning of the Victorian period in Sir William Hamilton's philosophy of the unconditioned. In 1858 it receives its classic Victorian formulation in H. L. Mansel's demonstration that a God who is both infinite and absolute is as logically indeterminate as the concepts of an infinitely divisible substance and of an indivisible atomic particle in physics. In the last decade of the nineteenth century the concept of indeterminacy receives another definitive formulation in the first book of F. H. Bradley's *Appearance and Reality*. The mind-made relations that T. H. Green had predicated of the real are shown by Bradley to be as incurably contradictory as Kant's paralogisms, hence the predicates of an indeterminate subject. Though Victorian poetic genres are increasingly indeterminate, their failure to satisfy the expectations they consciously set out to raise can be found in poems of every decade in the period. An early poem like 'The Lady of Shalott', for example, is generically indeterminate, because by using elision to block the normal representational aims of ballad poetry Tennyson creates a parable to which no single meaning can be assigned. When such techniques are practised on a large scale in *The Ring and the Book* they radically challenge representational norms. Some historians, Browning shows, try to read the facts recorded in a document like the Old Yellow Book as if they, like the world, were already coherently ordered. But such critics are continually frustrated in their efforts. When generic theorists try to do the same thing with *The Ring and the Book*, they are always in danger of betraying its mystery by resolving what is strange and indeterminate into something more stable and familiar than it really is.

In the third section of the book I suggest how some mysterious trouble spots in idealist theories of knowledge invite poetic solutions. Whereas Kant perceives the necessity for God in the moral order, Hegel finds the foundation of the world in a process of self-making which is really one aspect of aesthetic order. Apart from man and the world with its perpetual self-making, there could be no rational account of the Absolute. And apart from the Absolute, there could be no actual world, no arena for human creativity. The Absolute is larger than man, but it requires human activity to realize its nature. In an oracular or prophetic tradition in Victorian poetics, we find one partial answer to the question how this is possible. Because no finished product represents the average quality of the poet's thinking, it provides an example of a creation which seems other and greater than the individual poet. In a poetic creation, as in Hegel's Absolute, the individual finds himself judged and abashed by a power that is partly a product of his own unconscious mind. And yet the poet's inability to command the success of his operations suggests that poets are not truly the authors of what they write. Just as Hegel's Absolute both is and is not real before it is received and developed, so the poet, though a maker, is also a recipient. He is the oracle through whom the word somehow gets spoken. In placing art at the highest level of nature and at the lowest level of culture, Hegel is already consecrating the ideality of art. As ancient Symbolical art yields to the beauties of Classical art, and as Classical art evolves into the sublimity of Romantic art, the poet may feel humbled by something larger than himself, which he experiences like a vision of overwhelming happiness, when there are no more words but only the silence which marks the possession of all words. Many nineteenth-century and some modern poets who view themselves as poetic prophets or as prophetic poets are at least willing to entertain the proposition that art can be what it is only because it is as if the Hegelian theory of the Absolute, or something like it in Neoplatonic and Stoic thought, represented a system of possible truth. Because the oracular poet is encompassed by something 'incorrigibly real', as Denis Donoghue has said, something for which he is not responsible and which is not his invention, his 'words, after speech, reach into the silence' (1969, pp. 212–14). The heart of oracular poetry 'is in that silence'.

2 Education by Poetry

I asked a question at the beginning of this study to which I must now return at the end. In an age in which science occupies the same place in thought as did theology in the Middle Ages, how are the poet and critic to justify their vocation? In what sense, if any, can the poet give us knowledge? Why would Arnold, for example, want to make poetry and the classics rather than science the foundation of education? These questions seem to me as important today as they were a hundred years ago. For most Victorians the value and function of poetry are closely associated with the fortunes of a liberal education. The word 'liberal', like the word 'art', has both a negative and a positive implication. Negatively, a liberal pursuit like the pursuit of art is not engaged in for the sake of any immediate advantage. Positively, such a pursuit is carried on for its own sake because it is enjoyed or preferred. T. H. Huxley's objection to a literary education, like Bentham's objection to poetry, uses the merely worthwhile nature of such pursuits to trivialize them. Arnold, while conceding the same playful or disinterested qualities, uses them to praise literature for its supreme virtue of encouraging emotion and thought beyond the response to practical necessities.

Even after Hamilton and Mansel have demonstrated that God is unknowable, Victorian poetry may still be used to harness an oracular power that is proper to imagine but impossible to conceive. This division of labour between one's imaginative attitude to the world and one's analytic understanding of it originates with Kant. Art is properly located, along with Ideas of the Pure Reason, in a realm of the supersensible or the occult. A non-factual sense of wonder and awe is sustained and encouraged by poetry. A poem like 'The Vision of Sin' creates a purposiveness without purpose, and like other supreme fictions, including perhaps the idea of God, it may be good for one's soul. Oddly enough, the increasing demystification of the theory that the poet is God's scribe, a view Browning presents in 'How It Strikes a Contemporary', brings no demystification of the poet's role. On the contrary, if there is no science of God, then there is no science of art either. The poet's power is the new unknown: it remains a mystery even to himself.

Having freed art from the shackles of a mummified theology and metaphysics, Victorians like Arnold, Wilde, and Pater tend to identify the irreducible truth of poetry with its freedom from corruption. Poetry is pure because it resists manipulation. It cannot be made to mean something other than itself. The chief value of poetry is that, like the pursuit of virtue or a liberal education, it is conspicuously *not* useful. Though Arnold praises the delight the mind takes in the display and enjoyment of form for form's own sake, he is also conscious of poetry's educative function. It trains the mind to recognize patterns and to renew its capacity for seeing life steadily and seeing it whole. In becoming a part of the best that has been thought and said in the world, we take a disinterested, inclusive view. Arnold's removal of poetry into a sanctifying world of disinterested contemplation is reinforced in Pater by a tendency to think of both art and religion as a *vita contemplativa*, a contemporary refuge from the secular world. Once the Absolute is banished by personal idealists like Pringle-Pattison or by Wilde in *De Profundis*, art can be celebrated as a sacred activity, not because it is still tied to a specific theology or metaphysics, but because it occupies a spiritual territory from which the quasi-divine Hegelian Mind or the unknowable God of Hamilton and Mansel has been forced to retreat. Like a liberal education, a devotion to art for its own sake yields such cognitive pleasures as identifying patterns, deciphering symbols, and recognizing their originality, their strangeness, or even the unexpected similarity between a work of art and what it 're-presents'. For free rational beings there seems to be no higher sanction by which this educative activity can be justified.

Theories that the poet is the unconscious channel through whom God or the Absolute communicates with the world tend to celebrate a poet who is a rational agent but not wholly free. Conversely, theories of the poet's spontaneous expression and holistic theories of intuitively grasped unities which cannot properly be analysed into a system of parts celebrate the poet as an agent who is free but not wholly rational. Dallas argues in *The Gay Science*, for example, that poetic imagination is a scandalously irrational activity which, like many faithful accounts of how the mind operates, defies what we have been taught to think about the subject. Yet most Victorians prefer theories which allow poets and critics to be both rational and free. Arnold argues that, in seeing the poem as an object of disinterested contemplation, the critic has a chance to be fully lucid and rational. At the same time, through a free play of his intellect, he frees his imagination for the kind of generous response to the world that converts ordinary things into wonders. When Arnold says that it is the function of disinterested contemplation to 'see the object, as in itself it really is', he is not prescribing passive or detached receptivity. There is no reason why such contemplative viewing cannot be active rather than Olympian and detached. Arnold is simply insisting that the critic should have no partisan or ulterior motives.

But why does Arnold value poetry as a unique source of knowledge? To assert that poetry gives knowledge of the individual is to make a claim at once too large and too small. It is too large a claim because, as Grote's and Green's critiques of atomism make clear, a mere flow of truly unmediated sensations can never be an object of knowledge. But the claim is also too small, because it would exclude the poet's ability to modify experience, allowing it to possess a significance valid for many readers at many different times. If the study of poetry is a model for liberal education, as I believe it is, it is because, unlike the scientist, both the poet and the literary critic are an important part of the world they are studying. The knowledge of poets and critics is interpretive knowledge. It is capable of being 're-presented' in the interpreter's mind. But there can be no interpretation of physical nature, because physical objects are never an experience as such. They are always the mere objects of experience. In order to be an object of poetic knowledge, natural events must be viewed as the actions of some spirit or god immanent in nature. But immanent teleology is bad science. And though the geologist's knowledge of the earth may be chronological, it is not a knowledge of the geologist's own self-conscious response or of his own place in geological history. When Tennyson in *In Memoriam* re-presents the long perspective of geological time, sowing 'The dust of continents to be' (xxxv, 12), his knowledge of chronology is poetic rather than scientific, because his own response and place are an important part of what he knows.

To the anonymous knower of a science, poetry seems to express what everyone knew before in language too individualized for the knower of mere objective truth to decipher. And to the highly individualized reader of a poem, science seems to express a truth no one knew before in language that even the most anonymous inquirer can know and understand. Poetry's special claim has something to do with the injustice we feel when our individual experiences, which we believe to be unique to ourselves, are described in the abstractions of the psychological sciences or of ethics, which use concepts common to everyone. For a free rational being, the necessary and sufficient condition of poetry's educative value lies in the fact that this sense of loss may be diminished when a critic like Mill reads a poet like Wordsworth. In representing poetically what Mill calls the 'very culture of the feelings', Wordsworth reveals to Mill the condition of unselfish affection he shares with other men, but not as that affection is expressed in the common run of concepts. We know that a poem, like a psychological treatise, speaks to and for poets about our common humanity. But because a poem's representation is wholly individual, we may find in it an image of ourselves that is an invention in both senses of that word. It is something we come upon or discover, but also something we alone can make. Conservative hermeneutical critics like Keble and

Newman teach the Victorian interpreter to be loyal to his text. But in the more liberal hermeneutical traditions of Bradley and Strauss, the interpreter is reminded not to be too loyal. Even in escaping from the limits of his own personality by losing himself in impersonal scholarship, the interpreter must never forget that the knowledge he brings to interpretation is not just knowledge of the kind he can look up in a glossary or handbook. It is knowledge of the interpreter himself. Even in adhering to the letter of his texts, the good interpreter transforms the quality of our thinking and feeling. Though what the critic says is in some sense familiar, in another sense it is as if we were reading the poem he criticizes for the first time. Instead of merely paraphrasing a poem, he deepens its meaning in an idiom that is fresh and continues to strike us as saying something new. Neither the facts that form the moving targets of the critic nor the facts that recede beyond the frontiers of physics are solid and immutable. Because the facts can be changed by new descriptions and interpretations, both the scientist and the humanist are endlessly exploring untravelled worlds whose margins fade for ever and for ever, giving a feel for the strange and the inexplicable. But whereas a scientific knower is in principle identical with every other knower, poetic knowledge is unique to each interpreter. By including the knower's singularity as an important part of what is known, poetry can continue science or philosophy by other means. This is why poetry can illuminate the mysterious trouble spots of knowledge. Because the mystery of poetic knowledge, as compared, say, with a mystery in physics, comes not from anything bewildering in the world but from something unlimited in the subject, a poem like *In Memoriam* can even speak across the ages, across the reader's death, about the deepest puzzles in his own life.

Notes
Bibliography
Index

Notes

Chapter II   The Idealist Revolt

1 Isobel Armstrong establishes Fox's indebtedness to James Mill's new 'science of mind' in *Victorian Scrutinies* (1972, p. 16). Fox's theory of dramatic projection may reflect the influence of A. W. Schlegel's *A Course of Lectures on Dramatic Art and Literature* (1815), a work to which Fox's friend Browning was much indebted in *Aristophanes' Apology*, and of Friedrich Schlegel's *Lectures on the History of Literature, Ancient and Modern* (1818).

2 Browning says of a subjective poet like Shelley essentially what Carlyle had said in praise of Schiller. According to Browning, Shelley 'is impelled to embody the thing he perceives, not so much with reference to the many below as to the one above him, the supreme Intelligence which apprehends all things in their absolute truth' ('An Essay on Shelley', 1852, p. 1009). In a similar vein Carlyle had said that a poet like Schiller should 'leave to *common sense*, which is here at home, the province of the actual; while *he* strives from the union of the possible with the necessary to bring out the ideal' (*The Life of Schiller, 1898–1901*, vol. 25, p. 202). Browning's attempt to unite the virtues of the objective and subjective poets is also anticipated by Carlyle. Just as Shelley's poetry is praised by Browning 'as a sublime fragmentary essay towards a presentment of the correspondency of the universe to Deity, of the natural to the spiritual, and of the actual to the ideal' (p. 1014), so Schiller is praised for his ability to combine 'the earnest of his actions' with 'the sport of his imagination', uniting 'all sensible and spiritual forms' (p. 202). Unlike his Scottish contemporary Sir William Hamilton, who four years later gives an influential sceptical interpretation of Kant's teachings, Carlyle in his 1825 *Life of Schiller* offers a Platonic, Shelleyan account of Kant's influence. Despite the scepticism of Schiller's *Philosophical Letters*, which find a counterpart in Shelley's *The Necessity of Atheism*, Carlyle extols Schiller as a 'just and lofty spirit', just as Browning hazards the opinion that if Shelley had lived he would have been a convert to Christianity (p. 1013). Like Carlyle's own response to Schiller, however, Browning's response to Carlyle is complex. He seems to have been one of Carlyle's few friends who suspected the truth of Friedrich Nietzsche's devastating insight that 'Carlyle is an English atheist who wants to be honoured for *not* being one' (1968, p. 75).

Chapter IV   The Agnostic Imagination

1 Jerome C. Hixson and Patrick Scott, 'Tennyson's Books', *Tennyson Research Bulletin*, 2 (1976), 194.

Chapter V From Representation to Presentation

1 Because 'intuitive or aesthetic knowledge' defies logical translation, Benedetto Croce rejects all generic theory as 'the greatest triumph of the intellectualist error' (*Aesthetic as Science of Expression and General Linguistic*, 1953, p. 35). According to Collingwood, what mistakenly passes for a theory of genres is really 'a classification of kinds of pseudo-art', by which Collingwood means a hierarchy of crafts and techniques (*The Principles of Art*, 1938, p. 32).

2 'Putting to death the very thing which it engenders, [genre] cuts a strange figure: a formless form, it remains nearly invisible, it neither sees the day nor brings itself to light.'

Chapter VI The Victorian Reconstruction

1 From his free translation of the Latin, Jowett extracts the canon: 'We cannot understand Scripture without becoming familiar with it.'

2 According to the Sotheby Catalogue of the Browning Library, Browning's testimony of his father's high regard for Baruh was written in his father's copy of Baruh's book. Though I have not seen this copy, I am grateful to the Library of Hebrew Union College, Cincinnati, Ohio, for making another copy available to me through interlibrary loan.

Raphael Baruh's own identity is shrouded in mystery. He is not mentioned in the *DNB* or most of the other standard sources. Robert Watt's *Bibliotheca Britannica* (1824) simply cites Baruh as the author of *Critica Sacra Examined*, his only work. Baruh seems to have been an orthodox Jewish scholar who found Kennicott's Hebrew scholarship subversive or misguided. Like any scrupulous editor, Baruh wants to defend the Old Jewish Doctors, who were very reluctant to alter a text unless the change was 'corroborated and supported by a great number of ancient copies of known and established character' (p. ii). Typical of Baruh's procedure is his attempt to account for apparent discrepancies between versions of Solomon's prayer in I Kings 8 : 12–50 and in II Chronicles 6 : 1–39. Baruh assumes that Solomon's prayer to consecrate the temple was in fact a public speech or oration, and that 'several copies were made by sundry scribes' (p. 121).

Benjamin Kennicott (1718–83) was a prominent English biblical scholar, whose life was spent in the collection of Hebrew manuscripts. The book Baruh is examining, *Critica Sacra*, was published in 1774. Kennicott's major work was his two-volume *Vetus Testamentum Hebraicum Cum Variis Lectionibus*, published by Oxford in 1776 and 1780.

Chapter VII Hegelian Aesthetics

1 G. W. F. Hegel, *Lectures on the Philosophy of History* (1857), pp. 281–2.

'The principle of Socrates manifests a revolutionary aspect towards the Athenian State... When Socrates wishes to induce his friends to reflection, the discourse has always a negative tone; he brings them to the consciousness that they do not know what the Right is. But when on account of the giving utterance to that principle which was advancing to recognition, Socrates is condemned to death, the sentence bears on the one hand the aspect of unimpeachable rectitude – inasmuch as the Athenian people condemns its deadliest foe – but on the other hand, that of a deeply tragical character, inasmuch as the Athenians had to make the discovery, that what they reprobated in Socrates had already struck firm root among themselves.'

2 Baylor MS., RB to Furnivall, 25 April 1882. The reference is given in William Irvine and Park Honan, *The Book, The Ring, and The Poet* (1974), p. 582.

3 Grant's influence on Pater is explored at greater length by Frank W. Turner in *The Greek Heritage in Victorian Britain* (1981), pp. 352–4. On the influence of Hegel on Pater see Richard Wollheim, 'Walter Pater as a Critic of the Arts', *On Art and the Mind: Essays and Lectures* (1973), pp. 169–70: '*The Philosophy of Fine Art*, as Hegel's lectures on aesthetics are often known, was a work with which Pater was extremely familiar. He adapts some of its central themes in the essay on Winckelmann, but there are many literal borrowings from it, on the level of direct observation of works of art as well as on the more theoretical level, throughout Pater's writings.'

4 There are obvious parallels between Aquinas' aesthetic theory, which is most familiar to modern readers from Stephen Daedalus' lecture on art in James Joyce's *Portrait of the Artist as a Young Man*, and Ruskin's theories of the imagination. Achieving the *integritas* which Aquinas associates with the aesthetic object, the Imagination Penetrative is the faculty most consistently displayed by Ruskin's first and highest rank of poets. Corresponding to the *consonantia* or harmony of Aquinas' aesthetic object, the arrangement of sensory wholes is the function assigned by Ruskin to the Combining or Associative Imagination. The Contemplative Imagination is displayed by prophetically inspired poets like Milton and Shelley. It allows them to approximate what Aquinas calls the radiance or *claritas* of oracular vision. On Joyce's indebtedness to Ruskin, Aristotle, and Aquinas, see Sidney Feshback, 'Joyce Read Ruskin', *James Joyce Quarterly*, 10 (1973), 333–6.

5 In his essay on 'The Holy Spirit and Inspiration', Gore keeps pondering the wisdom or the folly of the early Church's branding as heretical the monatist doctrine that the Holy Spirit acts upon a man 'like a flute player breathing into his flute' or 'a plectrum striking a lyre'. In order to make more vivid the kind of energy ascribed by Gore to the Holy Spirit in his essay (*Lux Mundi*, p. 253), Swinburne in 'A Nympholept' introduces a comparison based not only on a similarity between 'the word of the wind' (l. 11) and the breath of God, but also on the synecdochic character of the flaming, running, fiercely invasive power of every wind. All breezes are pentecostal, he seems to be saying. And they are all like this one.

6 A. C. Swinburne, *William Blake: A Critical Essay* (1868), p. 166n. '"God is no more than man; *because* man is no less than God": there is Blake's Pantheistic *Iliad* in a nutshell.'

7 The original version is preserved in Ashley MS. 5262 in the British Museum. The lines read as follows: 'I the grain and the furrow, / The plough-cloven clod / ~~And the germ and the sod~~ / And ￪ the ploughshare drawn thorough, / The germ and the sod / ~~And the plough=cloven clod.~~' Swinburne has pencilled out the words I have indicated.

8 Some of my own comments on Browning and Bradley are anticipated by Sir Henry Jones's essay 'The Social Organism' in *Essays in Philosophical Criticism* (1883). In that essay, for example, Jones argues that if hedonism is too subjective, duty for duty's sake is too universal and abstract. 'The one ideal is a mere *seyn*, the other is a mere *sollen*. A proper ideal is found in the social organism, or rather in the moral organism which is embodied in various forms of society' (p. 203). The influence of Bradley's *Ethical Studies* is unmistakable, and suggests an approach to Browning that Jones himself does not provide in *Browning as a Philosophical and Religious Teacher*, despite the fact that Jones maintains in that book that Browning 'has a right to a place amongst philosophers, as Plato has to a place amongst poets' (p. 19). Bradley's affinities with Hegel will be immediately apparent to anyone who compares *Ethical Studies* with Hegel's comments on dissemblance in *The Phenomenology of Spirit*, especially with Hegel's analysis of contradictions in the moral view of the world and of the resolution of morality into its opposite.

Bibliography

Works quoted in the text

Aarsleff, Hans (1967), *The Study of Language in England 1780–1860*.

Abrams, M. H. (1953), *The Mirror and the Lamp: Romantic Theory and the Critical Tradition*.

—— (1961), review of Ernest Lee Tuveson, *The Imagination as a Means of Grace*, *Modern Language Notes*, vol. 76.

—— (1971), *Natural Supernaturalism: Tradition and Revolution in Romantic Literature*.

Allott, Kenneth (1959), 'Matthew Arnold's Reading-Lists in Three Early Diaries', *Victorian Studies*, vol. 2.

apRoberts, Ruth (1983), *Arnold and God*.

Armstrong, Isobel (1972), *Victorian Scrutinies: Reviews of Poetry, 1830–1870*.

Arnold, Matthew (1932), *The Letters of Matthew Arnold to Arthur Hugh Clough*, ed. H. F. Lowry.

—— (1960–77), *The Complete Prose Works*, ed. R. H. Super, 11 vols.

Austin, J. L. (1962), *How To Do Things With Words*.

Bacon, Francis (1955), *The Advancement of Learning, Selected Writings of Francis Bacon*, ed. Hugh G. Dick.

Ball, Patricia (1974), *The Science of Aspects: The Changing Role of Fact in the Works of Coleridge, Ruskin, and Hopkins*.

Barfield, Owen (1952), *Poetic Diction: A Study in Meaning*.

Barth, Karl (1933), *The Epistle of the Romans*, trans. Edwyn C. Hoskyns.

Barthes, Roland (1974), *S/Z: An Essay*, trans. Richard Miller.

—— (1975), *The Pleasure of the Text*, trans. Richard Miller.

Baruh, Raphael (1775), *Critica Sacra Examined: Or An Attempt to Show that a New Method May be Found to Reconcile the Seemingly Glaring Variations in Parallel Passages of Scripture*.

Bayley, John (1981), *Shakespeare and Tragedy*.

Bishop, Jonathan (1972), *Something Else*.

Biswas, R. K. (1972), *Arthur Hugh Clough, Towards a Reconsideration*.

Booth, Stephen (1983), *King Lear, Macbeth, Indefinition, and Tragedy*.

Bradley, F. H. (1874), *The Presuppositions of Critical History*; reprint, ed. Lionel Rubinoff (1968).

—— (1876), *Ethical Studies*; reprint, intro. Richard Wollheim (1962).

—— (1883), *The Principles of Logic*.

—— (1893), *Appearance and Reality: A Metaphysical Essay*.

—— (1914), *Essays on Truth and Reality*.

—— (1930), *Aphorisms*.

Brazill, William J. (1970), *The Young Hegelians*.

Brockie, William (1876), *Indian Thought: A Popular Essay*.

Browning Collections, The (1913), the catalogue of Sotheby, Wilkinson & Hodge, the auctioneers who dispersed the Browning library on the death of R. W. B. Browning.

Browning, Robert (1852), 'An Essay on Shelley', reprinted in *The Complete Poetical Works of Browning* (1895).

—— (1969), *The Letters of Robert Browning and Elizabeth Barrett Barrett 1845–1846*, ed. Elvan Kintner, 2 vols.

Bruns, Gerald (1974), *Modern Poetry and the Idea of Language: A Critical and Historical Study*.

Buckle, H. T. (1864), *History of Civilization in England*, 2 vols; originally published 1857.

Burke, Kenneth (1962), *A Grammar of Motives and a Rhetoric of Motives*.

Caird, Edward (1881), *The Problem of Philosophy at the Present Time*.

Caird, John (1904), *Introduction to the Philosophy of Religion*.

Carlyle, Thomas (1898–1901), *The Works of Thomas Carlyle*, centenary edition, 30 vols.

Christ, Carol T. (1975), *The Finer Optic: The Aesthetic of Particularity in Victorian Poetry*.

Coleridge, Hartley (1839), 'What is Poetical Description?', *Blackwood's Edinburgh Magazine*, vol. 45.

Coleridge, Samuel Taylor (1905), *Aids to Reflection*, ed. Thomas Fenby.

—— (1969), *The Friend*, ed. Barbara E. Rooke.

Collingwood, R. G. (1933), *An Essay on Philosophical Method*.

—— (1938), *The Principles of Art*.

—— (1946), *The Idea of History*.

Cousin, Victor (1852), *Course of the History of Modern Philosophy*, trans. O. W. Wright, vol. 1.

Croce, Benedetto (1953), *Aesthetic as Science of Expression and General Linguistic*, trans. Douglas Ainslie.

Culler, A. Dwight (1977), *The Poetry of Tennyson*.

Dallas, E. S. (1852), *Poetics: An Essay on Poetry*.

—— (1866), *The Gay Science*, 2 vols.

Daniélou, Jean (1960), *From Shadows to Reality: Studies in the Biblical Typology of the Fathers*.

Derrida, Jacques (1976), *Of Grammatology*, trans. G. C. Spivak.

—— (1978), *La Vérité en peinture*; Part II, 'Le Parergon', trans. as 'The Parergon', *October*, 9 (1979).

—— (1980), 'The Law of Genre', *Glyph*, vol. 7.

DeVane, W. C. (1955), *A Browning Handbook*.

Dobell, Sydney (1876), 'Lecture on the "Nature of Poetry"', *Thoughts on Art, Philosophy, and Religion*; lecture originally given 8 April 1857.

Donoghue, Denis (1969), 'T. S. Eliot's *Quartets*: A New Reading (1965)', *T. S. Eliot: Four Quartets: A Casebook*, ed. Bernard Bergonzi.

Douglas, James (1830), *Errors Regarding Religion.*

Eliot, T. S. (1932), *Selected Essays.*

—— (1964), *Knowledge and Experience in the Philosophy of F. H. Bradley.*

Fackenheim, Emil L. (1961), *Metaphysics and Historicity.*

—— (1967), *The Religious Dimension in Hegel's Thought.*

Ferrier, J. F. (1838–9), 'An Introduction to the Philosophy of Consciousness', *Blackwood's Edinburgh Magazine*, vol. 43.

—— (1842), 'Berkeley and Idealism', *Blackwood's Edinburgh Magazine*, vol. 51.

—— (1854), *The Institutes of Metaphysics: Theory of Knowing and Being.*

Feuerbach, Ludwig (1841), *The Essence of Christianity*, trans. George Eliot; reprinted 1957.

Flaubert, Gustave (1953), *Selected Letters of Gustave Flaubert*, trans. Francis Steegmuller.

Fox, W. J. (1831), review of Tennyson's *Poems, Chiefly Lyrical, Westminster Review*, vol. 14, reprinted in *Victorian Scrutinies*, ed. Isobel Armstrong (1972).

Frost, Robert (1968), *Selected Prose of Robert Frost*, ed. H. Cox and E. Lathem.

Frye, Northrop (1957), *Anatomy of Criticism.*

—— (1982), *The Great Code: The Bible and Literature.*

Glanvill, Joseph (1661), *The Vanity of Dogmatizing*; facsimile edn 1931.

Gombrich, E. H. (1960), *Art and Illusion.*

Gore, Charles (1904), 'The Holy Spirit and Inspiration', *Lux Mundi: A Series of Studies in the Religion of the Incarnation*, ed. Charles Gore; originally published 1889.

Grant, Alexander (1857–8), *The 'Ethics' of Aristotle Illustrated with Essays and Notes*, 2 vols.

Green, T. H. (1874), *Introduction to Hume's Treatise on Human Nature.*

—— (1906), *Prolegomena to Ethics.*

Grote, George (1869), *A History of Greece, A New Edition*, 12 vols; originally published 1846–56.

—— (1888), *Plato, and the Other Companions of Sokrates*, 4 vols; originally published 1865.

Grote, John (1865), *Exploratio Philosophica*, 2 vols.

Hallam, Arthur (1831), 'On Some of the Characteristics of Modern Poetry and on the *Lyrical Poems* of Alfred Tennyson'; reprinted in *Victorian Poetry and Poetics*, ed. Walter E. Houghton and G. Robert Stange (1968).

Hamilton, Sir William (1829), 'Review of M. Cousin's *Course of Philosophy*', *Edinburgh Review*, vol. 50.

—— (1861), *Lectures on Metaphysics and Logic*, ed. H. L. Mansel and John Veitch, 2 vols.

Hartman, Geoffrey H. (1980), *Criticism in the Wilderness: The Study of Literature Today.*

Hegel, G. W. F. (1857), *Lectures on the Philosophy of History*, trans. from the third German edn by J. Sibree; the edition owned by Tennyson.

—— (1892), *Hegel's Lectures on the History of Philosophy*, trans. E. S. Haldane and Frances H. Simson, 3 vols.

—— (1895), *Lectures on the Philosophy of Religion*, trans. E. B. Speirs and J. B. Saunderson, 3 vols.

—— (1965), Preface to *The Phenomenology of Spirit, Hegel: Reinterpretation, Texts, and Commentary*, trans. Walter Kaufmann.

—— (1970), *G. W. F. Hegel on Art, Religion, Philosophy*, ed. J. Glenn Gray: reprint of *The Introduction to Hegel's Philosophy of Fine Art*, trans. Bernard Bosanquet, *Lectures on the Philosophy of Religion*, trans. E. B. Speirs and J. B. Saunderson, and *Introduction from Hegel's Lectures on the History of Philosophy*, trans. E. S. Haldane.

—— (1975), *Hegel's Aesthetics: Lectures on Fine Art by G. W. F. Hegel*, trans. T. M. Knox, 2 vols; originally published 1835.

Helmholtz, H. (1873), *Popular Lectures on Scientific Subjects*, trans. E. Atkinson, intro. John Tyndall.

Hirsch, E. D. (1967), *Validity in Interpretation*.

Hixson, Jerome C., and Scott, Patrick (1976), 'Tennyson's Books', *Tennyson Research Bulletin*, vol. 2.

Hoge, J. O. (ed) (1981), *Lady Tennyson's Journal*.

Hopkins, G. M. (1935), *The Letters of G. M. Hopkins to Robert Bridges*, ed. C. C. Abbott.

—— (1959a), *The Sermons and Devotional Writings of G. M. Hopkins*, ed. Christopher Devlin.

—— (1959b), *The Journals and Papers of Gerard Manley Hopkins*, ed. Humphrey House and Graham Storey.

Hume, David (1888), *A Treatise on Human Nature*, ed. L. A. Selby-Bigge.

Huxley, T. H. (1893), 'On the Basis of Life', *Collected Essays*, vol. 1; originally published 1868.

—— (1893), 'Science and Culture', *Collected Essays*, vol. 3; originally published 1880.

—— (1893), 'The Progress of Science', *Collected Essays*, vol. 1; originally published 1887.

Irvine, William, and Honan, Park (1974), *The Book, The Ring, and the Poet*.

Johnson, Alexander B. (1836), *A Treatise of Language*; reprint, ed. David Rynin (1947).

Jones, Sir Henry (1883), 'The Social Organism', *Essays in Philosophical Criticism*, ed. Andrew Seth and R. B. Haldane; reprint 1971.

—— (1892), *Browning as a Philosophical and Religious Teacher*.

Jowett, Benjamin (1861), 'On the Interpretation of Scripture', *Essays and Reviews*.

—— (trans. and ed.) (1871), *The Dialogues of Plato*, 4 vols.

Kant, Immanuel (1881), *Critique of Pure Reason*, trans. Max Müller, vol. 2.

—— (1923), *Critique of Practical Reason*, trans. T. K. Abbott.

—— (1940), *Prolegomena to any Future Metaphysics*, reprinted in *From Descartes to Kant*, ed. T. V. Smith and Marjorie Grene; originally published 1783.

—— (1951), *Critique of Judgement*, trans. J. H. Bernard.

Keats, John (1958), *The Letters of John Keats 1814–1821*, ed. H. E. Rollins, 2 vols.

Keble, John (1812), 'On Translation from Dead Languages', Bodleian Library MS., Don. d. 67, folios 48, 53 and 54.

—— (1838), 'Review of Lockhart's *Life of Sir Walter Scott*', *British Critic and Quarterly Theological Review*, vol. 24.

—— (1840), 'On the Mysticism Attributed to the Early Fathers of the Church', *Tract 89, Tracts for the Times*, vol. 8, 1865 edn.

—— (1912), *Lectures on Poetry*, trans. E. K. Francis, 2 vols.

Kenner, Hugh (1965), *The Invisible Poet: T. S. Eliot*.

Ker, W. P. (1883), 'On the Philosophy of Art', *Essays in Philosophical Criticism*, ed. Andrew Seth and R. B. Haldane; reprint 1971.

Landow, George P. (1971), *The Aesthetic and Critical Theories of John Ruskin*.

Lange, John (1970), *The Cognitivity Paradox: An Inquiry Concerning the Claims of Philosophy*.

Langer, Susanne K. (1960), *Philosophy in a New Key*.

Lewes, G. H. (1842), 'Hegel's Aesthetics, Philosophy of Art', review of Hegel's *Lectures on Aesthetics*, *British and Foreign Review*, vol. 13.

—— (1845–6), *A Biographical History of Philosophy*, 4 vols.

—— (1857), *The Biographical History of Philosophy*, second edn, 1 vol.

—— (1865), *The Principles of Success in Literature*.

—— (1880), *The History of Philosophy from Thales to Comte*, fifth edn of *The Biographical History of Philosophy*, 2 vols.

Locke, John (1924), *An Essay Concerning Human Understanding*, ed. A. S. Pringle-Pattison.

Loewenberg, J. (ed.) (1929), *Hegel Selections*.

Mandelbaum, Maurice (1971), *History, Man, and Reason: A Study in Nineteenth-Century Thought*.

Mansel, H. L. (1851), *Prologomena Logica: An Inquiry into the Psychological Character of Logical Processes*.

—— (1867), *The Limits of Religious Thought Examined in Eight Lectures*, Bampton Lectures for 1858.

Masson, David (1856), *Essays Biographical and Critical, Chiefly on English Poets*.

Maurice, F. D. (1872), *Moral and Metaphysical Philosophy*, 2 vols.

Mill, James (1817), *The History of British India*, 3 vols.

—— (1869), *Analysis of the Phenomena of the Human Mind*, ed. John Stuart Mill, 2 vols; originally published 1829.

Mill, John Stuart (1962), *Earlier Letters, 1812–1848*, in *Collected Works of John Stuart Mill*, ed. J. M. Robson and Francis E. Mineka, vols 12 and 13.

—— (1969), *Essays on Ethics, Religion and Society*, in *Collected Works of John Stuart Mill*, ed. J. M. Robson and F. E. L. Priestley, vol. 10.

—— (1974), *System of Logic: Ratiocinative and Inductive*, in *Collected Works of John Stuart Mill*, ed. J. M. Robson and R. F. McRae, vols 7 and 8.

—— (1981), *Autobiography and Literary Essays,* in *Collected Works of John Stuart Mill,* ed. J. M. Robson and Jack Stillinger, vol. 1.

Milroy, James (1984), 'Hopkins the Purist (?)', *Vital Candle: Victorian and Modern Bearings in Gerard Manley Hopkins,* ed. John S. North and Michael D. Moore.

Morgan, Peter F. (1983), *Literary Critics and Reviewers in Early Nineteenth-Century Britain.*

Mulhauser, Frederick L. (ed.) (1957), *The Correspondence of Arthur Hugh Clough,* 2 vols.

Müller, Max (1869), *Chips from a German Workshop,* 4 vols.

Nagarajan, S. (1960), 'Arnold and the *Bhagavad Gita*: A Reinterpretation of *Empedocles on Etna*', *Comparative Literature,* vol. 12.

Newman, J. H. (1829), 'Poetry with Reference to Aristotle's *Poetics*', *The London Review,* vol. 1; (1871), reprinted in *Essays Critical and Historical,* vol. 1.

—— (1887), *Fifteen Sermons Preached Before the University of Oxford Between 1826 and 1843.*

Newsome, David (1974), *Two Classes of Men: Platonism and English Thought.*

Nietzsche, Friedrich (1968), *Twilight of the Idols and the Anti-Christ,* trans. R. J. Hollingdale; originally published 1889 and 1895.

Ogden, C. K. (1932), *Bentham's Theory of Fictions.*

Page, Norman (ed.) (1983), *Tennyson Interviews and Recollections.*

Pater, Walter (1893), *Plato and Platonism.*

—— (1900), *Studies in the History of the Renaissance, The Works of Walter Pater,* vol. 1.

—— (1900), 'Winckelmann', *The Works of Walter Pater,* vol. 1.

—— (1901), 'Style', *The Works of Walter Pater,* vol. 5.

Peacock, Thomas Love (1820), 'The Four Ages of Poetry'; reprinted in *Prose of the Romantic Period,* ed. Carl R. Woodring (1961).

Pearson, Karl (1892), *The Grammar of Science.*

Preyer, Robert (1961), 'Sydney Dobell and the Victorian Epic', *University of Toronto Quarterly,* vol. 30.

—— (1965), 'Two Styles in the Verse of Robert Browning', *English Literary History,* vol. 32.

Pringle-Pattison, Andrew Seth (1887), *Hegelianism and Personality.*

Raymond, W. O. (1950), *The Infinite Moment and Other Essays.*

Rorty, Richard (1979), *Philosophy and the Mirror of Nature.*

Ruskin, John (1903–12), *The Complete Works of John Ruskin,* ed. E. T. Cook and Alexander Wedderburn, 39 vols.

Sagan, Carl (1980), *Cosmos.*

Santayana, George (1968), *Selected Critical Writings,* ed. Norman Henfrey, vol. 1.

Saussure, Ferdinand de (1969), *Cours de linguistique générale.*

Schiller, F. C. S. (1903), *Humanism: Philosophical Essays.*

—— (1912), *Riddles of the Sphinx: A Study in the Philosophy of Humanism;*

originally published 1891.

Schlegel, Augustus William (1846), *A Course of Lectures on Dramatic Art and Literature*, trans. John Black; originally published 1815.

Schlegel, Friedrich (1971), *Friedrich Schlegel's Lucinde and the Fragments*, trans. Peter Firchow.

Schleiermacher, Friedrich (1928), *The Christian Faith*, ed. H. R. Mackintosh and J. S. Stewart, trans. of the second German edn.

Scholes, Robert (1982), *Semiotics and Interpretation*.

Schwegler, Albert (1871), *Handbook of the History of Philosophy*, ed. and trans. James Hutchinson Stirling.

Shaw, W. David (1976), *Tennyson's Style*.

Smith, Alexander (of Banff) (1835), 'The Philosophy of Poetry', *Blackwood's Edinburgh Magazine*, vol. 38.

Smith, William Henry (1859), 'Dr Mansel's Bampton Lectures', *Blackwood's Edinburgh Magazine*, vol. 86.

Sparshott, Francis (1972), *Looking for Philosophy*.

—— (1982), *The Theory of the Arts*.

Spencer, Herbert (1880), *First Principles*.

Stevenson, Robert Louis (1885), 'On Style in Literature: Its Technical Elements', *Contemporary Review*, vol. 47; reprinted in *English Prose of the Victorian Era*, ed. C. F. Harrold and W. D. Templeman (1938).

Stewart, Dugald (1827), *Elements of the Philosophy of the Human Mind*, 3 vols.

Stirling, James Hutchinson (1898), *The Secret of Hegel*.

Strauss, David Friedrich (1846), *The Life of Jesus, Critically Examined*, trans. George Eliot, 3 vols.

Sussman, Herbert L. (1979), *Fact into Figure: Typology in Carlyle, Ruskin, and the Pre-Raphaelite Brotherhood*.

Swinburne, A. C. (1868), *William Blake: A Critical Essay*; reprint, ed. Hugh J. Luke (1970).

Symons, Arthur (1919), *The Symbolist Movement in Literature*.

Tennyson, Charles (1949), *Alfred Tennyson*.

Tennyson, G. B. (1981), *Victorian Devotional Poetry: The Tractarian Mode*.

Thirlwall, Connop (1847), *A History of Greece*, 8 vols; first edition published 1835–45.

Thompson, Lawrance, and Winnick, R. H. (1971), *Robert Frost: The Later Years 1938–63*.

Trench, R. C. (1853), *On the Study of Words*.

Turner, Frank (1981), *The Greek Heritage in Victorian Britain*.

Tyndall, John (1889), *Fragments of Science: Essays, Addresses, and Reviews of John Tyndall*, vol. 2.

Vaihinger, Hans (1924), *The Philosophy of 'As If'*, trans. C. K. Ogden.

Wallace, William (1874), 'Prolegomena' to *The Logic of Hegel*.

Ward, W. G. (1841), 'Review of Arnold's Sermons', *British Critic and Quarterly Theological Review*, vol. 30.

Whitehead, Alfred North (1925), *Science and the Modern World*.

Wilson, David B. (1977), 'Concepts of Physical Nature: John Herschel to Karl Pearson', *Nature and the Victorian Imagination*, ed. U. C. Knoepflmacher and G. B. Tennyson.

Wilson, Edmund (1931), *Axel's Castle: A Study of the Imaginative Literature of 1870–1930*.

Wittgenstein, Ludwig (1961), *Tractatus Logico-Philosophicus*, trans. D. F. Pears and B. F. McGuiness.

—— (1972), *Philosophical Investigations*, trans. G. E. M. Anscombe.

Wollheim, Richard (1959), *F. H. Bradley*.

—— (1973), *On Art and the Mind: Essays and Lectures*.

Wordsworth, William (1963), 'Wordsworth's Prefaces of 1800 and 1802', *Lyrical Ballads: Wordsworth and Coleridge*, ed. R. L. Brett and A. R. Jones.

Poetry editions used

Arnold, Matthew, *The Poems of Matthew Arnold*, ed. Kenneth Allott (1965).

Browning, Robert, *The Works of Robert Browning*, centenary edition, vols 5 and 6 (1912). All quotations from *The Ring and the Book* are taken from these volumes.

Browning, Robert, *Robert Browning The Poems*, ed. John Pettigrew and Thomas J. Collins, 2 vols (1981).

Clough, Arthur Hugh, *The Poems of Arthur Hugh Clough*, ed. H. F. Lowry, A. L. P. Norrington and F. L. Mulhauser (1951).

Hardy, Thomas, *Collected Poems of Thomas Hardy* (1953).

Hopkins, G. M., *Poems of Gerard Manley Hopkins*, ed. W. H. Gardner and N. H. MacKenzie (1967).

Keble, John, *The Christian Year*, ed. Walter Lock, third edition (1904).

Morris, William, *The Collected Works of William Morris*, ed. May Morris, 24 vols (1910–15).

Patmore, Coventry, *The Poems of Coventry Patmore*, ed. F. Page (1949).

Rossetti, Christina, *The Poetical Works of Christina Georgina Rossetti*, ed. W. M. Rossetti (1904).

Rossetti, D. G., *The Works of Dante Gabriel Rossetti*, ed. W. M. Rossetti (1911).

Swinburne, A. C., *The Complete Works*, Bonchurch edition, 20 vols (1925–7).

Symons, Arthur, *Poems*, 2 vols (1902).

Tennyson, Lord Alfred, *The Poems of Tennyson*, ed. Christopher Ricks (1969).

Thomson, James, *Complete Poetical Works*, ed. Bertram Dobell, 2 vols (1895).

Wordsworth, William, *The Poetical Works of William Wordsworth*, ed. E. de Selincourt and Helen Darbishire, 5 vols (1940–9).

Index

Numerals in italic type indicate main discussions